René Lévesque
& the Parti Québécois
in Power

Graham Fraser

McGill-Queen's University Press
Montreal & Kingston · London · Ithaca

To the memory of
Blair Fraser
1909-1968

Who had hoped to write
part of this story himself,
and who inspired me
with his affection for Quebec

and to
Barbara Uteck,
who made this book possible,
with love and gratitude

Copyright © Graham Fraser, 1984
Second edition 2001

McGill-Queen's University Press
ISBN 0-7735-2310-3 (cloth)
ISBN 0-7735-2323-5 (paper)

McGill-Queen's University Press acknowledges
the financial support of the Government of Canada
through the Book Publishing Industry Development
Program (BPIDP) for its activities. It also
acknowledges the support of the Canada Council
for the Arts for its publishing program.

Canadian Cataloguing in Publication Data
Fraser, Graham, 1946–
René Lévesque and the Parti québécois in power

Includes index.
Bibliography: p.
ISBN 0-7735-2310-3 (bnd)
ISBN 0-7735-2323-5 (pbk)
1. Parti québécois.
2. Parti québécois — History.
3. Lévesque, René, 1922–
4. Quebec (Province) — Politics and government — 1960–1976.
5. Quebec (Province) — Politics and govenment — 1976–
I. Title

JL259.A57F7 1984   324.2714'093   C84-099032-4

First edition published by Macmillan of Canada, 1984, under the title
PQ: René Lévesque and the Parti Québécois in Power

Edited by Ivon Owen

Design: NewtonFrank

Printed in Canada

Contents

Part 4   The Politics of Humiliation

Preface

I can remember very vividly the sense of distance, foreign-
ness, and envy that I had towards Quebec French — and,
correspondingly, towards French-speaking Quebec — while
growing up in Ottawa. In Ottawa in the 1950s and 1960s, French
was both far and near; a familiar accent, but also an inaccessible otherness.

In the spring of 1965, shortly after I had turned nineteen, I
was walking into the National Gallery when a young man was
coming out. He looked unquestionably and irredeemably English Canadian: tall, with blond sandy hair, horn-rimmed
glasses, and a tweed jacket. But as he passed the security
guard he stopped and exchanged a few words: not the crisp,
European, t-crossed, i-dotted French of the classroom, but a
nasal sibilant whine that sounded almost like bagpipes.

To my ears, Quebec French sounded like an inaccessible
verbal code: as earthy, rich, and appealing as Cockney, as cool
and harshly musical as a Southern blues harmonica. And when
I heard this unmistakable Anglo exchange a few words and a
chuckle, words I could not separate from one another, let
alone understand, I was struck with envy.

That flash of envy, of desire to become someone who could
speak that exotic other language, was at the root of my desire
to go to Quebec and to come to terms with it. That summer, I
worked on an archeological dig at Fort Lennox on the Richelieu River, south of Montreal, and began a process of infatua-
tion and discovery that would ultimately result in this book.

I was struck by the contrasts of Quebec in 1965: a society
that, on the one hand, was bursting with nationalist energies
and, on the other hand, was still plagued with insecurities
and resentments. Similarly, I encountered two different English Montreals — one that I had known through my parents,
and during summers as a child in the Eastern Townships: a
gracious, greystone, tree-lined place, full of quiet streets and

good manners; and another: a place of harsh, fearful people who told me that there were "two types of French: those that are ignorant, and those that are so high-strung you can't reason with them", and warned me "they" were "taking over".

For the next two summers I came back to Montreal, and worked as an orderly at a mental hospital. I became fascinated by the social change that I saw occurring, watching the election and the hospital strike of 1966 close up.

As a student, I watched the vitality of the Union Générale des Étudiants du Québec, the student federation that would form a new political generation. Academically, I studied some of the roots of that change, and wrote a paper for Ramsay Cook on the producers' strike at Radio-Canada in 1958-9, a turning-point for René Lévesque.

In 1969, on a leave of absence from the *Toronto Star*, I followed Lévesque for a week as he toured English-Canadian universities, explaining his dream of sovereignty for Quebec and a new relationship with the rest of Canada. I was fascinated by him, and wrote an article on the trip for *Maclean's*.

A year later, I went to Montreal and did a radio documentary on the Parti Québécois during the 1970 election, and then left for Europe. Returning to Toronto, I became engrossed in urban politics until, in the summer of 1976, Peter C. Newman asked me to move to Montreal for *Maclean's*. It was an invitation I will always be grateful for.

When I came to Montreal, I watched Lévesque's election campaign, how he formed a government, how he juggled the dreams and fears of those who had elected him and the plans and ambitions of those elected with him: brilliant, complex men like Camille Laurin, Jacques Parizeau, and Claude Morin. I also watched the exceptional men who strove to defeat him: Claude Ryan, Robert Bourassa, and, of course, Pierre Trudeau.

In 1979, I was hired by the Montreal *Gazette* and moved to Quebec City, where I was able to watch the government close up. I agonized through the referendum period, and watched how Lévesque and his colleagues coped with defeat.

Less than a year after the referendum, the Parti Québécois was re-elected. The referendum had transformed it from a national movement into a provincial party, and René Lévesque from a national leader into a provincial premier. That election made the constitutional settlement possible: one of the great ironies of our history.

That series of events, in lock-step succession, ended an era that had begun on June 22, 1960, when Jean Lesage was elected Liberal premier of Quebec. The political dynamic of an expanding state in Quebec seeking more powers from Ottawa was abruptly ended: a dynamic that had continued, under four governments and three political parties in power in Quebec, for more than two decades.

The result was the end of an era in Quebec and Canadian history, and an attempt to come to terms with the new, harsh realities: realities which, ironically enough, resulted in the political resurrection of Robert Bourassa. It was a time of paradox, of pride and humiliation, of a dream that became battered by the realities of power.

Graham Fraser
June 1984

Preface to the Second Edition

When I was offered a job in Montreal with _Maclean's_ in the summer of 1976, I felt as if an opportunity I had been waiting for had suddenly arrived. I was thirty years old; my wife, Barbara Uteck, our two young boys, and I were living in Toronto, where I was an urban affairs reporter for the _Globe and Mail_. But we had always assumed that some day we would move to Montreal. We had fallen in love with the city, and with each other, in 1967; we both felt we had a rendezvous with Quebec.

On October 18, 1976, Robert Bourassa called an election; the day that the moving van delivered our boxes to our house in Montreal, I climbed on a campaign bus. Sometimes I feel as if I haven't got off it yet.

In 1984, Macmillan of Canada published this book, which had finally emerged after seven years of work. What had originally been planned as a pre-referendum book, and then as a book on the first mandate of the Parti Québécois, finally came out eight years after a stunned René Lévesque tried to calm the crowd in the Paul Sauvé Arena.

I had first met Lévesque in 1968. He had left the Liberal Party a few months earlier and was sitting in the National Assembly as an independent; I was a student at the University of Toronto, writing a paper on the Radio-Canada producers' strike a decade earlier. He was in Toronto to give a speech, and at first he said he didn't have time to talk to me; then he said, "What the hell, come on back to my hotel." So we sat in his room and talked, late into the night.

Then, in 1969, shortly after I started in journalism, I followed him for a week as he travelled alone visiting university campuses in English-Canada.[1] That intimacy of contact, while never repeated with the same intensity, gave me insights that shaped my reporting of him, and the writing of this book.

Over the years Lévesque dealt with me in various ways: with openness, distance, fondness, exasperation, frankness, suspicion, candour, irritation, and friendly teasing. He had known my father, who was also a journalist, and, I suspect, remembering my father's deep federalist convictions, always felt that, whatever my political sympathies were as a young man, they could not be relied upon. But that mercurial mixture was also a reflection of his restless vitality. He distrusted many of the people around him and could be distant, suspicious, and stubborn. In cabinet meetings, he could not sit still when a minister whom he did not take seriously was talking and would twitch impatiently.

The hardback edition of this book was launched on the eighth anniversary of the election, in the library of the Quebec Literary and Historical Society in le Vieux Québec. Tensions that had been brewing all fall inside the cabinet had not yet burst into the open, but the unease and black humour were obvious. A day or so earlier, when I had given Lévesque his copy, he quipped wryly that he hoped the book concentrated on the first four years in power: the good years.

I should have waited another year. Only a few days later, while I was on my book promotion tour, the long-simmering division inside the PQ exploded and one quarter of the Lévesque cabinet quit. The day the first resignations happened, I was in Toronto; I remember researchers running into the studio at CFRB, delivering the latest paragraphs ripped off the wire as the resignations were being reported.

Much has changed in the twenty-five years since ecstatic PQ supporters drove up to Westmount, honking their horns in delirious triumph. Some of the key figures in this book, such as Lévesque and Camille Laurin, have died, but the huge impact they both had on Quebec society lives on. Others, like Pierre Marc Johnson, Jacques Parizeau, and Bernard Landry, have gone on to become PQ leader and premier. Claude Ryan became an effective cabinet minister during the second Bourassa government and remains as rigourous and independent an analyst of Quebec society as ever. And Claude Morin's role as a paid informant for the RCMP throughout the period covered by this book has become known.[2] But many of the fault lines, factions, and divisions that mark Quebec society and the Parti Québécois today can be seen in clear relief in the months that led up to Lévesque's resignation and his death two years later. Events during the years that followed were, to some extent, variations on these themes.

IN THE SPRING AND SUMMER OF 1984, THE PROSPECT OF QUEBEC independence seemed more distant than it had for twenty years. As the National Assembly session ended and Lévesque prepared to go on holiday, he could already sense that things were in a state of flux.[3] But the political shift that would occur in the weeks ahead would transform the nature of politics in Quebec and set in motion a chain of events that would drive a stake into the heart of the Parti Québécois. For by early August, Brian Mulroney was clearly making serious inroads in Quebec, gaining significant support. He was viewed as having won the televised debates, and the polls were swinging in his favour. Then, even more significantly for Lévesque, at his nomination meeting in Sept-Îles on August 6 Mulroney gave a speech (written by Lucien Bouchard) in which he promised reconciliation and federal-provincial cooperation, vowing he would try to persuade the National Assembly to sign the new constitution "with honour and enthusiasm."[4]

The Sept-Îles speech provided Lévesque with the opening he had been looking for. Signing the constitution with honour meant repairing the humiliation of 1981-82. At a press conference in Quebec on August 9, three days later, he called it "a very remarkable opening," adding prudently, "A speech is a speech and the proof of the pudding is in the eating."[5]

But while he did not openly endorse Mulroney, he subtly distanced himself from both the Parti Nationaliste (a precursor to the Bloc Québécois, a pro-sovereignty federal party) and the decision at the PQ's June convention that the next election would be fought "principally" on sovereignty, saying that it was "perhaps not exactly skilful." At the same time PQ organizers were working with Conservative candidates (as were many provincial Liberals) more openly than ever before.

So when Lévesque saw the election results on September 4, not only could he delight in the defeat of the Liberals, he could see a door opening that made recovery seem possible. For months the polls had shown that people wanted cooperation between Quebec and Ottawa; now it was conceivable.

The election of Brian Mulroney's Progressive Conservatives with extremely strong representation from Quebec had suddenly and dramatically changed the nature of politics in the province and in the country.

The most vivid image of that change on election night was the report from Brome-Missisquoi. The television cameras showed the Conservative candidate, Gabrielle Bertrand, watching the results in her living room. Sitting on the floor by her knee was her son, the Quebec minister of communications, Jean-François Bertrand.

Suddenly, viscerally, a whole wing of the Parti Québécois felt differently about the federal government. They had friends in Ottawa. There had been fifty-eight Conservatives elected from Quebec, many of them with the help of PQ riding organizations, some of them people who had voted Yes in the referendum, and some of them highly successful — but unilingual, French-speaking — Quebec businessmen. The result would change the nature not only of the Conservative Party and the federal government but of the Parti Québécois as well.

Until the election on September 4, the Parti Québécois had faced a Liberal adversary in Ottawa throughout its sixteen-year existence (with the exception of the Clark interregnum in 1979-80). This common enemy reinforced the sprawling coalition that stretched from veterans of the Rassemblement pour l'Indépendance Nationale (RIN) to traditionally conservative nationalists from the Union nationale and Social Credit. At times they were united only by their common belief in Quebec primacy and their hatred of the Liberals.

Now the regime in Ottawa was not rouge, but bleu — and it brought into relief all the blue pieces in the PQ ideological mosaic. With the Conservatives in power those PQ members with Union Nationale roots, such as Bertrand, the minister of justice Pierre Marc Johnson, the minister of labour Raynauld Fréchette, and the minister of industy and commerce Rodrigue Biron, simply could not feel the same resentment toward the federal government that they had felt when the Liberals were there.

At first, Lévesque suggested that the next election would still be on sovereignty, but at a National Council meeting in Quebec City on September 22 he gave the first big hint of the change of direction he had in mind. It was the government's duty, he said, to deal with Ottawa in good faith. "One thing is certain: we have no right to practise 'la politique du pire,' that is to say, to refuse to play the game loyally by digging in our heels and hoping things go from bad to worse."

"So," Lévesque continued, "if federalism should function less badly, and even actually improve, doesn't that risk smothering our fundamental option and sending sovereignty to never-never land? Obviously, there is an element of risk. But it is a beautiful risk, and we don't have the luxury of not taking it."6 "Le beau risque" suddenly entered the language of politics in Quebec.

Later in the same speech, he said that decisions by the PQ conventions were "not gospel." It was a clear indication that he was preparing to make a change in the party's commitment to hold the next election on sovereignty.

Two people at the Council reacted angrily. Pierre de Bellefeuille, a member of the National Assembly, said that those who did not want to fight the next election on sovereignty should go form their own party. Robert Blondin, a delegate, agreed, complaining that the *agents provocateurs* were not in the ranks, but at the top, a reference to Lévesque's accusation in 1981 that the party had been infiltrated by *agents provocateurs* who had led it to take radical positions.7

But the moderates in the party and in the executive were relieved at the speech, and at the reaction. "It was a good speech," said one member of the executive. "He wasn't booed."

Lévesque had made it clear that he did not want his cabinet debating in public the question of whether the next election should be held on sovereignty. But over the next month cabinet members began forming into loose groups, setting the stage for a conflict that Lévesque himself would ignite.

Inside the cabinet, those committed to holding the next election on independence got a hint that something was afoot at the annual end-of-summer cabinet meeting, held at Fort Prével in the Gaspé a few days before the federal election. There was already talk that the party should abandon Article 1 of the PQ's program in order to be able to negotiate with Mulroney. Jean-François Bertrand said he could not understand why the PQ could not have federalists working with it, provoking Jean Garon to call him contemptuously "a mama's boy." During the same meeting Guy Chevrette observed, "A party exists in order to get elected."8

For the indépendantistes, this confirmed what they had suspected: a group in cabinet seemed to be laying the groundwork for Quebec to sign the constitution. In August, Michel Clair had even said in cabinet, "I am going to use iconoclastic language: what would it matter if we signed?"

Jacques Léonard was very concerned. Discreet, often indecisive as a minister, Léonard nevertheless had a fierce commitment to independence. (He had also never forgiven or forgotten that his law penalizing municipalities for accepting federal grants had been abandoned.) So he began making phone calls to the ministers he knew were still faithful to the cause, to organize a meeting.

After Camille Laurin notified Lévesque that the group was planning to meet (to offset any possible rumours of disloyalty), a small group gathered at Léonard's farm in the Laurentians on Thanksgiving Monday, October 8. Léonard had invited seven, and six were able to come: Laurin, Gilbert Paquette, Denise Leblanc-Bantey, Louise Harel, Marcel Léger, and Robert Dean. (Denis Lazure was unable to attend). They were the core of what became known first as the "Groupe des Laurentides," later as the Group of Twelve, and finally as "les orthodoxes."

They could sense the new electoral impatience in the cabinet: the previous Saturday, October 6, *Le Soleil* had published the fall SORECOM poll, which showed that the PQ was stuck at 23 per cent, the same level as in June. The Liberals had slipped 10 points to 58 per cent and, out of nowhere, the Union nationale had surged to 18 per cent. It was further proof, if tany were needed, that the election of Mulroney had changed things in Quebec, that Liberal support was soft, and that the PQ faced certain defeat if it campaigned on independence. But there was a cabinet moratorium on public discussion of the issue, and they all thought they had several months to work on a strategy. They were wrong: events began to unfold very quickly.

On October 16, the national assembly session opened with an inaugural address. Lévesque was tired; he had just come back from a trip to Asia where he had caught a flu bug he had not really shaken. As he had done so often before, he stressed the economy, job creation measures, and youth unemployment. He called for a re-opening of the constitutional issue in order to achieve "the correction of an injustice" and stated a desire for cooperation with the federal government. For the first time, there was no mention of sovereignty.

Two days later, on October 18, Johnson went to see Lévesque in his office to tell him that, after repeated requests, he had agreed to give an interview to Le Devoir as minister of Canadian intergovernmental affairs. He was sure, he told Lévesque, that he would be asked how he felt about holding the next election on sovereignty and he wanted to answer that question.

Johnson's feelings were no secret to Lévesque: the previous February Johnson had told the cabinet that if the next election were to be fought on sovereignty, he would not be a candidate. More than once, publicly and privately, he had indicated that it would not be unpleasant for him to spend time with his children. But two years before he had also told a former aide, André Sormany, that he had not put aside the idea of becoming premier and succeeding Lévesque.

He had talked to Sormany before going to see Lévesque and had laid out his options: if he could talk about his conviction that the next election should not be on sovereignty, fine; if not, he would either soldier on quietly or resign.

Lévesque agreed that Johnson could give the interview but said he would have to inform cabinet of what he said. Shortly afterwards Johnson gave an interview to Pierre Godin, who was doing a profile for *L'actualité*. Based on Johnson's description of the meeting with Lévesque, Godin concluded that Johnson had threatened to resign. It proved to be an embarrassing interpretation.

At the weekly cabinet meeting on October 24, Lévesque began by saying Johnson had something to tell them. When Johnson revealed that he had given the interview and had said that he did not think the next election should be on sovereignty, the debate that would preoccupy public life in Quebec for three months began. When the discussion ended, Lévesque said, "As you can see, the moratorium is lifted." And with the publication of a letter in *La Presse* from PQ executive member Jules-Pascal Venne the next day and the appearance of Johnson's interview in Le Devoir on October 27, the debate became public.

Lévesque knew that the result would inevitably force some people out of the party. This did not seem to concern him: "People in any party come in, go out, depending on evolution," he told a news conference on October 25. "I remember a lovely sad line — sad in a sense, lovely because it is the democratic conscience — a lovely line of party militants coming up to the microphone at one of our conventions and quite visibly tearing up their membership cards. Some have come back since. Some have not come back. It is bound to happen periodically, when there is a full democratic debate. When we come . . . to a decision that has to be made, well, let the chips fall where they may."[9]

But he clearly did not think the chips would be so big — or that they would tear the PQ coalition apart.

Although Johnson's interview attracted much attention, he actually said very little that one could grapple with. He declared that Quebec should embark on constitutional negotiations with Ottawa, and that in the next election, Quebecers should not "inflict another No on themselves."

In contrast, Venne — a Johnson supporter — argued that the PQ had made serious errors in its analysis of the very idea of independence by assuming that Quebec was in a similar position to the fifty-odd nations who had won independence from their former colonial masters in the 1960s and that the referendum-election process would work. In fact, he argued, the party had to recognize that the process of acceding to sovereignty had broken down: the PQ had to prepare for "a historic compromise" with the federal government on the constitutional question.[10]

Gilbert Paquette was quick to reply to Johnson and more declarations followed pell-mell, with Louise Harel saying that those who opposed an election on sovereignty were probably not indépendantistes, and Clément Richard comparing those who wanted to campaign on sovereignty to the ten thousand caribou who had drowned in the Caniapiscau River in September. "What the unconditional indépendantistes are proposing," he told Gilles Lesage of *Le Devoir*, "is a crossing of the river at the worst time, where it is widest and the current is strongest."

The "orthodoxes" who had met at Léonard's farm continued meeting at Denise Leblanc-Bantey's home to discuss strategy; they agreed they should produce a common statement. One by one, the group grew. LeBlanc-Bantey invited Parizeau to come. (At his first meeting, he said, "In case people might have doubts, if Mr. Lévesque announces his resignation, I would resign tomorrow morning. Is that clear?"[11] It was his way of saying that he was not planning a leadership campaign.)

Bernard Landry asked to be invited, as did Pauline Marois. Jean Garon came. Someone brought Guy Tardif, and François

Gendron came to one of the last meetings. The result was a statement by what was immediately dubbed the "Group of Twelve." The declaration was written by Paquette and Parizeau, and signed by Pauline Marois, Robert Dean, Denise Leblanc-Bantey, Camile Laurin, Denis Lazure, Guy Tardif, Jacques Léonard, Marcel Léger, and Louise Harel. (Later, Gérald Godin signed.)

The statement appeared, at first glance, to be an offer to compromise. It seemed to accept, in a backhanded fashion, the resolution from the June convention, saying that for most voters a vote for the PQ was a vote for sovereignty. But it suggested that the next election would inevitably be held "around a perception that the sovereignty of Quebec consists, sector by sector of our personal and collective life, in going farther than we have been able to go until now, and . . . ultimately as far as obtaining full powers."

What appeared to be a compromise in fact conceded very little. Claude Charron pounced on the suggestion that for "a very great majority of voters" a vote for the PQ had always been a vote for sovereignty. "That obviously wasn't the case in 1976 and 1981, and some of you would not even have been members of the National Assembly if it had been as you claim," he wrote in an open letter in *La Presse*.

Lévesque himself remained silent. Almost all of the Group of Twelve, however, remained convinced that he would come out with a statement that both sides could rally to. (Only Denis Lazure was sure that Lévesque would not bring out a consensus position.) By November 15 Lévesque had decided that a special convention would be required to endorse a new position, and he spent the weekend preparing a declaration for the party executive meeting on Monday night.

On November 19 it became clear that, far from seeking consensus, Lévesque had come down unconditionally on the side of the revisionists. Suddenly he was leading Pierre Marc Johnson's parade.

"We must surely resign ourselves, in my humble opinion, to the fact that sovereignty must not be at stake: neither in whole nor in more or less disguised parts, neither directly nor still less by replunging into the temptation to want to 'begin' piece by piece any process whatever, by starting again, in a week or in a month, with everyone pointing to his or her slice of the goal."

Lévesque acknowledged that he had contributed to the party's losing its bearings, in his view, after the shock of the patriation of the constitution; he said he had been forced to come to his senses and realize that things couldn't go on as they were. Sovereignty would remain an ideal, and Lévesque called on party members to keep the faith. But it seemed clear that he no longer believed that Quebec independence was on the public agenda for the foreseeable future. Sovereignty was, he said, an insurance policy.

The reaction among the ministers who had worked on the Group of Twelve statement was shock. Younger members of the group, such as Denise Leblanc-Bantey, wondered if they had been naïve; older ones, such as Camille Laurin, felt betrayed. Jacques Parizeau was astounded: he had worked with Lévesque for twenty years and, despite their differences, was unprepared for so blunt a disavowal. He was shocked by the idea that the ideal of independence was merely an insurance policy.

The next morning, November 20, there was a caucus meeting in Quebec. Usually cabinet meets before caucus on important questions, but Lévesque had much stronger support in caucus than in cabinet. Before the meeting began, some of those who had signed the Group of Twelve document consulted one another briefly. Had they understood? And were they bound by cabinet solidarity?

"Denise, there is no doubt," Bernard Landry told Leblanc-Bantey. "Your ministerial solidarity binds you. We have no choice. We have to accept that or quit." But they decided that if there was any flexibility, they would stay in cabinet.

The caucus was a stormy one; Gilles Baril, the youngest PQ MNA, told the veteran Pierre de Bellefeuille that he should quit the caucus, and de Bellefeuille was so furious at his impertinence that they almost came to blows.

At one o'clock, cabinet met to discuss ministerial solidarity. One of the Group of Twelve ministers felt that Lévesque did not want to force them to quit but that Yves Duhaime and Alain Marcoux were pushing him to enforce cabinet discipline. Finally, Lévesque said, "At the convention, I will have one government. Either you can live with that, or you do what you have to do."

Questioned in the Assembly, Parizeau and Laurin were terse and non-committal but indicated that they were reflecting. The Parti Québécois was in crisis.

On Wednesday November 21, de Bellefeuille quit the caucus. Thursday five cabinet ministers resigned: Parizeau and Léonard effective immediately, and Laurin, Leblanc-Bantey, and Paquette effective on Monday, November 26. All stayed in caucus, although Parizeau subsequently resigned his seat. Jérôme Proulx quit the caucus to sit as an independent.

On Monday, November 26, Leblanc-Bantey announced she was quitting cabinet and caucus to sit as an independent, and Jules Boucher, the MNA from Rivière-du-Loup, announced he was leaving the caucus to sit as an independent. On Tuesday Louise Harel announced she was resigning as minister of Cultural Communities, but remaining a PQ member of the National Assembly.

Lévesque was now playing his last hand. He had been warned a year earlier that ministers would resign and had not believed it, snorting cynically that ministers never quit. He was clearly stunned by the magnitude of the volcano he had provoked and particularly hurt by Camille Laurin's resignation. He saw it as his last battle with those committed to Quebec independence — a battle he had been waging in one form or another since the creation of the Parti Québécois. If he won, it was his final chance to win back what he had lost in the constitutional negotiations.

The humiliation he had suffered over the constitution had become a virtual obsession; he was embarking on a final transformation of the PQ to get the tools he needed for that last remaining job. To meet Mulroney's conditions for negotiations ("I'm not going to give away a plugged nickel until I find out what Mr Lévesque is going to do for Canada," Mulroney had said in 1983), he was putting the PQ through the wrenching test of a convention on January 19 to ratify his renunciation of an election on sovereignty. Riding associations had until December 19 to select delegates.

But Lévesque was much more alone than he had ever been. The people of his generation had resigned from the cabinet and he had a new, younger staff. Jean-Roch Boivin was gone, Michel Carpentier was gone. Their replacements, Martine Tremblay and Alexandre Stefanescu, did not have Boivin's seniority and toughness or Carpentier's years of intimacy.

The battle had taken its toll — and Lévesque was one of its victims. Some of those close to him have suggested that his decline began in the aftermath of the constitutional battle in

November 1981. It was at that time that Claude Morin told him he had been a paid RCMP informant for years, a disclosure that, it seems in retrospect, may have sparked one of the four or five heart attacks Levesque apparently had before the attack that killed him. His decisions had become more erratic and unpredictable and, after the resignations, the traumatic effect of the stresss became obvious. If before he had played Hamlet, now he seemed to be playing Lear.

His behaviour had always been dubious in formal situations: protocol seemed to bring out the childish streak in him and his after-dinner speeches during ceromonial visits always risked being an embarrassment. But television usually brought out his best — and for this reason his appearance on the Radio-Canada public affairs program Le Point on November 29 was particularly shocking. While complicated and full of digressions, his sentences usually made sense; that night, for long periods, he was totally unintelligible. He was clearly exhausted, dispirited, and unable to articulate his new vision for the PQ.

The next day he had recovered enough to give a lengthy interview to La Presse, and he convinced Michel Roy, who had known him for thirty years, that "the man is well and his health is good." But he could not shake the fatigue that had been accumulating since his trip to Asia in September. On top of this, he had suffered the trauma of separation from men and women whose dream he had shared and personified for seventeen years. In the weeks following the resignations his behaviour was punctuated by bizarre episodes: rambling speeches, interventions in the National Assembly when he clearly lost his train of thought, strange behaviour at Christmas parties. His back was bothering him: he conducted one five-hour cabinet meeting standing, saying it was too painful for him to sit down.

After one particularly strange performance in the Assembly, during which he dropped a cigarette in someone's water glass and was unable to remember the questions he was being asked, let alone answer them coherently, reporters began to write about his odd behaviour. His friends began to worry about him: to Lévesque's fury, his staff began to tiptoe past his office and peer in to make sure he was all right. Finally, at the urging of old friends, Lévesque agreed to leave on holiday early, after the last cabinet shuffle. Despite his sore back, which he said bothered him every year, Lévesque insisted he had not seen a doctor.

"I don't want a doctor around me because they can take you to a hospital, and then two months later you find that you didn't need that at all," he told reporters with a smile. "But they have just floored you for another six months."

He was not joking: Lévesque had a phobia about doctors. His father had died from complications following a routine operation and, except for obligatory medical exams when he went overseas during the wars he covered, Lévesque had seen as little as possible of doctors since he was fourteen. This only made people worry about his health all the more, which adding to the stress he felt.

After Christmas Lévesque, his wife, Corinne, his sister Alice, and her husband, Philippe Amyot, flew to Barbados. But Lévesque was still having trouble sleeping and his sister found that he wasn't himself. He flew back early, saying he had to prepare his speech for the convention.

Then, on January 10, something happened.

In his memoirs, Lévesque describes it this way: "The first evening back in Quebec I went to my office and there, while going through some dossiers, I had an experience the memory of which still today fills me with the sense of something bitterly unreal," he wrote. "I won't go into detail, but it was pure Molière with some Kafka on the side. To make a long story short, I was soon joined there by three persons who began to belabour me with friendly reproaches. The word 'tired, tired, tired' kept coming back like a leitmotif. I finally exploded. It was too much."[12]

Levesque wrote that he was "literally kidnapped and hauled off to the hospital"; what he did not say is that when he exploded, he punched his most senior civil servant, Secretary of the Executive Council Louis Bernard. The three men — the other two were Pierre Marc Johnson, and Bernard Landry — then summoned a doctor who gave Lévesque a tranquillizer and sent him to hospital.

The next day he was released — with his doctors declaring that while the premier was overtired, he was in good health — but not before rumours and speculations about what he might be suffering from had swept the province. From then on Lévesque's health remained a nagging question.

By the end of the year, the final result of the convention was not in doubt. With his usual serenity, Camille Laurin had acknowledged that the orthodox position would lose in what he called "a glorious last stand," using the phrase that the French had borrowed from the Arabs to describe the final battle before defeat, "un beau barroud d'honneur." He said it without bitterness: he felt that at least "les orthodoxes" would succeed in denying Lévesque the sort of massive endorsement he had received at the internal party referendum in 1982.

Laurin and the other orthodox ministers campaigned night after night at riding association meetings, warning that if Lévesque's position were accepted, Quebec would be negotiating with Ottawa from a position of weakness. They charged that Lévesque seemed to be submitting totally to Mulroney's authority. Jacques Parizeau went to only one meeting, in L'Assomption, and there he warned against what he called the "Union nationalisation" of the Parti Québécois.

The orthodox campaigners argued that they were not calling for a referendum or attacking Lévesque's leadership: they just wanted to be able to talk about sovereignty and campaign for sovereign powers in certain areas, such as a policy of full employment. (There were elements of either naïveté or cynicism in this argument, since the first element of an effective full employment policy is control of interest rates, and this had been given up in the idea of sovereignty-association.)

The campaign for delegates was intense, with both sides complaining about foul play and demagoguery at meetings. The emotions of the crisis carried everyone through to Christmas but over the holidays, as the politicians returned home, many of them had a sense of what they had lost.

In December, when they had sat out a vote of confidence and seen the government win by a mere seven votes, the nine PQ dissenters believed that they had the bargaining power to force Lévesque to compromise — either before the convention or in terms of legislation in the Assembly, But over Christmas many realized sadly that there could be no happy ending, The Humpty Dumpty alliance — the odd coalition of idealists and pragmatists, nationalists and social democrats, that had united behind René Lévesque in 1968 — was broken and could not be repaired. But their final battle would not be simply symbolic: in addition to registering their dissent, the orthodox members wanted to do what they could to stop Pierre Marc Johnson.

So, during the week before the convention, the orthodox leaders accused Johnson of having forced Lévesque to take the position he had, supporting their position by quoting from the Godin profile, which was now on the cover of *L'actualité*, thus putting Johnson's photograph on every newstand in Quebec. The attention was embarrassing to Johnson and increasingly annoying to Lévesque.

The convention itself was full of strange echoes of the 1967 Liberal convention, when Lévesque's position had been rejected by the Quebec Liberal Party. On Friday night, as had been the case in 1967, the initial skirmish was fought on the issue of whether to hold a secret ballot. And, as in 1967, the party leadership won and it was a secret ballot.

On Saturday morning the debate was over which of several groups or "blocs" of resolutions would be debated. This decision would have a decisive effect on the outcome of the vote. Laurin argued that Lévesque's position, expressed in "bloc A," "does not constitute putting sovereignty aside, but putting it to death"; he called for the support of "bloc B," "in the name of fidelity, pride, dignity, and the future." Emotions were high: when the revisionists spoke, the applause was punctuated with boos.

A Laval delegate, Denis Bertrand, said angrily, "The new political ayatollahs, the guardians of the faith, the orthodoxes, the neo-fascists of sovereignty, those who do not let people speak, those who have booed several times—today, they are wrong."

The focus of the anger was not Lévesque, however, but Johnson and, to a lesser extent, the other ministers around him. Johnson was in a difficult position: if he spoke, he would seem to be seeking the spotlight and the premier's job. If he didn't, he would seem to lack the courage to defend his position. It was even more awkward because La Presse had published a poll that day showing that under Lévesque's leadership the PQ would lose to the Liberals, 39 per cent to 53 per cent; but if Johnson were leader, according to the poll the PQ would defeat the Liberals, 47 per cent to 46 per cent. He did speak, saying clearly that "the next election should not be held, either directly or indirectly, in disguised fashion or approximately, on the option."

The vote was taken: the revisionist resolution received 869 votes and the orthodox resolutions received 469 votes.

After the ratification vote on the resolutions passed by 921 to 495, 65.1 per cent to 34.9 per cent, Camille Laurin went to the microphone. Under an agreement he had negotiated with the chair, he announced that he would be registering his dissent in a room nearby—and the 495 delegates rose and left the hall, singing and chanting. (They returned later.)

Throughout the day René Lévesque had not intervened in the debate, saving his speech to the end. He had known how it would turn out: his assistant, Alexandre Stefanscu, had made a prediction that was accurate to within a few votes.

"We have, for all intents and purposes, gone back to our roots," he said. "That is to say that we are still, as we have been since the begining, sovereignists, but with the realism that the special situation that history and geography have made in Quebec demands. It is not for nothing that from the beginning, seventeen years ago, we evoked not only associate states, but even—do you remember, a sort of new Canadian community."[13]

It was a reminder to the audience that Lévesque had fashioned the PQ not with the indépendantistes of the RIN but with the conservative nationalists of the Ralliement National; that he had talked about a "Union Canadienne" in his original proposition of sovereignty-association. This was his final victory over those who were more idealistic and less pragmatic than he was; his final fight to re-establish his own particular vision in the party he had founded, a battle that he had fought again and again since 1968. It was a fight whose aim had never been so clear before, because his vision had never been so clear before. In the past, each fraction of the PQ could see its own view reflected in the leader's dazzling ambiguities and contradictory reflexes. Now Lévesque had clearly rejected rupture on favour of conciliation, active striving for independence in favour of a passive belief in it.

Even before his speech was finished, the orthodox supporters wer making their way a few blocks east to the Union Française, where they cheered the small group of former ministers and chanted ecstatically at the sight of Jacques Parizeau. But while the parallel with Lévesque's departure from the Liberal Party was obvious, there was a difference, and they knew it. As Louise Harel put it, in 1967 there was a mass movement waiting for Lévesque; in 1985 there was massive disenchantment with politics. The *La Presse* poll had shown that support for sovereignty-association had dropped to 19 per cent, and support for independence had dropped to 4 per cent. The orthodoxes knew they had 35 per cent support for an election on sovereignty in the party—and 4 per cent in the population.

But they also knew that some of the 65 per cent vote resulted from personal support for Lévesque; many wanted to stay on in the party to fight the good fight again — after Lévesque had left.

Thus Lévesque had resolved little. He had won a decisive victory, but those he had defeated were lying low and waiting; he had received a clean bill of health, but he was being watched like a hawk by supporters, friends, and opponents alike. He no longer had to worry about his idealistic critics, but instead about his pragmatic supporters — who, having won the convention, increasingly felt that the old man had served his time and should step aside for someone the polls had shown could win: Pierre Marc Johnson.

But Lévesque continued to make it clear that he had no intention of stepping down. Nor was he amused by the constant focus on Johnson. (At the press conference after the convention, Lévesque was asked if he was concerned that Johnson was more popular than himself. "Yes," replied Lévesque, "And could I prevail on you not to insist too heavily on that, because you're in danger of hurting Mr Johnson, who I think deserves all his chances." His attempt at an impish grin fooled no one.)

Lévesque repeated that he preferred to wait until the fall of 1985 before calling an election; he still insisted that he would be leading the party into the next election and made it clear that he was determined to do his best to negotiate on the constitution with the Mulroney government.

Those who had resigned, such as Parizeau and Laurin, knew what some of Johnson's disgruntled backbench supporters seemed unable to comprehend: Lévesque had only months left to try to repair his place in history and, as long as he had the strength to continue, he was not going to retire simply because a pollster, some unhappy backbenchers, and some editorial writers or columnists thought he should. Many of those closest to him were deeply worried about him, and some of those most loyal to him felt that he would not be able to regain the strength he needed to govern and to lead the party into the next election, But they also knew how determined he was.

He had founded the Parti Québécois and had fought with it with all the intensity of a father battling a rebellious child. He had led it to victory twice and had suffered a terrible defeat that his own referendum had made possible. But, in part because he had a stronger commitment to Quebec itself than to the ideal of independence, he had forced the party to make a final change of direction that had pushed the idealists who had been at the heart of the party to the margin.

The transition had been a crisis for René Lévesque, for the PQ, and for the nationalists who had looked to the party for political leadership — but it was not a crisis for Quebec. The crisis was political and personal, but not societal. In fact, the PQ had, since the prescient conservatism of the 1981 election campaign, come to terms with the fact that there was no ideological debate in Quebec: all the political parties were elbowing for room on the centre right.

Lévesque again left on holidays — this time to Florida with Deputy-Premier Marc-Andre Bedard, who apparently tried without success to persuade him to resign. Before he left, one close collaborator worried that Lévesque would return rested, reassure his caucus and his cabinet of his determination and his ability to stay on — and then slip back to his exhausted state.

Exactly this began to happen — but less because of Lévesque's behaviour than that of those in his cabinet and his caucus. Beginning in late March, articles began to appear in different newspapers, first to the effect that a dozen ministers and MNAs would not run again if Lévesque remained leader, then that MNAs were preparing to confront him directly, and finally that he had decided to resign and would be announcing his decision at the National Council meeting — originally scheduled for June 8, then postponed to June 15, and finally to be held on June 22.

During that spring Lévesque had Louis Bernard put together a constitutional proposal: a long list of Quebec's so-called "traditional demands." Mulroney acknowledged them politely, and waited; he was in no hurry to negotiate with Lévesque, who was governing on borrowed time. But the speculation over his next move continued until the end of the session, as observers and politicians had become convinced that he would not resign but would take the summer to reflect on his future and decide whether or not to lead the party into the next election.

On June 20, 1985, the last day of the National Assembly session, the National Assembly marked the twenty-fifth anniversary of Lévesque's first election on June 22, 1960, and he was forced to listen to a series of eulogies and sit through two standing ovations, grimacing with embarrassment. But he rose to the challenge of acknowledging the speeches of congratulations, quipping, "Those whom you are burying with flowers are doing just fine."

There was a spontaneous standing ovation as the sixty-two-year-old premier sat in his chair, wincing and twitching, and looking as though he would rather be somewhere else.

Liberal Leader Robert Bourassa praised his opponent's "courage, determination, and great sincerity." He also made it clear that he had lost none of his respect for Levesque's political strength. "We are aware, Mr. Speaker, that after twenty-five years, the premier can always, when he wants to, be a formidable politician," he said.[14]

That night, Lévesque made known the decision he had made at Easter in a letter to party vice-president Nadia Assimopoulos, who received the letter at 11:10 p.m. "You surely assumed, like many others, that sooner or later I would quit the leadership of the party," he wrote. "Having weighed the alternatives as well as I can, I submit the following, which constitutes my resignation, which takes effect today. It is thus your responsibility, unless I am mistaken, to set in motion the process of replacement which is laid out in the statutes."

And, with a paragraph of thanks to the party volunteers and delegates and the National Council meeting, he was gone. He had succeeded in doing what every retiring leader wants: despite all the months of suspense and intrigue, despite having made the decision to resign at Easter, he had taken everyone by surprise.

In September, on the eve of the vote that confirmed Pierre Marc Johnson as his successor, the party gave Lévesque an around-the-world plane ticket — provoking a bittersweet joke from him to the effect that they obviously wanted him as far away as possible. Johnson governed for a few months and then called an election for December 2, 1985.

Given the disastrous poll figures earlier in the year, he managed to do well in getting 39 per cent of the popular vote although winning only twenty-three seats. Robert Bourassa led the Liberals back to power with ninety-nine seats.

On his return, Lévesque set to work to write his memoirs — which enabled him, literally, to turn the page on politics. Back in 1969 he had said that, if Quebec became independent, he would not stay on in politics, but would either become an ambassador or return to journalism. His return, when it came, was to journalism.

He met the late-July 1986 deadline, and, when the book was published, embarked on an extensive book tour. That tour revealed another of the paradoxes of his career: the man who had given the Quebec independence movement the respectability and legitimacy it had never enjoyed before was adored in English Canada. Thousands of people stood in long lines in front of bookstores to meet him and shake his hand.

At the Francophone Summit in Quebec City in September 1987, Lévesque was in attendance — as a reporter. It was startling at first to see him sitting at press conferences, asking questions, a colleague to those of us he had so fascinated and so eluded as a politician. He was obviously glad to be back in journalism for, despite all the years in politics, he had never lost his curiosity, his love of telling stories, or the dislike of protocol that he had acquired as a reporter and a foreign correspondent. The the transition was not yet complete: his TV producer kept pressing him to get an interview with French president Francois Mitterrand and Lévesque kept snapping that this wasn't in the contract. But when the last summit press conference was over, he was ushered up through the crowd to talk briefly to the French president and a dozen tape recorders were thrust into the encounter. When they replayed their tapes, reporters heard Lévesque suggesting an interview — to be conducted during the French elections the next March.

On Friday, October 30, Lévesque attended a fund-raising dinner for Canadian authors in Montreal and bumped into Pierre Trudeau. Lévesque was full of the projects he was embarking on: television documentaries in countries he had never managed to visit before, political reporting of one kind or another, For once, Trudeau seemed the less vigorous of the two: he had recently had knee surgery and was still using a cane to walk. It occurred to him that Lévesque was taking on too much.

On Sunday, November 1, 1987 Lévesque complained of indigestion. His wife urged him to go to the hospital, but, ever suspicious of hospitals, he would have none of it. During dinner, about 8pm, he collapsed. Frantically, Corinne Côté-Lévesque telephoned Urgence Santé, the emergency ambulance service, and, as a nurse stayed on the line, began giving mouth-to-mouth resuscitation and chest massage. The ambulance was stuck in traffic but a doctor arrived separately ten minutes after the call and tried to revive him.

At 8.35, twenty-two minutes after the call, the ambulance arrived, and the paramedics worked for another forty-five minutes before carrying him to hospital. He was dead when the ambulance arrived.

René Lévesque's death was an enormous shock, both in Quebec and in the rest of Canada. Thosands stood in line for hours in Montreal to pay their respects and, when the coffin was removed from where he had been lying in state to be brought to Quebec City for a state funeral, there was spontaneous applause, a last inarticulate gesture of respect, affection, and grief.

For millions of Quebecers, he was a cultural symbol as much as a partisan figure: a little guy, whose weaknesses and strengths were a reflection of all the contradictions in French-speaking Quebec. He was full of paradoxes. A man who hated political parties and was suspicious of serious people who liked going to meetings had presided over a party that was full of them. The man who invented the term sovereignty-association hated labels and definitions: he played with them sometimes, hinting, teasing, and flirting, but then would slip away from their constraints. He entered politics to do things.

And, while death meant his oratory was suddenly stilled, and his sentences no longer floated like the wisps of cigarette smoke that constantly surrounded him, his achievements remained. Hydro-Québec. The cleanest party fund-raising system in North America. A framework of progressive legislation, including agricultural zoning, anti-scab legislation, strong laws on health and safety in the workplace, provincial automobile Insurance. The renewed strength of the French language in Quebec. But, above all, a commitment to democracy. For Lévesque set a number of critical precedents that shaped the political culture in Quebec: he committed the province to the rule that only voters can contribute to political parties; he established the principle that a mandate from a majority of the population in a referendum is required to change the political regime; and he accepted the results of such a referendum in 1980.[15]

THE SHOCK IN QUEBEC AT LÉVESQUE'S DEATH WAS NOT MERELY personal. Politically, it had the seismic effect of an earthquake.

Pierre Marc Johnson, who had been in Paris when Lévesque died, was faced with a nationalist surge in his party; those who had left the party over the sovereignty issue in 1984-85 made it clear that they were reclaiming the Parti Québécois. On November 11, 1987, realizing that he could no longer fight the nationalist faction attacking him from outside the PQ, Johnson stepped down from the leadership of the party.

Four months later, on March 18, Jacques Parizeau became leader, unopposed. Vowing to talk about sovereignty "before, during, and after" elections, Parizeau re-energized the Parti Québécois and on September 25, 1989, while Bourassa won a second term with ninety-three seats, the PQ won twenty-nine seats. (Unhappiness in the English community following Bourassa's use of the "notwithstanding clause" to exempt Bill 89, the Liberal amendments to the sign provisions of the language law, from a decision by the Supreme Court resulted in the election of four members of the Equality Party.)

Despite the crisis of morale, membership, and fund-raising that had followed the departure of the separatist wing, and the revival in those three areas under Parizeau's leadership, the party's actual electoral performance did not alter much. Pierre Marc Johnson, whose leadership is viewed as the low-water mark for the PQ, won twenty-three seats and 39 per cent of the vote in 1985 while the Liberals won ninety-nine seats; in 1989, when the party congratulated itself for its miraculous recovery, it received 40.2 per cent of the vote.

On September 12, 1994, after nine years of a Liberal government that had become tired and unpopular, Jacques Parizeau led the PQ back to power, forming a government with seventy-seven seats and 44.7 per cent of the popular vote, only a hair ahead of the Liberals, led by Daniel Johnson (the older brother of Pierre Marc), who got 44.4 per cent of the vote but only forty-seven seats. Mario Dumont, who had formed the Action Démocratique du Québec with a group of disenchanted Liberal nationalists and conservative young people, succeeded in winning a seat and getting 6.5 per cent of the vote.

Once he was elected, it was clear that Parizeau was going to move to a referendum soon, despite the fact that the polls suggested that the Yes side would lose. Lucien Bouchard, who had left the Mulroney cabinet in May, 1990, before the collapse of the Meech Lake Accord and formed the Bloc Québécois that summer, pressured Parizeau to agree that the referendum should be fought on a softer question than Parizeau wanted.

Bouchard's eerie political aura was reinforced by the stunning turnaround of the campaign. From a position of apparent powerlessness, he forced Parizeau to change direction, sign an agreement with him and Mario Dumont in June, and give up his leadership in the middle of the campaign. His brush with death from a flesh-eating disease had made him a near-martyr and taken away nothing from his charisma or rhetorical intensity.

Parizeau was not in the same position. He prided himself on the clarity of his beliefs and made a point of calling himself a separatist when everyone else recoiled from the word. However, he was forced to claim that he had "evolved" to a position of supporting the partnership proposal, thus agreeing to a concept that he had considered irrational, and had to concede leadership in the campaign. He had to swallow his pride and convictions without expressing his displeasure.

Bouchard, on the other hand, by insisting on the idea of a partnership with the rest of Canada, revived Lévesque's contradictory ideal of sovereignty-association without using the word: independence but partnership; freedom but respect; secession but association. This ideal struck at the deep contradictory feelings and desires in Quebec for recognition and reconciliation, acknowledgment and association. Bouchard also stirred the wells of bitterness and resentment and feelings of rejection that many Quebecers felt over the Constitution and Meech Lake — sentiments hotly felt in the summer of 1990 returned with a vengeance.

The question was "Do you agree that Quebec should become sovereign, after having made a formal offer to Canada for a new economic and political partnershop, within the scope of the bill respecting the future of Quebec and of the agreement signed on June 12, 1995?" The margin of victory was less than 54,000 votes out of over 4.6 million votes cast; 50.6 per cent voted No, and 49.4 per cent voted Yes.

On referendum night, October 30, 1995 when the agonizingly close results were known, Parizeau let his bitterness show. "We are beaten, it's true," he told the crowd. "But by what, basically? By money and the ethnic vote."

It was a remark that shocked the party and the province; Parizeau had previously decided that he would resign if he lost. The next day, he did so. Three months later, on January 27, 1996, Lucien Bouchard was acclaimed leader of the Parti Québécois and was sworn in as premier on January 29.

During the years the Lévesque's government was in power, Bouchard had worked as the Quebec government's chief labour negotiator and had become close to Pierre Marc Johnson, who was then Quebec's minister of labour and later minister of health. Ironically, Bouchard would suffer a fate similar to that of both Lévesque and Johnson.[16]

As leaders of the Parti Québécois all three men tried to turn the party away from a rock-hard commitment to a referendum and tried to straddle the dream of independence and the political realities of the moment. All three faced pressures in the PQ from the true believers: Lévesque had one-quarter of his cabinet quit in 1984, Johnson resigned as leader in the face of a attacks from the nationalists, and Bouchard left behind a party that also reflects the tensions between pragmatism and purity of ideals.

In January 2001 Bouchard came back from a holiday with his family in Martinique, where he had completed several weeks' reflection on the impact of the November 27, 2000, federal election results: his nemesis, Jean Chrétien, had received more votes from Quebecers than his protégé, Bloc Québécois leader Gilles Duceppe. Saying that he had failed to revive the flame of independence, he announced his imminent departure from public life.

When he had become premier, almost exactly five years earlier, Bouchard tried to bring back some of those who had been closest to Lévesque: Jean-Roch Boivin, the gruff, tough-talking lawyer who had been the fixer and bad cop in Lévesque's office, and Michel Carpentier, the devoted aide to Lévesque who came back to be Quebec senior civil servant before suffering a terrible car accident. They, and an informal circle of others such as former justice minister Marc-André Bédard, were to be his link to the Golden Age of the Parti Québécois.

He also seemed to be trying to recapture some of Lévesque's ambiguity, trying to get some room to manoeuvre between the resistance to constitutional change in Ottawa and the impatience for independence in his party. While Bouchard's partisan rhetoric proclaimed his commitment to Quebec independence, he often showed signs of wanting to co-operate with the rest of Canada, befriending Ontario's Mike Harris and signing the 2000 health-care accord.

But the possibility of maintaining that ambiguity had died in 1984. The tensions that have marked the Parti Québécois since its creation remain constant—but the party has hardened, becoming both more conservative and more nationalist. The death of the Meech Lake Accord in 1990 made it impossible to sustain Lévesque's ideal of sovereignty-association. Sovereignty-hyphen-association became sovereignty. Period.

As premier, Bouchard was very conscious of the weight of responsibility left by his predecessors. At one premiers' conference, when he resisted pressure to join a consensus that he felt would allow the federal government too great a role in social policy, this feeling was particularly acute. He could almost see the spectres of now-dead former premiers—Jean Lesage, Lévesque, Bourassa—standing in the room like the ghostly baseball players in the film *Field of Dreams*. It was a powerful image of how haunted he had been by history.

His personal political trajectory had been, to say the least, uneven. He campaigned for the federal Liberals in 1968 and for the provincial Liberals in 1970 but, disillusioned by Pierre Trudeau after his invocation of the War Measures Act, had joined the Parti Québécois in 1972. He wrote the speech in which Mulroney commited his party to constitutional reconciliation with Quebec (the 1984 election promise that led to Meech Lake), ran as a Tory in 1988, and left cabinet in a rage in May, 1990. With the silent approval of Bourassa, himself a master of ambiguity who straddled Quebec's conflicting political emotions, Bouchard founded the Bloc Québécois. In 1995, as Bloc leader, he forced Parizeau to moderate his position, and emerged as the dominant force in the 1995 referendum.

Some English-speaking Canadian observers have denounced his changes as lies and betrayals;[17] others, more sympathetic, have spoken of his "successive sincerities." But Bouchard's mercurial nature, his pride, his sense of honour, his hunger for collective solidarity and reconciliation, his shifting sense of where and how his values would be best reflected—all these have been an uncanny reflection of the Quebec body politic over the last four decades.

BERNARD LANDRY, WHO SUCCEEDED BOUCHARD ON MARCH 2, 2001, has had no such bumps in his political history: he became leader of the PQ at his 120th National Council meeting. He had been with the party since the beginning, and his adult life had been a reflection of the evolution of the sovereignty movement.

Jean-Bernard Landry was born in 1937 and grew up in St. Jacques-de-Montcalm, a village outside Joliette, a small town northeast of Montreal. Landry was an only child until his parents adopted two younger girls. The family lived on Landry's grandfather's farm but his father was a jack of all trades, selling insurance and doing odds and ends.

Landry went to the Séminaire de Joliette—where Jean Chrétien, several years older, was also a student—and founded the student council. He was already a nationalist, devoted to the idea that Quebec was a nation and should become independent. While at the Séminaire, Landry was recruited to join the Ordre de Jacques Cartier. This powerful secret society, which died out in the 1960s, was an elite nationalist network. Known colloquially as La Patente, it played the same kind of role in Quebec that the Orange Lodge did in Ontario: campaigning secretly for nationalist goals and conservative religious values, infiltrating social organizations, and promoting the interests of its members.

Landry dismisses it as an influence on him. "(Joining) it was almost automatic," he said. "It was more of a mutual aid organization."[18] Alluding to La Patente's support for the Achat Chez Nous campaign to support French Canadian merchants, Landry quipped that this was a narrow view that he abandoned when he embraced free trade.

But the young man who left the Séminaire de Joliette at the end of the 1950s to go to law school at the Université de Montréal was a traditional conservative nationalist, influenced by the teachings of Lionel Groulx in some ways, but unusual in another. Lysiane Gagnon met him in 1959, when he was twenty-two, and recalled in *La Presse* that she was stunned by his deep commitment to Quebec independence at a time when only marginal right-wingers in the Alliance Laurentienne even thought about it.

At university, he met people who modified his conservatism, if not his nationalism. Fellow students such as Jacques Girard—later a deputy minister and now president of Montreal International—and Pierre Marois were urban and more progressive.

In 1960 Landry joined the Liberal party and worked in the election that defeated the Union Nationale. He then became active in student politics. In 1962 he was elected president of the students' council. Marois, his closest ally in student politics, was more emotional, more charismatic; Landry was harder. "Landry became the leader of everything he got involved in," observed Yves Duhaime, a fellow student and later cabinet colleague. Another student activist from the era recalls that Marois was more outgoing—but Landry was tougher. "Landry was tough, really tough," he said.

Landry was also moving in a different direction. Like many students from modest backgrounds, he joined the Canadian Officers' Training Corps and became an officer in the reserves, joining Le Regiment de Joliette, the 83rd Infantry battalion. "I carried on a fight for the French language," he says. "I remember being told, 'Lt. Landry, speak English! It's an order!'"

You can see the traces still: the posture, the rigour, the discipline, the organizational zeal, the determination to take command. Unlike many of his contemporaries, Landry stayed with the COTC, remaining an officer in the reserves for a decade, leaving only in the early 1970s.

It was in December, 1962, at the age of twenty-five, that Bernard Landry became a name to reckon with. His slogan in his campaign for student president had given a hint of his ambitions: "In the service of the students and the nation." His student council immediately started to shake things up—starting a student co-operative, getting students involved in the slums of Montreal, launching a student strike over tuition and cafeteria prices.

Seizing on public outrage at the remark by CN president Donald Gordon before a parliamentary committee in Ottawa that there were no French Canadians qualified for executive positions in the railway, Landry and Marois organized a massive student demonstration against Gordon. They went to see him and, when they emerged, talked to the press, poised and confident. Gordon seemed a symbol of the old order: aging (he was sixty-one and had not been well), unilingual, and out of touch.

Outside, thousands of students shouted their anger and his effigy was burned in protest. There was no violence, but the organizers had prepared with military precision: if the police, on horseback, had charged the students, they had bags of marbles ready to upset the horses. The precaution was never used.

Landry graduated in 1963 and married Lorette Jacquemin. While doing his bar admission course, he worked briefly for the Quebec Labour Federation on its human rights committee and founded the Human Rights League with his former law professor, Trudeau. But it was such a short tenure that he considered his first real job to have been with Lévesque.

A few days before Landry arrived for work, Lévesque had had a stormy meeting with a group of executives from the Quebec North Shore company, who objected to the minister's interventionist policies. Lévesque, furious, banged his fist on the table so hard he smashed a pane of glass — which had been intended for Landry's desk top. Apologizing for the cracked desktop, the office secretary offered to get it replaced. "Don't worry about it, madame," Landry replied. "It will remind me what the policy of the office is."[19] Lévesque and Landry would later refer to the incident as a symbol of the "creative tension" between the state and the private sector.

After a year working for Lévesque, Landry decided he needed more education and got leave to go to France to study economics and politics. Still technically a member of a minister's staff, he cruised around Paris in a white Renault cabriolet convertible and, to the delight of his companions, bluffed Paris gendarmes and talked his way out of traffic violations.

Landry, Marois, Duhaime, and Jacques Léonard were students in Paris together. A decade later, the four would be in the first Lévesque cabinet. (Of the four, Landry would prove to be the most ambitious by nature, the most technocratic in style, the most skilled in political manoeuvring, and the most persistent in hanging in against all odds when others had dropped out or moved on.)

In 1967 Landry went back to Quebec and back to work as a civil servant in the planning department of the Ministry of Natural Resources, working on the development of state-owned Quebec initiatives in the economy such as Rexfor (wood products) SOQUIP (gas and oil), and SOQUEM (mining). But he decided that under the Union Nationale Quebec could not make the changes he felt were essential. So he left government and returned to Joliette to practise law, planning to run for the Parti Québécois. He ran in 1970 and lost. In 1973, after his second defeat, he moved to Montreal to follow his wife, also a lawyer, who had been appointed to a position in the city. For three years, he practised law in the firm of Lapointe, Rosenstern White.

In 1976 he packed his law books into boxes and headed to Quebec City, where he became minister of state for economic development and, later, minister of external trade. During those years Landry developed policy documents—*Building Quebec* and *The Technological Transformation*[20]—whose recommendations and results can be seen in the present state of high-tech Montreal.

Landry remained loyal to Lévesque when "the orthodoxes" left the party, but kept lines open to them. He withdrew from the leadership campaign in 1985 when polls showed his cause was hopeless and served as Johnson's minister of finance for only a few weeks in 1985 before he lost his seat in the 1985 election. Many of his colleagues moved on, but Landry stuck to politics. He taught at the Université du Québec à Montréal and, thanks to his ability to speak Spanish, at the University of Guerrero in Mexico—but he became vice-president of the PQ and was always available to do whatever chore was required for the party, no matter how inconvenient.

In 1993 he was re-elected and in 1994 became a pillar of Parizeau's cabinet. He was cautious about the idea of a referendum in 1995, warning publicly that the PQ should not drive the car over a cliff, and saying that he did not want to be second-in-command in the charge of the Light Brigade. As premier, he has introduced his own version of sovereignty-association, saying that he wants to create "a confederal union" between Quebec and the rest of Canada, a term that carries its own ambiguities.

But it is possible to see flashes of bitterness. Even before his outburst at a Mexican hotel employee on referendum night, Landry looked like a man with a chip on his shoulder who could see a lifelong dream slipping away. Only days before becoming premier, with an insulting turn of phrase about the Canadian flag (calling it a "chiffon rouge," or red rag) he reminded Canadians of his flaws: his thin skin, his quick temper, his prickly manner. His more aggressive tone has had an invigorating effect on PQ memberships and Canadians may soon learn to be wary of his strengths: his intelligence, his stubbornness, and his lifelong commitment to making Quebec an independent country.

IN THE YEARS SINCE THE ERUPTION IN THE PARTI QUÉBÉCOIS IN 1984, many events have occurred. Conservative attempts to amend the constitution so that Quebec would sign—the Meech Lake and Charlottetown Accords—failed. Support for sovereignty surged after the failure of Meech Lake, and the referendum of 1995 failed by a hair's breadth. Since 1995 support for sovereignty and for sovereignist parties has gradually declined (although support for sovereignist parties has not dropped below 38 per cent, despite the weaknesses of the Bloc Québécois). The backlash that many (including me) expected from the federal government's Clarity Act never occurred, and the federal Liberals won a plurality of the votes in Quebec in November 2000.

But the party Lévesque created remains in power, his heritage remains intact, one of his protégés is premier, and the currents of opinion and sentiment which roiled his government, his party, and his society during his years in power remain relevant. The goal of a referendum on Quebec sovereignty remains clear. Speaking to the youth wing of the party in August, Bernard Landry renewed his commitment to hold a referendum after the next election, adding that he hoped Quebec would attend the Summit of the Americas in Buenos Aires in 2005.[21] The story of René Lévesque and the Parti Québécois in power continues to resonate.

Graham Fraser
August 2001

Notes

1   I wrote about this trip in "René Lévesque: The Anglais Cheer As He Calls for Canada' Break-Up," Maclean's, May 1969; reprinted in *Canada From The Newstands: A Selection from the Best Canadian Journalism of the Past Thirty Years*, edited by Val Clery (Toronto: Macmillan Canada, 1978), 196-202.

2   Claude Morin, Lévesque's Minister of Intergovernmental Affairs, admitted in a Radio-Canada investigative documentary by Normand Lester broadcast on May 7, 1992 that he had been a paid informer for the RCMP. For a sense of the shock that this news created, see Hubert Bauch, "The Schemer," *The Gazette*, May 9, 1992; Louis Falardeau, "Lisez, Puis Choisissez Le Titre: Claude Morin est un naïf dupé par la GRC, ou Claude Morin est un vulgaire informateur," *La Presse*, May 9, 1992; Robert McKenzie, "Morin Shakes the Soul of Quebec Independence," the *Toronto Star*, May 10, 1992 and "Witness Believes News of

Morin Gave Levesque Mild Heart Attack, *Toronto Star*, May 13, 1992; and Gilles Lesage, "Le Sphynx Déboulonné: Claude Morin est tombé d'un piédestal qu'il avait mis 30 ans à bâtir," *Le Devoir*, May 14, 1992.

3 Most of the following, on the period leaing up to the January 19 convention, is drawn from the epilogue I wrote for the paperback edition of *PQ: René Lévesque and the Parti Québécois in Power* (Toronto: Macmillan of Canada, 1985). In addition, I covered these events on a daily basis for the *Globe and Mail*.

4 *Globe and Mail*, August 7, 1984..

5 *Globe and Mail*, August 10, 1984

6 *Globe and Mail*, September 24, 1984.

7 *Globe and Mail*, September 24, 1984.

8 Conversations inside cabinet and at private meetings were quoted on the basis of confidential interviews done during the winter and spring of 1985 in the preparation of the epilogue of the paperback edition of this book.

9 *Globe and Mail*, October 26, 1984.

10 For an analysis of the Venne statement, see the *Globe and Mail*, October 27, 1984.

11 *Globe and Mail*, January 19, 1985.

12 René Lévesque, *Memoirs*. Translated by Philip Stratford (Toronto: McClelland and Stewart, 1986), 27.

13 "Discours de Monsieur René Lévesque au Congrès National Extraordinaire du Parti Québécois," text distributed at convention; my translation.

14 *Globe and Mail*, June 21, 1985.

15 I expanded on this theme in "René Lévesque et le paradoxe démocratique," in *René Lévesque: l'homme, la nation, la démocratie*, textes colligés par Yves Bélanger et Michel Lévesque avec la collaboration de Richard Desrosiers et Lizette Jalbert (Montreal: Presses de l'Université du Québec, 1992), 119-23. Also published in *Vous m'intéressez: Chroniques* (Montreal: Boréal, 2001).

16 An expanded version of this assessment of Lucien Bouchard's year in power appeared in the *Toronto Star*, "Haunted by History," January 13, 2001.

17 See Lawrence Martin, *The Antagonist* (Toronto: Penguin, 1997).

18 Comment, and much of the passage on Landry, is taken from my profile published in the *Toronto Star*, "A Separate View," January 26, 2001, based on interviews with Landry, Yves Duhaime, and other sources who asked not to be identified.

19 Landry recounts the anecdote in "René Lévesque et ses rapports à l'économie," in Bélanger et Lévesque, *René Lévesque*, 299-300.

20 Published as *Bâtir le Québec* and *Le virage technologique*.

21 *Le Devoir*, 20 August 2001.

Prologue:
November 15,
1976

*C'est cela la folie, se laisser
emporter par un rêve; le laisser
croître en toute liberté,
exubérant, envahissant.*
Anne Hébert

For over an hour, Paul Sauvé Arena had been filling up with ecstatic Parti Québécois campaign workers. At 8.40, Radio-Canada had announced that the unbelievable had happened, that the Parti Québécois would form a majority government. From all around the region of Montreal, people were heading for the hockey arena in the east end to cheer and shout and share their delight.

It was incredible; beyond their wildest dreams. Premier Robert Bourassa had lost his seat to a journalist and poet, Gérald Godin. René Lévesque, a symbol of change in Quebec for over sixteen years, who had stepped into the political wilderness in 1967 to build a new party and had suffered two defeats, in 1970 and 1973, would be premier. The small band of idealists who had been struggling to build a dream had now become a virtual army, and anything seemed possible.

The campaign song, "A partir d'aujourd'hui", boomed out of the loudspeakers as the results continued to pour in; up on stage, the co-hosts turned the wall of posters around, one by one, to show the faces of the winning candidates.

But René Lévesque was in a state of virtual shock. He had really not expected victory; he had looked for a breakthrough, thirty or forty seats, and a strong opposition to the Bourassa government, but not power. Not yet. He was stunned.

When Lévesque and his entourage arrived at Paul Sauvé Arena and made their way inside and into a small locker room reserved for senior party staff, Louis Bernard was sitting waiting, watching the results on television.

Bernard, a former Quebec civil servant who had worked as the senior researcher and chief of staff for the PQ parliamentary leader since 1970, was a totally unflappable person; he looked at Lévesque and said simply, as one might to a nervous Olympic diver, "Take your time, Mr. Lévesque." Aides who had been worrying about how incredibly tense Lévesque had become saw him visibly relax for the first time since eight o'clock.

Then all eyes turned to the television set. Radio-Canada switched to the Liberal headquarters on Gilford Street. Robert Bourassa had arrived and gone down to the basement to talk to reporters. It was jammed and noisy, with metal chairs banging together; the very kind of uncontrolled scene that Bourassa had always taken pains to avoid. But he responded with calm dignity.

"Dear fellow citizens," he said, as reporters clustered around, reaching at him with microphones, "I obviously accept the verdict of the population, which seems very clear, at least on the level of seats."

After congratulating Lévesque and thanking the Liberal candidates, Bourassa gave his explanation of the defeat: Quebec was an increasingly polarized society, making it more and more difficult to govern by taking the middle course. "It is clear that the Liberal Party was caught between the left and the right — the left finding that it didn't go far enough, and the right finding that it lacked firmness."

Then, Bourassa made a particular appeal. "I would like to address myself, in the name of all Quebecers, to the economic milieu, particularly to the business community and labour, and ask them, given the context, in the name of Quebecers — ask them to have a thoughtful reaction to the events of this evening."

It was a graceful, dignified gesture, and, sitting in the players' locker room in Paul Sauvé Arena, groping for what to say himself to move the triumphant and reassure the fearful, Lévesque was moved.

For almost another half-hour, closeted with Bernard, Lévesque tried to work out what to say as the campaign song continued to boom out through the arena. Then, at 10.28, a group began to push its way through the crowd. To a last crescendo of "A partir d'aujourd'hui, demain nous appartient", with people shouting and waving flags and weeping for joy, Lévesque moved slowly through the crush up to the stage.

He was embraced by the co-host, a comedian and an old friend, Doris Lussier, who then moved to the microphone. "The Parti Québécois is the key!" he intoned. "Power is the lock. You have just put the key in the lock which opens the door to our future! Here is René Lévesque!"

Standing in the bath of sound, with Camille Laurin on his right, Lise Payette on his left, Gilbert Paquette and Claude Charron behind him, and several dozen other party workers, security guards, and even a few reporters squeezed onto the stage around him, Lévesque looked mournful, almost grief-stricken by the emotional shock of the occasion.

Joan Fraser, a reporter for the *Financial Times*, was in the crush of reporters below the stage, only a few feet away, and was struck by Lévesque's expression. For a split second, she could swear that what she saw was fear. Real fear.

After fifteen seconds of wild applause and cheers, he tried to speak. "Je pense que . . . je pense que . . ." he croaked, but the overwhelming sound would not let up. There were then forty-five seconds of chanting—partly chanting for the cameramen in front to get down so that the crowd could see Lévesque — before he could try again.

"I don't think I need to say to what point I am incapable now of making any comment on the extraordinary gesture of confidence which was unhoped for . . ."

Again, he was interrupted by wild cheers.

"I must tell you with all my heart that we hoped, but we didn't expect it like that this year!" He paused, and then — "I have never, I have never thought that I could be so proud to be a Quebecer as this evening!"

The hall erupted for a whole minute of cheering and chanting; sheer shrieks of delight, and rhythmic chanting of the old indépendantiste line from the 1960s, "Le Québec aux Québécois!"

"I want to thank from the bottom of my heart all the electors in every corner of Quebec who were not afraid of the necessary changes in Quebec!"

Again, applause. The speech went on like that: one hoarse, often convoluted line after another, flung out with an almost desperate intensity and sincerity, as Lévesque talked about "the enormous weight that the confidence of Quebecers has just placed on our shoulders", and vowed that "we will carry that weight with all the energy and all the honesty and all the enthusiasm that we will be able to put into it," clenching his fists with each noun, and then grasping the double mikes in front of him. As Lévesque spoke, Claude Charron put his head on Gilbert Paquette's shoulder and wept, sobbing "C'est trop beau!" — "It's too beautiful!"

Vowing that they would keep all their promises, Lévesque began to repeat what he called "this central commitment" — but digressed to say that he and the party hoped "in friendship with our fellow-citizens of Canada, to succeed in giving ourselves a country, but with . . ."

When the applause and cheers and chanting died down, he continued. "But this country of Quebec will only come when an adult society, true to itself, will have approved of this by a clear and democratic majority in a referendum as we have promised."

Lévesque then congratulated Bourassa for his "extremely appropriate and courageous remarks" a few minutes earlier. After a word to the defeated candidates, he concluded: "I would like to say, in a very very calm and very very sincere fashion, to our adversaries in Quebec, to our adversaries and to those who here, elsewhere, who could have feared the results of the victory of the Parti Québécois: that we want to make, and we are going to work with all our energies to make of Quebec a homeland that will be more than ever a homeland of all Quebecers who inhabit, and who love it.

"Again, I don't know how to thank the voters for the confidence and the responsibility which they have granted tonight. It is in my humble opinion—I don't know how to evaluate it, but I am sure that it is pretty well, politically, the most beautiful and perhaps the greatest evening in Quebec history. Bonjour!"

And with that, he was gone.

In Montreal, a long night of celebration began. In English Canada, a sense of shock set in, as if there had been an earthquake, or a hostage-taking. An adventure was about to begin and no-one, least of all René Lévesque, was sure where it would lead.

1
Winning

ONE

The Greenhouse Years

"I've read all kinds of silly things . . . [that are] all part of that false dogma of the great darkness which is supposed to have reigned over Quebec until the blessed year of God 1960, as if we had all been a bunch of fools before 1960 and the light had appeared after Mr. Lesage took power. That's a completely distorted view of history. You had a lot of intelligent, free-minded people working seriously, before 1960, and you've had a lot of foolish people after 1960 proclaiming themselves apostles of enlightenment, who are the stupidest minds that I've seen at work."

Claude Ryan

When René Lévesque stood at the eye of the storm of joy at Paul Sauvé Arena, mournfully clutching the microphones on the crowded stage, he was riding the latest of the waves of nationalist reform politics that had swept through Quebec society in the previous half-century. Until 1960, those waves had fallen short, petered out, and been absorbed by the forces of stability.

In each successive generation, the educated French-Canadian élite seems to have relived the nationalist debate, playing out the drama and fears of an isolated minority that has stubbornly refused to assimilate and join the English-speaking majority of North America. The fact of the Conquest in 1760, the failure of the rebellion of 1837-8, the proposals for assimilation by Lord Durham in his 1839 report, the terms of Confederation, the hanging of Louis Riel, the gradual destruction of French-language rights in Western Canada, and the fight for the use of French in air-traffic control in Quebec — each of these events has become part of the great subject, re-argued and reviewed in the light of each generation's experience. Each generation has renewed its commitment to the survival of a French-speaking society in North America.

Shortly after the rebellion of 1837, the Roman Catholic Church had established a position of overwhelming ideological dominance in Quebec, which it maintained for over a century. The rebellion — an attack on the existing order which came as a climax to the economic crisis of the 1830s — had failed. As Denis Monière put it, the defeat of the Patriotes "hastened the process of inferiorization in French-Canadian society", bringing "a defensive conservative resistance and the ideology of survival".

The failure of the rebellion was a victory for the clergy. "From now on, the dominant ideology in Quebec would reflect the clergy's world view and interests, as well as its sources of power," Monière wrote. "It was the beginning of a century of obscurantism."

But during the 120 years between Durham's description of Canada as "two nations warring in the bosom of a single state" and the death of Premier Maurice Duplessis, every variant of nationalist aspiration was to be heard, from the creation of a separate French-speaking independent state, to a more autonomous Quebec, to a fuller role for French Canadians in the federal government.

The conservative clerical reaction reinforced the unwritten rule of the society created by the Conquest: business remained English-speaking; moral authority remained in the hands of the Church. Thus, the Ministry of Public Instruction, which had been formed after Confédération, was abolished by a Conservative premier in 1875, and its powers were transferred to the Church.

The challenge for Catholicism was to preserve this society and its faith against the threats of industrialization and urbanization — solidly identified with anglicization, assimilation, and loss of faith. The response, in the words of Michel Brunet, was "agriculturalism, anti-statism, and messianism".

The first nationalist to articulate clearly the idea that Quebec should break away from Confederation was an American-born ultramontane journalist named Jules-Paul Tardivel, who published his own paper, *La Vérité*, beginning in 1881, and waged merciless war on Liberals in general and on Wilfrid Laurier (federal Liberal leader from 1887) in particular. The hanging of Louis Riel in 1885 was a turning point for Tardivel, and led him to reject the Conservatives as well as the Liberals, and to decide on separation as the long-term necessity for French Canada. Indignation over Riel also led Honoré Mercier, the Quebec Liberal leader, to form a new National Party. As its leader, he became premier of Quebec in 1887.

As Monière points out, Mercier "gave official status and impetus to the idea that the province of Quebec was the French-Canadian national state", and argued for the need for non-partisan unity among French Canadians.

In counterpoint to the separatist nationalism of Tardivel and the autonomist nationalism of Mercier was the pan-Canadian nationalism of Henri Bourassa, who in a public debate with Tardivel in 1904 argued that "the fatherland, for us, is the whole of Canada, that is to say, a federation of distinct races and autonomous provinces. The nation we want to see developed is the Canadian nation, composed of French Canadians and English Canadians."

Bourassa, however, remained a vigorous critic of Laurier, the apostle of conciliation, arguing that Laurier had compromised too much of French Canada's crucial needs in education in Western Canada, and had sacrificed Canada's independence to the imperial loyalties of English Canada.

These four men, Tardivel, Mercier, Bourassa, and Laurier, dominated the debate on the role and future of French Canada for virtually forty years, personifying four enduring aspects of political thought in Quebec: Quebec independence, Quebec autonomy, pan-Canadian French-Canadian nationalism, and anti-nationalist conciliation.

But one of the most important figures in the articulation of a nationalist vision for French Canada was a slight, frail priest and historian, Lionel Groulx. For the generation reaching maturity during the Depression, Groulx played a crucial and formative role as a writer and teacher, giving a generation of Quebec intellectuals a sense of French Canada's sacred mission.

Groulx's life spanned eighty years of French-Canadian nationalism: he was seven years old when Riel was hanged and, as a boy, sang the songs of outrage penned in Quebec to the tune of "La Marseillaise"; he was an inspiration to the nationalist youth of the 1920s and 1930s; he lived to delight in the nationalism and expansion of the state in Quebec in the 1960s.

Groulx was part of the rich Quebec tradition of teacher-priests who invest almost parental affection in their students. A nationalist and a romantic, sometimes given to harsh and blinkered generalizations about ethnic cultural characteristics, he was clearly anti-Jewish while professing to be opposed to anti-Semitism.

Partly because of the length of his career, Groulx is difficult to categorize simply. He was attacked as a xenophobe, but he uttered no call to violence. While his habit of calling French Canadians a "race" was more nationalist than racist, there was a dark tone of exclusivity to his view of French Canada, and he legitimized the ethnocentric fear of the outsider, the foreigner, the immigrant. Groulx endorsed the corporatism of Salazar and Mussolini — but he cannot be called a fascist.

He was deeply conservative, but looked to the state for an expanded role in the economy. His influence on Quebec nationalism was enormous. When he died, Claude Ryan called him "a sort of spiritual hyphen between three generations of French Canadians" and "the spiritual father of modern Quebec". According to René Lévesque, Groulx gave Quebecers "by his work and by his actions a great lesson in practical and enlightened patriotism which guides us today in our present choices".

His was a messianic nationalism: a religious, almost mystic conviction of French Canada's Catholic, rural, and heroic mission. That it was profoundly ambiguous in its direct political implications only added to his influence.

A circle of young literary intellectuals sought out Groulx in the 1930s, forming Les Jeune-Canada, and men like André Laurendeau and Pierre Dansereau were to become controversial nationalist figures. They also made anti-Semitic speeches in this period that they would renounce and deeply regret in later years.

However, the movement was to split in 1937 over the very question of Quebec separatism, and Dostaler O'Leary formed Les Jeunesses Patriotes, which included Michel Chartrand, Jean-Louis Gagnon, and several others. It was in 1937 that Dostaler O'Leary wrote *Séparatisme: doctrine constructive*, which laid out the Catholic, corporate basis for an independent Quebec, rejecting liberalism as "an essentially Anglo-Saxon institution inspired principally by Protestantism", which "leads to communism and anarchy".

O'Leary wrote that it was necessary to "centralize power in the hands of leaders capable of acting", saying, "The corporate state must be, consequently, authoritarian, and not totalitarian. It will protect the collectivity before individuals; it will talk about duties before talking of rights. . . . People will use the word 'dictatorship' to describe such a government. Why be afraid of words? We are not liberals who call economic, financial, or other kinds of dictatorship liberty."

While the ravages of the Depression created a right-wing reaction against a system that was failing, they also resulted in 1934 in a breakaway from the provincial Liberal Party, Action Libérale Nationale. The ALN's program called for new laws on collective bargaining, a minimum-wage law, a sickness-insurance scheme, and housing programs to eliminate slums. But the core of the program was the determination to national-ize the private hydro-electric companies.

The ALN introduced the idea of planning and the growth of the state to Quebec. But in 1935 Maurice Duplessis, the leader of the provincial Conservatives, induced the group of idealists into a merger to form a new party, the Union Nationale. After winning the election of 1936, Duplessis ruthlessly excluded the three leading ALN figures from the cabinet. Abbé Groulx complained, "To have used three men, to have paraded them from one end of the province to the other as the greatest political asset, and then on the day of victory, to throw them overboard, I call that a uniquely dirty political act."

Not only did Duplessis succeed in swallowing up the ALN, he also drew in right-wing nationalists like Paul Bouchard, the separatist editor of *La Nation*.

He laughed at intellectuals, regardless of their politics;

Duplessis understood power and fear. He knew how little tolerance there was in Quebec for ideas that questioned the most
traditional values of the Church, and how little challenge there
would be to his 1937 Padlock Law, which authorized him as
attorney general to close up any building he determined was
being used for Communist propaganda.

Shrewd, cunning, earthy, funny, he had total control of not
only his cabinet, but the state as a whole: summoning university rectors for their grants, he effectively vetoed the appointment of professors who were not practising Catholics, or who
were critics of the régime.

Opponents were attacked as Communists, and Communism
was constantly presented as the great threat to public safety
and morality in Quebec. Unionized workers were attacked on
the picket lines by the provincial police.

Public works like roads, hospitals, and bridges were represented as "gifts" from the Union Nationale, and explicitly given
or withheld, depending on how a constituency had voted. In
the words of Jean Marchand, Duplessis made favouritism a
political doctrine.

He knew how to play off the different parts of the Church
hierarchy against one another, boasting that "the bishops
eat out of my hand," and observing wryly, "There is no great
difficulty in governing Quebec. All one must do is keep the
Jesuits and Dominicans fighting."

Duplessis attacked Ottawa in the name of provincial autonomy, while at the same time welcoming foreign capital. "This
is a régime," said André Laurendeau, "which defended provincial autonomy to make Quebec the paradise for monopolies,
the kingdom of low salaries, and the land of slums."

For his working arrangement, with foreign capital was explicit. When Herbert Lank, then president of Du Pont of Canada,
went to Quebec in the early 1950s on behalf of the Canadian
Chamber of Commerce to complain about the imposition of
provincial income tax, Duplessis turned on him. "I don't sell
you our natural resources, I don't rent them to you, I give
them to you!" he snapped. "And your managers want to complain about a little income tax?

"Secondly, manpower," he continued. "Quebec's costs you
less and causes you fewer problems than any other in Canada
— not to mention the United States, of course. And it's my
government, it's the Union Nationale that takes care of it. And

you have the nerve to come crying to me, you, the bosses!"

In 1939, Duplessis was defeated by the combined assault of the provincial and federal Liberals, and Adélard Godbout became premier. But the conscription crisis doomed the Liberal government to an indelible image of subservience to federal authority.

The conscription crisis stimulated the creation of a reform nationalist coalition, the Bloc Populaire. Led by Maxime Raymond, a former Liberal MP, and André Laurendeau, the Bloc drew together nationalists from both right and left, inheriting many of the progressives who had worked with the ALN, but, at the same time, many of the defensive ethnocentric reflexes of the nationalism of the 1930s. In between, men as different as Jean Drapeau and Pierre Trudeau were attracted by its idealism.

The Bloc dissolved in 1948, and André Laurendeau joined *Le Devoir*. But he remained an important figure for the rising generation. A nationalist, a humanist, a deeply sensitive writer, he represented a kind of bridge between the earlier generation of nationalists around Abbé Groulx in the 1920s and 1930s, and the younger generation, often critical of the traditional nationalism.

After Duplessis returned to office in 1944, he stayed in power for the remaining fifteen years of his life. It was a crucial period: an era of economic growth and expansion and a time when, in the rest of the Western world, the state was expanding with the economy.

The war broke the spell of defensive conservatism. A generation came to adulthood during and after the war who refused to accept the traditional verities of mainstream Quebec society.

In addition to Laurendeau, another influential opponent to what Duplessis stood for was Father Georges-Henri Lévesque, Dean of the Faculty of Social Sciences at Laval, a source of cheerful inspiration to the young men and women who left the faculty to work in the union movement, journalism, the universities, and government.

For during the fifteen years that Duplessis remained in power, the new university graduates felt blocked and frustrated. Business remained mostly inaccessible to French Canadians, and Duplessis kept the lid tightly in place.

Working to criticize and change society remained a marginal, almost underground activity. And yet the activity was taking place; as Jean-Louis Roy put it, "Quebecers under Duplessis lived through and sparked apparently marginal phenomena which, during and despite the long reign of the chief, transformed Quebec society."

Some were mobilized by the Catholic Action movement, a lay organization that attracted young intellectuals from across Quebec, men and women like Claude Ryan, Gérard Pelletier, Guy Rocher, Maurice and Jeanne Sauvé, Marc Lalonde, and Pierre Juneau. A group of these people, with Pierre Trudeau, launched the magazine *Cité libre* in 1950 as a forum for dissent — albeit a dissent that remained Catholic in inspiration.

Some, like Jean Marchand, left Father Lévesque's faculty to work in the union movement. Marchand proved to be a crucial catalyst in the Asbestos strike that exploded in 1949.

The strike began after the Johns-Manville asbestos miners became fed up with a succession of setbacks at the National War Labour Board during the war and at arbitration on a grievance in 1948. At a meeting on February 13, the workers refused to allow Marchand, the union organizer for the Canadian and Catholic Confederation of Labour, the forty-eight hours he wanted to meet with the minister of labour; they had had enough of the arbitration process.

The illegal strike that began that night lasted until July 1 — nearly five months — and ended after intervention by the Archbishop of Quebec, Monseigneur Maurice Roy, with a ten-cent-an-hour increase for the miners and a guarantee by the company to rehire all the strikers.

The strike was not primarily for money, but for dignity. In January 1948, the company had voluntarily raised the base rate from 58 to 85 cents an hour. But the strike became first an almost spontaneous vote of non-confidence in "the authorities"—the company and the government—and became a fight for the survival of the union.

It proved to be both a watershed and a rallying point. For the first time, Church leaders in Quebec expressed sympathy for strikers; the provincial police proved to be brutal in their protection of strikebreakers and their intimidation of strikers; links between the governments in Ottawa and Quebec and the asbestos industry were exposed.

The strike acted as a magnet for the critics of the Duplessis régime. Gérard Pelletier covered it for *Le Devoir*, Pierre Trudeau came as a volunteer, at Laval Guy Rocher, a student, and Maurice

Lamontagne, a faculty member, raised money for the strikers, and Father Lévesque spoke at a rally in their support.

Years afterward, the strike remained a symbol of opposition to Duplessis. In 1956, seven years later, Pierre Trudeau published a collection of articles on the strike; the contributors included Fernand Dumont, Jean Gérin-Lajoie, Charles Lussier, and Maurice Sauvé. Of that group, Dumont and Gérin-Lajoie would become indépendantistes; the others would become active federalists.

Other critics of the Duplessis régime, like Maurice Lamontagne and Marcel Rioux, were virtually compelled to work in Ottawa, because their views were considered too radical for Quebec universities. Rioux was disqualified explicitly because he declared himself to be an atheist; he was not allowed to teach in Quebec until after 1960.

But while some of them worked in Ottawa, they never felt at home there, or at ease with English Canadians. In one form or another, the feeling of humiliation in dealing with the English was a central emotional experience for many French Canadians of that generation.

"You know, every French Canadian has his own bitter memory of English insensitivity," Jean Marchand once remarked. "It remains carved in each of us for life." His own bitterest memory comes from childhood, when he used to spend summers along the St. Lawrence, near Trois-Rivières. Yachts would cruise past, and the owners would toss coins over the side for the boys to dive for, as the blacks used to do for the cruising tourists in the Caribbean. "There were times when I thought I would drown, reaching out for those bloody five-cent pieces."

Later, Marchand encountered some of the scars others carried, during the Asbestos strike in 1949 — a key struggle against the Duplessis régime. Everyone talked about the manager who kept a dog in his office and who, when annoyed, would sic the dog on the miners. It was several weeks before Marchand realized that this had happened twenty years before; the sense of outrage was so fresh it seemed to have happened a week ago.

Others remembered sales clerks refusing to serve them in French, or racial slurs. The world-renowned ecologist Pierre Dansereau, who grew up in Outremont, the home of Montreal's French-speaking élite, recalls that until the introduction of the dial telephone it was difficult, if not impossible, to use the

telephone without speaking English, since the operators usually spoke no French. He also recalls the condescension towards Quebec French. "It was bad enough being complimented
on one's English—but it was much worse to be complimented
on one's French, to be treated as some kind of superior exception to the rule."

As a young man, Jacques Parizeau lost his temper in a bar
when he was told to "speak White"; he broke his hand in the
ensuing scuffle and, ever since, the little finger on his right
hand has veered off at an angle.

In Ottawa, Marcel Rioux and Pierre Trudeau would talk about
"Greeks" when referring to potentially sympathetic French-
Canadian civil servants, for fear of being overheard.

It was a generation with a potent combination. In classical
college, they had benefited from one of the most rarified and
intense of classical educations; but the turmoil of post-war
change made them impatient of the traditions of passivity.
Business was closed to them, through prejudice, lack of openness to francophones — and lack of interest on their part.

For fifteen years, they were kept on the outside of positions
of authority. These were, in Gérard Pelletier's phrase, the years
of impatience. They had the effect of a greenhouse, isolating
and intensifying this generation. The intimacy of the classical-
college system formed an élite; the inaccessibility and repres-
siveness of the Duplessis régime kept it together, united in
opposition; the years of waiting gave it energy and forged its
ideas. The death of Duplessis in 1959 and the election victory
of the Quebec Liberals in 1960 took the lid off this generation
in waiting.

The ensuing explosion of energy not only transformed the
state in Quebec, but resulted in the transformation of government in Canada as a whole. United against Duplessis, this élite
divided over the national question, but retained, in Quebec
City and Ottawa, a remarkably similar vision of the state. The
head of steam that this generation built up in the 1940s and
1950s would carry them into power in the 1960s and keep
them dominant in Canadian life into the mid-1980s.

It was against this backdrop of evolving nationalism and a
rising generation that René Lévesque emerged as a magnetic
figure in Quebec.

TWO

René Lévesque:
Prelude to Politics

Every adult, whether he is a
follower or a leader, a
member of a mass or an
elite, was once a child.
He was once small. A sense
of smallness forms a
substratum in his mind,
ineradicably. His triumphs
will be measured against
this smallness, his defeats
will substantiate it.

Erik H. Erikson

By November 1976, René Lévesque was already a mythic figure in Quebec. A full-blown star for twenty years, first as a television host and then as the most outspoken member of the Liberal cabinet of Jean Lesage from 1960 to 1966, he projected a personality that seemed transparently honest, impulsive, mischievous, modest, outspoken, and provocative. His foibles — a chain-smoking sloppy dresser, he was a notorious night owl, working and then relaxing until the early hours — were as endearing as his strengths.

A study of Lévesque is, in large part, a study of language, gesture, and culture — for, in a homogeneous society with a strong oral tradition, Lévesque was a cultural force as much as a politician. An artist. A performer. A star.

In 1964, the novelist and filmmaker Jacques Godbout called Lévesque "Quebec's first lay teacher", and compared him to Quebec's symbolic hero, Maurice Richard. It was a telling comparison, for Maurice Richard, the dark, explosive hockey legend with the smouldering eyes, is a symbol of both pride and humiliation, remembered for his scoring triumphs, his martyred rage, and his bitterness against the NHL and Les Canadiens management. (Richard is the only hockey player whose suspension provoked a nationalist riot.)

Lévesque's career had been a torrent of words: a seemingly unending exhortation to Quebecers, emerging in a stream of prose that has been described as "an original mixture of joual, popular phrases, freshly coined words, American or English expressions that have been more or less gallicized, all expressed in long sentences plaited with an incredible association of ideas."

At his best, Lévesque personified simplicity and action: in place of the vanity and rhetoric of traditional politics in Quebec, he brought a new energy and openness. He spoke in provocative, firecracker phrases, constantly surprising, exciting, challenging his audiences. As a public figure, he seemed rumpled, casual, informal, and accessible. Lévesque was a constant smoker; cigarettes seemed part of his restlessness, together with his squint, his twitches, his shrugs; they filled his spaces, just as the rhythms of the smoke seemed to shape his looping sentence structure.

Politically, Lévesque would adopt labels and self-definitions —and then thrust them away impatiently. Ultimately, he lived his ideological commitment in an intensely personal way, forging his political decisions out of events rather than ideas. Long after he might have been isolated by his own celebrity, he remained intellectually curious, questioning ordinary people he met with a seductive intensity, reading widely and voraciously, bolting from people or ideas that might limit him.

But there is another side to René Lévesque. He is a restless, solitary man. Distrustful of many of the people around him, distant, suspicious, stubborn, he remembers slights, embarrassments, and grudges with slit-eyed bitterness years after everyone else has forgotten them. And despite his apparent casualness, he calls very few people "tu"; people who have worked with him for years call him "vous" and "Monsieur Lévesque".

Sometimes it seems as if there are two René Lévesques: one modest, witty, curious, tolerant and open, widely read and taking a spontaneous pleasure in new people and new ideas; the other distant, cool, suspicious, and narrow, with a vindictive streak. He seems to oscillate between humility and humiliation, pride and resentment, generosity and vengefulness.

Many people have remarked on his paradoxical impulses. Camille Laurin, the psychiatrist who was to become an important member of his cabinet, once described them vividly. It is a description that has remained valid over the years.

"Ever since I began working with him, René Lévesque seems to me to have understood and empathized with the contradictions facing every Québécois which compel him to strive for liberation and at the same time prevent him from achieving it. This is why he himself oscillates between the light and the dark, impatience and confidence, tenderness and severity, scolding and the call to self-betterment, whenever he thinks to himself or talks to others. This is why he plumbs his own depths when in need of counsel during times of crisis. This is why he is a symbol of contradiction in everyone's eyes, and an object of recognition, hatred, and love."

RENÉ LÉVESQUE WAS BORN ON AUGUST 24, 1922. HE HAS LISTED his birthplace as New Carlisle, the Gaspé village where his parents lived, but there was no hospital there — and he was actually born at the hospital in Campbellton, across the Baie des Chaleurs in New Brunswick.

His father, Dominique Lévesque, was a lawyer who had moved to the village in 1920 from Rivière-du-Loup, where he had been in the firm of Ernest Lapointe, the MP who was soon to be recognized as "Quebec lieutenant" to Mackenzie King, the new Liberal leader. This might have led to a political career. However, he was not a healthy man; he had never fully recovered from the influenza that he had caught in 1918. As his son put it, "He had to accept that with the wear and tear of politics, he would die very young. So he went down to the Gaspé because there was an opening for a country lawyer."

New Carlisle was a comfortable, predominantly English-speaking community of some fifteen hundred people. It was a decision-making centre for the English-speaking community in the Gaspé, with the courthouse, two or three general stores, and a Bank of Nova Scotia branch.

Paspébiac, four miles away, was a working-class French-Canadian village, and the headquarters of the fish company, Robin, Jones and Whitman Ltd. — universally hated in the Gaspé for its exploitative relationship with the fishermen.

Dominique Lévesque was a quiet, modest, diligent man: a country lawyer who did the daily grind of a country lawyer's practice. But his partner was a high roller.

John Hall Kelly lived in the biggest house in the village, and had made a fortune. He had founded the Bonaventure and Gaspé Telephone Company in 1905, and had headed a number of mining ventures in the Gaspé. Elected to the National Assembly in 1908 and 1912, Kelly resigned in 1914 to become a member of the Legislative Council, the appointed upper house of the legislature, and kept a suite at the Château Frontenac. It was in Quebec after the war that he met the young Dominique Lévesque, and persuaded him to come to New Carlisle to be his partner. Dominique did so, and even asked his Irish mentor to be godfather to his eldest son, René.

However, the relationship turned sour. Years later, Lévesque would describe his godfather as "a self-made millionaire, a plunderer of the Gaspé, a bandit". The Lévesques — particularly Dominique's wife, Diane—became convinced that, while Kelly was pursuing his business ventures, Lévesque was being exploited. The partnership ended. One man who knew the family in the Gaspé was to conclude that the experience embittered René Lévesque for life.

His childhood was marked by the contrasting tranquillity of his home, where his father was a constant reader who read aloud to his son, and the scrappy battles of the street, where French-speaking and English-speaking boys split into gangs and squared off.

Growing up in a coastal village, he learned to love the sea, and would return to it every summer he could—in the Gaspé, Maine, or Cape Cod. He also learned, at a very early age, to play poker — from his grandmother. "She must have been about seventy, and I was six," Lévesque said years later. "She and her old-lady friends were damn good. They taught me a lot. Few people are more devious than a group of old ladies playing poker."

Alternately dreamy and pugnacious, a precocious reader and a quick-tempered fighter, Lévesque was acquiring not only a taste for poker, but habits and instincts that were to last a lifetime.

His father had strung up an aerial so that they could listen to Montreal radio stations, giving Lévesque an early taste for broadcasting and for broader horizons than the village, and he developed a love of reading like his father's. He also adopted his father's habit of holding a pencil between his first and second fingers.

He learned English on the street, easily and without thinking about it, and attended a bilingual one-room schoolhouse which included all the Catholic children, English- and French-speaking, and where the teacher usually spoke better English than French. The French and the English children fought, but Lévesque and the others who remember the village now shrug off these scraps as normal rather than traumatic: "It all seemed quite natural, just part of growing up."

New Carlisle was seventy-five per cent English-speaking. Dominique Lévesque read widely in English, but he had learned the language as an adult, and spoke it with an accent that his son described later as "atrocious — you could barely understand what he was saying."

When Lévesque was ten, his father began to worry that his French was suffering — and decided that his son should go into boarding school so that he would learn to speak French properly. So René was enrolled at the Jesuit Collège de Gaspé. There he came into contact with what he later called "the first expression of Quebec nationalism in my lifetime, [which] came down through the Jesuit fathers". Meanwhile, his father had become disillusioned with the Taschereau government, and became caught up in the Action Libérale Nationale. Thus, dinner-table conversations at home were reinforced by the reform nationalism of the Jesuits at the college.

Lévesque's Tom Sawyer childhood — which had continued on holidays from boarding school — ended abruptly when he was fourteen. His father died of complications after an appendix operation.

It was a traumatic shock for Lévesque. The insurance didn't allow him to continue in boarding school; his mother sold the house, and moved quickly to Quebec City, where he was enrolled in a day school, Collège Garnier.

A few years later, his mother married Albert Pelletier, who worked on the nationalist journal *La Nation*. But Pelletier died, and Lévesque's mother never married again — joking, "I won't kill another one."

Lévesque's scholastic record was mixed. Expelled from Collège Garnier after he got one per cent on a mathematics exam, he completed his collège classique at the Séminaire de

Québec as a day student, ultimately getting his baccalauréat from the Faculty of Arts at Laval after writing supplemental exams in the summer of 1941.

In the fall of 1941, he enrolled in law at Laval. (He was to joke for years afterwards that he spent more time playing poker with Jean Marchand than attending classes.) During his two and a half years in law school he also did something he had first tried as a summer job at fourteen — he worked as a part-time radio announcer: first for CKCV, a private station, and then for CBV, the local Quebec City Radio-Canada station.

In December 1943, shortly before exams, he was suspended for smoking in class. He never returned.

The smoking incident was a useful pretext, for increasingly he had lost interest in law. Moreover, there was an additional pressure: his family very much wanted him to follow in his father's footsteps — an office had even been rented and held for him in the Gaspé — and he has always hated being locked in by people's expectations of him. His impatience and mercurial quality made him recoil from the waiting office.

With no desire to be conscripted, or to fight in His Majesty's uniform, Lévesque managed to meet the head of the American Office of War Information, in Montreal, and was offered a job. He went to New York for an interview with Pierre Lazareff, the head of the French-language division of the Office.

In May 1944, Lévesque headed overseas. In his two years in Europe, he lived through the Blitz in London and the Normandy invasion, and witnessed the liberation of Dachau. During this time, he lost his voice, from untreated laryngitis, and was left with a hoarse rasp — a quality in his voice which, strangely, only changed during the strain of the 1960 election campaign.

He also lost his oldest, closest friend. Lévesque had known Raymond Bourget both in the Gaspé, when they were children, and later in Quebec City; his father was a bank manager. They were in the same class, and were, in Lévesque's words, "co-conspirators in practically everything". In the war, Bourget was a captain in the British Army; he died near Caen, under accidental fire from Allied planes. Lévesque had to identify the body. It has been surmised that the pain of this loss closed him off to the intimacy of friendship.

In 1946, Lévesque returned to Montreal, a war-seasoned broadcaster, and began to work in the French-language section of the International Service of the CBC. A year later, he married Louise L'Heureux, whom he had known at Laval. She was a student in the Faculty of Social Sciences, and its dean, Father Georges-Henri Lévesque, married the young couple; two years later, their first child, Pierre, was born, followed a year later by Claude. A third child, Suzanne, was born in 1956.

In 1951, Lévesque was sent to cover the Korean War, and his material began to be used by the regular domestic service of Radio-Canada. When he returned, he put together a series on Korea, which made a great impression.

On the basis of those reports, Gérard Pelletier wrote in *Le Devoir* that Lévesque was "the radio discovery of the year, and the best French-language (and perhaps also English-language) commentator Canadian radio has ever offered us".

In 1953, Lévesque was one of the founders of the news service of Radio-Canada, which until then had used simply wire-service reports or free-lance contributors, and also began to program *Carrefour* (Crossroads). His co-producer, the late Judith Jasmin, observed that he had been a mature broadcaster at 23, when she first met him in 1946.

Although director of the news service, Lévesque remained a reporter, covering a wide variety of events, from the coronation of Queen Elizabeth in 1953 to Lester Pearson's visit to the Soviet Union in 1956. He was, by all accounts, a gifted reporter: his husky voice, his eye for human details, his curiosity, and his quick grasp combined to make him a distinctive and highly respected journalist.

However, despite his reputation, no radio journalist could reach all Quebecers; the competition was too great. Television was different. Lévesque became a TV star in 1956, with his program *Point de Mire* (Target, or Bull's-Eye).

As director of the news service, he had conceived the program; he then decided to resign as an employee of Radio-Canada to become the program's host, on a freelance contract. The program went on the air on November 4, 1956, with a half-hour show on the Suez Crisis.

The format was extremely simple: Lévesque, with a map, a pointer, a blackboard and chalk, film clips and interviews, explaining what was happening in the world. But the impact was enormous. While there were many radio stations in Quebec at the time, there was only one French-language television channel, and an audience hungry for information.

"It was the golden age of television," wrote Jacques Godbout, six years later. "Channel 10 [Montreal's first private French-language TV station] had not been invented. One single station, one single people, one single image, one single sound."

The program ended abruptly when, on December 29, 1958, the producers of Radio-Canada went on strike.

DURING THE TWELVE YEARS THAT LÉVESQUE HAD BEEN BACK IN Canada, he had remained, in spirit if not in fact, a foreign correspondent; his preoccupations were international, not local. While his contemporaries were working virtually underground — in the universities, in the labour movement, at *Le Devoir*, and meeting to put out *Cité libre* — Lévesque was reaching a mass audience, and talking about the world: Suez, Hungary, Algeria, Formosa, the American elections, the creation of the Fifth Republic in France. Furiously researching during the week, Lévesque would synthesize, explain, clarify, bringing the world to French Canada with a raspy intensity that few who saw him could forget. The program dealt with Quebec affairs only occasionally — though often enough to enrage Duplessis.

In the recollections of Lévesque's contemporaries, one can detect a tinge of disdain for his celebrity and his internationalism. "During the decade of the 1950s, René didn't get involved in the social questions of Quebec," recalled Jean Marchand. "He didn't pay much attention, and didn't get involved in the strikes, or in the foundation of *Cité libre*, or in [the liberal reform group] Le Rassemblement. He was totally involved in his job as a TV commentator."

In fact, his first encounter with *Cité libre* and Pierre Trudeau was not happy. Gérard Pelletier, by then working for the Catholic labour federation, the Confédération des Travailleurs Catholiques du Canada (the precursor of the Confédération des Syndicats Nationaux), was with Trudeau in the CBC cafeteria when they saw Lévesque coming through, with a cup of coffee in one hand, a cigarette in the other, and papers under his arm. Pelletier introduced them.

"You talk very well, I've heard you on television," Trudeau said, in what Pelletier considered a supercilious tone reminiscent of Trudeau's classical college, Jean de Brébeuf, and, in Lévesque's recollection, looking down his nose. "But can you write?"

When Lévesque looked taken aback, Trudeau said that he gathered Lévesque had been asked to contribute to *Cité libre*. Lévesque said apologetically that this took time, and Trudeau interrupted. "And ideas, of course. I realize that. But if you try . . ."

Lévesque swore at him, apparently making a joke of Trudeau's condescending tone, but he never forgot the insult.

The event that was to bring Lévesque together with his contemporaries — and push him past them at the same time — was the producers' strike.

Since the introduction of television five years earlier, the producers had been at the centre of an explosion: Radio-Canada produced at least sixty per cent of the programs it broadcast, and Montreal was the third-largest TV production centre after New York and Hollywood. Toronto had fewer than half as many producers as Montreal — forty compared to eighty-five.

However, there was no clear definition of a producer's job, and as time went on, producers' authority was eroded by the growing bureaucracy; they lost control of casting, script selection, negotiation of fees, and so on. Producers could rarely choose their own programs, and were often shuffled or overloaded with assignments. In addition, at the time of the strike, almost a third of the producers were without a contract; the administration had been too inefficient to renew contracts on a regular basis.

The situation was tense. In early December 1958, the producers met and decided to form a professional association. However, the director-general for Radio-Canada, André Ouimet, refused to recognize the association, and on December 23, the producers voted to strike. On December 29, Radio-Canada offered the producers three unacceptable choices, and the producers decided to fight for recognition as a bargaining unit by the corporation. The strike began that evening. It was to last sixty-eight days.

The strike began as a relatively minor dispute on the fringes of collective bargaining, but before it ended it became one of the symbolic strikes of the century in Quebec, joining the mythological struggles like the Asbestos strike in 1949 and Murdochville in 1957. But there was a difference. The strike paralysed the most important cultural instrument in French Canada.

When it became clear that the federal government was indifferent to this, the strike became a symbol not merely of a new white-collar militancy, but of French-Canadian nationalism and English-Canadian insensitivity.

The strike was a turning point in Lévesque's development as a nationalist, and, as so often happened with him, the change in his attitude was forged in the heat of action. But equally, the strike pointed the direction for white-collar public-sector unions in Quebec for years to come, laying the groundwork for the militancy of the 1970s and 1980s.

As happened in Asbestos and Murdochville, the strike became a rallying point for a generation of Quebec intellectuals. Lévesque, Marchand, and Pelletier were crucial figures in it, as were the actors Jean-Louis Roux and Jean Duceppe. Supporters included Pierre Trudeau, who travelled with the strikers to Ottawa, and Claude Ryan, who as president of the Canadian Institute for Adult Education sent a telegram of support.

During the Duplessis years, intellectuals in Quebec tended to look to Ottawa and federal institutions for refuge. But in 1958 John Diefenbaker was prime minister, and Quebecers in his cabinet had little influence. For the first time, the Radio-Canada strike focused intellectual anger not against Duplessis but against the federal government.

At the beginning, Lévesque was not involved; he was a freelancer, not an employee. Moreover, he did not believe in journalists becoming involved; he believed in objectivity. However, his participation was viewed as essential by the strike organizers.

"We knew that as long as he stayed aloof, many people would doubt there was any merit to the cause," Gérard Pelletier recalled later. "Jean Marchand was instrumental in bringing him in, challenging him. And when Lévesque was convinced this was a just cause, it was a tornado. There was not one minute left for anything else."

With Pelletier, he worked on writing press statements and a brief to the federal government; every night, he was on stage at the Comédie Canadienne, as part of a show presented by the producers to raise funds. He went to Ottawa with the strikers, and was arrested on March 3 when the police charged the picket lines.

When the strike ended on March 7, with limited recognition for the producers as a bargaining unit, hundreds of strikers and supporters hit the streets again — this time in triumph. However, the bitterness was not gone.

That day, René Lévesque's burst of anger hit print, fuelled by his rage at an editorial in the *Montreal Star* that blamed the strikers for the police attack on the picket lines a few days before.

After pointing out that the police moved in first, Lévesque accused the *Star* of having an attitude "fundamentally hostile to any attempt by French-Canadians at anything but prover-bial 'pittoresque' and quaintness." He quoted a federal minis-ter to the effect that if the strike had affected English-language television, it would have been settled in a matter of hours, not weeks — and concluded on a sarcastic note that expressed something of the turning point he saw the experience to be, even then.

"Never before have we felt that our affairs are bound to be either tragically or comically mismanaged as long as they remain in the hands of men who have no understanding of them and make it quite clear that they don't consider this any kind of personal flaw," he wrote. "And even at the risk of being called a 'torrid nationalist', we feel that at least once before this conflict is over, we have to make plain our deep apprecia-tion of such an enviable place in the great bilingual, bicultural, and fraternal Canadian sun."

The change the strike had wrought in him was dramatic and clear. "After the strike, René Lévesque was another man," observed Jean Duceppe. "It was the strike that caused a break-through in his social conscience. The direction he took started right then."

Maurice Duplessis was amused by the strike; both sides were his adversaries. He would never have tolerated Lévesque. But the CBC's handling of the strike effectively erased any feeling of loyalty that Lévesque might have had to the federal institu-tion. And if Lévesque was speaking, for virtually the first time, in tones of nationalist rage, others could see the long-term implications of the strike.

"It is almost always this way that nationalism begins," wrote André Laurendeau in *Le Devoir*. "The man who is treated like a second-class citizen, like a colonial as opposed to a strong and inaccessible metropolis, like a nigger whose suffering stirs no sympathy in his all-powerful master: this man is either crushed and consents to a state of moral slavery, or, on the other hand, he rightfully demands the restoration of his shattered dignity. In any case, he feels wounded. A lot of us felt something like that."

In 1959, Duplessis died, to be succeeded by Paul Sauvé. Sauvé, in his speech on taking office, used the fateful word "Désormais" — from now on — to indicate that the time for change had come. The Liberals were disheartened; for the past few years, Pelletier's "years of impatience", the Liberals under Georges-Émile Lapalme and the new leader, Jean Lesage, had been working to become a rallying point for change. Now it looked as if they would lose yet again. But only three months later, Sauvé died, to be succeeded by the much weaker, rather ineffectual former minister of labour, Antonio Barrette.

Lesage wanted Lévesque to run in the election that was expected in the spring of 1960, and sent his confidant and political adviser, Bona Arsenault, to see what his terms would be.

At that first meeting with Arsenault, Lévesque wanted a commitment that a Liberal government would nationalize the private electricity companies. But in the early months of 1960 the discussion broadened to include other possible candidates. The question was which of the intellectuals who had contributed to rewriting the party program were actually prepared to run.

"Lesage finally got in touch with us," Lévesque recalled later. "He wanted to know if any of us in this indecisive group connected with *Cité libre* and the unions were interested in being candidates, because the elections were just around the corner. We got together and talked it over a number of times."

However, most of the group had commitments or steady jobs, and were not in a position to take risks. So they dithered. Finally, after the second week of the election campaign, Lesage said that they had to decide that night, since there weren't many ridings left without candidates.

Lesage waited in a room at the Windsor Hotel, at Peel and Dorchester, while, a few hundred yards north, Trudeau, Pelletier, Marchand, Lévesque, and a couple of others talked it over in Marchand's room at the Mount Royal Hotel.

"In the end, I was the only one who went," Lévesque recalled later. "At midnight or one o'clock, I phoned Lesage and went to the Windsor. 'Here I am,' I said. 'The others just aren't ready.'"

The six months of discussions that had begun with the chat

with Bona Arsenault were over, and Lévesque had made the plunge. However, he did so with lingering misgivings — not about running for office, but about joining a political party. He retained deep suspicions about the motivations of those who worked for parties: suspicions that were to shape his attitudes to politics.

Lévesque chose the Montreal riding of Laurier because he had enjoyed doing on-the-street interviews in Saint-Hubert Plaza in the riding. He plunged into campaigning—and quickly became an election issue himself. The Union Nationale denounced him as a Communist, pointing to his interview with Khrushchev during Pearson's tour of the Soviet Union. Lévesque replied by mocking the old Duplessis red-baiting excuse for the collapse of the Trois-Rivières Bridge.

Despite the fact that Barrette was the third Union Nationale premier in less than a year, and by far the weakest of the three, despite the general sense that an era was ending, despite the vigour of the Liberal campaign and the relative fatigue of the government, the vote was extremely close. Lévesque won by only 129 votes, Paul Gérin-Lajoie won in Vaudreuil-Soulanges by 149, Harry Blank in Saint-Louis by 101, Claude Jourdain in Gaspé-Nord by 11, Laurent Lizotte in Montmagny by 9, Bernard Pinard in Drummond by 101. If only 400 Liberal votes had gone the other way in those six ridings, the UN would have stayed in power.

When the votes were counted, the Liberals won 50 seats and 51 per cent of the popular vote, and the Union Nationale won 44 seats and 47 per cent of the popular vote. Lesage was triumphant. "The people deserved this victory," he told supporters. "They wanted, despite the chains that bound them, to shed themselves of the régime that held them in slavery. The people had confidence in us. They had confidence in our program. The province is liberated."

In Laurier, another René Lévesque, put up by the Union Nationale, won 910 votes; and *Le Devoir* estimated that five thousand UN votes were stuffed into ballot boxes in the riding. After his victory was official, Lévesque went on television, saying that he had seen Provincial Police officers directing thugs into polling stations six at a time. He vowed that the era of rotten election tactics was over.

He thanked the electors, said he hoped he would deserve the honour that they had given him—and couldn't resist concluding on a mischievous note, with a cheeky allusion to the producers' strike. "In conclusion, let me add that I am happy to be here, this evening, to do a program on Radio-Canada!"

It was, as Gérard Filion called it in a front-page editorial in *Le Devoir* the next morning, "la fin d'un ère politique" — the end of a political era.

THREE

Whirlwind
on the Margin

*The art of government is the
organization of idolatry.*
George Bernard Shaw

Shortly after the election, René Lévesque was at home
recovering from the campaign when he got a call from someone in Hydro-Québec who had heard a rumour that he would
be named the minister responsible for Hydro.

At that point, Hydro-Québec was a small government-owned
electricity company which had been created sixteen years
earlier when the Liberal government of Adélard Godbout had
taken over Montreal Light, Heat and Power. Lévesque agreed to
see the man. In their discussion he learned that there were
plans for a power dam on the Ottawa River, and that a letter of
intent had already been given to a construction firm in Boston:
part, as Lévesque put it later, of "the slush fund tradition . . .
they had a list of firms that contributed to the party. One firm
had bridges in Montreal, another had roads — and this Boston
firm had power plants."

The Hydro man told Lévesque that the contract was crucial,
and that the government had to get out of the letter of intent—
which could be done easily. "If this is done by an American
firm, it means that all the experience, all the engineers, all the
sub-contracts will be American," the man said. "We need that
kind of experience here; we're building a huge project at
Manicouagan in a few years, and if we don't have Quebec people with that kind of experience, we'll be sunk."

Lévesque thought this made sense, and raised the question
when he was named to the cabinet. "Do you know how long it
took me to fight that through?" he asked, telling the story
years later, his voice rising in indignation. *"Two months!* As
soon as I brought up the issue in cabinet, I got a call from the

senior lawyer of the Liberal Party, the chief fund-raiser—who was also a corporate counsel for this goddam Boston firm!"

It was a quick, tough lesson in political realities for the new minister of hydro-electric resources and public works, who soon decided that since, as a journalist, he did not have the skills or knowledge to take on the private electricity companies, he had better surround himself with some people who had. Soon after being sworn into the cabinet, he telephoned Father Lévesque at the Laval Faculty of Social Sciences, to ask him if he knew of any bright young economists who could give him policy advice.

The result was that Michel Bélanger, then working for the Department of Finance in Ottawa, joined Lévesque's department in August 1960. He soon became the man in charge of showing Lévesque how he could finance the acquisition of the private electricity companies. Bélanger was not alone—Lévesque consulted Jacques Parizeau, then an economics professor at the École des Hautes Études Commerciales (HEC), and Douglas Fullerton, a financial consultant—but Bélanger prepared the briefing books that Lévesque used to persuade his reluctant colleagues that the idea was possible.

In taking on the private electricity companies, Lévesque was reviving a dream of the ALN reformers who had been swallowed up by Duplessis in the Union Nationale in 1936. Lévesque was also tackling one of the traditional preserves of English-Canadian economic power in Quebec. As early as 1936, a Royal Commission had criticized the companies' abusive privileges, and Godbout had publicly called the directors of Montreal Light, Heat and Power bandits.

In October 1960, Lévesque had his first confrontation with the electricity companies when he announced to representatives of Shawinigan Water and Power that the rates for renting the government's reservoirs in the Saint-Maurice basin, which had been unchanged since the beginning of the century, would be raised. Three times the representatives said that the company could not accept an increase. Finally, one said, "But, Mr. Minister, Shawinigan contributes to the economic progress of the province!" Lévesque exploded, banging his fists in anger, and breaking the glass pane on his desk. He coldly told his visitors that they were doing Quebec no special favour; that in a free economy, this was precisely what one expected from free enterprise.

"After we started talking with the companies about nationalization, I remember this middle-level executive at one of them saying, 'Do you people really think you can run this company as well as we can?' " Lévesque recalled years later. "He was so filled with contempt. Of course, he was English-speaking, and the company was English-owned, as they all were. I remember thinking, 'You bloody so-and-so. You're just like the British were a few years ago, saying the Egyptians could never run the Suez Canal.' It was the same paternalistic contempt — the colonial master speaking to the backward native. 'We'll show you, you bastard,' I thought. And we did."

It was a story he would tell, in different ways, again and again over the years; it would play a central part in his referendum speeches in 1980.

Starting in the fall of 1960, Lévesque began to put the future of the electricity companies on the public agenda. In early December, at a conference on resources, Lévesque called the situation an unhealthy one which Quebec should reverse "at any price". Pierre Laporte, then a reporter at *Le Devoir*, spotted the phrase, and pointed out in the next day's paper that "at any price" could mean expropriation. It was the beginning of a campaign by Lévesque, fought inside and outside the cabinet, to win support for the idea of nationalization of the private companies. Publicly, Lévesque made a commitment on February 12, 1962, to "integrate" the private companies, and have them "unified" by Hydro-Québec. He did not succeed in convincing the cabinet until a cabinet meeting at Lac-à-l'Épaule over the Labour Day weekend of 1962. At that meeting, Lesage agreed to fight an election on the issue.

With a slogan of "Maîtres Chez Nous" (Masters in Our Own Home), a phrase with a long history of Quebec nationalistic rhetoric, the Liberals made the election a referendum on nationalization of the private companies. Lévesque travelled the province with a blackboard and chalk, selling a new vision of Hydro-Québec to the voters.

It was a vigorous debate. Pierre Trudeau, who met with Lévesque, Marchand, Pelletier, and Laurendeau in regular sessions at Pelletier's Westmount house or Marchand's Saint-Denis Street apartment, needled Lévesque, saying there were better ways to spend the money, and that he was being driven by traditional nationalism rather than good sense.

This was an argument that troubled André Laurendeau, who

questioned whether an election campaign on the question was necessary. However, nationalization had privately won some major converts: Jean-Jacques Bertrand of the Union Nationale supported it, and Daniel Johnson, the Union Nationale's new leader, promised to nationalize two of the power companies — after a referendum.

On November 14, 1962, the Liberals were re-elected with 63 seats and 57 per cent of the popular vote. The Union Nationale won 31 seats with 42 per cent of the popular vote.

Ten days after the election, Douglas Fullerton joined Louis-Philippe Pigeon, Lesage's legal adviser, Parizeau, and Bélanger to work on the final details. At six o'clock on December 28, 1962, Lesage announced the decision: the government was acquiring the shares of Shawinigan Water and Power, the largest private power company, for $600 million. It was incorporated into Hydro-Québec, which now became the symbol of Quebec's will to take control of its resources and modernize. Lévesque encouraged, cajoled, and convinced Quebecers that they were capable of doing it.

But while Hydro was the symbol of change that the government chose to campaign on, the Lesage administration was bursting with energy in other areas. Road construction, liquor licences, and the provincial police — all nests of patronage — were cleaned up.

All the energies that had gone into the intellectual dissent of the 1950s were now concentrated on catching up with the rest of the Western world and creating a modern state. The Quebec government was vigorously recruiting civil servants from Ottawa, private industry, the United Nations, and, of course, the universities — thirty from Laval alone. But if this will for change created unanimity among the élite of intellectuals who had been fighting Duplessis and whose eyes lit up at the prospect of putting their ideas into action, it unnerved many, including many members of the Liberal cabinet, who were cautious and conservative by nature and experience.

It was a time of turmoil. While the Liberals were reshaping the state, the Rassemblement pour l'Indépendance Nationale was attracting large crowds to rallies and demonstrations in Montreal. Chansonniers like Félix Leclerc, Gilles Vigneault, and Raymond Lévesque were capturing the imagination of a generation of restless young people, singing songs of pride.

When the RIN bogged down in an internal squabble between conservatives and progressives in 1962, a group of young people lost patience and decided to adopt terrorist methods. The Front de Libération du Quebec (FLQ) was formed in January 1963, and through the winter and spring a series of bombs were set off. The Wolfe Monument on the Plains of Abraham was toppled, armouries were bombed, mailboxes were blown up. A night watchman was killed and a bomb demolition expert maimed for life.

Less violent but almost as surprising for the rest of Canada was the election in 1962 of twenty-six Créditiste (Social Credit) members of Parliament from Quebec, led by Réal Caouette, a flamboyant car salesman from Rouyn, and Gilles Grégoire, a shrewd Quebec lawyer. The sudden success of this right-wing group came as a shock. It was clear that, across the political spectrum, a debate was raging in Quebec about its future.

Lévesque played a crucial role in this debate. He was a one-man whirlwind campaign for change. Living on his nerves, operating on the outer margin of cabinet solidarity, spending as little time in the legislature as he could, he tossed out his ideas like stones in a pond, seeing how far the ripples would go. It was a risky game that often enraged his colleagues, who watched angrily while Lévesque mobilized public opinion to support his fights inside cabinet. Lesage often lost his temper at Lévesque's tactics, but was a shrewd enough politician to sit back and let him take the heat before acting.

Lévesque continued to meet with Marchand, Pelletier, Trudeau, and Laurendeau, arguing, listening, shrugging, giving and getting shots of intellectual energy. He fired off angry letters to company presidents, attacking them for the small number of French-speaking executives in their firms, and sent shock waves through the business community as he mused aloud the need for an expanded economic role for the state. To English Canada his instinctive preoccupation with Quebec conveyed his indifference to the rest of Canada.

Thus, in 1961, he casually told a Laval medical-faculty banquet that "some time or other" there would have to be a ceiling on doctors' fees and salaries. In January 1964 he told a meeting on the eve of the opening of the legislature that he intended "to keep this non-controversial" since the Speech from the Throne the next day was "kind of delicate" — and then proceeded to discuss almost every aspect of government policy. And, in 1965, to the liquor-board strikers who were defying the government and asked his advice, he said, "Lâchez pas" — "Hang in there."

Lévesque's impetuousness was born partly of temperament, and partly of frustration. He had no Liberal roots, and no base of support in the party organization. Thus, when he thumbed his nose at the traditions of cabinet solidarity, he was reinforcing the political base he did have: in the media, the unions, and public opinion. He had no compunction whatever about attacking the Liberal Party.

"The big problem is that the party, like every other party, has its people who believe in the program, and others who wish that the party would behave like its predecessor and dish out the gravy," he told one journalist. "These latter people, if they can't be re-educated, have to be discouraged or die off. They are an older element who are cynical about politics generally, an attitude which they describe as 'being realistic'. This education in political morality is the most important part of our program, for if it is not absorbed the program is useless. But it's the toughest job of all."

Later, Lévesque was to shy away from ideological labels, but in 1961 he was less wary. "The ideology of the Liberal Party is non-existent," he snorted, when Peter C. Newman asked him about it. "We're starting from an ambiguous base, with a wide range of options in cabinet. I'm on the far left, of course. If this government doesn't reflect the views of the left, it won't be here long."

He was similarly provocative on the subject of Canada and Confederation. The thrust of all his work since the Radio-Canada strike had been broadly nationalist, but his remarks were often ambivalent.

He summed up his ambivalence in an interview with Jean-Marc Léger in *Le Devoir* in July 1963, when he said that political action in Quebec should start from two fundamental facts: firstly, that French Canada was a true nation, and secondly that it was not politically sovereign.

"It's not a matter of examining for the time being whether we should be or not: we're not," he said. "Thus, an authentic nation, but a nation that does not possess its sovereignty. It is from these two poles, or in terms of these two realities, that we must work."

In May 1963 he told Pierre Berton in a television interview that he "wouldn't cry for long" if Quebec separated. But in

January 1964, he told a Laval student audience that he believed "the time will soon come when this national state [Quebec] will be incorporated in a new Canadian nation," adding, "We [in the Liberal government] are not at all convinced of the necessity of separatism." In May, he told a student conference that the only status appropriate for Quebec would be that of an "associate state", saying that this would have to be negotiated with the rest of Canada "without rifles and without dynamite as much as possible . . . if they refuse this status to Quebec, we should separate."

This remark resulted in vigorous criticism, and Lévesque felt obliged to denounce terrorism and express his solidarity with the Lesage cabinet. But in December 1964, he told an audience in Plattsburg, New York: "I am not a separatist—but I could become one."

The dynamic of the Lesage government set ever higher expectations for the state in Quebec, and, as a result, ever higher demands from the federal government for increased power and jurisdiction. During this period, the federal government tended to blame Lévesque for their problems in dealing with Lesage. Over dinner in Ottawa, in 1964, the minister of trade and commerce, Mitchell Sharp, asked André Laurendeau, then co-chairman of the Royal Commission on Bilingualism and Biculturalism, if Lesage really controlled his cabinet.

"They have the impression that Lesage makes an agreement in good faith, and then René Lévesque forces him to retreat, which makes all serious negotiation almost impossible," Laurendeau noted in his diary. "We ended up talking for a very long time about René Lévesque, about the fact that he is not doctrinaire, that he is himself being pushed by a part of nationalist opinion, that he has a sense of realities and wants to establish a position of strength before negotiating."

Two days later, Laurendeau had dinner with Lévesque, and noted that, while Lévesque had not confided in him, "it seems to be clear that he has separatist gut reflexes." Yet he added that "he seems to perceive the future in confederal terms."

The most dramatic of the federal-provincial fights was over the introduction of the Canada Pension Plan and the creation of the Quebec Régie des Rentes and the Caisse de Dépôt.

In the federal election of 1963, the Liberals had promised "better pensions for all", and when Lester Pearson became prime minister, his government set to work to try to implement the absurdly unrealistic promise that a national contributory pension plan would be established before the end of "sixty days of decision" (another campaign gimmick) following the election.

In July, September, and November, the federal government presented drafts of pension proposals, and received a cool response from the provinces. By a unanimous vote of the legislature, Quebec made it clear it would be staying out of the federal scheme. But, convinced that the English-speaking provinces could not resist and prepared to cope with Quebec later, the federal government pushed ahead with its plan. At the same time, Lesage's economic adviser Claude Morin, who became the first deputy minister of federal-provincial affairs in 1963, and a Quebec City actuary, Claude Castonguay, were working on a Quebec pension plan.

At a federal-provincial conference in Quebec at the end of March 1964, Ottawa presented a non-negotiable tax position, saying that no further concessions to the provinces were possible. The conference was already failing to reach agreement when the pension issue came up, and Lesage dramatically unveiled the five-hundred-page report from the pension task force.

As Richard Simeon put it, "the plan caused a small sensation." For not only was the Quebec plan more generous than the Ottawa plan, but it covered more people and created the enormous cash-reserve fund that was to become the Caisse de Dépôt, or the Quebec Deposit and Investment Fund.

The conference broke up with no agreement, and the mood was pessimistic. René Lévesque was struck to see Blair Fraser, the Ottawa journalist he had known since his days in radio, sitting in the Salon Rouge of the legislature, where the conference had been held, slumped in his chair. "With his long face and his long legs sticking out on the carpet, he looked like the Voice of Doom of English Canada," Lévesque recalled later. " 'Lévesque,' he said, 'this may be the end of Confederation.' "

Fraser was not the only one to think so. "I think we suddenly realized at the Quebec Conference that, by God, the country might break up," a senior Liberal cabinet minister told Simeon. "It was a really dangerous situation, and the only way to deal with it was to make concessions to Quebec."

For as Pearson said later, the issue "could have broken up our country. If Quebec had gone ahead with a pension plan of its own that bore no relation to the national plan, it would have been a disaster."

After a week of frantic secret diplomacy between Quebec and Ottawa, a deal was reached. Quebec won a striking victory. Ottawa agreed to a transfer of payments instead of the federal family-allowance plan, a greater provincial share of income taxes, and Quebec's own pension scheme with the accompanying tool, the Caisse de Dépôt.

"For the past month I have lived a terrifying life," Lesage told the legislature. "I have made use of all the means which Providence granted me ... so that Quebec, at last, could be recognized as a province which has a special status in Confederation, and I have succeeded."

The resolution of the crisis, with the creation of the Caisse de Dépôt, was both a monument to Lester Pearson's co-operative federalism and an enormous lever for the new Quebec. For the Caisse was to be for Quebec what the Alberta Heritage Fund was to become a decade later: a tool and a symbol of autonomous development.

The creation of the pension fund was to be considered, by people as various as Lesage, Claude Morin, and Jacques Parizeau, the major achievement of the Quiet Revolution. In 1966, René Lévesque called the fund the only state institution created by the Quebec government that challenged somewhat the economic dominance of the English-speaking minority.

As Laurendeau had told Mitchell Sharp, Lévesque had his own pressures to deal with from the nationalists. For the Rassemblement de l'Indépendance Nationale had become a force to reckon with, as had the student organizations. The mood of impatience and dissent was being heard on the streets.

The RIN had been formed in September 1960 by a group that included Marcel Chaput, a chemist at the National Research Council, and a former *Hansard* translator, André d'Allemagne. A few weeks later, a young actor named Pierre Bourgault joined the group. In 1961 Chaput published *Pourquoi je suis séparatiste*, which became an instant bestseller. Fired when he defied his superior and spoke at a Laval University conference, he left the RIN in 1962 to create the Parti Républicain du Québec.

Bourgault became president of the RIN in 1964, a post he held until the party's dissolution in 1968. It was a period in which the RIN was in the streets and in the media; turbulent

years in which Bourgault, an electrifying orator, helped politi-
cize a generation.

Students demonstrated against Donald Gordon of the CNR
in December 1962 for saying that French Canadians were not
qualified for executive positions in the CNR, and there was an
even more dramatic protest in the fall of 1964, when the Queen
visited Quebec, and police clubbed demonstrators.

Lévesque disliked Pierre Bourgault and the RIN intensely;
he thought Bourgault was a demagogue, and his tactic of leading demonstrations unnerved him. In addition, the RIN's pressure on him made him uncomfortable.

Lévesque did begin to forge links with the student activists.
He hired Bernard Landry, the president of the Association
Générale des Étudiants de l'Université de Montréal, who led
the march on Gordon's office. Later, impressed by the arguments of Landry's successor, Pierre Marois, during a student
strike in 1962, Lévesque phoned him up and suggested that
they meet for a drink. It was the beginning of a friendship and
a working relationship that lasted almost twenty years. Marois
also went to work for a Liberal minister, Paul Gérin-Lajoie.

During this period, Lesage was considering acceptance of
the Fulton-Favreau formula for constitutional patriation and
amendment. The formula, which evolved from a proposition
made by Davie Fulton, the Conservative minister of justice,
and modified by his Liberal successor, Guy Favreau, was agreed
upon unanimously by the ten premiers and the prime minister on October 30, 1964. It called for limitation of the federal
amending power, said that no change to the constitution in
fundamental areas would be possible without the agreement
of all eleven governments; in other areas, agreement of the
legislatures of two-thirds of the provinces representing at least
half of the population would be required. In January 1965,
Lesage announced that the legislature would debate a resolution to ratify the formula.

This provoked a broad nationalist campaign against it.
Nationalists argued that Quebec's only bargaining power for
obtaining more power for Quebec was English Canada's desire
to patriate the constitution, and they insisted that greater
powers must be obtained before Quebec agreed to patriation.

The leader of the Union Nationale, Daniel Johnson, accused
Lesage of betraying the Quebec nation, and argued that the
formula would make special status for Quebec impossible.

Claude Ryan attacked it as an "unacceptable compromise". Lévesque and Pierre Laporte were asked by Lesage to defend it at the Université de Montréal on March 18, 1965, in a debate with the professor of constitutional law, Jacques-Yvan Morin. There had been some discussion between Bernard Landry and Pierre Marois and the student leaders at the university about whether or not this was wise — but Lévesque shrugged and said he would go.

At that point, for all his firecracker phrases about Confederation, Lévesque did not take the constitutional debate very seriously. Three years before, in a round-table discussion with Trudeau, Laurendeau, Frank Scott, and Jean-Jacques Bertrand, he had said, "I am neither a lawyer nor a constitutionalist, but it's incredible how whether we patriate or whether we don't patriate leaves me cold. Basically, isn't it a political problem?"

That was roughly his argument to the students. "We must be careful to avoid throwing ourselves headlong into the wrong battle at the wrong time at the wrong place," he said. "A dynamic reality can't be restricted by legal phrases. Those who are playing up the dangers of this formula probably don't understand the realities of Quebec."

He and Laporte argued that the formula would protect Quebec against a federal offensive. The students were not impressed. "Opportunist!" one shouted. For the first time, René Lévesque was booed by a student audience.

To add insult to injury, Jacques-Yvan Morin, fastidious in manner, speech, and legal argument, picked Lévesque's arguments apart. He argued that Lévesque and Laporte, both supporters of associate statehood for Quebec, were defending a constitutional formula that would make such a thing impossible. It was a humiliation Lévesque would never forget, and a warning that he would eventually be forced to take sides.

On the way out, Lévesque bumped into Claude Ryan, who had vigorously opposed the formula in his editorials, and gave him a lift home in the snowstorm. "It was an interesting evening," Ryan observed dryly. "But I think you would be wise to pay more attention to constitutional questions. They could become more important than you think this evening."

In January 1966, Lesage told the legislature that the Fulton-Favreau formula was no longer under consideration, and it died automatically.

In 1960, Lévesque had been the only one of his circle to

commit himself to joining the Liberal Party, and he often felt isolated and impatient in the cabinet. The collegial brainstorming atmosphere with Marchand, Pelletier, Trudeau, and Laurendeau was dissolving, as they were being pulled in different directions. Laurendeau had become co-chairman of the Royal Commission on Bilingualism and Biculturalism, and in October 1965 Marchand, Pelletier, and Trudeau announced that they were running as Liberal candidates in the coming federal election. Paradoxically, this increased Lévesque's awareness of his own isolation; privately, he advised Marchand to make sure he didn't go alone.

Lévesque had been given a new portfolio in October 1965, becoming minister of family and social welfare. Together with Eric Kierans, who had moved from Revenue to Health, he was determined to transform social policy. Lévesque announced flatly that family allowances should come under provincial jurisdiction; Lesage followed up on this in the 1966 Speech from the Throne, saying that Quebec intended to take control of the whole field of social legislation. But these plans ended with the defeat of the Lesage government on June 5, 1966.

Lesage had become over-confident after six years in power, and insensitive to the silent toll his vanity was taking on his government's popularity. Daniel Johnson, on the other hand, was a shrewd, canny politician who had succeeded in capitalizing on Lesage's pretensions in their exchanges in the legislature. A lawyer and a minister under Duplessis, and a man of great personal charm, Johnson elevated ambivalence to a fine art. In 1965 he had published a book with the provocative title of *Égalité ou indépendance* which flirted with the idea of independence, while insisting that he believed in "the possibility of dialogue". Separatism, he said, was like a strike — a measure of last resort — but, "should it be necessary, the Union Nationale would be the only party capable of achieving independence in an orderly fashion, with respect for individual liberties and acquired rights."

It was a masterpiece of ambiguity, which allowed Johnson to persuade the strong federalists in his caucus that it was simply a device to defend Quebec's autonomy, and at the same time to imply different things to the party's quasi-indépendantistes. Significantly, his proposal was virtually identical to what René Lévesque would propose as sovereignty-association, two years later.

Johnson sensed that the Liberals had moved too far too fast, and that Lesage had become a liability. He ran a careful riding-by-riding campaign, and to Lesage's stunned disbelief on election night, the Union Nationale won 55 seats with 41 per cent of the popular vote, while, with 47 per cent of the popular vote, the Liberals won only 51 seats. The Liberals had suffered losses in smaller rural ridings, and won their victories in more populous urban ridings, especially in the West Island of Montreal, which contained a concentration of English-speaking voters. As Johnson crudely put it on election night, "If you take away the English-speaking vote in Montreal, if you take away the votes that are English, Jewish, I am sure that the Union Nationale had a very strong majority of the francophone vote."

But while the Liberal defeat was partly due to rural dissatisfaction and electoral boundaries that gave more weight to rural than to urban voters, a crucial factor was a completely new element in Quebec politics: the emergence of a separatist vote.

A political party since 1964, and no longer just a movement, the RIN campaigned hard. In addition, Johnson had struck a deal with Bourgault on the day the election was called: neither party would present strong candidates where the other stood a good chance of winning a seat. While the RIN failed to elect a candidate, it won six per cent, an all-important fraction of support, from students and intellectuals who might otherwise have gone to the Liberals.

In addition, there was a right-wing separatist party, the Ralliement National, led jointly by a Créditiste, Laurent Legault, and Dr. René Jutras, who had broken away from the RIN in 1964 because he found it too left wing, and had formed the Ralliement National. Liberal strategists had hoped that the Ralliement would attract some potential Union Nationale voters, but it won only three per cent of the popular vote, and had little impact on the Union Nationale.

The Liberals were suddenly in opposition, and René Lévesque had the time to wrestle with his differences with the Quebec Liberal Party.

FOUR
Leader

*The prince must consider
how to avoid those things
which will make him hated
or contemptible. . . . It
makes him contemptible to
be considered fickle,
frivolous, effeminate,
mean-spirited, irresolute,
from all of which the prince
should guard himself as
from a rock, and he should
endeavour to show in his
actions greatness, courage,
gravity, and fortitude.*
Machiavelli

René Lévesque was now simply the Liberal member for Laurier, in opposition. He was not comfortable in opposition; he never liked the legislature much, and he was not comfortable in the Liberal Party. Much of parliamentary life struck him as an archaic waste of time, and he spent more time preparing his weekly column for *Dimanche Matin* than participating in debates in what the new government would rename the National Assembly.

However, the fact of being in opposition forced Lévesque — and the rest of the party — to think about issues that had been put aside during the intensity of day-to-day government. In defeat, the Quebec Liberals were tearing each other apart. At their convention in November 1966, Lesage blamed the election defeat on the "idealistic illusions" and "perfectionism" of some people. As Dominique Clift observed, everyone understood this to be directed at Lévesque, Kierans, and Gérin-Lajoie.

39

Even more explicitly, the outgoing party president, Dr. Irenée Lapierre, said in a CBC interview that Lévesque should quit the party.

However, the party was in no mood for this. The reform elements had gathered around Lévesque and Kierans and their slate for the party executive. Despite Lesage's speech, Kierans was elected to the presidency of the party, and an apology was exacted from Lapierre by the delegates. Lesage, who had come close to throwing Lévesque out of the cabinet after the "lâchez-pas" incident, clearly did not have the power to throw him out of the party. Still, even the relationship of Kierans and Lévesque as reformers in the cabinet and their personal friendship could not maintain their alliance. Lévesque was to evolve in a direction that Kierans would not follow.

There was a new intensity to the nationalist debate; with the election of Daniel Johnson, tensions between Quebec and the federal government moved to a new stage. Instead of dismissing Claude Morin, who had done Lesage's strategic planning on the federal-provincial front, Johnson kept him on; Morin became even more influential than before. At his first federal-provincial conference, Johnson stunned English Canada by calling for one hundred per cent control of personal income taxes, succession duties, and corporation taxes on natural-resource firms by 1972. The implied threat was clear.

In this new stage of the debate between Ottawa and Quebec, Pierre Trudeau, Jean Marchand, and Gérard Pelletier were no longer meeting Lévesque to argue; they were in Ottawa as MPs — Marchand was minister of manpower and Trudeau parliamentary secretary to the prime minister, Lester Pearson — and advising the finance minister, Mitchell Sharp, on how to repel these attacks.

On the weekend of April 1–2, 1967, there was a weekend meeting of some twenty reform Liberals at Mont Tremblant to discuss new policy directions for the party. It was here that Lévesque presented the first germ of what was to become sovereignty-association: a call for dramatically more powers for Quebec — although the word "sovereignty" was not mentioned.

After Mont Tremblant, Lévesque began meeting with a smaller group that included Jean-Roch Boivin, his law partner Rosaire Beaulé, labour lawyer Marc Brière, André Brassard, and a young MNA, Robert Bourassa. Although the issue of Quebec sovereignty had not yet entered their discussions, there was already an indication of the direction Lévesque's thinking was going in. Readers of his column in *Dimanche Matin* could see his views becoming firmer. He began to write about the demographic threat that immigration represented to Quebec — since immigrants were being overwhelmingly assimilated into the English-speaking minority — and about the failure of Confederation to protect the interests of Quebec, and the interests of French Canadians. But he had tossed off bitter remarks about federalism and the federal government for years; he only dropped hints of where he was evolving. He concluded one column: "Where does that lead us? In any case, certainly not to a second centennial."

When Lévesque went off on holidays to Maine, he told Jean-Roch Boivin and the others that he would write a statement of the position he was still groping for. He didn't get around to it, but when he got back, things suddenly began to move very quickly. For on July 24, Charles de Gaulle shouted "Vive le Québec libre!" from the balcony of the Montreal City Hall. Lévesque was, if anything, annoyed. He didn't want his statement to seem inspired by this incident. At Lesage's insistence, the Liberal caucus passed a motion criticizing de Gaulle, and François Aquin resigned from the party as a result. Lévesque tried to persuade him not to quit; he wasn't ready — yet — to leave. His ideas were still coming together.

In August and September, the group he had been discussing things with had been meeting at Robert Bourassa's house. At the last meeting they were to hold before Lévesque's riding-association meeting, he read a thirty-five-page statement that he had finished in Bourassa's basement. It called for "the essential components of independence", and "the complete mastery of every last area of collective decision-making" along with economic association with the rest of Canada. "This means that Quebec must become sovereign as soon as possible."

Despite the months of discussion, Lévesque's blunt statement took the group by surprise. André Brassard and Jean-Roch Boivin were hesitant. Lévesque had hoped that Bourassa would support him — he had a great deal of respect for Bourassa's economic expertise — but Bourassa took him aside and said, "René, I can't join you. You don't seem to realize that political independence goes with monetary independence. Quebec cannot be sovereign and pay its bills with Canadian dollars."

Lévesque shrugged. "Monetary system, economic system,

all this is plumbing. One doesn't worry about plumbing when one fights for the destiny of a people."

But even then the rupture was not complete. The statement remained a policy which he was going to present to the Laurier riding association to be endorsed as a proposal for the Liberal Party policy convention.

On September 18, Lévesque's statement was ready for the riding-association meeting, which had already been postponed once so that he could finish it. The constitutional debate had picked up in intensity: the Progressive Conservatives had held their leadership convention ten days earlier, choosing Robert Stanfield but rejecting the concept of "two nations" which had emerged at a Conservative policy conference that summer, and which Stanfield supported. The Ontario premier, John Robarts, had asked the other provincial premiers to a "Confederation of Tomorrow" conference in November. The Friday before, the newspapers had reported Jean Lesage as accusing Pierre Trudeau — by now minister of justice — of intransigence; over the weekend, Senator Maurice Lamontagne had urged the federal Liberals to accept the idea of special status for Quebec.

So the debate ranged from the functional pragmatism of the Progressive Conservatives and federal Liberals to the explicitly anti-colonial "liberation" arguments of the RIN.

When Lévesque rose to make his presentation of a resolution that his riding association would endorse for the party convention in October, he made a wide-ranging three-hour speech.

Often expanding on his text, he talked about how he felt more at home in the United States than in English Canada; about how diminished people felt when they were told "I can't speak French" in stores in Montreal; about how the French explorers gave "lessons of audacity and heroism" and how, as a boy of thirteen, he had spent weeks drawing up an outline for a novel about the soldier and sailor Pierre Le Moyne d'Iberville, who defeated the English in Hudson Bay.

While managing to cover every possible justification for breaking the federal link, Lévesque still emerged with a formula for independence that remained ambiguous. For if there was an appeal to pride and history in his speech, there was also a kind of frustrated pragmatism. Stronger than his nationalist message was the suggestion that he could accomplish a great deal for Quebec if it weren't for the waste of energy caused by the bickering and squabbling of federal-provincial relations.

"Either we have to modify [the system] profoundly, or else build another, because it's paralysing," he said. "There is a vital minimum, a prudent minimum, a vital minimum of change [needed] to assure our collective security. And this is a minimum which, for the rest of the country, is a completely unacceptable maximum."

The next day, the *Toronto Star* ran a major front-page story on the speech, along with a background piece which began, "Partisans of Quebec independence waited seven years for René Lévesque. He arrived last night."

On Friday night, October 13, the Liberal convention opened at the Château Frontenac in Quebec. Kierans was chairing the meeting as president, but had arranged to withdraw for the procedural wrangles. Lévesque's supporters were pushing to get a secret ballot on the constitutional question, but this was defeated overwhelmingly. On Saturday, there were some last-minute abortive attempts to mediate. On Saturday afternoon, as he came into the ballroom, Lévesque was greeted by delegates chanting "Lévesque dehors! Lévesque dehors!" (Lévesque out.) Walking beside him, Jean-Roch Boivin said, "I'm nervous; this is the first time I have physically felt hatred."

"You should have been nervous before the decision," Lévesque replied. "Once it's taken, it's all right."

Bourassa came up to him and, in a last attempt to keep him in the party, reminded him that Aneurin Bevan had stayed in the Labour Party when his position on nuclear arms was rejected.

After making his presentation and seeing that it was going to be defeated overwhelmingly, René Lévesque made a short statement and walked out of the ballroom of the Château Frontenac, and out of the Quebec Liberal Party.

Doris Lussier, an old friend, followed, sadly removing his delegate badge and dropping it in a hotel ashtray, looking, in the words of a reporter, "like an American student burning his draft card". In the press section, a twenty-one-year-old student named Claude Charron, accredited with the Université de Montréal student paper, said, "That's enough." He whipped off his press badge, and headed after Lévesque.

Followed by a cluster of supporters and a crowd of reporters,

Lévesque walked across Place d'Armes to the Clarendon Hotel, and held a press conference. A reporter asked him if he would be founding a political party. "I don't know," Lévesque replied. "We're going to meet. But if we do, we'll get twenty per cent of the vote." There was a burst of laughter.

After the press conference, Lévesque's group went for dinner at the Old Homestead Restaurant on Place d'Armes. At the end of the meal, Jean-Roch Boivin grabbed a place-mat and said, "I'm going to make you all sign, in case it becomes historic."

Lévesque signed at the top left corner; thirty-eight others signed with him. An era had ended; a new one had begun.

THE PERIOD BETWEEN 1967 AND 1970 WAS TRANSITIONAL; A SUBSTANTIAL change in political leadership occurred both in Canada and in Quebec.

Lévesque had ambiguous feelings on leadership. On the one hand, he carefully adopted a non-leadership style: an apologetic shrug, a modest "sorry-to-bother-you" manner. When a journalist described him as a "national leader" in 1969, Lévesque wrote him a letter, saying, "if you *do* have to make me any kind of leader (ugh) — I'd much prefer you made me 'party l[eader]'. But, please, not 'national leader'!" But on the other hand, he could be harsh and resentful towards those who did not give him total loyalty.

During these years, three men in particular were to act in counterpoint with Lévesque: sometimes enraging him, sometimes provoking him, and sometimes defining him. The three were Pierre Bourgault, Pierre Trudeau, and Robert Bourassa. All three were graduates of the best-known élite character-shaping Jesuit classical college in Quebec: Collège Jean-de-Brébeuf.

Bourgault had been an actor and a journalist when, in 1960, almost by accident, he found himself at an RIN meeting. But suddenly, he found his vocation: he was an orator. There was an icy brilliance to his style: a theatrical, precise rhetoric that had none of the slang or joual that marked the speech of many Quebec politicians.

He had an intensity that was almost frightening, and a style that shone with its simplicity. He often began his speeches with the Conquest: Quebecers were a conquered people, a colonized people. Confederation was imposed upon them. It worked to their constant economic disadvantage, having been designed for Ontario. From there, he would look at other countries. Independence was not something outrageous, but something normal. Why was it something appropriate for the Swedes and the Dutch, the Mexicans and the Brazilians — but not Quebecers?

It was a provocative question that stirred the imagination and the indignation of thousands. But Bourgault was not simply a powerful orator, he was a fiery, impulsive personality, living on adrenalin, fighting to keep the often divided party together, and often with no fixed address. He was a homosexual — a fact he would not discuss publicly until fifteen years later, but which gave Lévesque the creeps.

The indépendantistes dreamed of Lévesque and Bourgault working together; the prospect unnerved Lévesque. Whatever happened, he was determined to keep his new political organization as far away as possible from the RIN.

Similarly, Lévesque had never liked Pierre Trudeau. He found him arrogant, condescending, élitist, and exasperating. Trudeau's cold Jesuitical logic infuriated him. But while Lévesque was leaving the Quebec Liberal Party and setting out to build a political organization that he could control, Trudeau was engaged in a process that would result in his taking over the Liberal Party of Canada, and controlling it. The arguments the two men had always had would become a central part of the dynamic of politics in Canada and Quebec over the next fifteen years.

Of the three, Lévesque was closest to Bourassa, and had most hoped that he would join him. When Bourassa didn't, Lévesque was hurt, feeling that Bourassa had made his decision for careerist reasons. But others who were at the meetings at Bourassa's house in the summer and fall of 1967 suggest that the idea that Bourassa was on the point of joining Lévesque has been exaggerated; that Bourassa always made his disagreement clear. He tried to keep Lévesque in the party, and when Lévesque left, Bourassa said sadly, "The party will no longer be insured against lapses into bourgeois complacency."

ON APRIL 20, 1968, PIERRE ELLIOTT TRUDEAU WAS SWORN IN AS prime minister of Canada. Gérard Pelletier was sworn in the same day as a minister without portfolio, joining Jean Marchand in the cabinet.

That same day, in Montreal, there was a convention of the Mouvement Souveraineté-Association at the Maurice Richard Arena, and already splits in the movement were beginning to show. It had started very spontaneously and idealistically. The night of its conception over dinner at the Old Homestead, Jean-Roch Boivin had later dropped in to a Liberal suite at the Château Frontenac, where Pierre Laporte told him that he could not take the idea seriously because of Lévesque's insistence that there be no secret election fund, financed by corporate donations. But at Lévesque's riding office on Saint-Denis Street, the mail began to pour in: between five and six hundred letters, many containing dollar bills and two-dollar bills. Nervously, Lévesque and his friends decided that the movement could hire a student as a secretary, at fifty dollars a week.

After inviting everyone who had written or got in touch, Lévesque held a public meeting at the Dominican monastery on Côte Sainte-Catherine, on the weekend of November 18–19, and the Mouvement Souveraineté-Association was founded. He began gathering together academics and civil servants, while developing a platform and consulting Jacques Parizeau in some detail on the economic proposals. In January 1968, the September 18 speech, fleshed out, was published as a book: *Option Québec*. This provided the basis for speeches, debates, interviews, all aimed at laying the groundwork for the April convention.

By the time of the convention, the MSA had a provisional executive, and a set of policy proposals, ranging from the essentials of sovereignty-association to the creation of new ministries of planning, compulsory civic service for young people, a modest army, and the suggestion that all lawyers should be employed by the state.

The delegates debated various parts of the proposed program — but the big fight was on language. The proposal from the policy committee said that the state of French in Quebec "reflects sadly enough the very state of a threatened nation" — and made its restoration "a question of dignity, certainly, but also a question of life itself. Quebec will be the country of a people speaking French."

The specific recommendations called for French as the only official language of a sovereign Quebec, but gave the right to add English to French in municipalities that held a referendum on this, and also gave the right to anglophones to communicate with the public administration in English. Non-French-speaking immigrants were to be required to pass a French test before becoming citizens.

But the mood of the convention was not conciliatory. A paragraph in the preamble saying that Quebecers "should make it a point of honour to show great respect for the rights of its important linguistic minority" was deleted by a vote of 418 to 240.

This led to a dramatic floor fight between Lévesque and his fellow-independent in the National Assembly, François Aquin, who made a motion calling for stricter measures: a special tax on any company seeking to use English in a sign, or operate an English TV or radio station; the cutting off of social-security payments to any immigrant who did not enrol his or her child in a French school. Another motion called for the phasing out of state support for English-language schools.

Lévesque urged generosity, saying that to adopt the motions would be to imitate the most repugnant aspects of Anglo-Canadian repression of the French minorities outside Quebec. Aquin replied, saying that the English minority was different. "It has economic control. It is the best-off minority in the world," he said. "I don't want vengeance, I simply want to create a French society." He was cheered.

The debate raged on: some arguing that there would be no minorities in an independent Quebec, and that they might as well stay in Confederation if they were going to "pamper the English" and encourage "the cancer of bilingualism"; others argued that such a policy was unacceptable, and proof of an inferiority complex. Those opposing the amendment were booed, those endorsing it were cheered.

Then, at 11.10 p.m., Lévesque came to the microphone and made it clear how crucial he felt the movement's language policy to be. "The result [of the vote] will require a period of reflection on my part," he said. "For my name is attached to the movement."

Aquin came to the microphone to repeat that state funding for English-language education was not a right but a privilege, but Lévesque's implied threat had turned the tide. Aquin's amendment was defeated, 481–243.

Once the convention was over, the next job to be done was to resolve the question of negotiations with the RIN. Lévesque's chief negotiator was Jean-Roch Boivin, and neither he nor Lévesque wanted to fuse their movement with Bourgault's party. They didn't like his style: he had made too many inflammatory remarks, led too many demonstrations. So Boivin's main tactic was to stall. In June, two events gave Lévesque and Boivin the pretext to break off negotiations.

The first was the involvement of the RIN in the language dispute in Saint-Léonard, a largely Italian suburb in northeastern Montreal. The school board had refused to permit an English high school to be built, which had provoked the fury of the Italian community. This, in turn, had drawn the attention of the nationalist groups to Saint-Léonard as an example of their fears of immigrants assimilating into the English-speaking minority. The Mouvement pour l'Intégration Scolaire was formed, which demanded that all courses in Saint-Léonard be taught in French. In June, the MIS occupied a school, and RIN members participated, arousing Lévesque to accuse them of over-dramatizing the situation.

Then, on June 24, the day before the federal election, violence erupted during the St. Jean Baptiste parade in Montreal. Pierre Trudeau stayed on the reviewing stand, grimly refusing to retreat from the hurled bottles and stones — a gesture of personal courage widely thought to have sealed his parliamentary majority next day. The riot lasted five hours; 292 people were arrested, and 96 policemen injured. One of those arrested was Pierre Bourgault.

Lévesque was outraged, and broke off discussions with the RIN, whose members became convinced he had never wanted a fusion. "They were right," he told an interviewer, years later. "We weren't exactly eager to merge with them because of their image. Political realism was what we needed to fashion something new. . . . We were already getting members [from the RIN], except for the off-fringe."

In fact, he had always hoped that the RIN — or some other formation — would develop to the left of his movement, to draw off the idealists and ideologues who harassed and undermined him. Increasingly, he wanted the PQ to have a solid, middle-class base of support from what he was later to call "normal people". After the breakdown of negotiations with the RIN, he pursued discussions with Gilles Grégoire, the former Social Credit MP who had become the leader of the right-wing indépendantiste Ralliement National in the fall of 1966.

At the same time, work was continuing for the fall convention that would found a new party: preparation of party statutes and party policies. Lévesque and the group of people around him who had left the Liberal Party, like Boivin, Beaulé, and Marc Brière, were worried that the disruptive elements of the RIN might take control of the party. On the other hand, younger intellectuals who had been in the Liberal Party but had become very disenchanted with its authoritarian structure were determined that the new party should be controlled by its members, and not by a small élite working on a "political commission" named by the leader. This conflict was to mark the new party throughout its first years of existence.

In the months that led up to the October convention that founded the Parti Québécois, a group of young researchers had been drawing up possible constitutions for the party. André Larocque was a political scientist working on his doctorate at the Université de Montréal who, thanks to a sympathetic department head, was able to work virtually full-time on politics. He had assembled a range of examples, stretching from what he considered the authoritarian model of the Quebec Liberals to much more decentralized, member-controlled parties. He argued that in the Quebec Liberal Party policy was usually dictated by the political commission, while in more democratic parties policy was worked out at the grassroots.

The MSA executive consisted largely of former Liberals, and Jean-Roch Boivin was in charge of party statutes. Boivin was a tall, earthy, tough-talking lawyer. Born in Bagotville, he had graduated from the Université d'Ottawa and studied law at the Université de Montréal. He had worked with Lévesque since 1962; he remained totally loyal to his interests. Boivin was dead set against the kind of grassroots control of the party that Larocque was pushing for, but he was even more worried about the nationalist left taking over the first executive.

Boivin and Rosaire Beaulé invited Larocque and a colleague to lunch, and proposed a deal. They were prepared to accept Larocque's constitution, with its idealistic commitment to grassroots control of the party, if Larocque would agree that there should be no left-wing challenge to the proposed executive. Larocque agreed. The deal gave Boivin and Lévesque the executive they wanted at the foundation of the party, but it laid the basis for a continuing debate between the leadership and the membership.

On the weekend of October 11-14, 1968, in Quebec City, the Parti Québécois was founded, and delegates spent the weekend debating hundreds of resolutions that had been submitted by riding associations to modify the draft program drawn up at the April MSA convention.

Formally, the party was a fusion between the MSA and Gilles Grégoire's Ralliement National. However, this was an illusion; Grégoire had lied in claiming that there were fifteen thousand members in his right-wing nationalist-Créditiste party, and many RIN members had already left the floundering left-wing party to join Lévesque.

Lévesque had hoped that the new party would be called the Parti Souveraineté-Association, or the Parti Souverainiste — and those were the only names on the ballot. But, by lobbying furiously, Grégoire managed to get enough people to write in the name Parti Québécois to give it a majority.

The creation of the PQ meant the end of the line for the RIN. At a special convention ten days later, there was a vote to dissolve the party, and Bourgault urged the members to join the PQ, concluding "For the last time in my life I say 'Vive le RIN' — and for the first time in my life I say 'Vive le Parti Québécois!' "

The RIN members were to bring a strong commitment to a social-democratic program to the PQ. But they were also to bring an intensity and a partisan rigour which unnerved and irritated Lévesque. When Bourgault and the RINistes joined the party — and by 1972 it was estimated that seventy-two per cent of the RIN members had — they strengthened the uncompromisingly indépendantiste wing against Lévesque and the moderates. This remained a fundamental conflict in the new party.

In the months that followed the formation of the Parti Québécois, Lévesque worked to give it a reassuring image of stability and competence. At the 1969 convention, he asked the delegates to vote for unity and moderation in electing the executive — a hint that he did not want Pierre Bourgault elected. The convention responded, electing Claude Charron, then twenty-three and a student leader, to the executive instead of Bourgault. The party's goal of respectability was immeasurably bolstered in September 1969, when the economist Jacques Parizeau announced that he would be a candidate for it in the next election.

THE DEPARTURE OF RENÉ LÉVESQUE DID NOT SOLVE THE PROBLEMS of the Quebec Liberal Party. On August 28, 1969, after some public criticisms of his leadership, Jean Lesage resigned. On October 17, 1969, Robert Bourassa announced that he was a leadership candidate. The other candidates were Claude Wagner, forty-four, the former minister of justice and a tough law-and-order man, and Pierre Laporte, forty-eight, the former minister of municipal affairs.

Bourassa was then thirty-six. The only son of Aubert Bourassa, a modest civil servant in the federal ministry of transport who had died suddenly when his son was sixteen, he had been a scholarship student at Brébeuf. After studying law at the Université de Montréal, where he graduated in 1956 with the Governor General's Medal, and being admitted to the Bar, Bourassa won a fellowship to Oxford, where he read Philosophy, Politics, and Economics. He also became interested in British politics, and worked for the Labour Party while he was at Oxford. This was followed by a year at Harvard studying taxation and fiscal law in the International Tax Program.

From 1960 until 1963, Bourassa worked in Ottawa for the Department of National Revenue as a fiscal adviser, and taught economics and public finance at the University of Ottawa. Then, from 1963 until 1965, he was secretary and director of research for the Bélanger Commission on Taxation, which was studying the Quebec fiscal system. In 1966, he returned to Ottawa with a team of specialists studying the Carter report on tax reform, but he did not stay long.

For in June 1966, encouraged by Jean Lesage, Bourassa won the Montreal riding of Mercier, and was appointed opposition finance critic. It was then that he became friendly with Lévesque and tried to mediate between him and the less nationalist Liberals.

When he declared his candidacy for the leadership, he had one major asset. Paul Desrochers, the secretary-general of the Quebec Liberal Party, had commissioned an American polling firm, Social Research Inc. of Chicago, to do a massive study of the opinions of Quebec voters. The party officials were surprised to learn the importance the voters placed on the economy; the poll showed they were looking for a leader who could stimulate an economic recovery. Moreover, they saw such a recovery as the solution of another major preoccupation: the generation gap. In summary, according to Social Research, the ideal leader was seen as "helping bridge the gap between the generations . . . a good representative of the Quebec people, the kind of man who could be strong enough to deal with Ottawa, the titans of finance, and most aspects of a highly sophisticated world."

"We were stupefied," a senior party official said later. "The identikit sketch resembled neither Laporte nor Wagner. The leader people were looking for was a young businessman, with a very detailed knowledge of the economy. The man who best corresponded to the picture was Bourassa. I barely knew him at the time, but without knowing him, I agreed he should become leader."

Armed with the poll and the power that his position in the party gave him, Paul Desrochers went to work to set the stage for Bourassa to succeed Lesage. Bourassa seemed like a fresh alternative to old, tired, familiar faces. Claude Ryan wrote approvingly in *Le Devoir* that "The rational functionalism of this man who studies before speaking, who knows not only how to count but how to read, who maintains a responsible tone in every circumstance, makes for a man who is superior to his two rivals." On January 17, 1970, Bourassa won the Liberal leadership on the first ballot, with 53.2 per cent of the vote.

Two months later, Premier Jean-Jacques Bertrand called an election.

FIVE

Three
Elections

Nothin' improves a man's
manners like an election.
Sam Slick (T. C. Haliburton)

The Union Nationale government was clearly in trouble.
Jean-Jacques Bertrand, a decent, colourless man, had been
unable to avoid the language crisis that exploded over the
conflict in Saint-Léonard in 1968, and his 1969 law, Bill 63,
which gave freedom of choice in the language of education.
The economy was in bad shape, with unemployment over
nine per cent, and the finance minister, Mario Beaulieu, had
not presented a budget before the National Assembly was
dissolved.

The Union Nationale ran an erratic campaign, trying to be
more nationalist than the Liberals (whom they portrayed as
federal puppets) but to appear more responsible than the Parti
Québécois (whom they described as revolutionaries). When
the polls showed the UN running third, Bertrand lashed out
in a tantrum against the corporate élite, accusing them of
using the Montreal newspapers to defeat the UN and elect
Bourassa. In a paragraph he did not actually read but which
was distributed to reporters, he charged that the public-opinion
polls had been faked. But the only obvious fake was an elaborate gesture which became known as the "coup de la Brinks".
On April 27, at dawn, eight Brink's trucks loaded with millions of dollars' worth of securities drove off to Toronto. A
Gazette photographer was tipped off, and the pictures made
an enormous impact.

That night, the justice minister, Rémi Paul, told an audience
in Terrebonne that when they got home they would learn of
the millions being moved out of Quebec. "That's the result of
political instability in the province, the threat of independence,

53

separatism," he said. "René Lévesque is the Fidel Castro of Quebec."

Bourassa campaigned on a slogan of "Non au séparatisme," promising a hundred thousand jobs. The PQ ran a positive, almost therapeutically affirmative campaign, with a slogan of "Oui!" Lévesque told an ecstatic crowd in Paul Sauvé Arena on April 27 that victory was possible. "But in any case — the object was not necessarily to take power right away," he added, "it was not necessarily to jump right into soft jobs in a powerless province; it was to smash, once and for all, the ice of our fears, our complexes, our impotence!"

But sometimes the positive mood cracked. A *Montreal Star* editorial compared Lévesque to Kerensky, the Russian democrat who was deposed by Lenin and the Bolsheviks, and alluded to "the propensity of Quebec leaders, throughout history, toward authoritarianism and dictatorship".

The next night, speaking in English at a public meeting in his own riding, Lévesque let his outrage pour out. He described the editorial as the "first lovely confirmation" of the English community's view that "we, basically, are not civilized enough as a society for self-government."

"That's an insult, a collective insult to a civilized people which in fact has no goddam lesson to get from the *Montreal Star*, or from any of the exploiters of both the English and the French groups in Quebec — and they're among the worst!" he raged. "And I'd like to say that we've got no lesson on that score to take . . . from anyone that has been dominating Quebec like a bunch of Rhodesians — the white group. If we had colours here, you'd feel it."

The Liberals won a sweeping victory, taking 71 out of 108 seats: the biggest victory they had won since 1931, the strongest majority since Duplessis won 72 out of 93 seats in 1956. The UN became the official opposition with 16 seats, the Créditistes won 13 seats and the PQ only 7. Six of these were in Montreal: Dr. Camille Laurin was elected in Bourget; Robert Burns in Maisonneuve, Claude Charron in Saint-Jacques, Charles Tremblay in Sainte-Marie, Guy Joron in Gouin, and Marcel Léger in Lafontaine. The only seat off the Island of Montreal was Saguenay, won by Lucien Lessard.

English Canada reacted with euphoria: The Toronto *Telegram* ran a banner headline saying "Quebec: A vote for Canada." But the reaction in the PQ was bitter resentment, and a feeling that they had been cheated by the electoral system. For with 24 per cent of the popular vote the PQ had won less than 6 per cent of the seats; the Liberals had won 65 per cent of the seats with 44 per cent of the votes.

With his shy grin and boyish cowlick, Robert Bourassa seemed to be a portent of a new generation of technocrat politicians — unpretentious, contemporary, and accessible: a politician-expert more at ease with job-creation statistics than with the deceptive reassurances of campaign rhetoric. As newly elected premier, he continued to stay in a $9-a-day room in Old Quebec, drifting unrecognized among the youngsters on the rue Saint-Jean.

The October Crisis changed all that.

WITH THE KIDNAPPING OF THE BRITISH TRADE COMMISSIONER, JAMES Cross, on October 5, 1970, and of Pierre Laporte, Bourassa's labour minister, on October 10, the imposition of the War Measures Act and the arrest of over 450 people, and the subsequent discovery that Laporte had been murdered, Quebec's political life was thrown into chaos.

René Lévesque was appalled. When he heard the news that Laporte had been killed, he sat in his office at the PQ headquarters and wept. Laporte had been a friend. When he had run as an independent in 1956, Lévesque had covered his campaign; Laporte had covered Lévesque's for *Le Devoir* in 1960. They had played tennis together regularly as cabinet colleagues.

Lévesque and Claude Ryan both opposed the proclamation of the War Measures Act, and were part of a group that called on the federal government to negotiate with the FLQ. This became the basis for the suggestion, made to Peter C. and Christina McCall Newman, that there was a plan to replace the Bourassa government with a "provisional government".

The October Crisis did harden lines in Quebec, but the identification of independence with terrorism, which Lévesque had feared so much, did not happen — or, if it did, it did not last. Some people, like Pierre Marc Johnson, the late premier's son, decided that Pierre Trudeau was defining all nationalists as terrorists and, in their anger, decided to join the PQ. And only a few months after the crisis, in the by-election to fill Pierre Laporte's seat, Pierre Marois ran and held his vote from six months earlier. But the short-term effect of the October Crisis on reform politics was devastating. The War Measures Act virtually eradicated FRAP, the municipal reform party in Montreal, giving Mayor Jean Drapeau a complete victory at the polls. And it transformed Robert Bourassa.

The $9-a-night room vanished overnight in favour of the premier's suite; security became a constant fact of life, with Bourassa moving into the recently completed, impregnable premier's office that was quickly dubbed "le bunker", and functioning in a swirl of bodyguards, walkie-talkies, limousines, and helicopters.

BOURASSA'S FIRST MANDATE, FROM 1970 TO 1973, WAS A STORMY mixture of explosive conflicts, ambitious plans, sweeping reforms — and breathtaking sellouts to foreign investors. The growth of the state had continued unabated for a decade. For ten years, Quebecers had increasingly looked to the state to provide equipment, institutions, infrastructure. Under Lesage, Hydro-Québec was expanded, and the Ministry of Education, the Caisse de Dépôt, SIDBEC, Quebec's steel corporation, and SOQUEM, Quebec's mining corporation, were all created. Under the Union Nationale, the trend had continued, with the province taking control of the church-run hospitals, and the creation of Radio-Québec and the government-owned oil and gas company SOQUIP.

Now began a decade of conflict over social issues: language, immigration, power. Under Bourassa, with Claude Castonguay as his minister of social affairs, the great social reform was a full medical-insurance plan, with a whole centralized system of delivering social services, and the creation of a network of social-service centres: Centres Locaux de Services Communautaires (CLSC).

But the conflicts came quickly. The Union Nationale had lost its credibility on the issue of language; Bourassa tried, and failed, to end a General Motors strike in which the right of workers to use French at work was a key issue. He postponed introducing a language law of his own, saying that he was waiting for the report of the Gendron Commission that had been set up to examine the question.

In 1971, Bourassa at first agreed in principle, along with the other nine provincial premiers, to the "Victoria Charter", the federal government's proposal for patriating and amending the constitution. Under the Charter Ottawa would have had to consult the provinces on a range of decisions, and a province could opt out of federal social programs. Opinion in Quebec, led by Claude Ryan in *Le Devoir* and encouraged by the Parti Québécois, demanded that the province should receive from Ottawa the financial equivalent of programs from which it opted out. After a week of hesitation, Bourassa announced that he would not sign the Charter; thus acquiring a reputation for weakness both in Ottawa, for having vacillated, and in Quebec for not having won.

MEANWHILE THE PQ WAS HAVING ITS OWN PROBLEMS. CAMILLE LAURIN, an imperturbable psychiatrist highly respected in the party, became parliamentary leader. Robert Burns, a tall, cheerful labour lawyer, became House leader. Laurin had to spend a great deal of energy easing the tensions between the caucus and Lévesque, who, having been defeated at the polls, was back in Montreal, writing a daily column and leading the party.

But soon the party gained a major asset. Louis Bernard, the assistant deputy minister for intergovernmental affairs, resigned in June to become Laurin's chief of staff, and his presence was to provide technocratic expertise at the heart of the party.

The tensions between Lévesque and the caucus were not the only ones. The bitterness of the 1970 election defeat and the October Crisis surged onto the convention floor in February 1971. Again, Lévesque vowed to resign if a language resolution calling for an end to subsidized English schools were passed, and urged the delegates to elect a "harmonious" executive. The language resolution was defeated — but this time Lévesque could not keep Pierre Bourgault off the executive.

In an electrifying five-minute speech, Bourgault won over the convention. He summed up in a nutshell the party's unease about what the members saw as the increasingly cautious pragmatism of the leadership, and attacked that pragmatism openly and directly, accusing the party of seeking security instead of liberty, respectability instead of solidarity. He concluded with a series of metaphors that appalled Lévesque, confirming every prejudice he had against Bourgault; he listened with his face in his hands.

"Ho Chi Minh was not respectable; he became so. Castro was not respectable; he became so. De Gaulle was not respectable; he became so. Because they remained faithful to the dreams of their youth!" he shouted. "And that is what I want the Parti

Québécois to do — to remain faithful to the dream that it has given birth to!"

There was a storm of applause. The speech had drawn lines very clearly inside the party; Ho Chi Minh and Castro were certainly not part of Lévesque's dream. Lévesque was also challenged for the presidency — for the first and last time — by André Larocque, who used the campaign to argue the "participationist" position, as it was called — that more power should be given to the membership of the party.

Lévesque won handily, but the convention established a pattern of giving him most of what he wanted, but not everything. The divisions became even clearer, as labour unrest grew in Quebec. There was tension between Lévesque and the caucus, where men like Burns and Charron were urging the party to become more involved with the labour movement.

The unions had become increasingly radicalized, developing a neo-Marxist ideology and a sweeping critique of the government. Labour unrest exploded in the fall of 1971, first with a strike at *La Presse,* and then with a general strike in the public sector after the leaders of the three union federations, Louis Laberge, Marcel Pepin, and Yvon Charbonneau, were jailed for urging strikers to defy an injunction ordering them back to work.

Robert Burns argued vigorously that the PQ should join a march on *La Presse* on October 29. Lévesque, who had been warned by a union official that the march might become violent, was strongly opposed. The PQ executive backed Lévesque — by one vote. Burns marched anyway. By the end of the march, several buses were burned, eight policemen were injured, seven demonstrators were in hospital and thirty under arrest. One demonstrator died of an asthma attack.

A month later, the party held a closed-door national council meeting to clear the air, and issued a lengthy statement by Lévesque, clearly dissociating the party from violence and the excesses of the labour movement. And, although the debates continued inside the party over the next few years, as the 1973 election drew near the party pulled together, bolstered by the presence of "respectable" candidates like Claude Morin.

IN SEPTEMBER, BOURASSA CALLED AN ELECTION FOR OCTOBER 29. FOR the first time, the PQ campaigned on the assumption that it could win. The major party figures travelled together across the province, and were greeted by huge rallies of wildly cheering supporters. But it was a deceptive enthusiasm, and journalists sympathetic to it failed to see the electorate's fear of a Parti Québécois victory.

The PQ provided the Liberals with one heaven-sent opportunity. To reassure people of the financial safety of independence, the PQ executive decided (over his objections) that Jacques Parizeau should produce a model budget for an independent Quebec. The result was the notorious Budget de l'An 1. The document assumed that economic growth would continue after a PQ victory, that there would be a 9.5 per cent increase in GNP. The Liberals pounced on it, found miscalculations, mocked the optimistic assumptions, and succeeded in putting the PQ on the defensive.

Lévesque had often repeated since the 1970 defeat that the only way for the PQ to win power would be for the Union Nationale to disappear. This was one of his major arguments for a moderate campaign: that it was essential to win over UN supporters. He was wrong. In 1973, the Union Nationale and Créditiste support collapsed — and the result was a Liberal landslide of 102 out of 108 seats. The PQ increased its share of the popular vote to thirty-three per cent — and won one seat less than in 1970, losing three members (Camille Laurin, Guy Joron, and Charles Tremblay) and gaining two, Jacques-Yvan Morin and Marc-André Bédard. Lévesque again failed to win a seat. At the election-night rally in Paul Sauvé Arena, Laurin put his head on Lévesque's shoulder and wept uncontrollably.

The defeat was traumatic — even more so than in 1970, because it was more unexpected. Lévesque was particularly disheartened; Pierre Marois had again failed to get elected, and when Lévesque thought about quitting he wished that Marois had been elected so that he could succeed him as leader.

The defeat further widened the gap between the PQ national office and the parliamentary wing. Camille Laurin could no longer play the role of father-confessor and go-between. The caucus had split three-three between Jacques-Yvan Morin and Burns for the parliamentary leadership, and Lévesque broke the tie in Morin's favor. Unfortunately Morin did not have Laurin's skills, or his respect from all sides of the party. This split only contributed to the festering of the bitterness on the left of the party about Lévesque's leadership. The tension between his faction and Burns's became more intense.

The 1974 convention was marked by an uneasy compromise agreement on a referendum on sovereignty-association which left the indépendantistes unhappy. Also at that convention, Lévesque asked Burns to go on the party executive, which Burns thought would be a waste of time. Finally they struck a deal: Burns would go on the executive if Lévesque would come to Quebec City for caucus meetings. But Lévesque would not keep his part of the bargain. He had his own grievance: by then he was working full-time for the party for only $18,000 a year. The pension he was entitled to as a former MNA was going entirely to his estranged wife.

Tempers flared after he refused to run in a by-election, and the organization of the by-election was a shambles. The party's fundamental problem was a small parliamentary group in Quebec City with an unelected leader in Montreal. While the overworked caucus was forced to make its decisions on the fly in the assembly and in committees, the party's prestigious spokesmen, Lévesque, Parizeau on the economy, and Claude Morin on intergovernmental relations, were free to speak out at their leisure. The results were often contradictory, with Lévesque casually reversing positions that had been fought for strongly in the National Assembly.

But the Liberals suffered even more than the PQ from the problems created by the 1973 landslide. First, there was an accumulation of accusations of patronage and favouritism. A Liberal MNA was forced to resign because of a conflict of interest; Bourassa's wife and his brother-in-law, Tourism Minister Claude Simard, were part owners of the holding company that owned Paragon Business Forms, which did a million dollars' worth of government business. More substantially, the government failed to negotiate from strength with the construction unions building the massive James Bay hydro-electric project, or those building the Olympic Stadium. The Cliche Report found that the union goons who had sabotaged the James Bay LG2 site had benefited from a private deal with Paul Desrochers, Bourassa's chief adviser.

Bourassa began to appear manipulative and image-obsessed, hiring a hairdresser as his bodyguard. The American ambassador Thomas Enders privately compared him to Richard Nixon, saying they were "both creeps". While the comparison was tempting, it was fundamentally unfair; Bourassa was not paranoid, but blandly confident he could reach an agreement with everyone.

He did not hate his adversaries, he called them "tu", offered them jobs or cabinet posts, and assumed he could undercut their support, absorb their passion, contain and redirect their energies. Were his opponents and critics social democrats? So was he. Were they conservatives? He could slow the pace of change. His was the arrogance of consensus, the ultimate Liberal belief that all differences could be ironed out, all problems could be solved, all setbacks and failures rationalized and explained.

By 1976, the constituent parts of the Liberal consensus were falling away, and Robert Bourassa appeared a weak, cynical, Machiavellian figure; the people in his office, whizkids in 1970, now seemed to be cynics, sycophants, or liars.

Bourassa's language legislation, Bill 22, became the ultimate disaster in consensus politics: it outraged every constituency of the language issue, and satisfied virtually no-one. The English were horrified at the prospect of any restrictions in access to the English school system, and angry at the regulations making knowledge of French compulsory in various professions. Quebec nationalists were appalled that any immigrant or francophone child who could be coached to pass a test could enter the English, rather than the French, school system.

The most devastating critique of Bill 22 — and of Bourassa — came from Pierre Trudeau. On March 5, leaving lunch with Bourassa in Quebec City, Trudeau quipped "He only eats hot dogs, that guy" — a mocking reference to a recent magazine cover showing Bourassa with a hot dog on a silver platter. That night, for an hour, Trudeau was scathing in his treatment of Bourassa in a speech, saying how hard Bill 22 made it for Liberals to sell bilingualism to the rest of Canada. He also attacked Bourassa's handling of the Olympics and the constitution.

IN THE SPRING OF 1976, QUEBEC NATIONALIST ANGER FOCUSED ON THE rule that French-speaking pilots must talk to French-speaking air-traffic controllers in English. It was a question that struck at the heart of the French fact in Canada, and cut across all party lines.

The conflict had been brewing since 1975, when a Bilingual Communications Project (BILCOM) recommended to the federal ministry of transport that bilingual air-traffic control services be extended in Quebec. The Canadian Airline Pilots

Association (CALPA) and the Canadian Air Traffic Control Association (CATCA) objected. After a year of increasingly heated argument, and the formation of a new association, Les Gens de l'Air, to represent Quebecers in aviation, CATCA voted to go on strike on June 20, arguing that the extension of bilingual service threatened air safety. The pilots decided to support the air controllers.

The result was chaos in Canadian airports before a peak holiday period and just before the Olympics. Worse, it revealed a profound sense in English Canada, where there was heavy support for the strike, that French was a cultural luxury with no place in a technological environment. The fact that English-speaking pilots might hear French between another pilot and the control tower was seen as a threat to safety; the fact that a French-speaking pilot in a private plane had to use a second language to speak to the tower was not.

As Trudeau put it, "We can't force Quebecers to learn English, and if they don't want to within their own province, they will say 'Well, this is basically the separatist issue. If we can't operate even within our own language, then what the hell are we doing in this country?' Do you know the answer to that? I can't answer the separatists."

When the federal transport minister, Otto Lang, signed an agreement with air controllers and pilots on June 27 to end the strike, and conceded the controllers a virtual veto over the introduction of bilingual air-traffic control, there was outrage in Quebec. Jean Marchand resigned, saying he could "not stay in a government that is prepared to negotiate bilingualism".

The reaction in Quebec was spontaneous and massive. As John Saywell observed, "It is possible that there has never been such unanimity among Quebec francophones in the history of Canada." A massive public campaign in support of the Gens de l'Air gathered steam during the summer, and two Liberal MPs, Serge Joyal and Pierre de Bané, joined the Quebec labour lawyer Clément Richard as counsel for the association. The two committees of support were chaired by active PQ members: Claude Morin in Quebec City, and Guy Bisaillon in Montreal; Pierre Péladeau donated full-page advertisements in his tabloids for endorsations by figures as various as Dominique Michel, a TV star, and the hockey idol Maurice Richard. The unanimity of the outrage added to the sense that the

Liberals had failed to protect the French language, either in Quebec or in Ottawa.

Ironically, the Gens de l'Air fight added to the growing tensions inside the PQ leadership. During the summer, Lévesque began to view the non-partisan common front with suspicion. He distrusted Joyal and de Bané, and disliked Bisaillon, a union activist working on the campaign full-time. As a result, a special executive meeting at the Auberge Handfield in Saint-Marc-sur-le-Richelieu at the end of August ended in a major explosion. Lévesque came to the meeting with a paper calling on the executive to urge PQ members not to get involved with the Gens de l'Air, arguing that they would end up being manipulated by the federal Liberals working in the campaign. When tempers began to flicker, Lévesque banged his fist on the table and said, "We're going to settle this."

Burns, who has as much of a hair-trigger temper as Lévesque, flared up and uttered the caucus's complaints: they weren't being consulted, they were being embarrassed by Lévesque's shoot-from-the-hip policy-making; Lévesque had broken his agreement to come to caucus, and it had all gone too far. "I don't recognize you as my leader any more, it's as simple as that," Burns said. "You have no idea how to work as part of a team."

"You're right, I don't believe in it," Lévesque said bluntly. "That's the way it is."

Burns was appalled. He felt he had offered to go halfway to work with Lévesque, but on the condition that there be some commitment to the idea of teamwork. Now Lévesque had confirmed his worst suspicions. Lévesque's paper on participation in the Gens de l'Air was shelved, and there was a motion of confidence in his leadership, which he won — by one vote.

Michel Carpentier, Lévesque's executive assistant, left the meeting devastated. He was convinced that if there were no election that fall, the tensions would blow the party apart at the convention scheduled for the spring, and Bourassa would win again. If that happened, Lévesque would clearly be unable to survive as leader.

THE IDEA OF CALLING AN ELECTION IN THE FALL OF 1976, TWO YEARS before his mandate expired, had been maturing in Bourassa's mind over the summer. The federal-provincial discussions of constitutional reform which had ended with the failure of the

Victoria Charter had resumed in 1975. Through the winter and spring of 1976, Trudeau began talking about the need to patriate the BNA Act. Traditionally, Quebec had always opposed this until a new division of powers was agreed on. Through the summer and early fall, Bourassa became convinced that Trudeau was determined to proceed with unilateral patriation, and came to the conclusion that the only way to stop him was to hold an election on the issue.

In mid-September, he made a list of factors in favour of a fall 1976 election, and those favouring waiting until fall 1977. In support of September 1977, he came up with three reasons: it would be a normal four-year mandate; it would mean waiting until the memory of the strikes of 1976 had faded; and he knew that there were severe tensions inside the PQ which might boil over at the 1977 convention. He listed eleven reasons in favour of an earlier election, including the fact that the Union Nationale had climbed from eight to fourteen per cent in the polls over the summer; the government's borrowing was up and would go higher; the Olympic finances had left a mess and an arrangement for payment would have to be imposed on Montreal; there was a police contract coming up in the spring of 1977 which looked as if it would produce a strike; the economy was facing a downturn because of an expected slackening of investment after the American presidential elections; unemployment was expected to climb higher through the winter with the post-Olympic construction slump in Montreal; his leadership was increasingly contested. The overriding reason, though, was the threat of unilateral patriation of the constitution by Trudeau.

His cabinet expressed strong opposition at a meeting in Sherbrooke on September 29, but Bourassa did not change his mind. His decision was confirmed when, in the Speech from the Throne, Trudeau made it clear that he was determined to proceed with unilateral patriation. On October 18, the election was announced.

For the Liberals, the campaign was a disaster. Quebecers began to see TV clips on the news of Bourassa being jostled by Hydro-Québec strikers in Saint-Jérôme, and mobbed by angry Alcan strikers in Jonquière. Meetings began to be disrupted by loud, persistent hecklers. There was an unnerving sense of passions barely under control, of currents of rage and contempt towards Bourassa swirling around smaller currents in the English and ethnic communities of resentment, feelings of betrayal, and fear of the Parti Québécois. Instead of dying down, anger over Bill 22 began to intensify, and wide divergences in the party became public.

The election campaign proved to be exactly what the Parti Québécois needed to submerge the anger and internal conflict of the previous three years. Lévesque campaigned vigorously, attacking the government for having won "the Triple Crown: the championships of unemployment, taxes, and debt", but did so with the calm conviction that he could not win more than forty seats.

Lévesque himself coined the phrase "On a besoin d'un vrai gouvernement" (We need a real government) — the main slogan of the campaign. The other slogans were "On mérite mieux que ça" (We deserve better than that) and "René Lévesque: un vrai chef".

A key element in the PQ's platform was the commitment to hold a referendum on Quebec's future. In the dying days of the 1973 campaign, the PQ had promised a referendum taking out full-page advertisements on the last day of the campaign. But it was not until after that election that the question of a referendum was actually debated by the party. At the convention of 1974, the party committed itself to hold a referendum to ratify the constitution of an independent Quebec — indicating that this would be after independence was declared. Now, just as he had watered down the party policy in 1973, Lévesque changed this to mean that a PQ government would not proceed towards achieving independence until it had got the authorization of a referendum.

Lévesque focused the campaign on the announcement of a series of commitments: policies that had been developed by Louis Bernard, Jacques-Yvan Morin's chief of staff, and a party official, Claude Malette. They were nitty-gritty, bread-and-butter promises: free drugs for people over sixty-five, new industrial health and safety legislation, agricultural zoning, stringent election-financing legislation, the reform of municipal financing, and a promise to change the language law, Bill 22.

Like Bourassa, Lévesque and Carpentier had underestimated the revival of the Union Nationale. Its new leader, the tall, bearded political neophyte, Rodrigue Biron, succeeded in capitalizing on public disenchantment with the Bourassa government and unease with the PQ, making the election of the first Lévesque government possible. But the phenomenon of the revival of the moribund Union Nationale with its sewer-pipe-maker leader is explicable only by the rage and sense of betrayal in the non-French-speaking community.

Bourassa began to worry that English-speaking anger would create a split vote; in the middle of the campaign, he introduced changes to Bill 22, and, after a speech at the Canadian Club on November 8, made a personal appeal to the *Gazette* publisher, Ross Munro. With Bryce Mackasey, he talked with Munro for a couple of hours, impressing upon him the danger of a split vote, and warning him that, having just moved to Montreal from Edmonton, he should know that there were reporters on his staff sympathetic to the PQ. In addition, Arnie Masters, Mackasey's campaign manager, prepared an analysis of thirty-one ridings that the Liberals could lose because of the erosion of English and immigrant support.

Munro was impressed; more so when, on Wednesday, November 10, the Hamilton-Pinard poll was published showing that a PQ victory was probable unless there was a massive shift of undecided voters to the Liberals. Upset by the prospect, Munro sat down and, in a white heat, wrote an editorial which began, "The central issue in Monday's provincial election is separation." It was an awkward, passionate, sometimes ungrammatical diatribe, which argued that the election of the PQ would be a disaster for Quebec.

Faced with the prospect of an argument with his editorial-page editor, Tim Creery, Munro signed it and took it to the news desk. No-one dared edit it, and it ran as a front-page editorial on Saturday, November 13. On page 3, there was an advertisement taken out by thirty-six reporters publicly dissociating themselves from Munro's position.

Excess became the order of the day in that last week. In the north-end Montreal riding of Crémazie, Education Minister Jean Bienvenue distributed voting cards which said in Italian that Quebec was in peril because "they want to separate from Canada" and that only a Liberal vote was a guarantee against losing old-age pensions, family allowances, and health insurance.

Ross Munro was not the only prominent member of the English-speaking community to succumb to the Liberal pressure. Charles Bronfman, of the distilling family, had also talked with Bourassa and heard him at the Canadian Club, and he became more and more upset. At a special election meeting in the Allied Jewish Community Services Hall on Côte Sainte-Catherine, his rage and frustration exploded. "Don't vote with your heads — your heads tell you that Bourassa's a bum. But he hasn't done such a bad job," he said.

He told his audience that, unbelievable as it might seem, Bourassa was not aware of the "injury, pain, and distress" Bill 22 had caused. "I swear to God this is true! It's incredible to believe, but the premier just didn't know. *He knows now!*

"If we turn our backs on the Liberals," he continued, "we are committing suicide. It would be worse than a disaster, it would be criminal — putting spears and daggers into our own backs. The election *is* the referendum . . . the referendum on whether we live or die . . . because they are a bunch of bastards who are trying to kill us!"

No-one was to express so dramatically the mood of near-panic that gripped parts of the English-speaking community in Montreal at the prospect that the Parti Québécois might take power.

ON ELECTION DAY, NOVEMBER 15, LÉVESQUE WAS TIRED BUT QUIETLY hopeful; he thought he would probably win his own seat, and he felt that the PQ might, at last, make the breakthrough, and win as many as forty seats. Robert Bourassa had a more realistic sense of how things were going; the night before, his chief of staff, Jean Prieur, had told him that he would lose his own seat. Bourassa prided himself on being a cerebral, rational man; he believed it, and he was not particularly upset. It had happened before, he told himself, to Mackenzie King. Nevertheless, it had made it harder to get to sleep.

Both men spent the day touring their ridings, visiting the polls, shaking hands with the election workers. At four o'clock, the campaign committee had its final meeting at party headquarters as campaign director Michel Carpentier briefed Lévesque for the last time on how the voting had gone during the day, and what the latest projections were.

Throughout the campaign, the organizers had kept themselves from being too optimistic, refusing to believe Michel Lepage and Pierre Drouilly, their own poll-takers, who had projected victory. At the meeting, Carpentier presented three possibilities. The PQ might, as a minimum, get between 20 and 25 seats if only the most successful candidates pulled through. If things went better, they might get between 40 and 45 seats. Or, if the most optimistic scenario worked out, the party might get over 60 seats and form the government. Lévesque listened to the breakdown and then said, "We can forget about that last one."

At seven o'clock, the polls closed. Until three minutes earlier, Bourassa was still touring the polls. Finally, two minutes before they closed, having greeted the voters standing in line at a poll on Saint-Urbain Street, he climbed back into the limousine. As he had done in 1970 and 1973, he went first to the Centre Notre Dame, an athletic centre opposite St. Joseph's Oratory, for a swim. His mind swirling, speculating on the range of possibilities, Bourassa decided to swim a little more than his usual third of a mile. He wanted to be as relaxed as possible, and he wanted to have some news when he got out.

When he climbed out of the pool and walked dripping into the locker room, shortly after 7.30, he was struck by the fact that none of his entourage was there waiting. The news must be bad, he thought; there was only his son François, white-faced with shock.

"Papa, I think you're beaten," he said.

"Why?" replied his father, still breathing hard from the exertion and towelling himself off.

"It's six to one for the Parti Québécois," the boy replied.

"That's it," Bourassa thought. He dressed and headed off to visit his eighty-year-old mother, who was staying with his sister in Saint-Bruno, on the south shore. She was almost relieved at the news.

In Longueuil, René Lévesque arrived at the campaign office in a small shopping centre about 6.45. He listened intently to the early returns on the radio, and when the first results came in for Taillon showing that he had a substantial lead, he gave a sudden little jerk of joy with his fist, his face breaking into a glow of triumph. It was one of his few smiles of the night.

About 7.15, Lévesque turned to his campaign aides and said abruptly, "We're going upstairs." With Jean-Roch Boivin, Robert Mackay, and Pierre Bellemare, he headed up to a small apartment above the storefront office and turned on the television set. Someone offered him a Scotch; he took a glass of water instead, and sat down at a small round table opposite the television set. Boivin, Mackay, and Bellemare sat on a sofa, and found they were watching Lévesque as much as the television.

The results began to come in quickly. At 7.33, the PQ was leading in 21 seats, the Liberals in 18. Five minutes later, the PQ was leading in 27, the Liberals in 19. Getting tenser and tenser, Lévesque was almost twitching as he smoked one cigarette after another. "C'est pas possible, c'est pas possible," he muttered.

At eight o'clock, Bernard Derome announced that Pierre de Bellefeuille, a journalist and former director of Expo 67, had defeated the most nationalist member of the Bourassa cabinet. Denise Filiatrault, a popular actress who was the co-host at Paul Sauvé Arena, began to jump up and down with delight before running to the microphone to make the announcement.

The reaction was delirious. No-one had expected the PQ to win Deux-Montagnes; the announcement was a quick, sudden cue to everyone inside the party organization that this was a victory. In Longueuil, Lévesque violently stubbed the cigarette he was smoking and reached for another. Robert Mackay said quietly, "Those polls that Drouilly and Lepage did — perhaps they are not as stupid as all that." There was a ten-second silence, and Lévesque snapped, "Stop exaggerating."

But a minute or so later, Bertrand Bélanger, a senior party organizer working in the riding, came up to the apartment and said to Lévesque, "You'd better get to work on the 'miracle' speech, because that's what it looks like."

Similarly, Deux-Montagnes was all the news that Michel Carpentier needed; as soon as he heard, he decided he didn't need to wait any longer, and left Paul Sauvé Arena to drive to the party headquarters and start the wheels in motion for the transition: getting in touch with the Quebec police force so that the security could take over immediately, getting on the phone to Lévesque, and waiting for the key people to arrive back at headquarters and get to work.

At 8.40, Bernard Dérôme made the announcement: the Parti Québécois would form a majority government. That night, the PQ won 69 seats—and two more were added later on recounts for 71. The Liberals were reduced to 26 seats, the Union Nationale won 11, the Créditistes 1, and the Parti National Populaire 1. It was a sweeping victory; when Lévesque finished speaking to the ecstatic crowd at Paul Sauvé Arena, throngs poured onto the streets.

The newly elected members and party organizers made their way to PQ headquarters, where euphoria was total. But more than one person was struck by Lévesque's silence. He congratulated a few people, but said little, staying for about an hour, subdued and serious in the sea of elated faces. Then he headed home to brood on his too-sudden victory. Already, the new job had begun: Roland Giroux, the president of Hydro-Québec, had phoned and asked Lévesque to show up at the Hydro-Québec office the next morning to be briefed on a major international bond issue.

In the streets of Montreal, there were the sounds of triumph: honking horns and whoops of joy. Along the rue Saint-Denis and in Old Montreal, exuberant celebrants rode on the hoods of cars, waving Quebec flags.

About four in the morning, the last revellers left the Lasalle Hotel, where the Montreal Centre ridings had been having a victory party, and climbed into their cars. Then, without any previous discussion, they headed west.

It is an old custom in rural Quebec that after elections, the victors parade past the homes of the losers. Spontaneously, a line of cars formed and headed north, into Westmount, up past the brick townhouses, up the tree-lined streets where the houses grew larger, up to the symbolic peak of Upper Westmount, Summit Circle. And there, at the top, the cars drove around and around, honking their horns in taunting, nose-thumbing delight.

2
The Politics of Pride

SIX

Forming
a Government

*No duty the Executive had
to perform was so trying as
to put the right man in the
right place.*

Thomas Jefferson

Shortly after nine o'clock on the morning of November 16,
1976, René Lévesque walked up the steps of the Hydro-Québec
building on Dorchester Boulevard, to discuss a $50 million
private loan for Hydro-Québec with its president, Roland
Giroux.

It was symbolic that Lévesque's first gesture should be a
visit to Giroux, like a king kneeling to an archbishop for coronation and blessing. Giroux, the bulky, gravel-voiced man with
the calm assurance of an aging turtle, was a giant in the Quebec
economy; Hydro-Québec was a financial force of mythic proportions inside Quebec, with no mean reputation on the international money markets. The two men were also old friends.

Once the briefing on the loan was finished, Giroux had a
message for Lévesque: cool it. He advised him to move quickly
to calm the excited and even panicked reactions to the election
results, which had stirred the imaginations of headline writers
and the anxieties of investors across Canada and around the
world. "SEPARATISTS TAKE QUEBEC," shouted the London
Evening Standard; "SEPARATISTS WIN IN QUEBEC," echoed
the New York *Post*. The stock market reflected this, and the
Canadian dollar quivered on international money markets.

At his press conference that afternoon at the Méridien Hotel,
Lévesque spoke in almost poetic terms of broken ancestral
chains and the fear of change. But while he spoke of the laborious steps that had brought the PQ so far, he was also at pains to
make it clear that nothing precipitate would happen on the

national question, stressing the party's profound respect for democracy.

From the wandering, parenthetical sentences, one could sense Lévesque's desire to reassure, calm, and conciliate. He used sweeping metaphors for change, which he then qualified and subtly defused. He repeated his commitment to hold a referendum "on the national future of Quebecers", saying "Quebec turned a page of its history yesterday to begin a new chapter." He added that it would be just as important to "write this chapter . . . in a new association between equals with the rest of Canada." In the meantime, Lévesque promised to provide a provincial government that would be honest, efficient, and humane. It would be, he said, "a government of all Quebecers, of all origins, of all milieux. There is a place among us, and a place which should not only be just, but also welcoming, for all those who live in, give life to, and love Quebec."

But he also showed that he had moved from the party program, which called for immediate negotiations with Ottawa, and a referendum if those negotiations failed. This was a position that Lévesque himself had maintained, only a few months before the election, in an article in *Foreign Affairs*. Now, he was hinting that the referendum would come first; in response to a question about the program's references to negotiations, he described it as "outdated", and said that it would have to be amended at the next party convention.

At noon, as was his custom, Claude Ryan had given a post-election luncheon speech to the Chambre de Commerce de Montréal. Ryan told his audience that Lévesque would probably present a motion to the National Assembly to allow him to begin negotiating the patriation of all powers to Quebec, and then start negotiating with Ottawa for sovereignty, according to the party program. He clearly did not expect that Lévesque would postpone all negotiations until after a referendum.

But what radio broadcasters seized on were two throw-away remarks.

"We are heading towards a very interesting period — a period for men, and not for children," he said. The audience laughed contemptuously, seeing the insult to Bourassa. Ryan added that the Liberals had a problem. "I think we have to hope that Mr. Bourassa submits his resignation as soon as possible."

Bourassa heard the remark on the radio that afternoon and winced; he felt it was a cheap shot, coming so soon after his

defeat. "Dehors, enfant d'école!" (Out, schoolboy) he muttered
— and decided then that he would resign.

On Thursday, November 18, Lévesque met Bourassa in the
premier's office for lunch. Bourassa was one of the relatively
few people who called Lévesque "René" and "tu"; in the intimacy of the moment, perhaps the last time the two men would
meet alone, he gave Lévesque some advice on forming his
cabinet. He suggested that Lévesque name Claude Morin as
minister of finance. Parizeau, although brilliant in debate, was
erratic on what Bourassa considered fundamental questions
of financial judgement.

"René, the premier is so taken up with crises and mini-
crises that he can't be concerned with the day-to-day," Bourassa
said. "It is the minister of finance who does the day-to-day."

Morin would not, in fact, have been an unrealistic choice.
While his reputation was in intergovernmental affairs, he had
written all Lesage's budget speeches. Lévesque did not raise
the idea with Morin, but he did pause before he gave Finance
to Parizeau, and considered Bernard Landry for the job. Part
of the juggling act he had to perform was to balance the forces
for change against those for stability, the instincts for rupture
against those for continuity. Parizeau, a brilliant, daring
romantic, and one of the few in the PQ not to shrink from
calling themselves separatists, was a force for rupture; Morin,
a shrewd, cautious academic and former civil servant, represented stability.

Lévesque also had to deal with the left, personified by Robert
Burns. Tall, with thinning hair and a walrus moustache, Burns,
at forty, had the grin and the informality of a younger man.
(He was the only cabinet minister to call Lévesque "tu".)

While Parizeau was one of the few not to avoid the word
"separatist", Burns was one of the few to define himself clearly
as a socialist. He was born in Pointe-Saint-Charles, a working-
class English-speaking community in Montreal; his English-
speaking father died when he was three, and he was raised by
his French-speaking mother. Elected in 1970, he soon developed a reputation as a powerful debater and a dangerous
adversary, raising the scandals that dogged the Bourassa
government. He was the muckraker, the digger, the fighter —
and saw himself as such.

To help him steer between these conflicts and to form a
government, Lévesque relied on Louis Bernard, the chief of

staff for the PQ parliamentary leader. Bernard was the ideal person to be charged with the organization of the transition. Then thirty-nine, he had been a respected high-ranking civil servant in the late 1960s. Brilliant, calm, unflappable, and discreet, he had kept in touch with his former colleagues; they were to be invaluable in easing the difficulties of the change of government.

Born in the east end of Montreal, Bernard grew up in Saint-Henri, where his father had a small printing shop. He was the eldest of four children, but managed to go to the Jesuit Collège Sainte-Marie.

Sainte Marie was more activist and more political than Collège Jean-de-Brébeuf, the college of the affluent Outremont élite. Bernard was in the same class as Robert Burns, and was an outstanding student.

He went on to the Université de Montréal and studied law; at the same time, he was the editor of the newspaper of the Catholic Action movement, *Présence*. "He is the best example of a fine tradition: the Catholic intellectual," remarked Bernard Landry, who knew him at university.

After graduating, and articling at the prestigious Montreal law firm Stikeman Elliott (John Turner's firm at the time), Bernard went to the London School of Economics to get his Ph.D. in administrative law, writing his thesis on Canadian federalism and the mechanisms of co-operation that allowed it to work.

In 1964, Claude Morin, then deputy minister of federal-provincial affairs, was looking for staff. On the advice of an ex-classmate, he hired Bernard. At twenty-seven, with his thesis barely completed, Bernard returned from London to become assistant deputy minister. Over the next six years, Federal-Provincial Affairs — renamed Intergovernmental Affairs by Daniel Johnson — became a key area. Every question that dealt with another government passed through "Affaires Inter", as it was known. Bernard became one of the most impressive young civil servants. Claude Morin provided the strategy, Louis Bernard the administrative detail.

Thus, it was an enormous shock to Bourassa and the senior civil service when, in June 1970, Louis Bernard, the consummate technocrat, decided to take a $7,000 a year cut in pay — from $24,000 to $17,000 — to become chief of staff to Camille Laurin, the PQ parliamentary leader. In 1976 he was the obvious and automatic choice as Lévesque's first chief of staff, and the first and most important architect of the shape of the new government.

On Friday, November 19, the day Bourassa had his last cabinet meeting, Bernard met with Guy Coulombe, the secretary of the Executive Council — Quebec's top civil servant — and three other senior civil servants to test his plan for a new structure for the cabinet. Bernard wanted better planning and greater co-ordination between ministries. So he designed a plan for a priorities committee, and a group of ministers of state, who would be responsible for planning and co-ordinating areas between ministries, without ministries of their own to run. They would chair inter-ministerial committees, thus reducing the traditional competition between government departments.

It was a plan that Bernard hoped would put policy planning firmly in the hands of the politicians, rather than the senior civil servants. As he explained it later, "the civil servant is to the politician what the engineer is to the architect"; he felt it was essential that politicians should not merely have the power to rubber-stamp or veto policies prepared by civil servants, but should be involved at every stage of the elaboration of policy.

Coulombe was in favour of the plan; he had already strengthened the system of inter-ministerial committees. The deputy minister of education, Pierre Martin — the ex-classmate who, twelve years before, had recommended Bernard to Claude Morin — reported on some of the problems a similar system had in Ontario, where the so-called super-ministers felt isolated, and removed from the limelight, because they planned and co-ordinated, but did not administer, departments and did not produce legislation. So Bernard decided that in his system the ministers of state should be given special mandates to produce laws and defend them in the legislature.

There was only one dissenter at the meeting. Roch Bolduc, the deputy minister of municipal affairs, argued strenuously that this would make politicians rather than civil servants responsible for preparing dossiers. He put his finger on a problem at the heart of the PQ government. Rather than politicizing the bureaucracy, it was doing the precise opposite: bureaucratizing the politicians. From the beginning, the government would be a government of rational planning, bureaucratic reforms, and structural changes.

What remained was to sell the idea of the new structure to René Lévesque.

WITH ENORMOUS SECRECY, LÉVESQUE WITHDREW FROM MONTREAL on Sunday, November 21, to go to North Hatley, and settle into the Hatley Inn to design his cabinet. He was joined by five advisers — Louis Bernard, Jean-Roch Boivin, Michel Carpentier, Michel Maheu, and Claude Malette — and three newly elected members: Pierre Marois, Claude Morin, and Marc-André Bédard. Soon after, Jacques Parizeau and Robert Burns arrived.

Bernard laid out his plan for a priorities committee, and ministers of state responsible for social development, economic development, cultural development, land-use planning, and parliamentary reform. The reaction was mixed. The only members-elect present with experience as senior civil servants were Morin and Parizeau — and they were both dubious. But both could see Lévesque was leaning towards the idea.

Finally, on Monday morning, Lévesque made his decision. "I don't want the old structures," he said. "I knew them, and they don't work." From then on, the question became who would fill what job. The session became a continuous shifting series of meetings, with Lévesque periodically retiring to his room to draw up lists, which he would show to various people — including, once, the wives who had come to North Hatley.

One of Lévesque's initial ideas was to have Marois for Justice and Bernard Landry for Finance, with Bédard minister of state for social development and Parizeau minister of state for economic development and president of the Treasury Board.

Marois baulked; he felt a surge of insecurity, and suggested that he would be better simply as an adviser. Lévesque, exasperated at Marois's modesty, insisted; Marois became minister of state for social development, while Bédard got Justice.

On Saturday, Bédard had quietly sounded out someone close to Parizeau to see if he would be interested in the new super-ministry, but when Parizeau arrived at North Hatley he made it clear that if he did not have Finance and Treasury Board he would sit as a backbencher. Parizeau and Morin both understood how much power a minister derives from a real ministry, and they were both wary of being caught by an experiment that failed.

Lévesque wondered whether to give Jacques-Yvan Morin Education and Camille Laurin Cultural Development, or vice versa. By late Monday, when Laurin arrived, he was offered Cultural Development, and accepted.

Bernard Landry also arrived late at the meeting. Before leaving for a weekend skiing, he had heard rumours that he would be offered Finance, but dismissed them as idle speculation; when he arrived at the Hatley Inn, Lévesque offered him the Ministry of State for Economic Development. "Yes, but, Mr. Lévesque, what if it doesn't develop?" Landry joked nervously. "If it doesn't develop, then we're all in trouble," replied Lévesque, amused. Landry accepted.

In addition to the cabinet, there were two other major questions to be decided. What should be the relationship between the party and the government? And what should the government do about the federal-provincial conferences coming up in two weeks?

On the first question, Lévesque decided that the party could not be allowed to block or to impose government decisions. The government, he was to stress, was responsible to its electors, not just the party. However, the National Council (a meeting of four hundred delegates from all ridings, which met four times a year) would act as a kind of watchdog on the government, and a forum for party members to cross-examine ministers on their performance.

The question of Quebec's participation in federal-provincial conferences required a key decision, which would shape the government's approach to federal-provincial relations before the referendum. The decision couldn't wait, for there were to be a finance ministers' conference on December 6 to discuss federal-provincial fiscal arrangements, and a first ministers' conference on December 13.

How should the government handle the question of fiscal arrangements, which had been discussed over the last few months? Should they argue that they should not be bound by what Bourassa's finance minister, Raymond Garneau, had agreed to, and block agreement? Or should they co-operate, and remain part of what had become a provincial "Common Front" against the federal plan to reduce transfers to the provinces?

It was decided that the government should co-operate, on the grounds that its major commitment was to provide good government. Thus, it would continue to attend federal-provincial meetings as previous governments had done, and negotiate as well as they could in the existing context. By providing good government, the argument went, the Parti Québécois would be able to prove its capacity to manage Quebec with the full powers of an independent state.

On Wednesday night, November 24, Pierre Trudeau made a televised address to the nation. The Quebec election had shown the strength of democracy, he said, stressing that Quebecers had voted for a new government and not a new country, and making it clear that there was no question in his mind of using force to keep Quebec in Confederation.

"I have known René Lévesque for many years, some twenty years," he said. "I personally know many of his colleagues. I respect their intelligence and their dedication." They all believed in equality, liberty, and democracy, he said, but disagreed profoundly on the means to achieve these goals. His disagreement with Lévesque, which dated back some ten years, was based on his conviction that there is room in Canada for all Canadians.

"He, on the other hand, probably not without regret, perhaps even with sadness, . . . believes the opposite," Trudeau said, and then added the dig, "he has therefore surrounded himself with a strong corps of blood-brothers, and he speaks to the rest of the country as one speaks to good neighbours."

Blood-brothers. It was a one-word glimpse of Trudeau's feeling about Quebec nationalism in general, and the post-1960 resurgence of Quebec nationalism in particular; it was the kind of reference to tribalism that enraged Péquistes.

THE NEXT MORNING, THURSDAY, NOVEMBER 25, LÉVESQUE LEFT NORTH Hatley and drove to Quebec, where he was sworn in as premier, and completed the last touches to the cabinet before it was to be sworn in on Friday afternoon. One by one, the candidates were summoned to his hotel suite. Some were too inexperienced to realize they were about to be offered cabinet jobs; others were taken aback at the jobs they were given.

Louis Bernard spotted a bewildered Jean Garon on the Grande Allée, shortly after he had seen Lévesque. A rotund, gravel-voiced man, Garon was a professor of fiscal law at Laval.

"Are you pleased?" asked Bernard.

"I don't know," rumbled Garon. "Agriculture! I don't know anything about it. I didn't think I would be named to the cabinet, and if I were, I thought it would be Revenue. But Agriculture!"

"Listen, Jean," said Bernard. "You've got exactly the qualities that are needed for Agriculture. These days, agriculture is a matter of economy and law. The legal aspect is very important because of all the marketing-board plans, and so on. You can't have a farmer — and besides, you have a little farm."

Garon listened dubiously, muttering "Ouais . . ." (Yeah . . .). He was to suffer a rough initiation, but would emerge as the government's strongest asset in rural Quebec.

On Friday, November 26, the cabinet was to be announced. But at two o'clock Lévesque made an unprecedented gesture towards the senior civil service. He summoned all the deputy ministers to the cabinet room and made a clear statement that there would be no purge of the civil service. On the other hand, he said, the government did have an ideological direction that the civil servants should be aware of.

"That having been said, there is no question of a great housecleaning," he said. "It is up to you to make a decision whether you can work in conscience with this government."

There was a silence, and everyone turned towards the dean of the deputy ministers, Arthur Tremblay of Intergovernmental Affairs. Tremblay assured him of their allegiance in the exercise of their functions, regardless of their own opinions about the future of Canada.

At 3.30, the new ministers all gathered in the lieutenant-governor's chambers to be sworn in. There were some surprises; Jacques Couture, a worker-priest from Saint-Henri, was minister of labour, and, despite some initial hesitations because of his public criticisms of his leadership, Lévesque had included Claude Charron in the cabinet as minister responsible for the high commission on youth, recreation, and sports.

It was the first time they had all gathered together; they grinned, shook hands, and slapped shoulders: clusters of men (and one woman, the former TV host Lise Payette) who had worked together for years, now together in what they believed would be their greatest adventure in teamwork.

When he presented his cabinet to the dignitaries, reporters, and live TV cameras in the Salon Rouge at four o'clock, Lévesque stressed that a cabinet job was a temporary one, by its nature. He emphasized that a minister's first job was as an elected representative; everyone should understand from the beginning that being a cabinet minister was not a lifetime job, and that some would be asked to step down to make room for others. After explaining his new system of ministers of state,

Lévesque made a hyperbolic appeal for support and understanding that made the stakes very clear.

"Never in human memory has a group of men and women carried so many hopes at the same time," he said. "If we should disappoint Quebecers, it would collectively be our confidence in ourselves as a people that would risk being injured. In other words — it's simple — we haven't got the right to fail.

"If we all do our best, " he concluded, "we can make Quebec a country where people are happy to live. A country which maintains harmonious relations with its neighbours. A country which treats its minorities with justice and fairness. A country which develops its resources with respect for the environment, and for the benefit of its inhabitants first. A country which treats its older people, who have earned it after a long life, with recognition, and a tangible recognition. A country which houses its families with decency, and which assures its workers not only a job, but adequate working conditions."

It was perhaps the clearest statement of Lévesque's dream: a dream of reconciliation, justice, abundance, and equity; a dream of drawing together all Quebecers, regardless of their language, class, background, or origin; a dream of a new nation, born without conflict.

It was a dream of such idealism and such vulnerability that Lévesque would only recoil in anger if it were greeted with scepticism, and would instinctively view those who opposed him not as critics, or representatives of opposing interests — but as exploiters, traitors, or whores. The very fragility of the ideal would compromise its hopes.

Then he presented his cabinet: twenty-two men and one woman. They were, by any reckoning, an impressive lot. Eleven had taught at university; six had done graduate work in France, three in England, and five in the United States. (None had studied in English Canada.) They came from a wide range of the ideological spectrum, but were united by their nationalism and by the consensus that the Parti Québécois had forged over eight years. On the left, there were Robert Burns, Jacques Couture, Denis Lazure (social affairs), Louis O'Neill (cultural affairs and communications), and Pierre Marois, minister of state for social development. Their priorities differed, but they shared a gut commitment to transforming society.

On the right was Rodrigue Tremblay (industry and commerce), a conservative economist. Other ministers who were more cautious and conservative in their thinking included Marc-André Bédard (justice), Denis de Belleval (public service), Jean Garon, Lucien Lessard (transport and public works), and Marcel Léger, minister responsible for the environment.

But the bulk of the cabinet, though they might lean to the left or the right, were moderates: ideological pragmatists, politically liberal, favouring a strong interventionist state.

There was a similarly broad ideological spectrum on the national question, stretching from those like Claude Morin who had been led to the party primarily because of the concept of association, and were suspected of viewing sovereignty-association as a bargaining position to achieve special status — and those like Jacques Parizeau, who were committed to Quebec independence and accepted sovereignty-association as a political and electoral necessity.

But, despite these nuances, the cabinet, the caucus, and the PQ itself all had two fundamental things in common which gave them a common framework. The first was a commitment to Quebec as a political society. The second was an overwhelming amount of experience with the public sector — and virtually none with the private sector. The PQ leaders came from what the French academic Robert Lescartet has dubbed "l'industrie de la parole" — the word industry — teaching, journalism, law, the civil service. The lawyers were labour lawyers and public-interest lawyers; the economists were academics and civil servants. And, beyond the cabinet in the caucus, those in the PQ with roots in the labour movement (Burns, Marois, Guy Chevrette, Guy Bisaillon, François Gendron) came from the public sector: the teachers' unions, or the CSN.

WHEN RENÉ LÉVESQUE HAD HIS FIRST CABINET MEETING ON DECEMBER 1, he gave his colleagues two pieces of advice. "First, don't get lost on twenty-five projects at the same time," he said. "Pick one, and stick to it. Secondly, learn as fast as you bloody well can how to work with your deputy ministers."

He meant it. Despite his provocative behaviour as a minister and his often cavalier interpretation of cabinet solidarity, he prided himself on his ability to work with civil servants. Some of the new ministers never understood this; others grasped it immediately. Those who did understood an essential fact: deputy ministers work for their ministers, but they are named by and responsible to the premier.

Some tension with the civil service is inevitable with a new government. In the PQ's case trouble arose from the fact that ministers were coming to office with an elaborate program which they had been working on for eight years.

On November 29, Pierre Marois's first working day as minister of state for social development, a civil servant came into his office with his arms piled high with documents.

"What's all this?" Marois asked.

"It's a series of projects ready for presentation to cabinet," the man replied. "They're all ready; you simply have to sign them."

Marois had not planned to spend his first day on the job signing bills prepared for the Liberal government. After going through all the documents, Marois told the civil servant that the legislation was not, in fact, ready.

"You might go through this to get a sense of the way we approach things," Marois said, sliding a PQ program across his desk. Wide-eyed, the civil servant walked away muttering.

The next day, Claude Morin issued a memo to the staff of the Ministry of Intergovernmental Affairs, along with a photocopy of the memo he had sent his staff on September 29, 1971, when he had quit as deputy minister.

"With my decision, I am not closing a book, but turning a page," he had written in 1971. "I am not leaving, but absenting myself." In his new memo, he wrote, "This absence is now over. I have returned."

Morin told his first staff meeting clearly that the government's goal was sovereignty-association. If that created problems of conscience for the civil servants, he said, they should talk to him about being transferred to a less sensitive area.

When the meeting was over, Morin ushered Arthur Tremblay into his office for a private session. "Well, what do you think of us?" Morin asked his successor as deputy minister.

"You know, this may surprise you," replied Tremblay, "but it's a matter of punctuation."

"How's that?"

"This business of sovereignty association," said Tremblay. "If it is sovereignty comma association, sovereignty has priority over association; if it is sovereignty hyphen association, they are in equilibrium. And you haven't said yet which it is."

"That's funny," smiled Morin. "I never thought of that."

The first days of a new government—particularly one with a sense of mission—are often full of electric excitement. Minis-

ters do not yet have the ingrained caution that experience
brings; they have not yet learned not to say what they think,
or to surround themselves with protective layers of tight-lipped
aides. Immediately after the PQ victory, there was a flurry of
announcements, as the ministers explored their new authority,
and let their dreams be known. With a flick of a pen, auto-
routes were stopped, threatened day-care centres were saved
from demolition, and charges against the abortionist Henry
Morgentaler were dropped.

The labour minister, Jacques Couture, promised "a new social
contract" which would stop management from thinking only
about making money, and would give workers power, dignity,
and happiness. Marcel Léger, responsible for the environment,
said that six million Quebecers would become their own environmental inspectors. The cultural affairs minister, Louis
O'Neill, said that culture would be "democratized", and that
the only people who had to fear the PQ government were "the
parasites of the ancien régime". The social affairs minister,
Denis Lazure, said he wanted to institute compulsory two-year
service in remote areas for graduating doctors, and he hoped
for the day when doctors would be on salary. And, at a press
conference where he said that he liked to consider the Ministry of State for Parliamentary Reform as "the Ministry of
Democracy", Robert Burns introduced his staff to reporters:
from André Larocque, his chief of staff, to Robert Ouimet, his
chauffeur. ("I don't like the word chauffeur; I prefer to call
him my travelling companion.")

As for Lévesque, he seemed a different man from the cranky,
irritable leader who had lashed back at Burns at the August
meeting in Saint-Marc-sur-le-Richelieu. He was relaxed, pa-
tient — the first cabinet meetings were eight-hour marathons
— preoccupied with the issues of the party program, totally at
ease with the demands of being premier.

Burns mentioned it to Camille Laurin, amazed. "You're a
psychiatrist, Camille — how do you explain it?"

Laurin sensed Lévesque's enormous satisfaction at being
back in power after a decade in the political wilderness.
"Imagine a lumberjack who has been in the bush for weeks
and weeks, eating terrible food," he said. "He comes into the
city, and eats a first-class meal. He is transformed."

JUST TEN DAYS AFTER THE CABINET WAS SWORN IN, PARIZEAU AND
Morin went to Ottawa for the finance ministers' meeting on

December 6. At stake was the hideously complicated question of "fiscal arrangements": the process by which some $9 billion was transferred annually to the provinces by the federal government. This year, the federal government planned to eliminate "revenue guarantees" — a set of guarantees of revenue for the provinces which had cost the federal government $6 billion the previous year.

The federal government's argument was that the guarantees had been intended as a temporary measure in 1972; the provinces replied with a proposal they had agreed on secretly in Toronto in October. In exchange for giving up the guarantees, they demanded four "tax points" — worth about $5.5 billion over five years. Quebec was somewhat detached from the debate, since in 1964 it had withdrawn from the twenty-seven joint programs. But the first decision in North Hatley had been to co-operate with the other provinces, and Parizeau and Morin were determined that Quebec should not be penalized.

For both men, it was a triumphant return to an arena they had both known as civil servants and advisers only a few years before. Parizeau took a mischievous pleasure in coming to the conference as an indépendantiste finance minister. He joked that they were "fathers of de-Confederation".

"Just because we are 'séparatisses' doesn't mean we are going to say 'Go to hell', we are going to sweep all the pieces off the table," Parizeau told reporters on Sunday night. But he made it clear that in his mind this was a temporary alliance. "In 1964 we got opting-out of twenty-seven joint programs," he said. "Now we are preparing for the opting-out of Quebec."

The next morning, Claude Morin spoke to the meeting. He made no mischievous remarks; he scrupulously avoided any suggestion of rupture, adding to the ambiguity of two members of an indépendantiste government contributing their technical expertise to the discussions of the hideously complex question of fiscal transfers. This was no mere façade: Morin had a horror of the politics of rupture. But his performance made it all the more difficult for representatives of the other provinces to believe his government was, in fact, determined to lead Quebec out of Confederation.

The message Morin delivered to the meeting was a complex one, which the PQ never really succeeded in making clear. On the one hand, they were committed to sovereignty. On the other, they were determined to respect the majority will of the population. Thus, as long as Quebecers had not voted to leave

Confederation, Quebec would continue to participate in federal-provincial conferences — conferences, as Morin said, which are "situated within the federal-provincial framework. We are very well aware of this and we shall in consequence thereof act loyally but with dynamism and also — why not? — with imagination."

The conference ended in a stalemate; the provinces stuck together, and there was an $800 million gap between the federal offer and what the provinces were seeking.

Morin was very pleased. It was the strategic position he liked best: if the Common Front held, it would prove that Quebec could negotiate with the rest of Canada; if the other provinces gave in to Ottawa, it would show that federalism didn't work for Quebec.

Three days later, he explained why the provincial Common Front did not change his fundamental belief that Quebec was the only province that did not want to centralize powers in Ottawa. "There are Common Fronts of the provinces — there always have been. But either they don't last, or there are very specific factors at work."

In fact, Morin felt that provincial Common Fronts against Ottawa were dangerous for Quebec. "The Common Front which exists when Quebec is in means that Quebec and the provinces are holding to a strict common denominator," he said. "But to the extent that one province, let's say Quebec, is culturally and demographically different from the others, and it enters into a Common Front, it means that it abandons those differences. And it becomes a province like the others." They were prophetic words.

On December 13, the first ministers met on the same issue. At 9.30 a.m., René Lévesque slipped into the Conference Centre — the cavernous hall of the old Union Station in Ottawa. In the midst of a crush of reporters and cameramen, Lévesque and Trudeau shook hands. They had not seen each other since Daniel Johnson's funeral in 1968.

After an ironic exchange of barbed banalities, Trudeau led the premiers upstairs to a fifth-floor room for a private session, where Trudeau and Lévesque exchanged their contradictory visions before getting down to haggling over tax points and revenue guarantees. The premiers were impressed by Lévesque; he was charming, good-humoured, co-operative, and witty. But that view changed dramatically when tempers flared that night over dinner at 24 Sussex Drive.

In response to insistent questioning about the PQ's intentions for Quebec by New Brunswick premier Richard Hatfield, Lévesque snapped: "My intentions are to get out!"

The phrase stunned most of the premiers, who had assumed that Lévesque had been using independence as a lever to bargain more power and money from Ottawa. Prince Edward Island Premier Alex Campbell made a note on a scrap of paper with letters three-quarters of an inch high: OUT.

Newfoundland Premier Frank Moores began to question Lévesque. He started by saying how much he loved Canada, and how committed he was to it. Lévesque responded by talking of his patriotic feeling for Quebec. Then, Moores switched to talking about the impact the PQ was having on investment.

When Lévesque tried to reply, Moores flipped back to his patriotic appeal. It was, as one premier observed later, a skilful political performance: "It was heart-wallet, heart-wallet, heart-wallet. And he got Lévesque coming and going."

Finally, Lévesque lost his temper. "What I do in Quebec is none of your damn business," he snapped.

"What you're trying to do to Canada is my goddam business!" shot back Moores.

Lévesque refused to give a hint about the referendum date — "thirty days to four years," he quipped — but said that if the first referendum were lost, there would be another and another.

That night, the provincial Common Front was blown apart. The premiers had planned to stick together — but suddenly feeling the depth of Lévesque's hostility to federalism made them pull back. Reluctantly, they toned down their objections. A deal was struck the next day, and the fiscal arrangements were settled for another five years. When the crunch came, they were not prepared to join Lévesque in attacking Ottawa.

Angrily, Lévesque said Quebec had been "gypped" and "robbed". Trudeau said flatly, "I can never be flexible enough to suit him. His flexibility is Quebec opting out of Confederation."

Lévesque left quickly on Tuesday morning for the opening of a mini-session of the National Assembly, which was required to pass some budgetary provisions, and legislation needing annual renewal.

SYMBOLICALLY, THERE WERE A NUMBER OF INDICATIONS THAT THIS was a different kind of government. Speaker Clément Richard was in a dark suit, not robes. There was no prayer, but a moment of silence. The PQ members did not bang their desks, as generations of parliamentarians have delighted in doing, but applauded. And the inaugural address, delivered by the lieutenant-governor, was in French only.

The mini-session proved to be a first testing ground for neophyte ministers. Jean Garon seemed to be floundering with Agriculture, as did Jacques Couture in Labour, and Rodrigue Tremblay in Industry and Commerce. But the greatest burden fell on the shoulders of Guy Tardif, the criminologist and former Mountie who had been named municipal affairs minister. He had to introduce three important pieces of legislation, including a law requiring Montreal to impose an Olympic tax. He told reporters that the New York credit-evaluating firm, Moody's, had already insisted the previous June that Montreal pay its share of the Olympic debt to keep its "A" rating. But the law succeeded in annoying virtually every interest group in Montreal.

IN THE NEW YEAR, TWO EVENTS TOOK PLACE WHICH MARKED THE end of the beginning of the Parti Québécois in power: a speech and an accident.

On January 25, 1977, Lévesque spoke to the Economic Club of New York: his first major address outside Quebec, and the most important. For once, he did not write the speech. Parizeau, Morin, and Bernard collaborated on it, each one writing a different part. The result was a kind of manifesto.

"Exactly two months ago, a new government assumed power in Quebec," Lévesque began. "This government was born of a young political party which had gained strength during the two previous elections, with political sovereignty as its prime objective."

The room froze. Lévesque knew it, but he was stuck with his text; he simply had to plough on. Comparing Quebec's situation to that of America before the Revolution, he gave an overview of Quebec history from the Conquest to modern times. It was not a question of whether, or even when, Quebec would become independent, he said, but how.

More specifically, he said that Quebec was considering nationalization in the asbestos industry, but that this would be the only area for state take-over, since the PQ was "pragmatic".

As a speech, it was quite eloquent, and the francophone reporters who went to New York to hear it were moved and impressed. But the reaction of the businessmen was glacial.

They had no interest in any gratuitous comparisons with the American Revolution, and the claims of pragmatism left them cold.

Back in Quebec, Lévesque blamed what he called the "fifth column" of Canadians in New York for privately distorting his message to their head offices. But he had no illusions about the disaster. Never again would he face an audience with a text that he had not either written himself or substantially reworked to his taste.

However, the tone had been intentional. And, while it had not helped the government with the Americans or with English Canada—the Baltimore *Sun* titled an editorial "Lévesque lays an egg" — it reduced the pressure on the government from nationalists, who had been looking for some indication that independence was not forgotten. Louis Bernard concluded that the speech gave them the manoeuvring room to be a good government.

Ten days later, on February 5, Saturday night, Lévesque and Corinne Côté had dinner at the home of Yves Michaud with a few friends. They stayed until almost 4 a.m.

At 3 a.m., while the party was still going strong, Edgar Trottier arrived at the Queen Mary Veterans' Hospital, very drunk. He was a derelict: a 62-year-old veteran who had been banished from the Old Brewery Mission three months earlier as a habitual bedwetter. He wanted a place to sleep; three nights earlier, he had tried an old ruse of lying in the street, which had earned him a night on a stretcher when someone brought him to the hospital. But this time, a security guard called the police when Trottier became obstreperous.

Two constables from Station 15 took him away in a patrol car and, after trying two hostels unsuccessfully, took him out of their district and dropped him on McDougall Road, part of the drive down Côte des Neiges. Trottier tried his old trick again. He lay down in the street, in the hope that, being taken for an accident victim, he might get back to a hospital.

A driver spotted him, stopped, and tried to flag down the next car. Lévesque, who was driving without glasses (although his licence required them, he didn't own any), swerved to the left to avoid the man, and struck Trottier. Trottier died instantly.

For Lévesque, the accident was a jarring personal shock. Since his election, he had been able to escape the bodyguards and chauffeurs on the weekend. This was no longer possible.

Suddenly, his private life was no longer private. Peter Desbarats had disclosed in the biography published that fall that Lévesque was no longer living with his wife; his six-year-old relationship with Corinne Côté, which he had always been discreet about, was now public knowledge.

Lévesque cancelled all his appointments on Monday, and told advisers he would have to resign. An aide called Judge Robert Cliche, and pleaded, "You are the only person who can really talk to him — tell him he mustn't resign." Cliche persuaded Lévesque not to quit.

It was testimony to his popularity, and his virtual immunity from critical press scrutiny at that point, that the general public reaction was sympathetic. The political impact of an incident that might have destroyed another politician was negligible. There was no public inquiry, no public outcry. Nevertheless, the brutal jolt of the accident put an end to the charming illusion that Lévesque could step outside the demands of the job. From then on, provincial-police security agents sat a discreet distance away in restaurants; a large limousine waited outside any party he might attend. The first days were over.

SEVEN

Camille Laurin
and the Politics of
Language

*Their language is their point
of honour, as well as
their lever of power. So
long as they keep it, they are unconquered.
When it ceases to be spoken
by their children, a
greater loss than Montcalm's
will be felt.*

D'Arcy McGee

While the Parti Québécois ministers, their political staffs, and their senior officials were preparing legislation, some of which would not be ready for another two and a half years, the first months of the PQ government were dominated by a single preoccupation: the language law.

As Camille Laurin was minister of state for cultural development, language legislation was his responsibility; from the beginning, his idea was quite clear. He wanted French to be the defining reality of Quebec; not simply the only official language, but, as he put it in an interview on December 9, "in actual fact, the language of work and communication. In this sense, we want the milieu to be French. We want everyone to know that French is becoming . . . necessary, useful, profitable, and in particular that the immigrants and the ethnic groups realize that Quebec is French, and to earn their living, the language of promotion, the language of professional advantage, is French. That is our aspiration."

This aspiration was to determine the approach of the Parti Québécois to legislation: not just the language law, but legislation in general. For the language law that Laurin was to draw up was not simply intended to promote the use of French; it flowed from a set of assumptions that were deeply rooted in Quebec's intellectual traditions: assumptions shaped by Catholicism and the Napoleonic Code, to which Laurin and his colleagues brought a set of anthropological and psychiatric theories.

Camille Laurin was the oldest member of the Lévesque cabinet. Born on May 6, 1922, he was almost four months older than Lévesque himself. The fourth in a family of fourteen, he was born in Charlemagne, a village just across the river from the eastern tip of the Island of Montreal where his father was a small businessman, who ran everything from a restaurant to a fleet of trucks. Laurin's father could not afford classical college for his academically promising son. He sought out the village curé, who found a benefactor in Paul Gouin, the leader of the Action Libérale Nationale, who was to pay for the boy's studies.

In 1934, at the age of twelve, Laurin became a boarder at the Collège de L'Assomption, a rural college with a fine reputation, of which Wilfrid Laurier had been an illustrious graduate. He was a serious student: a musical boy (former schoolmates remember him as having a beautiful soprano voice), and a voracious reader fascinated by literature, nature, and science. Laurin graduated in 1942, and was awarded prizes in scholastic philosophy, French, physics, philosophy, the college prizes for general success and success in exams — and shared prizes for philosophic dissertation, apologetics, philosophic debating, and contributions to the naturalists' club. In addition, he won a share of an intercollegiate prize for an essay on "The share of French Canadians in the functioning of Confederation".

Laurin had decided to become a priest, and enrolled at the Grand Séminaire de Montréal. However, after eight months, he concluded that he was not made for the priesthood; theology seemed too specialized and narrow. He decided to become a doctor. His switch by no means signalled a crisis of faith; he saw medicine as a similar career of help and love, "another career in which I can examine the mystery of the link between the soul and the body, between mind and matter." Enrolling in the Faculty of Medicine at the Université de Montréal, Laurin also became very active in student affairs and worked on the student newspaper *Le Quartier Latin*, where he acquired a reputation for utopian speculation.

"Sometimes, coming into the newsroom, I find Camille Laurin deep in meditation," wrote Pierre Lefebvre, clearly only partly tongue-in-cheek, in 1947. "It is the moment when great projects for the future grow in this great mind, where plans are laid out for the ideal community, whose potentate would be one Camille Laurin, experienced, venerated, dispenser of social reforms and generous largesse."

That same year Laurin wrote, "It's a question of retaking lost ground. Our population has its natural leaders here, in the province. Let these understand the needs, take the initiative of social reforms — sometimes draconian — which are needed, and they will be followed. Our French and Catholic character will be safeguarded much more surely by these than by the loud proclamation of principles, warnings, and useless complaints."

After two years in Geneva from 1948 to 1950 as administrative secretary of Entr'aide Mondiale (World University Service), he did postgraduate work in psychiatry: first in Paris, then in Boston. In 1957, he returned to Montreal, where he was hired by the Institut Albert Prévost. This was a small private hospital which had been founded by two doctors in 1919. Laurin arrived like a hurricane, launching a campaign on behalf of Freudian psychiatry, and soon clashing with the director, Charlotte Tassé. A nurse when the hospital was founded, she had inherited it. By the mid-1950s, she was an aging grande dame.

An extremely strong personality, with extraordinary energy and a legendary capacity for work, Laurin was bent on reform. "I wanted to transform this hospital, which was more of a rest home for members of the élite in difficulty, into a public hospital, for everyone, a research hospital," he says.

Laurin's differences with the hospital director became irreconcilable and in May 1962 his contract was not renewed, causing the whole psychiatric team to resign in solidarity. Laurin hired a friend as his lawyer — Marc Lalonde. The matter became a public issue, and the Lesage government named a commission of inquiry. While Laurin won his job back, and significant reforms of the hospital, the experience was a turning point for him. "I had all the élites against me," he recalled. "The religious élites, the medical élites, the administrative élites. But since I had good sense on my side and social democracy on my side, the Liberal government was finally forced to give in. I say 'forced', because they didn't want to."

Laurin concluded that the Liberals' concession was based on opportunism, not on conviction — and his political position became crystallized. In addition, he felt excluded from the university and the Canadian medical organizations he participated in. "I was not part of the club. I found myself more or less excluded. In fact, I came to the idea that there was a new order of things to be established."

Thus, despite his friendship with strong federalists like Pierre Trudeau, Gérard Pelletier, Maurice and Jeanne Sauvé, Marc Lalonde, and Pierre Juneau, "it was in 1961 that I separated from them." However, it was another six years before he openly committed himself. His analysis evolved — influenced by the description of the two cultures in the 1965 *Preliminary Report* of the Royal Commission on Bilingualism and Biculturalism. With the formation of the Mouvement Souveraineté-Association in 1967 and the Parti Québécois a year later, he became publicly involved. He was immediately a major figure in the party: a member of the first executive, a serious intellectual voice in the party, and parliamentary leader from 1970 to 1973. During this period he retained his connection with the Institut Albert Prévost. His therapeutic experience shaped his political analysis and had a marked influence on the party and, after November 15, 1976, on the government.

Laurin's first act on becoming the minister of state for cultural development was to select a team to work with him on the preparation of the White Paper on language and the language law. He sought out a number of like-minded people: Guy Rocher, a sociologist at the Université de Montréal, Fernand Dumont, a sociologist and philosopher at Laval, Henri Laberge, a PQ activist working for the teachers' union, and David Payne, a humanities teacher. It was an impressive group — Rocher and Dumont were two of the most respected academics in Quebec — but strikingly homogeneous. All its members were left-leaning Catholic intellectuals from small-town backgrounds. Laurin had known them all very well for a long time. They were all abstract thinkers.

Guy Rocher, then fifty-two, had known Laurin since they were schoolboys. After graduating from the Collège de L'Assomption, he had spent four years working full time with Catholic Action, from 1944 to 1948. He then went to Laval to study sociology at the school of social science under Father Lévesque; later he did a doctorate at Harvard. In the 1960s, he worked on the

Parent Report, which transformed the education system in Quebec. His political turning point was in 1970. He was the chairman of the "Group of Eight" — the group including Claude Ryan and René Lévesque that had tried to seek a negotiated solution to the October Crisis — and he had travelled across Canada. The apathy and hostility that he discovered left him with an overwhelming feeling of Quebec's isolation.

The following year, after analysing the federal multiculturalism policy and its implications for bilingualism, he concluded that "the creation of an independent French-speaking Quebec appears as the last chance for a French-speaking North American nation whose future is uncertain anyway."

Fernand Dumont's political turning point had occurred much earlier. The son of a Dominion Textile worker in Montmorency, outside Quebec City, Dumont studied at the Petit Séminaire du Québec, graduating in 1949. He had gone on to Laval, getting an MA in social science in 1953 before doing a doctorate at the Sorbonne. A sociologist, he was also a poet, a deeply religious man, and a widely eclectic thinker. When Laurin persuaded him to leave Laval to come to work for him, the two had known each other for thirty years.

Henri Laberge, thirty-seven, was born in Sainte-Foy when it was a farming village, and was active in the farm organization of Catholic Action. In the early 1960s, he had gone to work full time for Catholic Action in Montreal. Later in the 1960s, he joined the RIN and ran against Jean Lesage in Louis-Hébert in 1966; he was on the executive that tried to negotiate fusion with the MSA. A teacher, he went to work for the union. Throughout the 1960s and 1970s, he was active in the campaigns over the French language: the campaign against Bill 63 in 1969, and the Mouvement Québec Français in the 1970s. He was a PQ candidate in 1970, and president of his riding association.

David Payne, thirty-two, had first met Laurin in Rome in 1967. Born in Yorkshire, Payne had become a priest and was working at the Vatican as executive assistant to the English bishops when he met Laurin. Payne was extremely impressed with the erudition and culture of this Quebec psychiatrist who could talk about Palmerston, Disraeli, and Wilson with the same apparent ease as he could discuss Freud, opera, Beethoven, or Vatican II. Payne immigrated to Canada, became a teacher, and joined the PQ.

This group created a powerful atmosphere of religious zeal and intensity. The result, combined with Laurin's incredible capacity for work, was almost stifling. One member of his staff, after leaving, observed, "The priesthood doesn't interest me. It really requires a vocation to follow him."

The group brought a number of common assumptions to the language question that shaped their approach and sometimes reinforced the negative attitudes of the non-francophone communities. Laurin's primary assumption was the validity of a therapeutic, psychiatric model for resolving the language problem. In his practice, he had concluded that most of his francophone patients were suffering from what he called a "feeling of incompleteness and [a] flawed identity", which he decided was "a collective inheritance that only collective psychotherapy could resolve", shaped by the experience of conquest and domination, frustration and insecurity. The result was a pattern of minority behaviour reinforced by the patterns of authority that the Church had established in the family and at school — a reaction to "the weakness, the disorganization, and the vulnerability of the French-Canadian man".

Within the family, parents reproduced the model of defensive authority which they inherited from the Church. This ideology of retreat, he argued, simply magnified the threatening image of the English: the dominant, Protestant, mercantile, powerful Other. Thus the English became "an envied and dreaded paternal substitute" before whom the French Canadian felt "the full extent of his weakness, of the poverty of his powerlessness and his destitution." Laurin began to feel that those who opted for independence had succeeded in breaking this pattern, a conviction that motivated him to work for Quebec independence. He saw language legislation as a kind of shock therapy, or, as Evelyn Dumas put it with Laurin's agreement, "a cure in intensive care" for Quebecers: therapy which would give French-speaking Quebecers a sense of their identity, and bring the English-speaking community "to its real proportions". He dismissed the 326 francophone businessmen who signed a critique of the language law as "inféodés" — feudal vassals to the English-speaking élite.

In addition to Laurin's psychiatric assumptions, Rocher and Dumont brought a set of sociological — or, more properly, anthropological — assumptions about language to the debate — assumptions which Laurin shared, and which would permeate the rhetoric of the White Paper. These two men had emerged out of an intellectual tradition that leaned more to global, philosophical theorizing than to the smaller-scale approach. "The sociologists who have been shaped either by Catholic influence or by Jewish influence have a greater tendency towards a sociology of large concepts than the sociologists who have been shaped by Protestant influence," Rocher observed.

In addition to this general approach, Rocher and Dumont both fell within the "Whorfian" tradition of linguistic anthropology: the belief, identified with Benjamin L. Whorf, that thought, and therefore culture, are inextricably linked with language. It was a conviction reflected in George Steiner's argument that "All developed language has a private core. . . . [Words] encode, preserve and transmit the knowledge, the shared memories, the metaphorical and pragmatic conjectures on life of a small group—a family, a clan, a tribe. . . . A language . . . is secret towards the outsider and inventive of its own world." This was contrary to the linguistic ideas of Edward Sapir and Noam Chomsky, who argued that language and culture are not causally related but autonomous, and, more generally, opposed the tradition of North American pluralism.

Laurin, Rocher, Dumont, Laberge, and Payne brought another shared experience to their work. They had all been — and Laurin, Rocher, and Dumont still were—practising Catholics. They were not uncritical of the Church, but they were Catholic, not secular, intellectuals.

Their nationalism — a strong belief in a Quebec that was almost mystically French and at the same time tolerant of non-French-speaking minorities — was similar to their sense of Catholicism: they were extremely devout, but committed to dialogue with non-Catholics.

The careful, earnest, theological sense of faith and dialogue that underlay the ideas these men brought to the language question created an intellectual framework that English-speaking non-Catholics were only dimly aware of. To the extent that they recognized it, it was dark, foreign, and threatening, reminding them of the narrow ultramontane nationalism that dominated Quebec for the century following the uprising of 1837, conveyed in the classic phrase "la langue, gardienne de la foi [language, guardian of faith]".

There was another set of unarticulated assumptions which added to the conflicting reactions of francophones and non-

francophones to the language legislation. The law was based
on the Civil Code, which was derived from the Napoleonic
Code. It flowed logically and inexorably from a set of principles;
once the principles were accepted, the terms of the legislation
followed with irrefutable, almost Euclidean inevitability.

"In the final analysis, the legislation was drawn up more as
a law à la française than as a law in the British tradition,"
Rocher said later. "And, moreover, that was the basis of cri-
tiques we received from jurists, who told us 'Canadian juris-
prudence will not understand this law. It doesn't correspond
to the British legal tradition.'"

The difference between the French Civil Code approach to
legislation and the English Common Law approach is one of
the greatest underlying, and most rarely analysed, sources of
misunderstanding between French and English Canada. The
Civil Code is written law, based on a set of principles; it is
rational, logical, Cartesian. The Common Law system, on the
other hand, is pragmatic, evolutionary, and based on precedent.
It elevates "common sense" into law, building precedent upon
precedent like the rings that form a tree.

The conflict in attitudes towards legislation was rarely so
clear as in the debate over the language law. In addition to
disagreements over the policy's explicit goal—to make Quebec
as French as Ontario is English, and to do away with official
bilingualism — these underlying assumptions, psychiatric,
anthropological, religious, and legal, all combined to elevate
the language law — and Laurin himself — to the status of a
symbol of reassuring protection for most francophones, of
dark threat, rigidity, and menace to most anglophones.

Laurin put his finger on the ambiguous symbolism of the
law when he said in an interview that it would not legitimize
xenophobia but rather eliminate it by diminishing the insecurities of Quebecers that gave rise to racism. "In the same way
that a champion boxer is often, in everyday life, a very gentle
man," he said. "He knows that he is strong, and he does not
need to use his strength all the time. It is the same thing
collectively."

Three ideas lay at the root of the desire for language legislation: the economic inferiority of francophones, the tendency
of immigrants to assimilate with the English-speaking community and further threaten the demographic balance in Quebec,
and the desire to make a symbolic affirmation of Quebec as a
French-speaking place.

The Royal Commission on Bilingualism and Biculturalism had established in the 1960s that French Canadians earned less than English Canadians in Quebec. This was confirmed by a study for the Gendron Commission, which described Quebec's economic structure as a pyramid: unilingual francophones on the bottom, unilingual anglophones on the top, and the bilingual in between. Moreover, the more educated an anglophone was, the less likely he was to speak French, while the more educated a francophone was, the more likely he was to speak English. The Gendron Commission also found that francophones were seriously under-represented in head offices — and the under-representation increased at higher salary levels.

Laurin had to decide how his law would deal with this. Would it be aimed at promoting the French language as the language of work? Or would it be aimed at promoting and protecting francophones? One of the officials assigned to Laurin in the first weeks of the new government was Gaston Cholette, who had been the first president of the Office de la Langue Française. Cholette's recommendation to Laurin in early December was that the legislation be modelled on American "affirmative action" programs, giving priority to francophones in hiring and promotion. At first glance, Laurin was impressed, and in one of his first interviews said that one of the flaws in Bill 22 was that it did not protect francophones. William Tetley, who had lived through the language debates in the Bourassa cabinet, spotted the implications immediately, and wrote that such a policy would endanger the Human Rights Code.

However, when Laurin's team was assembled, it began to question the validity of the "affirmative action" approach. It would require quotas — and, more difficult, a definition of a francophone. Was a francophone someone who could speak French? A French-speaking Quebecer? A French Canadian? Someone educated in French? Cholette eventually conceded that a rat's nest of problems would result.

The language of education was an even more complicated question. It had its roots in the demographic analysis made by Jacques Henripin in the 1960s, which concluded that, at the most pessimistic rate of assimilation of immigrants to the English community, the proportion of francophones in Montreal would drop from 66.4 per cent in 1961 to 52.7 per cent in the year 2000. Henripin himself was later to reject this melodramatic picture, saying that he had failed to take into account the fact of anglophone migration from Quebec, but it became a fundamental part of the nationalist view of francophone Quebec as a vulnerable, hemorrhaging community.

There was a consensus: immigrants should be assimilated into the French-speaking majority. But if "free choice" was no longer politically acceptable, how to determine who had the right to go to English schools? The Liberals' Bill 22 had introduced the criterion of competence in English, which had resulted in the odious spectacle of inspectors testing terrified five-year-olds to determine whether their command of English entitled them to schooling in that language. More insidiously, it implied clearly that successful children could go to English schools, and the failures would be relegated to French schools.

The PQ policy had been to allocate English school places in proportion to population. The Laurin team soon abandoned this quota system, just as they had abandoned affirmative action in the workplace. They reached a consensus based on the idea that the French language was more than just a means of communication in Quebec; it was a way of life, an environment, and a collective self-definition. Everything would flow from that basic precept: that Quebec's defining force was the French language, and that it would be the only official language of the state and the public environment. The law would therefore fully extend French as the complete expression of life in Quebec, and affirm that everyone had the right to have a full and complete existence in French in Quebec. There was to be respect for other languages and cultures, but on the assumption that the connecting link between those minorities would be French, not English. Bilingualism—which gave official and equal status to French and English, thus diminishing the symbolic importance of French and giving English recognition as a common language for non-francophones — was to be explicitly rejected. But, having agreed on these principles, they still had to decide who would have access to English schools.

Claude Benjamin, who had been an adviser to the Liberal government on language, was now working for Jacques-Yvan Morin, the minister of education — and argued against basing any policy on "mother tongue", because of the problem of defining and verifying a child's mother tongue.

The idea then emerged of defining the right to access to English schools in terms of the language in which the parents had been educated. Laurin's team agreed on this as the formula:

if one parent had been educated in English in Quebec, this could be easily verified, and there would be no debate over whether or not that person belonged to the Quebec English-speaking community. Since education was a purely provincial jurisdiction, control would be simple.

There was a similar discussion on signs. Everyone was unanimous on the object: the public face of Quebec had to be French. Many French-speaking Quebecers were embarrassed that in parts of Montreal it was difficult to tell from the signs that this was the second-largest French-speaking city in the world. The problem was deciding on exceptions. Some argued that signs in other languages should be allowed in areas with a certain proportion of non-French-speaking residents. However, others felt this thinking smacked of the ghetto.

Throughout these discussions, drafts of the law were prepared by a legislative drafter in the Executive Council office, and sent on to cabinet. When Laurin first presented the policy to cabinet, the reaction was mixed. On the whole, the majority of the cabinet seemed favourable. Some expressed their total support: Parizeau, de Belleval, O'Neill, Jacques-Yvan Morin, Landry, Couture. Others were concerned about the effect that the policy might have on business and on the economy: Rodrigue Tremblay and Lise Payette. Only one had a totally negative attitude, and could see no value whatever in the sweeping nature of the policy: Claude Morin. At that meeting, René Lévesque did not express an opinion.

From the first presentation of the policy to cabinet until Bill 1 was presented in its final form, there were fourteen drafts that went back and forth between cabinet and the legislative drafting office, with different sections being referred back to Laurin's office for more work, or additional supporting argument. The areas of disagreement were substantial.

On the question of signs, Lévesque insisted that there be exemptions for businesses employing fewer than five people; he had a horror of imposing French signs on corner stores.

On the question of the language of the courts, Lévesque could see no reason for challenging Section 133 of the BNA Act, which said that either English or French could be used. Laurin turned to Henri Laberge, who had been pushing hardest to make French the only official language of the courts and the legislature.

Laberge argued that Section 133 of the BNA Act did not protect individual rights. An individual, he argued, could take a company to court and find that the company did all its pleading in English, which he could not understand. Claude Charron was very responsive to this argument; his mother had had that very experience, feeling embarrassed and humiliated that she could not follow the proceedings after bringing a company to court. Lévesque gave in: the language legislation was to contain a direct challenge to the BNA Act—a challenge that was later overturned by the Supreme Court.

However, the toughest fight in cabinet was over what became known as the "Quebec clause" versus the "Canada clause". Lévesque was very uncomfortable with the idea of closing off English schools in Quebec to the children of parents educated in other provinces in Canada, while Laurin and his people argued that education was under the sole jurisdiction of Quebec, and that there should be no distinction made for those educated outside Quebec.

The weeks dragged on; the White Paper kept being postponed; dribs and drabs of the cabinet debate emerged in the newspapers. Finally, the White Paper was tabled on April 1. The public debate over language policy began again.

The document — illustrated with a pinstripe-sleeved arm reaching to put an acute accent on the word Quebec — presented a gloomy view of the status of the French language in Quebec. In the 1950s, the White Paper said, Quebecers found that "the French, like their language, were dominated; their existence was threatened; corrective measures based solely on good faith and goodwill were powerless to cope with this threat."

The White Paper was a skilful, eloquent document, written by Fernand Dumont and a former journalist, Hélène Pelletier-Baillargeon. The worst assumptions of Quebec nationalism were presented as self-evident truths, supported by the studies for the Gendron Commission, done five years earlier, and sometimes backed up by quotations from the Report of the Royal Commission on Bilingualism and Biculturalism—some of them taken from public meetings held twelve years earlier.

The structure and style led the reader on with devices like the omnipresent use of the passive voice ("Language is used in so many different instances of private and social life that for a long time it was not known how to improve the critical situation"), suggesting the gradual, inevitable growth of a consensus on government action to bring about official French unilingualism in Quebec.

From the diagnosis and the apparent consensus, the White Paper laid down four principles: the French language was "not just a means of expression but a medium for living"; there had to be "respect for the minorities, their language and their culture"; it was "important to learn languages other than French"; and finally, "the status of the French language in Quebec is a question of social justice." Learning languages other than French was to be encouraged, but the monopoly of English as the automatic second language, and the presumption of bilingualism, had to be broken.

And, as a matter of social justice, "what Quebec's French-speaking majority must do is reassume the power which is its by right, not in order to dominate, but to regain the status and latitude proper to its size and importance."

From the propositions flowed the principles; from the principles came the Charter.

The authors began by criticizing the Liberal language law, Bill 22, for pursuing what they described as two divergent aims: making Quebec a French-speaking society and, at the same time, establishing institutional bilingualism. This approach was rejected. "These ambiguities must be removed," the White Paper said firmly.

Then came the passage that planted the flag in the clearest possible fashion:

> The Quebec we wish to build will be essentially French. The fact that the majority of its population is French will be clearly visible —at work, in communications, and in the countryside. It will also be a country in which the traditional balance of power will be altered, especially in regard to the economy; the use of French will not merely be universalized to hide the predominance of foreign powers from the French population; this use will accompany, symbolize and support a reconquest by the French-speaking majority in Quebec of that control over the economy which it ought to have. To sum up, the Quebec whose features are sketched in the charter is a French-language society.
> There will no longer be any question of a bilingual Quebec.

From that declaration, all else flowed. The White Paper announced that the law would declare the fundamental rights of every Quebecer to work in French, receive his education in

French, and be informed and served in French. Every part of the public administration would function in French. Their addresses, their contracts, their communications, their agendas, and their minutes would be in French. The Office de la Langue Française would have the power to impose francization programs on any part of the public administration.

The law would directly affect the private sector as well as the state. Every firm with more than fifty employees would be required to prepare a francization program to ensure a satisfactory knowledge of French among management and staff, French manuals and catalogues, the use of French in communications with employees and suppliers, the use of appropriate French terms, and the use of French in advertising (except in media of another language).

To obtain access to an English school, a child had to have one parent educated in English in Quebec, or educated in English elsewhere but resident in Quebec when the law was passed. Individuals would be able to use English before the courts, but corporations would be required to use French.

The document concluded on a note of idealism and optimism: the language policy would be liberating and transforming, changing the outlook and attitude of Quebecers towards themselves and towards the world.

"The time has come for us to stop thinking of our future in terms of shaky survival and to recapture the conviction of our true importance: the rightful participation in one of the great linguistic and cultural traditions of this vast world, a world of which we, as Quebecers, are citizens."

The document expressed a vision of Quebec as a French society that struck an immediate, almost unconscious chord with thousands of French-speaking Quebecers, federalist or indépendantiste. Many, without ever fully articulating it, resented the afterthought, subtitle quality of bilingualism, resented the unquestioned omnipresence of English in the environment: elevators labelled "UP" and "DOWN", faucets marked "H" and "C". They silently burned at the fact that supermarkets were scrupulously bilingual in communities with no English-speaking residents, while they were unilingually English in communities with thousands of French Canadians in other provinces.

The Charter was published in its entirety in *Le Devoir*, *La Presse*, the *Montreal Star*, the *Gazette*, and the *Globe and*

Mail. Most of the French-language press responded extremely favourably. The great exception was Claude Ryan in *Le Devoir.* More than any other gesture, the White Paper on Language placed him in opposition to the Parti Québécois.

Ryan had, by and large, supported Bill 22. He hadn't liked the application of English proficiency tests, but he thought the law basically sound. But from its first publication, he rejected completely the approach, the methodology, the argument, and the recommendations of the White Paper. His criticisms—which were to continue as the debate evolved with the legislation and the parliamentary hearings — were to mark him as the major opposition to the government as he broke once and for all with the attitude of measured support he had displayed since endorsing the Parti Québécois in November.

In his first editorial on April 2, he argued that the rights of the English-speaking community would be seriously diminished by the severity of the criteria for access to English schools, the suppression of Article 133 of the BNA Act, and the restrictions on signs, which he found offensive, "frankly abusive and contrary to the most elementary principles of freedom of expression."

Over the weekend, Ryan was able to check out the White Paper's use of the Gendron Commission studies, and he was appalled. On Monday, he accused the authors of twisting the studies and misquoting them to make the use of French in business seem dramatically more limited than it actually was.

The authors of the White Paper said that Gendron had found that eighty-two per cent of communication on the job was in English. In fact, sixty-four per cent of francophones used only French at work; eighty-two per cent of the anglophones polled used only English. "The style [of the White Paper] is, in effect, often honey-coated," Ryan wrote. "But the thinking is rigid, monolithic, possessive."

The political reaction to the White Paper was varied. The Parti Québécois was ecstatic: Laurin was given a standing ovation at a National Council meeting the day after the document was tabled. The only PQ member to express any disagreement publicly was Gérald Godin, who told an audience that he hoped the law would be more flexible with regard to the English minority, and that he felt English Canadians from other provinces should be able to have access to English schools in Quebec.

The Quebec Liberals immediately attacked the policy. The

leader of the opposition, Gérard-D. Lévesque, talked about totalitarianism, authoritarianism, state planning, and intolerance.

In Ottawa, Pierre Trudeau waited a few days before commenting, and then told a press conference that he thought the policy was "narrow and retrograde" and that the PQ had shown its "true colours" at last — those of a party seeking the establishment of "an ethnic society". The document confirmed his prophecies, he said. "An independent Quebec will not only seek independence, but also the creation of a monolithic society, dominated by a single language."

Once the White Paper was tabled, Camille Laurin set out on a series of tours across the province to explain it. Pale, heavy-lidded, in dark suits, with an incongruous head of dark shiny hair above a lined face, Laurin became the personification of the language policy, explaining it with hypnotic patience.

He provoked contradictory reactions. French-speaking audiences found his manner soothing, his legislation rational, necessary, and generous. His parish-priest style, latinate sentence structure, and Cartesian reasoning were familiar and reassuring. After almost every speech Laurin made in French that spring, someone marvelled at the fact that he hadn't lost his temper at the provocation from the English and urged him to carry on his mission.

The English, on the other hand, largely found the policy discriminatory, intolerant, authoritarian, petty, inward-looking, vengeful, and unnecessary. Laurin's fabled serenity seemed to them to be, in a word, creepy. The only time he expressed real anger was on April 18, when Earle McLaughlin, president of the Royal Bank, said the law reflected "a spirit of oppression and vengeance". Laurin accused McLaughlin of treating francophones as "inferior specimens of humanity."

Suddenly, the emotional context of the White Paper became clear. While the *Montreal Star* reporter who called Laurin for reaction was astonished at the flash of toughness, after weeks of almost hypnotic serenity, some of the people who knew him best were not surprised at all.

"I would say about him that he has the elements of a French-Canadian peasant," Guy Rocher observed. "That is to say he has the will, the tenacity of a peasant, who knows what he wants. He has great respect for the little person, the immigrant; he will do everything to avoid having them pushed around. But when the big shots, the rich want it all their own way, they won't be forgiven. A French-Canadian peasant will never allow a big rich banker to try and teach him a lesson."

Camille Laurin became more than an enigma; rather, he was a virtual ikon: a diabolical figure in the eyes of the minorities in Quebec, a figure of cultural salvation for thousands of French-speaking Quebecers. There has been no other figure in Canadian politics, with the possible exception of John Diefenbaker, who was regarded in two such wholly contradictory fashions, who was painted in such unrelieved shades of black or white.

He was certainly not an ordinary politician. He was a man of rare erudition, and equally rare stubbornness. However, there was also a touch of pretentiousness. After the election, when asked what ministry he wanted, Laurin replied, "Any ministry where one fights for the betterment of a conception of Man." Three days before the tabling of the White Paper, a journalist was surprised to see him in a chic hair salon in Montreal, having his hair dyed black.

At a press conference held by Pierre Trudeau and René Lévesque in Quebec in December 1977, Laurin sat on a table at the side of the room, looking at them silently and intensely, smoking his Buckingham cigarettes to the end, squinting slightly, looking for all the world like an owl on a barn beam.

When the conference ended, Laurin came up to Trudeau from behind and touched him on the shoulder. Trudeau turned, and his face lit up in surprise and spontaneous pleasure at seeing an old friend. They chatted for only a moment or so before Trudeau headed off, but their mutual affection was obvious, neither forced nor feigned.

A reporter noticed the encounter, and asked Laurin about it; Laurin explained that he and Trudeau had always been very good friends. "We spent countless evenings chatting on the streets of Outremont, or at my house, or at his place."

Other reporters gathered, and one asked Laurin if it bothered him that Quebec was reaching an agreement with Ottawa — an economic-development arrangement which Trudeau and Lévesque had announced at the press conference.

"Not at all," Laurin replied. "In an occupied country, one has to deal with the occupying force." Suddenly, brutally, an encounter with an old friend was transformed into a heavy-handed allusion to France under Nazi occupation.

On April 27, Bill 1 was tabled in the National Assembly, and it became clear that the law was the legislative mirror of the White Paper. In fact, in committing the principles to legislative form, the drafter, Bertrand Rioux, had sharpened and tightened them. In the preamble, Laurin himself had written a phrase that many non-French-speaking Quebecers were to find not only inaccurate but offensive: "The National Assembly, being aware that the French language has always been the language of the Quebec people, that it is, indeed, the very instrument by which they have articulated their identity . . ."

Le Devoir described the law in its headline as "impératif, rigoureux, contraignant" — imperative, rigorous, restrictive. It contained 177 articles, including one — quickly denounced by the Human Rights Commission — giving the law precedence over the Quebec Charter of human rights.

Laurin had said that there would be no changes on the basis of public reaction until after the parliamentary hearings—but one substantial change was introduced. Lévesque had been unhappy with the "Quebec clause" for access to English schools, and kept pushing for wider criteria. At cabinet, Denis de Belleval broke the log-jam by suggesting a formula of reciprocity, linking the eligibility of English Canadians from other provinces to the rights of francophone minorities in their provinces. Quebec would offer to make bilateral agreements with other provinces to guarantee the right to education in the minority language for those who migrated. Lévesque accepted this compromise.

The hearings of the parliamentary committee began on June 7, 1977. They lasted a month, with twenty-one sessions hearing sixty-two briefs. It was a carefully structured display, with the critics of the bill played off against the wholehearted supporters. But as the committee hearings dragged on into July, the government began to worry that it would not be able to get the bill passed in time for the beginning of school in September. Louis Bernard had lived through the PQ opposition filibuster of Bill 22, and he assumed that the Liberals would adopt the same tactics.

Bernard came up with a plan to avoid using closure and, at the same time, get the legislation through in time. Instead of forcing the bill through committee, the government would introduce a new bill and leave the old one to die on the order paper.

On July 12, Laurin introduced the new Bill—Bill 101. It had been substantially rewritten, but the basic principles and major restrictions remained unchanged. However, some of the coercive elements were modified. The clause giving the law primacy over the Charter of Rights and Freedoms was removed, and Laurin's sentence in the preamble was changed to read: "Distinctive language of a people that is largely French-speaking, the French language permits the Quebec people to express their identity." References to Quebecers, which had peppered Bill 1, were removed; the inspection and monitoring process was loosened, and exemptions were permitted for the francization of head offices.

But the manoeuvring backfired. The switch of bills was bungled, and the National Assembly ground to a halt in procedural wrangling. In an extraordinary gesture, given that the strategy had been conceived in his office, René Lévesque seemed to pass the blame for the upheaval to Robert Burns, the House leader, saying, "C'était pas la trouvaille du siècle." (It wasn't the invention of the century.) Burns never forgave him.

Reciprocity with regard to language of education was to make its first and last entry into the interprovincial political arena at the premiers' conference at St. Andrews, N.B. Traditionally, the annual summer meeting of the ten premiers was a social get-together. But that changed in 1976, when the premiers had solidified their position on the fiscal arrangements at Banff. In 1977, Premier Richard Hatfield of New Brunswick was host, and set out quietly to undermine the potent idea of reciprocity. As premier of Canada's only officially bilingual province, Hatfield was deeply committed to the idea of bilingualism, and felt that reciprocity would be an acceptance of unilingualism and a political victory for the PQ. He hoped that they could take the wind out of the reciprocity offer with a commitment to improve the state of minority-language education.

Without telling Lévesque, Hatfield began putting together a consensus among the other premiers. So, at the private meeting that Lévesque thought would be discussing reciprocity, William Davis of Ontario proposed a resolution that the premiers commit themselves to reviewing the state of minority education, and then ensure the provision of minority-language education.

Lévesque was taken aback. "For the love of God, at least take the trouble to read the texts we've submitted," he said. "Bill

101 exists, and it will be adopted in third reading very soon. If you want an opening on the Canadian dimension, it's up to you."

Lévesque tried again to win a hearing for reciprocity, but to no avail. Claude Morin was unperturbed: reciprocity would prove that negotiations were possible; rejection of reciprocity would prove that Quebec had no place in Canadian federalism. Heads I win, tails you lose.

But Lévesque seemed genuinely upset, and was caustic about the likelihood of the premiers achieving anything concrete for francophone minorities. Privately, he was convinced that Trudeau had phoned the premiers personally to persuade them not to support reciprocity. (He hadn't.) Apart from the occasional joking reference at future meetings ("I've got the reciprocity forms here, if anybody wants to sign") he never pursued the idea with the premiers again.

A few days later, back in Quebec, Lévesque rose in the National Assembly to begin the debate on third reading of Bill 101. As he got to his feet, backbench Liberals began to bang their desks in mimicry of a tribal tom-tom.

But Lévesque gave a lukewarm, half-hearted speech. He had said in the spring that he felt "humiliated" at needing to pass such a law; his embarrassment was palpable. It would take Pierre Trudeau's plan to amend and patriate the constitution, rendering parts of Bill 101 invalid, to transform Lévesque into a spirited defender of the law.

On Friday, August 26, Camille Laurin ended the debate on third reading, calling the *Charte de la langue française* "nothing other than the gesture of a people determined to live its life". The bill was passed 54 to 32. Of the opposition, only the independent Fabien Roy supported the bill; the Liberals and the UN voted solidly against. Bill 101 became law. François-Albert Angers, a veteran nationalist, was to call it "the greatest moment in our history since the founding of Quebec in 1608".

Bill 101 was to become a divisive code, conveying one message to most francophones and quite another to most non-francophones; reassuring to the one group, and threatening to the other. But it did work a transformation. For the first time, the Quebec government said to its school system, "You are no longer the defensive preserve of an ethnic group: you are an open, integrating force in society." For the first time, Quebec French-language schools took on the traditional mission of the educational system in North America: taking thousands of immigrant children from Europe, Asia, and Latin America, and turning them into citizens. French-speaking citizens.

The effect of the accelerated francization caused by Bill 101 proved to be massive. Companies in Montreal did adapt, francization committees were established. French became, to an ever greater extent, the reflexive public language in Montreal — the language people automatically spoke when buying a newspaper, climbing into a taxicab, ordering a meal.

The price was considerable. Thousands of anglophones, given the choice between adapting to an increasingly French-speaking environment and moving, moved. An incalculable number of others, who might have moved to Quebec as part of the constant migration that is part of North American life, chose not to. Many of those who stayed felt isolated, vulnerable, and harassed by the bureaucratic application of the law.

A large number of the changes in the workplace demanded by the legislation did occur. Corporations began to promote young francophones to positions that would otherwise have gone to older anglophones. Memos to employees appeared in French as well as English. Francophones lost the habit of switching automatically to English when an anglophone joined the conversation. Interests were at stake — and the government had legislated to create a situation favourable to one of its most important constituencies: young, well-educated, upwardly mobile, middle-class francophones.

But for many of those non-francophones who stayed — the vast majority — the things that they cherished about life in Quebec remained as pleasant as ever, if not more so. Chips dropped off shoulders. Quebecers began to acquire a social skill that the rest of North America had been learning for over a century: how to listen to one's language being spoken with a foreign accent. In that regard, Bill 101 represented a step towards greater pluralism in Quebec society.

But there was little public recognition of this shift. Much more attention was given to bureaucratic excesses in the enforcement of the law: the nurses who spoke French fluently but failed written language tests, the shopkeepers charged for defying the sign provisions of the law. In non-French-speaking communities, the law was tolerated at best, despised and resented by most.

The language law can be seen as an ideological twin to the proposal for sovereignty-association. Like sovereignty-association, it was regarded by its supporters as a humane, rational, generous compromise: a project marked by such an all-encompassing and logically self-evident social vision that it could not be rejected, except by the most narrow-minded; but like sovereignty-association, it was not a bargaining position, but a final offer. All the compromising had been done; the logical chain of reasoning was closed. Those presented with the policy — whether companies, English-speaking citizens, or provinces being offered reciprocity for minority-language education rights — had only two choices: they could accept, or reject. There was no middle ground.

In this regard, the language law was far from being a freak accident. It was the reflection of a particular vision, a vision shaped by psychological, sociological, religious, and legal assumptions that were almost totally foreign to English Canada. But its all-encompassing nature, and the sometimes excessive rhetoric that surrounded it, made it more than just a law; it became a symbol. As the years passed, and the details of the legislation faded from the public consciousness, its symbolic quality grew.

Undermined by Supreme Court decisions and massively attacked by the constitutional Charter of Rights, Bill 101 left the realm of legislation and public policy, and entered the world of myth. This was to be its ultimate potency, and its terrible divisiveness.

EIGHT

Flying High

*Experience has taught
me that following an election
and the formation of a
government, and for a
relatively short period, it is
possible to get parliament
to vote really innovative
laws. After this period,
everything becomes more
difficult.*
Gaston Defferre

René Lévesque's great asset on taking power was his enor-mous personal popularity. During the frantic months of the first year, it was an asset he protected carefully. Moody, volatile, distant, apparently impulsive, he was in fact not impulsive at all. Intuitive, but not impulsive. Politically, he took as few risks as possible.

The people working for him were bright, but not challenging; they were characterized by their loyalty and their discretion. Louis Bernard, Jean-Roch Boivin, Michel Carpentier, Claude Malette, Robert Mackay, Gratia O'Leary — they were all bound to Lévesque by deep ties of time and loyalty.

Not all the hirings proved to be a success. In seeking a liaison person to deal with the English community, he turned down two experienced English-speaking journalists in favour of a naive, politically inexperienced young woman from Ontario. Beverley Smith, a former translator, was shocked at the intensity and the work addiction. After six months on the job, she resigned. The mystery was not that she had quit, but that she was ever hired. The appointment seemed to indicate not only

113

incomprehension of the English-speaking community in Quebec, but contempt for it.

Lévesque kept the language law at arm's length; he had warned Laurin at the beginning that, if the situation blew up, he would be on his own. It was a position he adopted with all his ministers: they had considerable freedom to work out their legislation and defend it. Lévesque was the final arbiter in cabinet, but he proved to be brutal in dissociating himself from a minister, a policy, or a decision that proved unpopular, as Robert Burns learned during the parliamentary manoeuvre changing Bill 1 to Bill 101.

Lévesque was very conscious of the enormous expectations the election had produced, and walked a swaying tightrope, trying to defuse those expectations and fulfil them simultaneously. Distrustful of ideology, wary of dogmatism, he felt his way by flashes of intuition and insight, many of which he got while touring the province, meeting and talking to people.

Thus, Lévesque's interest in decentralization was fuelled by his discovery that there was no city hall in Sainte-Marguerite-du-Lac-Masson, and that the village council met at the local school, where, one night, they were thrown out. That kind of journalistic human detail made more impact on him than a dozen studies.

That was his most effective function: acting like the boy who observed that the emperor was naked, responding to and conveying the common sense of the ordinary people he talked to. His commitment to "common sense" was his strength as a politician. As a party leader, he feared party conventions simply because he doubted their capacity for political common sense. And as an administrator he believed in planning, co-ordination, and discussion — which often made for a wordy, long-winded process when combined with the Cartesian search for first principles that shaped the reflexes of many of his colleagues. The result, as he said in a rueful appraisal of the first year, was "a year, let us say, of a lot of words".

THE REFORM THAT LÉVESQUE CHERISHED THE MOST WAS THE election-financing legislation, Bill 2. Indeed, he expressed more emotion about political fund-raising than about anything else: federalism, sovereignty-association, or language. His face would screw up with contempt, and his vocabulary would suggest the swamp: "slime", "ooze", "shadowy".

What he called "the old slush-fund tradition" was part of Quebec's political folklore; donations were secret, and were quietly repaid with government contracts. This was one of the reasons for the Liberal government's unsavoury reputation: a crime-probe witness saying in 1973 that underworld figures had contributed to Bourassa's leadership campaign, and Bourassa lamely conceding the possibility; police investigations of a Liberal MNA for Election Act violations in 1973; police leaks during the 1976 campaign alleging extortion from lottery distributors.

When Lévesque gave Burns the mandate to draw up the election-financing law, he knew it would be tough; Burns had constantly harassed the Bourassa government on the question, and had held up the PQ funding approach as a model. Partly from conviction, partly by necessity, the PQ raised money by going from door to door, and made the donors' names public. In fact, fund-raising was a major part of the party's organizational activity. Burns set out to make party practice into law, and produced the very first piece of legislation in the session: Bill 2, the tightest piece of election-funding legislation in the Western world.

In January and February, Burns and an all-party committee visited Washington, Sacramento, Toronto, and Ottawa to examine four examples of similar legislation, and studied the problems each had encountered. The result was a sweeping bill based on a bluntly simple principle. Only voters would be allowed to contribute to political parties. Corporations, companies, clubs, associations, unions, co-ops would no longer be allowed to make contributions.

This was strongly opposed by the Chambre de Commerce, the Liberals, and, more importantly, the Human Rights Commission, whose chairman criticized the draft law as restricting freedom of opinion, expression, and association, and objected to the powers of search and seizure that were given to the new body being created, the office of the Directeur Général du Financement des Partis Politiques.

Burns quickly announced that the provisions for search and seizure would be changed, and that all ambiguities suggesting that the restrictions would apply to citizens' groups would be lifted. But he would not budge on the fundamental question, saying that the government was determined to abolish secret election funds, "and no recommendation, no matter where it comes from, will make it back off on the subject".

The law reflected the PQ belief that corporate donations were a crucial, almost occult factor in Quebec politics. Bill 2 was intended to sever the link between corporate wealth and political parties. The Péquistes never thought that the Liberals would be capable of raising money from door to door; in fact, they did learn to do so. The result was to transform the nature of partisan politics in Quebec.

This same concern about private funds shaping the political debate could be seen in Burns's White Paper on referendums, tabled on August 26. As early as December 1976, Burns was thinking of tight restrictions on spending. "Do we permit the Société Saint-Jean-Baptiste and the Montreal Board of Trade to plunge in?" he mused. "I don't know. We have to look at it."

What emerged was based on the British referendum legislation, but designed much more tightly. Referendums were to be strictly controlled by the Yes and No committees, which had to be presided over by members of the National Assembly. No money could be spent that was not accounted for by those committees.

In addition to controlling money, the new government did its best to shape the nature of information coming out of Quebec. Thus, on March 26, 1977, the industry and commerce minister, Rodrigue Tremblay, released a 222-page report which, he claimed, showed that the federal government had taken $4.3 billion more out of Quebec between 1961 and 1975 than it had invested.

This was an elaborate public-relations coup: it was timed on Friday afternoon, so that journalists would have little time to check the figures. Along with the dense technical report, Tremblay circulated a twenty-five-page statement giving his interpretation of what it really meant. The interpretation was simple: Quebec was being robbed blind. Overwhelmingly, this was the version that was reported.

In fact, the report compared federal revenue from Quebec with the direct federal investment in the province — but did not take into account any investment outside Quebec that might benefit the province. It also showed that Quebec was taxing its citizens twice as much per capita as Ottawa was; while the federal government was taking 32.3 per cent of the tax dollar in Quebec, the province, the municipalities, hospitals, and pensions were taking 67.7 per cent.

Then, on April 12, 1977, Jacques Parizeau presented his first budget. Concluding with the words "the road to independence needs healthy finances", Parizeau's début was austere, belt-tightening, and conservative: a "banker's budget". The uncommon grace and wit with which it was written only sweetened a bitter pill for the most highly taxed citizens in the country. The costly promises were postponed, borrowing was reduced, and taxpayers were hit with higher licence fees, increased sales taxes on restaurant meals, and, perhaps toughest of all, an eight per cent sales tax on children's shoes and clothes. There was little in the way of job-creation measures for the 237,000 unemployed in Quebec, except for increased investment in James Bay, a Quebec purchasing policy, and some small municipal construction projects. "When you don't have money, you can't do miracles," Parizeau said.

His real audience was on Wall Street, and he got applause where he needed it most. Calling it "restrained" and "disciplined", traders were pleased. "The market . . . is interpreting the budget bullishly," a New York broker observed. Five months later, Parizeau could see the results: Quebec kept its AA credit rating on Wall Street.

In May, on the eve of the PQ convention, Lévesque made another gesture to dissociate his government from extremism and make a commitment to mediation and dialogue. For three days, beginning on May 24, Lévesque played host to the first "economic summit", at the Manoir Richelieu in Pointe-au-Pic.

Although little concrete was achieved, the summit brought business, labour, and government leaders together for informal chats as well as formal meetings. They reached unanimous — albeit pious — agreement that something should be done about job safety. More importantly, Lévesque was able to make it very clear to the business community that his government was not in the hands of the labour movement. Of the three labour centrals represented, two — the Confédération des Syndicats Nationaux (CSN) and the Centrale de l'Enseignement du Québec (CEQ)—took very tough left-wing stands criticizing the government. As a result, Lévesque was able to keep his distance, and show the businessmen that he was having nothing to do with the left-wing labour leaders, calling them "professional Cassandras who are killing themselves trying to predict that the apocalypse is coming tomorrow morning if the entire economic system is not immediately abolished".

On the other hand, Louis Laberge of the Fédération des Travailleurs du Québec was a bundle of roly-poly charm and diplomacy; businessmen were overheard in the bar marvelling at how "sympathique" he was.

It was a public-relations triumph for Lévesque, and gave birth to a virtual summit industry: a continuing series of conferences on economic questions. The results of these sessions, held on everything from furniture to apple-farming, and clothing to tourism, were sometimes difficult to identify, but they were part of the flowing river of apparent events in economic policy-making: a field full of conferences, colloquies, summits, white papers, policy studies, and plans. At times, the process seemed to have more to do with adult education than with economic management.

THE NEXT MAJOR HURDLE THAT LÉVESQUE HAD TO DEAL WITH WAS the biennial Parti Québécois convention: the first since the party had taken power. It opened on Friday, May 26, in Montreal. Some fifteen hundred delegates, five hundred observers, and hundreds of reporters, cameramen, anchormen, interviewers, and foreign correspondents streamed into the Vélodrome beside the Olympic Stadium on Friday night to hear Lévesque make an appeal for realism and restraint, for responsibility and an appreciation of "the constraints of power".

Then the delegates settled into the endurance test of poring over two thousand resolutions with Talmudic intensity, enduring the dense cigarette smoke, the bad acoustics, the detailed resolutions, and the claustrophobic confinement with equanimity. For the PQ in congress was overwhelmingly serious. Few delegates left their seats to chat, or seek out bars and old friends; the fifteen hundred pages of the "cahier de résolutions" turned in unison.

Lévesque was in a pretty good mood. He had found the economic summit at Pointe-au-Pic the week before an enormous success; legislation was beginning to emerge from the machine in Quebec City: the automobile-insurance program had been announced in outline, the language legislation was about to go to committee, the budget had been well received. But party conventions always unnerved him.

For about six months, resolutions had come up from constituency meetings to regional meetings to the convention, doggedly argued all the way. At the convention they were argued again, first in workshops and then in plenary session. The result was characteristic of any social-democratic or reform party, especially one in power. For there is a fundamental tension between pragmatism and principle, the responsibilities of office and the ideology of the membership.

At this sixth convention the party leadership was worried that there might be too much criticism of the budget, or the partial automobile-insurance scheme, and too much embarrassing pressure on the national question, which might tie the government's hands in preparing the referendum strategy. But, despite a decision that all speakers on a resolution should be chosen by lot, so as to prevent ministers from monopolizing the microphones, the leadership was largely successful.

Telling his workshop that the change was necessary for "strategic reasons" related to the referendum, Claude Morin succeeded in introducing the principle that the PQ should work for greater Quebec autonomy within Confederation as long as Quebec was part of Canada. The convention gave passionate support to anti-scab legislation, which the government was working on, and the language law. For the bulk of the party program, the government's position was approved without serious challenge.

However, on women's issues, the party leadership was outmanoeuvred and outvoted. The national office had broken up a lengthy feminist resolution and scattered it; a group of women led by Louise Thiboutot carefully put it back together, and shepherded it out of the workshop and onto the convention floor. The resolution, in effect, called for abortion on demand, described as "the right to motherhood by free consent", and the removal of all references to abortion from the Criminal Code.

When the package came to the convention floor, Lévesque was furious. Personally opposed to abortion himself, he felt it was insane to take a position on something so divisive, which was in federal jurisdiction anyway. When the vote was called, he looked at the executive, making a "get-your-hands-up" gesture; they all voted with him except Burns. However, the convention voted solidly to give women "the right to decide their maternity"; no count was required. Louise Thiboutot and Lise Payette embraced for joy as the "militantes" jumped and shouted with glee.

Lévesque was equally annoyed by the new executive: Guy Bisaillon was elected, as were Thiboutot and the young MNA from Îles-de-la-Madeleine, Denise Leblanc-Bantey.

Fully half the new executive stood grim-faced and unsmiling as Lévesque angrily lectured the convention in his closing remarks. A resolution recognizing aboriginal rights had been defeated. He made it clear that the government would not be bound by that vote or the one on abortion.

However, he had won much more than he had lost. The party did not criticize the "banker's budget"; no-one had challenged the government's referendum strategy of concentrating on "good government"; the program had been changed to allow the government to continue the Quebec tradition of seeking more "autonomy" inside Confederation.

On the other hand, the women's victory was a dramatic indication that the women's movement was virtually the only pressure group that had not, in some way, folded up its tent with the election of a PQ government. Labour, the ecology movement, the urban community groups—none put as much pressure on the PQ as they had on the Liberals.

THE FIRST YEAR IN POWER WAS AN INCREDIBLE FLURRY OF ACTIVITY for virtually all the ministers as they grappled with their new jobs. They had to learn to cope with extraordinary expectations and demands on their time and energy: from their staff, their civil servants, the National Assembly, their constituents, the media, the cabinet, and, least obvious but crucial, the premier. Some flowered; others wilted under the strain.

To everyone's surprise, Claude Charron adapted quickly to the job, picking up intuitively how to deal with his civil servants in Sports, Recreation, and Youth.

Lucien Lessard had originally been slated to give up Transport to make room for Pierre Marc Johnson, but he handled a truckers' strike with such poise that this plan was dropped. Denis de Belleval was one of the few with government experience, but colleagues began to resent his constant advice.

A number of others took a long time to adjust. Rodrigue Tremblay quickly became a laughing stock for his vanity, his rigidity, and his knack for saying the wrong thing; Jean Garon seemed to flounder at first in Agriculture; Denis Lazure was incautious and undiplomatic in Social Affairs.

Other ministers were in serious trouble. Jacques Couture

alienated everyone involved in labour during his time as minister, and was hampered by his lack of administrative experience. As minister of cultural affairs and communications, Louis O'Neill was a disappointment to Lévesque and the premier's staff, and he began to be undermined by rumours about his weakness as a minister.

The laws that emerged varied. Some which appeared awkward and controversial at first proved to be great successes; others became the legislative equivalent of eight-cylinder convertibles: heavy pieces of machinery more suitable for an era of economic expansion and cheap money.

One of the most controversial turned out to be the most successful: Lise Payette's automobile-insurance plan. Payette had been a popular television talk-show host, active in various causes. She had organized the famous St. Jean Baptiste concert on Mount Royal in 1975, and had led the campaign of support for Tricofil, the experiment in worker ownership of a textile firm in Saint-Jérôme. A progressive indépendantiste, she plunged into the complexities of the auto-insurance issue as minister of consumers, co-operatives, and financial institutions.

In April she produced a White Paper, which laid out the government's plans. Trying to avoid both the high costs and the battles with the insurance industry incurred by Manitoba and British Columbia, the plan left insurance for property damage in the hands of the private insurance companies, while setting up a state-run no-fault plan for personal injuries.

However, even this provoked outrage in the industry and the legal profession — unnerving her colleagues considerably. At a two-day retreat at Sainte-Marguerite at the end of the summer, she was grilled for three hours by the cabinet. Marc-André Bédard argued that the plan should be delayed for a year; someone else said two years. Bédard and Bernard Landry argued that it would make the PQ lose the referendum and the next election. But finally Lévesque intervened. The plan would go ahead.

Then, with the catchy slogan "La personne avant toute chose" (People before anything), Payette set out to tour Quebec to defend the proposal. The Bar Association dug in for a long fight — a very high proportion of small-town lawyers' incomes came from fighting insurance claims — but Payette stuck to her guns. The law was passed, and came into effect on March 1, 1978.

Although it was a partial system, and Quebecers still paid more in premiums than the residents of any other province, it was one of the most successful innovations of the first mandate. The Régie des Assurances Automobiles turned out to be an efficient operation, with rates remaining at $85 for three consecutive years. To her colleagues' surprise, Payette was one of the most effective ministers in the first year.

One of the most idealistic pieces of legislation was the Youth Protection Act, introduced by the minister of state for social development, Pierre Marois. It had bogged down in interministerial conflict during the Bourassa government; precisely the kind of law that the ministers of state were created to produce. It was far-sighted, compassionate, and enlightened. It was also expensive, unwieldy, naive, and manipulable by a street-smart punk.

The law recognized the rights of children before the law, forbade placing juveniles in adult prisons, and created a network of youth-protection officers who could intervene to remove mistreated children from their homes without a court order, investigate cases of child abuse, and have a court decision on a child's future within five days.

The legislation was launched with a publicity campaign showing a child saying "Maintenant j'ai ma loi" — Now I have my law. However, no-one was prepared for teenage purse-snatchers chanting the slogan as they dashed away from their victims, or unruly drug-peddling teenagers taunting their parents with the protective clauses in the law. Within a few years, youth workers were complaining that the bill was "a Cadillac with a Volkswagen engine"; facilities were not available, and the mechanisms bogged down in paper work.

"This is a very good law for the victims of child abuse," observed a youth-court judge in 1981. "But concerning juvenile delinquents, it's been a fiasco." Part of the act was thrown out by the Supreme Court, and it had to be amended in the second mandate.

Like the language law, the Youth Protection Act followed a characteristic pattern. Virtually every reform in the PQ's first three years established a code or charter defining rights, and created a new para-governmental body to oversee, supervise, or enforce. The PQ proved to be a government of rights-definers, code-makers, charter-writers, and agency-creators. Repeatedly, its legislation by-passed the civil service and set up a new parallel bureaucracy of administration and regulation. The strength in this approach was its intellectual rigour; the weakness was its highly bureaucratic approach, which often had unwieldy results.

Two other acts stood out as part of the PQ's effort to transform Quebec in the first year: the anti-scab law, and the decision to acquire Asbestos Corporation. Both were heavy with symbolism.

On Friday, July 22, 1977, a trio of armed security guards in front of the Robin Hood Multifoods plan in Montreal fired on strikers, sending eight men to hospital. Pierre Marc Johnson had been named minister of labour only two weeks before; it was his first taste of the tension and potential for violence in the labour scene. In fact, the shots in the shipping yard were helpful; they dramatized the situation that the government's first labour law was intended to deal with: Bill 45, the anti-strikebreaking legislation.

The law prohibited the use of strikebreakers, guaranteed the right of strikers to get their jobs back, imposed the Rand formula of obligatory contribution of union dues, and compelled the use of a secret ballot in strike votes. It was already drafted, and undergoing a storm of business criticism, when the violence occurred at Robin Hood; such an incident could only help.

Johnson, then only thirty-one, was ideal for defending the new law. He was the son of Daniel Johnson, the late premier, and defined himself as a "bleu" — a conservative. Articulate, fully bilingual, both a lawyer and a doctor, he exuded the charm and confidence of a man who had spent his life preparing for politics — which, in a sense, he had. He was twenty-two when his father died; old enough to know his father intimately and learn from his political experience, but liberated early from what can be the crushing shadow of a famous father. He had an intuitive sense of politics, a knack for the kind of showmanship required in the Assembly to put down opposition questioners, and a sense of how labour leaders wanted to be treated.

Johnson managed to keep the basic sympathy of the unionized workers, while keeping a distance from the radicalism of the CEQ and the CSN. However, both labour and government knew that whatever public debate might occur over different pieces of legislation, the real political test of the government would come in two years, in the negotiations with the Common Front of public-sector unions. Until then, the government could administer or plan in relative comfort: it would be in 1979 that the crunch would come as the government would have to settle with all its employees in Quebec's extraordinarily centralized exercise in public-sector union negotiations.

But of all the government's actions in the first year, probably the most symbolic (except for the language law) was the announcement that the government would be acquiring the Asbestos Corporation.

In Quebec, asbestos was the stuff of myth and symbol. As Yves Bérubé, the minister of energy and resources, told a Toronto audience in 1978, asbestos represented hard times, death, and foreign economic exploitation: "The holes left in the ground and the piles of dust are a symbol of wealth that could have been, and never showed up."

Beginning in the 1920s, Quebec governments had considered ways of putting an end to the massive exportation of raw asbestos and jobs to the United States. But nothing came of it. In the words of the *Encyclopaedia Britannica,* "Canada is the major source of asbestos fibre, and the United States leads in the manufacture of asbestos products." As Eric Kierans put it, "Since the 1880s, the asbestos companies have done pretty well what they wanted and told everyone else to go to hell. Asbestos is a needling sore in the psyche of this place, and in the psyche of anyone who cares about this place."

None of the mining was Canadian-owned, and fully ninety-seven per cent of the mined asbestos was exported, raw, to be converted into asbestos products outside Quebec. As a result, there were 1,500 asbestos manufacturing jobs in Quebec — and 150,000 elsewhere.

The symbolism was not only economic, but political and cultural. The Asbestos strike in 1949 was the first major labour resistance to the Duplessis government, and had brought Jean Marchand, Gérard Pelletier, and Pierre Trudeau to the town of Asbestos.

One of the most vivid images of industrial paternalism in Quebec occurs in the film *Mon Oncle Antoine,* set in the asbestos town of Black Lake. At Christmas, the mining company's local boss is shown being pulled through the town on a sleigh, and throwing Christmas presents for the children on the snow in front of the employees' houses. Angry and humiliated, the workers stand and watch silently as the sleigh moves down the street.

So when Lévesque travelled to Thetford Mines with Yves Bérubé on October 21, 1977, to announce the decision to acquire the Asbestos Corporation before a packed hall of 2,500 applauding asbestos workers and their families, he was clearing a psychic debt.

The party program was explicit. It called for Quebec majority control of the industry, a marketing bureau, and a secondary asbestos industry. What Lévesque announced was a compromise between idealism and budgetary constraints. The government created the Société Nationale d'Amiante and announced that it would acquire control of the Asbestos Corporation. This was considerably less than outright expropriation or nationalization.

Bérubé, a tall, lanky man with a trim beard, was the architect of the plan, and argued strenuously that the crown corporation, along with the research and development body the government would create, would force the development of secondary manufacturing.

Bérubé had come to the Parti Québécois with a bitter sense of rejection. A brilliant student in classical college, he had shared Pierre Trudeau's belief that French Canadians should prove their worth by excelling and competing with the best.

"I was a nationalist; a federalist, but a nationalist," he said in 1978. "I wanted to prove that there was a place for a Quebecer in industry, and so I set out to get the best education possible.

"After classical college, I didn't study in Quebec, I went to the United States, because the greatest university at that time in engineering was there. I was sure I would come back [from the Massachussetts Institute of Technology] with such a good education that the world would open to me."

He returned with his degree in 1963.

"Well, the world didn't open," he laughed. "I was forced to realize that the world opens up when you have personal contacts, when you know people, that it's a world of interrelations. And you realize very quickly that we don't have interrelations with the anglophones. It is an anglophone world closed in on itself, and a francophone world closed in on itself."

So after a brief unhappy period with Iron Ore of Canada, Bérubé returned to MIT to do his doctorate. He came back in 1966 to teach metallurgical engineering at Laval. In 1969, he was asked by the federal minister of energy, mines, and resources, Donald Macdonald, to join an advisory group on a national minerals policy. Bérubé wrote a lengthy report on the absence of French Canadians in the field, and the lack of funding to French-language universities.

"It was in French, of course. It was never distributed; it was never discussed," Bérubé said, the bitterness still audible. "I realized that there was no place in Ottawa for a policy that would be developed in terms of Quebec's problems—that they would always be based in terms of Canadian problems."

These two experiences were critical in his decision to join the PQ in the early 1970s. In 1976, he was putting up signs for Claude Morin when he was asked to become the PQ candidate in Matane. A few weeks later, he was in the cabinet, working to bring Quebec into what he considered "the club" of the asbestos industry.

But General Dynamics, the American multinational which owned the Asbestos Corporation, had no interest in selling. It fought the acquisition every way it could, taking the government to court on a technicality, and dragging out the process for almost four years before a deal was finally struck.

The ultimate settlement kept General Dynamics as a partner; what had been planned as a nationalist symbol, like Hydro-Québec and James Bay, emerged as simply another hilltop in the rolling landscape of state enterprise. There was an increase in secondary production, but the slump in the world asbestos market meant that within five years many of the workers who had applauded so vigorously that night in Thetford Mines were laid off.

THE CLIMAX OF THE FIRST YEAR IN OFFICE WAS LÉVESQUE'S VISIT to Paris in November. Nine months after the frosty reception of his speech in New York, official Paris opened its arms to him in the fullest endorsation of Quebec independence since the de Gaulle speech in 1967. Proposing a toast to him, the president of the National Assembly, Edgar Faure, praised Quebec's effort "to rid itself of colonization".

Clearly, but delicately, the French made their sympathies known, undermining the Canadian ambassador, Gérard Pelletier, without publicly humiliating him. When Lévesquc met Pelletier at the airport, he couldn't help gloating: "Salut, espèce de chialeux!" (Roughly, "Hi, crybaby!")

The enthusiasm was not without its awkward moments: the band struck up "Alouette", as Lévesque arrived at the Élysée Palace, rather as if Muhammad Ali were greeted with "My Old Kentucky Home". But on the whole the trip was a personal and political triumph. The French had responded precisely as he had hoped: with sympathetic support and an enthusiastic ambiguity which responded precisely to the ambiguity of sovereignty-association.

But there was no such ambiguity in the reaction in English Canada to the PQ's first year in office. While the Quebec government was flying high in the months after the election, bursting with energy and action, English Canada was thrown into a state of anxiety and confusion. The rising tide of resentment of bilingualism, so visible in 1976, seemed to vanish overnight. English Canadians groped for an appropriate response. Conferences called Destiny Canada and Options Canada; groups called One Canada, the United Canada Movement, Option Canada, Decision Canada, Commitment Canada, and Quebec-Canada; and existing groups like the Council for Canadian Unity, all flowered, producing buttons, bumper stickers, rallies, and petitions. Few lasted.

In Quebec, it seemed as if every imaginative federalist politician had sponsored his own group, like some kind of political pee-wee hockey team. George Springate, Liberal MNA for Westmount, launched a group called Team Canada; his colleague from Gatineau, Michel Gratton, started the Quebec-Canada Movement. Dr. William Shaw, the UN MNA for Pointe-Claire, helped inspire the Provisional Committee for an 11th Province.

Three other groups emerged that became the basis of something more permanent. However, they were less "unity groups" than groups trying to mobilize the English community in Quebec in response to the language law.

The Positive Action Committee was born at the University Club in Montreal. With Alex Paterson, a lawyer, and Storrs McCall, a McGill philosophy professor, as co-chairmen, and a stockbroker, Reford McDougall, taking a leave of absence to work full-time, it spoke with the accents of a certain well-intentioned and well-established Montreal.

Participation Quebec was the creation of a group of McGill law students led by Michael Prupas and Eric Maldoff, who were determined to try to define a place for English Quebecers in a French-speaking Quebec. These two groups became the nucleus, four years later, of Alliance Quebec.

Ralli-Canada was the most militantly opposed of the three to any language law. It was the first mobilization of what was later to become the Freedom of Choice Movement, and then Quebec For All: militant English-rights groups.

The multitude of different unity groups continued until December 1977, when there was an umbrella group established as the Quebec-Canada Pre-Referendum Committee to co-ordinate the various groups in preparation for the referendum campaign. But during their year or so of existence, the groups did not suffer from lack of media attention.

When a *Toronto Star* reporter in Montreal asked an organizer about one of the more spontaneous unity groups that had sprung up in Quebec, he was astonished to be told, "Well, I went to university with Marty Goodman [then editor-in-chief of the *Star*] — and he suggested that I do this." Similarly, a *Globe and Mail* reporter in Montreal was taken aback when a senior editor told him, "On this issue, I'm a Canadian first and a journalist second."

For English-Canadian journalists covering Quebec, there were times when 1977 felt like war. Mark Harrison inadvertently summed up the mood in an unfortunate phrase quoted in *Maclean's* when he said that in becoming editor of the *Gazette* after the election, he felt like Errol Flynn "riding to the sound of the guns". Reporters covering Quebec for English-language publications could sense the anxiety their editors felt, and the desire they had to discredit the new government.

A senior editor at *Maclean's* summed up the frustration many editors felt in an angry note to a correspondent: "We are not dealing with a government like any other. We are dealing with a constitutionally elected group of men and women who are determined to break up the federation of Canada. You can't get away from that by conjuring up the phony alternative of Sovereignty Association."

Maclean's certainly reflected that anger and frustration in its writing. In the months following the Quebec election, its senior Toronto-based writers called Lévesque "a midget" and "a fanatic in a rented tux". It referred to the Parti Québécois as "already a revolutionary body" and to its followers as "deluded". Sovereignty-association was called "a fallacy" and — in a column by the editor, Peter C. Newman (headed "Quebec let

Lévesque dupe them once. Will they let him do it again?")—"a cruel hoax".

It was reminiscent of the most unpleasant kind of wartime propaganda, and reflected the profound fears that the election of the PQ had provoked in English Canada. But the most unpleasant of all was the experience the Canadian Broadcasting Corporation had to endure. For it became clear that many Liberals in Ottawa held the CBC — particularly the French network — responsible for the PQ victory. Beginning in mid-February, the Liberals started a systematic campaign attacking Radio-Canada as a nest of separatists.

It soon became clear how some defined the network's responsibilities. The urban affairs minister, André Ouellet, saw it clearly as the propaganda arm of the federal government, and didn't mind saying so.

"I don't want to see Radio-Canada on the fence, presenting, as a neutral body, two sides," Ouellet told Peter Gzowski at the end of April 1977. "Those working there at the time of the referendum should be clearly on the side of the pro-Canada."

"Mr. Ouellet, what if I were to use the word 'propaganda'?" Gzowski asked.

"Well, when it comes to the survival of our country, I don't think we should be afraid of words."

"Propaganda?" repeated Gzowski, clearly not believing his ears.

"Indeed, sure," Ouellet replied.

On March 4, 1977, Pierre Trudeau asked the chairman of the Canadian Radio-Television and Telecommunications Commission (CRTC), Harry Boyle, to establish an inquiry to look into the question of whether the CBC was fulfilling its mandate.

Rather than point the finger at separatists in Radio-Canada, Boyle made a swift, sweeping, and piercing critique of public broadcasting in Canada, accusing it of a centralized vision of the country, and of assuming that English Canadians "could not care less about what happens to French Canadians and vice versa". The result, he said, was "cultural apartheid".

During this period, the federal government had to make some key decisions about how to respond to separatism. Should there be an election? A Royal Commission? In the months after November 15, 1976, a small group of senior officials developed strategies for tactics, information, and policy. These were to lay the groundwork for the federal response to the

Quebec referendum campaign in 1980, and the constitutional negotiations immediately afterwards.

The first step was to establish a working group to act as a clearing house for all the ideas. It had no formal name, and a membership that included senior civil servants and political aides. It was called simply "the co-ordinating committee", and met in the Langevin Block, the offices of the Privy Council Office (PCO) on Wellington Street, every Thursday at 5 p.m.

The members included Michael Pitfield, the clerk of the Privy Council, Gordon Robertson, his predecessor, who was then secretary to cabinet for federal-provincial relations, Jim Coutts, the prime minister's principal secretary, Paul Tellier, Robertson's deputy, DeMontigny Marchand, then deputy secretary to the cabinet for operations, Bob Rabinovitch, George Anderson, and Claude Lemelin from the PCO, Eddie Goldenberg, a senior aide to Jean Chrétien, and two or three deputy ministers.

Some of the meetings were long, freewheeling discussions; some were brisk summaries to bring people up to date on what had happened in the previous week. At a minimum, the meeting was a briefing on public-opinion polls in Quebec, and the policy planning being developed. However, virtually every federal initiative towards Quebec over the next four years was discussed at those meetings.

As time went on, smaller groups were formed to devote all their energy to the questions of national unity and federal strategy. The first of these, the Tellier Group, was headed by Paul Tellier, an impressively bright civil servant in his late thirties who had worked for Robert Bourassa as deputy secretary to the Quebec cabinet in the early 1970s.

Tellier worked on the whole range of federal initiatives that touched Quebec and national unity, from the July 1 celebrations to the negotiations on immigration policy. But the first job for the group was to advise Gordon Robertson and the prime minister on whether or not there should be some kind of pre-emptive action by the federal government. George Anderson, a bright policy specialist in his early thirties who had done graduate work in Oxford and Paris, set to work on a strategy paper.

In favour of pre-emptive action were the fears about leaving the PQ free to fight the referendum on its question, at its time, on its ground, with its rules. In addition, some of the senior civil servants thought that the economic consequences of the

PQ election might be devastating, halting investment, causing a massive emigration of capital, English-speaking Quebecers, and high-income earners.

Against this was the feeling that the PQ was and would be stronger during its first eighteen months in power than it ever would be again. If the federal government moved first, it might be blamed for forcing a confrontation before the situation had become clear. They were well aware, as one civil servant put it, that "even people who were not Péquistes were walking six inches off the ground."

In developing the strategy, the Tellier Group had to evaluate the PQ chances of winning the referendum and develop a fall-back strategy in case the situation changed. But after studying the polls carefully they concluded that, despite the election, opinion on the constitutional question remained stable. There was a basic alignment of PQ voters with the Yes option, regardless of the question, and of non-PQ voters with the No option, regardless of the question. The more data they got, the more they became convinced of this. Thus, the decision was taken in the spring of 1977 that there would be no early election. The federal government would let Quebec make the first move.

As a fall-back position, the Tellier Group prepared a referendum bill, which was tabled in the House of Commons and debated in committee — but died on the order paper in 1979.

In the meantime, however, the government decided to make some symbolic gestures and to wait for the Quebec government's honeymoon to subside. These included publication of a Green Paper reviewing the Official Languages Policy, entitled "A National Understanding", and the presentation of a $3.5 million televised spectacular on July 1 for Canada Day — only a year after the festivities had been cancelled as a cost-cutting measure.

Similarly, the government introduced a resolution on national unity in the House of Commons on July 5, 1977. In his speech on the resolution, Trudeau announced what had already been rumoured widely in the press: the creation of a task force on national unity, headed by Jean-Luc Pepin and John Robarts.

The debate occurred as the federal Liberals were at a historic high point in the polls, over fifty per cent for the first and only time since the election of 1974. Jim Coutts was begging Pierre Trudeau to call an election in the fall.

In his speech on the national-unity resolution, Trudeau told the House that "we are fighting to preserve a great and precious country" — and then listened in astonishment to the leader of the opposition, Joe Clark, say that bilingualism "by definition does not unite", and that the implementation of the federal program had been "a disaster".

"If that's the way Clark would hold the country together, we could win an election and lose a country," Trudeau told the caucus the next day. Although the final decision was not made until fall, the Clark speech helped swing Trudeau against the idea of an early election.

The idea for the task force that Trudeau announced in the speech had been floating about for some time. Pitfield had suggested a central organization to answer the question "What can we do?" being heard across Canada.

There were two natural candidates to head such a group: the former Ontario premier, John Robarts, who had been reflecting publicly on Canada's future and had privately let Trudeau know that he would be available, and Jean-Luc Pepin, the former Liberal cabinet minister who was head of the Anti-Inflation Board. When Pitfield suggested the co-chairmanship, Pepin was intrigued. However, the key question was the mandate.

Trudeau was absolutely opposed to establishing a commission with a mandate to tell him what shape the country should take, and how powers should be distributed. Pepin had no interest in heading a public-relations operation.

Finally, Pepin added a clause to the rough mandate Pitfield had drawn up: "to provide its own recommendations on the solutions" — and gave it to Coutts. "Oh, no problem at all," Coutts said.

With that phrase, Pepin succeeded in getting exactly what Trudeau did not want: a successor to Laurendeau-Dunton with a mandate to make recommendations on the future shape of the country.

After some delay in completing its membership, the task force quickly agreed that it would not co-ordinate the unity groups.

On September 20 the executive director of the task force, Reed Scowen, told a group of journalists that the Pepin-Robarts constitutional proposal would be "much closer to sovereignty-association than to the status quo". From that moment on, in the words of one task-force staff member, "war was declared between Marc Lalonde and Pierre Trudeau and Jean-Luc Pepin". Lalonde tried, and failed, to have Scowen fired.

The principal reaction to the task force was scepticism. Few observers thought that it could succeed in doing more than observing yet again the nature of the problem. Few imagined that it could reach a consensus on a substantial proposition for constitutional change; most assumed that it would be what Pierre Trudeau had intended it to be: a way of appearing to deal with the problem without actually doing anything.

In January 1978 an event occurred in which the federal government was powerless to do anything. On January 6, Thomas Galt, the president of Sun Life, announced that the 107-year-old company would be moving its head office from Montreal to Toronto. Galt blamed Bill 101.

"We do not believe the separation of Quebec from Canada is likely," he said. "However, since it is now evident that the language of the province of Quebec is by law to become very largely French, we can no longer envisage our ability to recruit, or retain in Montreal, or to bring to Montreal from outside Quebec, sufficient people with the necessary qualifications and competence in English to transact the daily business of the company."

The ensuing uproar was to focus on the whole question of the responsibilities of business in Quebec, and the role that business had played in creating the resentment that fuelled the independence movement.

Jacques Parizeau was furious. He had not been notified in advance by Sun Life — Jean Chrétien broke the news in a midnight phone call — and he had to track down Galt himself by phone for confirmation. (Galt's excuse was that the executive who was supposed to tell Parizeau had a dentist appointment.) He called Sun Life "one of the worst exploiters of the Quebec economy", and threatened to force the company to return to Quebec the $400 million in active policies held by Quebecers.

René Lévesque attacked Sun Life's "cowardice" in announcing that the shareholders' meeting would be held in Toronto, not Montreal, calling the move "a political gesture" and "a bitter refusal to accept the normal evolution of Quebec and the Quebec milieu which had nourished it for well over a century".

A symbol of anglo Montreal conservatism and power, Sun Life was now a symbol of corporate anglo panic. The reaction in French-speaking Quebec was an angry mixture of "Good riddance!" and "How dare you?" The FTQ called for a boycott; Sun Life business in Quebec plummeted.

Civil servants were calmer. Bernard Bonin, an economist analysing the economic basis for the association part of sovereignty-association, observed, "It was certain there would be flights of capital. It was also probable that English-Canadian capital would be the first to go. Multinationals capable of living with the governments of Brazil and South Korea have no trouble with Quebec's."

Bonin saw the political impact of the move as substantial. "Every time companies like Sun Life leave, the greater are the chances the government will win the referendum."

Later, like Bonin, Parizeau saw referendum benefits in the decision. With startling frankness, he explained the government's tactic of vehement reactions. "We must emphasize these actions and traumatize them right now, so that any repetition close to the referendum will appear simply old hat," he said. "I much prefer to see the corporations provocative now than later."

By emphasizing and traumatizing, Parizeau meant the nationalist gift for the politics of humiliation: the ability to fix upon an event and transform it into a mini-drama of national humiliation, usually with public denunciations, boycotts, constant references in speeches, and sometimes buttons, posters, and graffiti.

Sun Life was to join the list of painful incidents that have punctuated Quebec's history and shaped its nationalist rhetoric since the hanging of Louis Riel in 1885. It was a list that would grow over the next few years, reaching a climax with the constitutional agreement in November 1981.

Federalists instinctively sensed the emotional impact of the Sun Life decision. Pierre Trudeau summoned Galt, and the chairman of the board of Sun Life, Alistair Campbell, to 24 Sussex Drive to see if they would change their decision. All he got was a deferral of the shareholders' meeting from January 27 to April 25.

The delay gave Richard Holden, a Montreal lawyer, the opportunity to organize a protest on behalf of four hundred shareholders in Montreal.

Throughout the controversy, Sun Life was silent. At the shareholders' meeting on April 25, Holden was jeered; the move was endorsed by an 84 per cent vote. A bitter chapter in the history of English-Canadian business in Quebec was closed; another bitter phrase entered the political language of Quebec. The Montreal business community learned, if it did not know before, that it should leave Quebec as quietly and discreetly as possible.

NINE

Mr. Ryan
Goes To
Gilford Street

*Party leadership and the
conducting of a great journal
do not harmonize.*
George Brown, May 13, 1867

When Robert Bourassa resigned the leadership of the Quebec
Liberal Party, he left a shambles behind: a demoralized, dis-
organized, rudderless rump. As interim leader, Gérard-D.
Lévesque worked to establish a coherent presence in the
Assembly, with the former speaker, Jean-Noël Lavoie. But neither man had the stature to unite federalists in the province.
The Liberals' disarray showed almost daily. It took all the
interim leader's skills to keep the caucus together on such
divisive issues as language policy. He managed it, establishing
mother tongue as the criteria for admission to English-language
schools, but the shaky consensus was not enough to provide
leadership.

There were three problems hovering over the choice of a
new leader. The veterans of the Bourassa government were
discredited; anyone coming from the federal Liberals would
be too closely identified with Ottawa; and choosing someone
with no political experience was an enormous risk. The unanimous hope was for someone of unquestioned stature, with the
intelligence, experience, integrity, and charisma to tackle René
Lévesque in the referendum campaign.

Some names began to emerge. Raymond Mailloux, the member for Charlevoix, liked the idea of Michel Bélanger, the former senior civil servant who was president of the Provincial
Bank. Others suggested Claude Castonguay, social affairs minister under Bourassa, who had left politics in 1973 with his

reputation intact. The only person in the caucus with serious leadership ambitions was Raymond Garneau, the former finance minister. Young, highly competent, he had worked for Jean Lesage before running in 1970. He had chafed under Bourassa's leadership; now he wanted his shot.

Michel Gratton, a straight-talking engineer from outside Hull, decided to tackle the question head on. He had founded the Quebec-Canada Movement on February 2, 1977. In March he had dinner with Ryan in Old Montreal. Gratton, like so many politicians before him, wanted to pay his respects. He didn't expect to win Ryan's wholehearted support, but he hoped he could at least prevent an outright editorial attack on his new movement.

Over dinner, Ryan asked Gratton about the names being discussed by the caucus. Gratton said that Garneau and Bélanger were mentioned; he personally favoured Jean Chrétien, but it was obviously a kiss of death to come from Ottawa. To his surprise, Ryan said, "Chrétien's candidacy may not be as far-fetched as all that."

Encouraged, Gratton visited Chrétien, whom he had never met before, in Ottawa, and urged him to run. Chrétien was intrigued, attracted by the idea, but non-committal. Latter that spring, he visited Ryan in his office at *Le Devoir* to discuss federal policies. The subject of the Liberal leadership came up, and Ryan began a sentence with "Well, whoever is the next leader of the Liberal Party, whether it is Castonguay, or you, or me . . ." It was thrown in so casually that Chrétien thought it was merely rhetorical; he could not imagine Ryan as an effective politician. But later he would remember that casual remark as the first indication that Ryan was thinking seriously of becoming leader of the Quebec Liberal Party.

At first glance, it seemed as incongruous as having the curé take over the town bordello. There was a ponderousness to the man in public, a self-righteousness, a physical awkwardness, which seemed to disqualify him from political life. Although he was three years younger than Lévesque and six years younger than Trudeau, he looked and sounded a generation older.

It was somehow characteristic of the man that his editor-in-chief, Michel Roy, who had worked with him for fifteen years, called both Trudeau and Lévesque "tu" — and called Ryan "vous".

Ryan was notorious for being tight-fisted; on trips, he stayed at monasteries or at the YMCA, and sometimes dressed down his staff for staying in expensive hotels. The reporters at *Le Devoir* joked that his favourite restaurant was Saint-Hubert Barbecue.

He had a reputation for being tough and authoritarian; in the Liberals' depression after the weak leadership of Bourassa, this was no handicap. But those who were familiar with his painfully scrupulous habits of consultation wondered how he would function as a political leader. Others wondered about his explosive temper. Before the Progressive Conservative leadership convention in February 1976, Ryan had endorsed Brian Mulroney and praised Flora MacDonald and Joe Clark; he had vigorously opposed Claude Wagner. But when there had been a heavy swing to Clark away from Wagner on the final ballot, Tories were astounded to see a furious Ryan shouting at Flora MacDonald and Richard Hatfield, accusing them of betraying Quebec by supporting Clark against Wagner.

Ryan was capable of generosity of spirit — he hired the former FLQ intellectual Pierre Vallières, saying that he knew Vallières would not do the same for him — but he could be mean-spirited, and would never forget a slight. Years later, he recalled how Marc Lalonde had personally delivered a reply to an editorial criticizing the planning of Mirabel Airport — and had tromped into his office without taking his snowboots off. As an adversary, he could be ferocious: "He's not content with getting his opponent down, he has to gouge his eyes out," a journalist who had negotiated with him said bitterly.

In the summer of 1977, a group of reform-minded Liberal MNAs like Claude Forget, André Raynauld, and Thérèse Lavoie-Roux began to meet regularly with other Liberals like Claude Castonguay and Jean-Paul L'Allier to discuss directions that the party should take at the policy conference in the fall. In July, Michel Robert had lunch with Ryan to discuss the idea that Ryan should be the keynote speaker.

Robert, a tall, red-bearded lawyer and chairman of the party's policy commission, was determined that the conference should be part of a whole process of Liberal renewal. But the key element in this reform was the choice of a leader to personify a renewed, rebuilt party that would wipe out the memories of the Bourassa years.

Increasingly, Robert felt that Ryan was the man to do this, that the party needed his integrity and intellectual stature to break with the past and play its proper part in the referendum. In addition, he believed that Quebec was tired of the frequent changes of the last twenty years, and that the time had come for a leader who represented stability.

In early September, Robert met with Philippe Casgrain, another Montreal lawyer of aristocratic bearing and impeccable Liberal credentials. They agreed on Ryan; soon afterwards, Casgrain approached Ryan with the idea. Then the group of MNAs who had been meeting over the summer began to get involved, and a core took shape: Robert, Casgrain, Forget, Lavoie-Roux, Castonguay, Gilles Hébert, Pierre Mercier, and a widening circle of their friends in the party. Similarly, federal Liberals close to Pierre Trudeau began to think Ryan would be appropriate, and discouraged Chrétien from running.

Then, on November 7, Ryan issued a statement saying that he would be "happier and more useful to my fellow citizens" at *Le Devoir*, concluding: "My decision regarding the leadership of the Liberal Party of Quebec is firm and irrevocable." The group that had been pushing him to run was stunned. Some of them, only a few hours before, had felt confident that he would ultimately decide to run.

Part of Ryan's reason had been his fears of shadowy backroom figures like Paul Desrochers — but part was the state of his wife's health, which seemed precarious after a worrying diagnosis. It had been this that provoked the statement. It was only when he learned that his fears were unfounded that he allowed himself to reconsider.

The pressure to change his mind came almost immediately. His keynote speech at the policy conference was given an overwhelming ovation, though it was an arid statement of his constitutional views. It was as if he were saying, "This is the man I am, and I won't change," and the delegates were saying, "You're the man we want." Ryan was moved to say privately, "The door is closed, but not locked."

Meetings between Ryan and the group urging him to run resumed, with people trying to allay his fears about Desrochers, who had held a meeting of three hundred Liberal organizers, and polled them on their favourite candidate. Ryan won by a 3 to 1 margin — which so appalled him that he almost withdrew again.

Over the holidays, Ryan decided to run, but drew up a list of conditions: a full and unqualified commitment by the people compaigning for him until the end of the campaign, a commitment to honest campaign methods, a commitment to give first loyalty to him should he differ with the federal Liberals. He also made it clear that he would not be bound by the resolutions of the policy conference, which he had found too doctrinaire and right wing. He required a salary equivalent to what he was getting at *Le Devoir*—reportedly $42,000—and, in case of defeat, a guarantee that it would continue for three to six months after the convention.

After a meeting on January 4, those who attended felt confident that it was settled: Ryan would be a candidate. However, in the days that followed, he came within a hair of withdrawing completely. On Friday the 6th, he learned that an organizer he was counting on was close to Desrochers. Worse, he got a phone call from Brian Mulroney, an old friend. He had lunched at the Saint-Denis Club, and overheard Desrochers at a nearby table attacking Ryan, saying, "He's the one to beat; he never was a Liberal. We don't need a guy like him." When Michel Roy got back from lunch, he found Ryan in a rage. He had written an article saying why he would not run, which he wanted published in the Saturday paper.

"Look, Mr. Ryan, thousands of people are counting on you," Roy protested. "At least take the weekend to think it over."

The next day, Ryan drove with his family to stay with his in-laws in Lévis; there he met with Julien Giasson, a Liberal MNA and former cabinet minister. Giasson assured him that Desrochers's influence was waning, but Ryan was still undecided, and plagued with worries about the world of politics.

On Sunday, Giasson drove up to Montreal and, with two Ryan loyalists familiar with the organization of the party, Gilles Hébert and Pierre Mercier, met with Ryan. The organizer whose loyalties had been questioned was summoned, and the misunderstanding worked out. Shortly after midnight, Ryan sealed his decision. He was a candidate.

On Monday, January 9, 1978, Raymond Garneau announced that he was running. He had been thinking about it for some time, but there was one shadow hanging over his head: rumours that he had been guilty of improprieties in dealing with the Quebec Liquor Corporation as finance minister. On December 1, 1977, he had made an impassioned appeal in the Assembly to the justice minister, Marc-André Bédard, to bring forward the evidence and end the rumours. It was a highly emotional speech — some said the most emotional moment in the Assembly since Jérôme Choquette had burst into tears in 1970, when asked about the death of Pierre Laporte. On December 21, Bédard told the Assembly that no MNA would be charged; Garneau said that he could then take "an objective decision" on the leadership.

Garneau had been a prominent Liberal since 1966, when he joined Lesage's staff. Born in the small town of Plessisville, he bore a striking resemblance to the former Canadien hockey star Yvan Cournoyer, and had the battered face of a man who had spent his youth on skates. An economist, he had studied in Geneva before returning to Quebec, and had worked briefly for the Desjardins life insurance company before going to work for Lesage.

But even before Ryan's announcement it was clear that the bulk of the caucus was already committed to him. Garneau had only one former cabinet minister with him, Victor Goldbloom, and three members of the caucus: Michel Pagé, Georges Vaillancourt, and Richard Verreault.

While Garneau was making his announcement, Ryan was telling his colleagues at *Le Devoir* of his decision, and writing his letter of resignation as publisher. He presented the letter to the board of directors that night. As the final cord was cut with the newspaper he had served for more than fifteen years, Claude Ryan wept. The decision had been, he said later, "as painful as childbirth".

The next day, when Ryan said good-bye to the newsroom at *Le Devoir* and climbed into his brown Chevrolet Bel-Air with two journalists and a TV cameraman to drive over to the Méridien Hotel to announce his candidacy, he was immediately the front runner. His integrity was unquestioned, his intellectual abilities and capacity for hard work were undisputed.

Only two major doubts lingered. Garneau had earned loyalty in the party, and some wondered how the ordinary Liberal would react to this Montreal publisher who had told Quebecers to vote PQ in 1976.

The other question was adaptability. For all his intellect and honesty, Ryan could be dry, detailed, tedious — in a word, boring. He had never had to work in a political party, where people's egos needed stroking and where the devotion to frugality was less pronounced than at *Le Devoir*. He had a reputation for being authoritarian, a fighter. How would he react to the pressure of constant media attention, the fragile egos of political life, the media hunger for terse wit, and the intangible but crucial element of personal style?

As Ryan drove home that night with his eighteen-year-old son Paul after an open-line radio show with Yvon Dupuis on CKVL, a reporter accompanying him observed that it seemed at this point in the adventure he was embarking on that he might either succeed in capturing the public's imagination, as Pierre Trudeau, another political neophyte, had done ten years earlier, or, like Robert Stanfield, he might fail.

"Ah, yes, yes," Ryan said. "I've asked myself that question. If I failed, I wouldn't mind being compared to Mr. Stanfield. Mr. Stanfield left a fine testament."

CLAUDE RYAN WAS BORN IN MONTREAL ON JANUARY 25, 1925, THE second of three boys. His mother, Blandine Dorion, was the daughter of a prosperous businessman who had hoped that she would become a lawyer. The death of both her parents made this impossible, but she grew up with an iron will. She needed it; Henri-Albert Ryan, whom she married at the age of twenty-two, got a job with International Paper, moved the family to Dolbeau on Lac Saint-Jean, and then abandoned her with three small children. In 1931, after two years as a single parent, she returned to Montreal. Her husband never returned, and died in an accident in 1939.

It was a difficult childhood, growing up in poverty in Montreal, and instilled in Ryan stubbornness, scrappiness, personal austerity and contempt for wealth, disdain for authority, and personal insecurity that he overcame with ferocious work and self-discipline.

Blandine Ryan pushed and scrambled, instilling discipline and pride into her three stiff-necked sons, and supplementing the municipal relief she was forced to accept by typing letters at night for lawyers, doctors, and local merchants. Years later, Ryan said that he had derived his fundamental principles from her: the need for personal discipline, the importance of having principles, and the respect for different languages and backgrounds, particularly French and English.

Ryan grew up not only precociously intelligent but a dogged individualist. Attending Collège Sainte-Croix in the east end of Montreal, he would bring *Le Devoir* to the study hall every night, and only open his books for the last half-hour, completing the homework before the study period was over.

He had many arguments with the priests, ending in his refusal to compete for the provincial academic prize for graduating classical-college students. "If you think I'm going to win that for you after all the problems you've given me, you're mistaken!" he told them.

His stubbornness made him decide against going into the priesthood, as his mother had hoped, after he spent two weeks at the Saint-Benoît-du-Lac monastery. "I was too hard-headed and stiff-necked to accept the vow of obedience," he said later.

Similarly, his obstinacy made him refuse to take his exams at the School of Industrial Relations at the Université de Montréal because he felt the standards were too low, and that the degree they were granting was an "intellectual fraud". And it was his curiosity that led him to investigate the Co-operative Commonwealth Federation (CCF), the forerunner of the New Democratic Party. He was involved with the CCF for a year, meeting with leading figures like M. J. Coldwell, David Lewis, Frank Scott, and Tommy Douglas, and immersing himself in the writings of British socialism: the Webbs and Harold Laski.

But another tradition exercised a stronger pull on his loyalties. As an adolescent, he had been deeply influenced by the classic writers of the Church, especially St. Augustine and St. Thomas Aquinas. Now he was caught up in the wave of Catholic thinking that rejected reactionary conservatism. In 1945, when he was still a student, Ryan left the CCF and accepted the job of national secretary of l'Action Catholique Canadienne, where he was to stay, with only one break, for seventeen years.

He worked with many people in the lay Catholic movement who were later to move to politics and government: Gérard Pelletier, Maurice and Jeanne Sauvé, Pierre Juneau, Fernand Dumont, Guy Rocher, and Marc Lalonde — and others, like Pierre Trudeau and Camille Laurin, who were close to many in the movement.

In 1951-2, Ryan studied church history at the Gregorian Pontifical University in Rome. While he was there, Pierre Trudeau passed through Rome on his way to Asia, and the two had lunch. Ryan felt Trudeau was groping, and gave him some advice. "You're in Rome," he said. "There is something you are missing, perhaps, in order to be happy. You are a rich young man." He quoted scripture, urging him to give away his wealth. "The thing that distinguishes you from the rest of us is that you have no problem of security. This would be the place, in Rome, to take a decision like that."

Trudeau was sufficiently moved to consult friends at home about the idea; they told him he should keep his money so that he could do political work. It was not the last time he would reject Ryan's advice.

After a year, Ryan returned to Catholic Action in Montreal. As secretary-general of a movement that included the Jeunesse Étudiante Catholique (JEC), Jeunesse Ouvrière Catholique (JOC), and the Jeunesse Agricole Catholique (JAC), Ryan was part grass-roots organizer, part adult educator, part lobbyist and pressure-group leader, part intellectual, part lay religious leader. The work gave him a model for political action.

"I wrote a booklet on the intellectual life of a Christian militant that is very very close to what I am trying to do now," he said in 1978, a month after becoming Liberal leader. "The fundamental concern is the same. I felt that in order to be a good witness to the Christian religion, you have to have a strong intellectual content in your religious experience. You have to come up with a strong intellectual justification for your faith, and your involvement in the work of the Church."

In the booklets that Ryan wrote in this period, the ideas he would bring to the Liberal Party leadership are clearly laid out, with his insistence on hard work and intellectual rigour.

At times, there was almost a military tone to his writings. "Action, in the strong sense of the term, is always a struggle, a combat, where there is an enemy, a real obstacle to fight and conquer," he wrote in 1959. "It is never a pure gesture of benevolence. It demands the best energies and resources of each person. Defeat always involves the elimination of the vanquished."

Every activist should have a personal library, he said, and keep reading as widely as possible. He should carry a notebook at all times, make notes of significant information, and write up and file the notes later. "The real activist is a type who *works* when he attends a meeting, when he lives in his milieu, when he chats with someone," he wrote. "Every important thing is noted in his notebook, and he revises and disposes of them later in a moment of solitude."

In *Le Contact dans l'Apostolat*, the last of three brochures

published in 1959, Ryan wrote about the enormous importance of personal contact. More than the others, this expressed
ideas that he would transpose to political organization, basing
the renewal of the Liberal Party, the referendum campaign,
and the election campaign of 1981 on personal contact. What
had long been a canvassing technique of the PQ, and, before
it, the New Democratic Party and the CCF, Ryan invested with
spiritual intensity. His picture of the ideal activist, which carried over to his view of the *Le Devoir* reader and the Liberal
Party member, was of a serious, well-intentioned, often self-
taught, religious person who was active in community life and
in the workplace, and was trying to raise a family well.

He also believed in diversity, and had no patience for the
idea that devout Catholics should avoid the company of non-
Catholics. However, he didn't always adhere to the ideals of
openness and diversity he expressed in the brochures. In 1949,
he launched a one-man campaign to have a woman stricken
from the Canadian delegation to an international conference
on adult education on the grounds that he had heard she was
"a militant Communist". Renée Morin hired Frank Scott as
her lawyer, sued for slander, and won on appeal in 1957.

In 1958, Ryan decided he ought to get married. "I was thirty-
three, I was still a bachelor; several friends urged me to start a
home," he said later. "I was getting older, I had to choose what
I was going to make of my life. Besides, I didn't want to pass for
a bloody homosexual.

"I looked around my work environment, and then I said to
myself that Madeleine Guay would make a good wife. So one
night I invited her to a little restaurant near our offices at the
corner of Cherrier and Saint-Hubert. I didn't want to waste
her time. I told her right away, quite simply, that I wanted to
go out with her because I found that she had all the qualities
to establish a household."

Six months later they were married. In two years they had
their first child, and there were four more over the next eight
years.

In the early 1960s, Ryan began to feel that the time had come
to move on from l'Action Catholique. Then, in 1962, Gérard
Filion, the publisher of *Le Devoir*, invited Ryan to join the edito-
rial board with the possibility of succeeding him as publisher.
The board of directors had only one reservation about him.
"You probably feel that we are too nationalistically inclined,"

Filion said. "We in turn feel that you are not enough of a nationalist to be a fully reliable associate editor."

For Ryan was seen as an anti-nationalist. He had been greatly impressed by Pierre Trudeau's attack on the independence movement in *Cité libre*, and was resented by Abbé Groulx. However, though he did not have André Laurendeau's pen or his nationalist vision, Ryan was not insensitive to the emotional pull of Quebec nationalism, and Trudeau's detached logic would lose its appeal.

A year after Ryan joined *Le Devoir*, Filion left the paper to head Marine Industries. After a brief and unhappy period when the paper was run by a triumvirate, Ryan became publisher in 1964, and, when Laurendeau took a leave to head the Royal Commission on Bilingualism and Biculturalism, editor-in-chief as well. He quickly became the most authoritative editorialist in Quebec. Carefully weighing the facts and arguments in three long columns, he would pronounce on virtually every current subject, major or minor.

He threw the pages of *Le Devoir* open to the debate on independence, and carefully weighed and measured the arguments with scales and calipers on the editorial page. In 1964, he chose what he called "the thesis of two cultures" over the idea of two nations, or independence; in 1967, in a special Centennial supplement, he broadened the idea of cultural duality, calling for a new constitution which would allow Quebec "to dissociate itself without being penalized by Ottawa financially or otherwise".

In September 1967, as Lévesque's departure from the Liberal Party approached, Ryan's attitude seemed to stiffen. He attacked Pierre Trudeau for rejecting the "two nations" thesis, saying bitterly, "The Pierre Trudeau of the 1950s would have at least taken the trouble to study the propositions and discuss them with precision." He welcomed Lévesque's decision, while continuing to support federalism as a better vehicle for protecting freedom and personal liberties.

When Pierre Trudeau sought the federal Liberal leadership in 1968, Ryan was opposed to his candidacy; he had intended to support Mitchell Sharp, and when Sharp backed Trudeau, he endorsed Paul Hellyer. When Trudeau called the election, he seriously considered being a candidate for the Progressive Conservatives, as his brother was. The possibility ended with the sudden death of André Laurendeau. However, Ryan did

René Lévesque as a child of three and in his teens.(Canapress Photo Service)

Lévesque as a correspondent for Radio-Canada during the Korean War, 1951. (Public Archives of Canada)

Lévesque as a member of Jean Lesage's Liberal cabinet, 1960. (Canapress Photo Service)

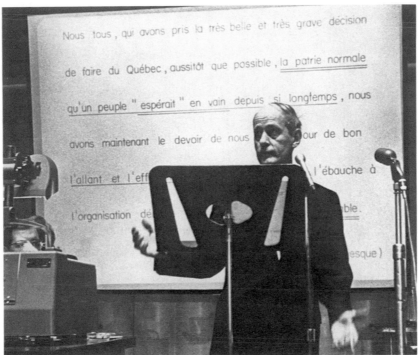

First policy meeting of the Mouvement Souveraineté-Association, April 22, 1968. (Canapress Photo Service)

Lévesque walks through demonstrators picketing during the Saint-Léonard school crisis in September 1968. (Canapress Photo Service)

Third annual convention of the Parti Québécois, February 1971. Left to right: Camille Laurin, Jacques Parizeau, and René Lévesque. (Canapress Photo Service)

Announcement of the Parti Québécois Budget de l'An 1 three weeks before the 1973 election. Left to right: Camille Laurin, Jacques Parizeau, René Lévesque, and Claude Morin. (Canapress Photo Service)

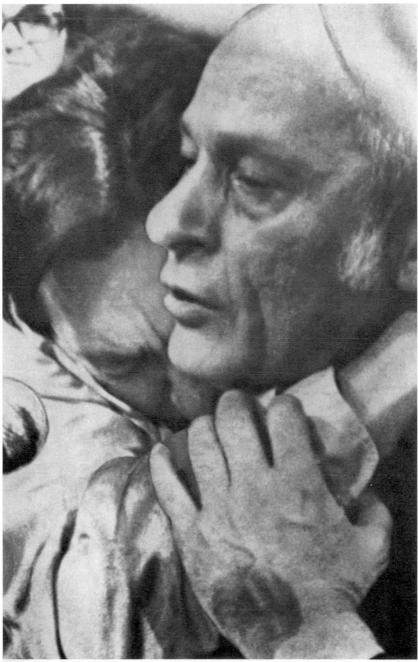

Lévesque comforts Camille Laurin after they both lost their bids for seats in the 1973 election. (Canapress Photo Service)

The face of victory, November 15, 1976. René Lévesque holds up his hands in a plea for silence at Paul Sauvé Arena. With him is Lise Payette. (Canapress Photo Service)

Outgoing premier Robert Bourassa and newly elected premier René Lévesque meet the press, November 18, 1976. (Canapress Photo Service)

Pierre Trudeau and René Lévesque shake hands while Quebec Intergovernmental Affairs Minister Claude Morin looks on, at the first Federal-Provincial Premiers Conference in Ottawa after the PQ victory, December 1976. (Canapress Photo Service)

Minister of Finance Jacques Parizeau. (Jacques Nadeau)

Claude Morin, minister of intergovernmental affairs and chief strategist of the 1980 referendum. (Jacques Nadeau)

Pierre Marc Johnson, first minister of labour, then minister of social affairs, and finally minister of justice, is considered a possible successor to René Lévesque. (Jacques Nadeau)

support the Conservatives under Stanfield, whom he had endorsed for the leadership in 1967.

Just as it was the principle of personal liberty that was the bedrock of Ryan's support for federalism, it was the suspension of civil liberties during the October Crisis of 1970 that put the greatest strain on his federalism. Throughout the crisis, Ryan was Trudeau's principal critic. Day after day, *Le Devoir* hammered away, calling for negotiations and exile for the kidnappers and the exchange of Cross and Laporte for the "political prisoners" the FLQ wanted.

The editorials provoked considerable anger from Trudeau and his supporters, and from English Canada. This pleased Ryan; he felt it put an end to any misunderstanding of him. "People often support you because they don't understand you," he wrote. "Better to be understood and disapproved of."

Trudeau, sneering that Ryan had been corrupted by powerlessness, insinuated that he had advised the government to capitulate. Ryan angrily retorted in print that Trudeau was lying.

But one of the most extraordinary episodes of the October Crisis was the so-called "provisional government plot". The rumour swirled through Ottawa that there was an attempt brewing to overthrow the Bourassa government, and install a provisional government. Peter C. Newman, after talking to Pierre Trudeau and Marc Lalonde, wrote a story saying that this was the reason for the imposition of the War Measures Act. On October 23, before the story ran, *Toronto Star* publisher Beland Honderich phoned Ryan for his reaction. Ryan was appalled, and told Honderich he totally rejected journalism that slandered someone under the cover of anonymous sources. The story ran the next day, with no by-line and no names mentioned.

The rumour had developed from a series of events. Bourassa had phoned Ryan the night Laporte was kidnapped, and Ryan recommended that he bring new people into the government. At the Sunday afternoon editorial meeting at *Le Devoir* the next day, Ryan and his colleagues discussed three possibilities: the invoking of the War Measures Act, Bourassa bringing someone into the cabinet and keeping control of the situation, or the creation of a unity government made up of diverse political elements. Ryan then visited Lucien Saulnier, Drapeau's right-hand man and an old friend, and they discussed the third idea. Saulnier felt the situation had not reached that extreme, and Ryan agreed. That night, Bourassa appeared on television with what seemed to be an offer to negotiate. So the idea died.

For a time it looked as if the October Crisis might prove to have been a turning point for Ryan in his continuing reassessment of federalism. He suggested as much in the spring of 1971. "More than ever the federal option has become relative, a question of means," he wrote. "I should have no hesitation in preferring an independence that would be responsive to real democratic values over a federalism dominated by interests that would make the realization of my people's destiny impossible."

Certainly the PQ thought Ryan was moving their way. However, Ryan remained suspicious of them. "The so-called alliance with Lévesque [during the October Crisis, when both men were on the committee urging negotiations] was only circumstantial," he said later. In fact, he concluded from the experience that he would always have difficulty in working with Lévesque. "In committee he's a man who doesn't yield himself easily, you know. He doesn't speak very much and he seems to keep some cards in his hands. He doesn't seem to lay all his cards down on the table. We had a couple of misunderstandings during that period. I thought to myself, 'I don't like that.' "

But Ryan's new tone led Lévesque to ask him to be a PQ candidate in the 1973 election. Ryan refused immediately. He had become resentful of the pressure he was feeling from nationalists he had never felt comfortable with. Not only did he refuse to be a candidate, he endorsed Bourassa.

The Parti Québécois was furious. In the aftermath of the defeat, a number of key figures in the party, including Jacques Parizeau and Yves Michaud, decided to launch a daily newspaper, *Le Jour*, partly to provide the party with a favourable press — and partly to exact revenge on Ryan and *Le Devoir*.

Ryan's endorsation of the PQ in 1976 did little or nothing to heal that breach. When the Liberals began to sound him out on the possibility of becoming a leadership candidate, he was established as the clearest, most articulate voice of opposition to the Parti Québécois government.

THE LIBERAL LEADERSHIP CAMPAIGN INVOLVED NOT ONLY TOURS across the province to meet Liberal delegates, but nine regional meetings where both Ryan and Garneau spoke. Both men managed to surprise: Ryan with his earthy manner when he threw away his text, Garneau with his intellectual depth. With only two in the race, pressure mounted on the caucus: by the end of January, Michel Gratton and John Ciaccia phoned Chrétien to say they could wait no longer, and that they had to declare. On February 2, they both announced support for Ryan. They both regretted it later.

Ryan campaigned saying he could attract PQ voters; he got some of his loudest applause when he told audiences about the letters of support he got that included torn-up PQ membership cards. At each meeting, he repeated that the Liberals lost in 1976 because of a "catastrophic weakening in leadership" and made it clear he did not exempt Garneau.

Garneau, on the other hand, campaigned as a spokesman for free enterprise, against excessive regulation, and for an unqualified commitment to Canadian federalism. He presented his experience, his financial ability, his administrative record, his years of work for the party.

Garneau was clearly more conservative than Ryan, calling for the return of automobile insurance to private enterprise; similarly, he was more aggressively anti-nationalist and anti-Péquiste. Ryan refused to be pushed into any dogmatic positions, saying he would examine the files carefully before making any rash decisions.

For the first part of the campaign, relations remained straightforward and aboveboard. But as Ryan began to pull inexorably ahead, the campaign turned bitter. Garneau complained that Ryan's organization had mounted "a psychological war" against him, circulating insinuations about his health. (Ryan apologized.) Ryan's supporters, on the other hand, were furious at the Garneau organization: first for ignoring the rules of a televised debate and organizing a noisy demonstration for the cameras, and secondly for an internal campaign document entitled "le kit du parfait vendeur" — the perfect salesman's kit — which detailed Ryan's endorsations for non-Liberals, going back to his support of Charles Taylor of the NDP against Pierre Trudeau in 1965, Stanfield against Trudeau in 1968 and 1972, and, of course, the PQ against the Liberals in 1976.

The kit suggested that Garneau was more effective on television than Ryan, that "Ryan represents the same psychological profile as René Lévesque," that his new team was full of

Bourassa confidants, and, worst of all, that both Ryan and Lévesque espoused "pink Marxism". Ryan was outraged. He never forgave Garneau.

THE CONVENTION ORGANIZERS HAD A PROBLEM IN ROBERT BOURASSA. They couldn't ignore him: he had, after all, been premier for six years, and won the greatest electoral victory in the history of Quebec. But they were terrified that, if he actually spoke to the convention, he might be booed.

The solution was a speech by Jean Lesage on Friday afternoon, April 14, 1978, and, in the evening, a $50,000 film of the last four leaders. As the lights went up, the ex-leaders were on stage: Georges-Émile Lapalme, Jean Lesage, Robert Bourassa, and the interim leader, Gérard-D. Lévesque. "It was $50,000 well spent, just to be sure that we could get Robert in and out of there without incident," said one party official wryly.

Then Gérard-D. Lévesque gave the keynote speech: a passionate, tub-thumping, Peq-bashing, unreservedly federalist, crowd-rousingly partisan barn-burner of a speech. Each camp used the applause to chant and shout their man's name. Claude Ryan conducted his own cheering section, waving his Ryan handkerchief, a silly grin on his face, chanting "Ry-an! Ry-an!"

Lysiane Gagnon, a *La Presse* reporter on strike, was appalled at what she was seeing in the Colisée du Québec. "Claude Ryan, the man of l'Action Catholique, of *Le Devoir*, and of *devoir* with a small d, frugal, austere, and studious, Claude Ryan was waving a scarf with his picture on it, frenetically, his arms outstretched, now back and forth like an incense pot, now in front of him like a flag," she wrote.

"In time with his own supporters, he chanted his own name: 'Ry-hi-an . . . Ry-iii-an'. Without anyone asking him, he climbed on top of his seat, lifting his wife up beside him, holding onto her with one hand, and with the other, waving his scarf, a little awkwardly, a little diminished by the pleasure which climbed and stretched across his face.

"Transformed, an ecstatic smile, his eyes shining, Claude Ryan exuded the smell of power, that smell which is, they say, more unnerving than that of any of the other passions, that smell which all true politicians can sniff, sense and follow."

The results were a foregone conclusion. The only questions were the margin of victory, and the style the victor adopted. As the voting ended on Saturday afternoon, a Garneau supporter asked Léonce Mercier, a key Garneau organizer, how it was going. "We'll get about eight hundred," he said. "It will be two to one." The supporter was stunned, silent with shock.

In another part of the arena, Michel Robert made his appraisal. "We've got about 1,700 votes," he said. The realities were hard to hide in a two-man race: the final tally was 1,748 for Ryan, 807 for Garneau.

Garneau went down with courage. He promised Ryan his support.

Ryan's speech to the delegates had been a dogged reading of a 23-page text, in which he rushed through applause lines; his victory speech was marked by his anger and bitterness towards the Garneau campaign. He plodded determinedly through an endless list of people to thank, and did not mention his defeated rival.

Garneau's supporters could not hide their bitterness. They felt they had been fighting a myth, that the delegates had refused to listen to their man, that the party had been taken over by a distant, intellectual nationalist.

In a storage room beneath the Quebec Coliseum, where Garneau's people gathered after the result, Auguste Jean, a major organizer, was crying. "We tried, we tried. What can you do against a myth? We were fighting a myth."

Garneau was fighting off tears of anguish. "Enough crying," he said with a crooked smile. After consoling his wife and daughter, he loosened his tie and looked at the people who were waiting for him to say something. "They never listened," he said flatly. "Right from the start, they never listened."

A few days later, the Liberal caucus met with Ryan at the Reform Club, beside the Plains of Abraham in Quebec. As the senior member of the eight people in the caucus who had ended up supporting Garneau, Victor Goldbloom made a gracious little speech, promising Ryan his full collaboration and support, and that of the whole caucus. Ryan looked straight ahead without responding. "Next!" he snapped, when Goldbloom finished.

Within a year, Garneau had resigned; within eighteen months, Goldbloom had followed suit. The Liberal Party was now Claude Ryan's party. Liberal headquarters on Gilford Street in Montreal was now Ryan's office.

TEN

Jacques Parizeau
and the
Sales Tax War

*En matière d'état, il
faut tirer profit de toutes
choses, et ce qui peut être
utile ne doit jamais être
méprisé.*

Cardinal de Richelieu

The emergence of Claude Ryan as a leadership candidate coincided with and helped provoke the government's first major slump in popularity. Ministers were exhausted from the pace of the first year in office, and Ryan began to look like the victor in the coming confrontation. More than one observer was reminded of British Columbia, where the New Democratic government had increased its popular vote, but lost the election because the opposition was united. The second inaugural address on February 21, 1978, had little that was new, and Lévesque acknowledged "a mixture of confidence and anxiety" in his opening words.

The February federal-provincial conference on the economy in Ottawa had been depressing; Lévesque had got into a bitter shouting match over federal housing policy with André Ouellet, and had been hammered. "C'était catastrophique," a senior aide admitted. Shortly afterwards, Lévesque walked out of the conference, saying, "I was simply tired of wasting my time."

For the first time, Lévesque was showing signs of indecision. In September, he had said there would be a substantial cabinet shuffle; in October, he said it would be decided on "during the holidays"; more stories to this effect emerged in early January, as members of his staff began to speculate. Then, in February, he said that the shuffle would be after the federal-provincial conference. When it finally happened, it was an enormous anticlimax. Denis Vaugeois became minister of cultural affairs — half of Louis O'Neill's double portfolio. And that was all.

Suddenly, little gaffes, slips, and signs of weakness seemed to multiply. The minister of tourism, fish, and game, Yves Duhaime, gave out a map of Quebec in Washington that showed Quebec and Canada as two separate entities, and Labrador as part of Quebec — in a press kit that listed Quebec's "foreign" offices, and included Toronto with New York, Tokyo, and the others. The introduction of television into the National Assembly was postponed — a setback for Burns. The government's critique of federal urban policy, the so-called "dossier noir", was embarrassingly shallow.

As Jean-Claude Picard wrote, "The Parti Québécois government suddenly seems morose and worried. From the great heights and ambitious projects of the days following the victory has now followed a painful period of groping, or moral uncertainty."

But one of the most embarrassing episodes was the fuss that surrounded the White Paper on Cultural Development being prepared for Camille Laurin by Fernand Dumont. In an article in *Maclean's*, David Thomas wrote about its sweeping nature. Without his knowledge, the story was headed "Quebec: a grand design for a New Order", suggesting the French fascist party, Ordre Nouveau, and rewritten to suggest that the policy called for "compulsory assimilation" of linguistic minorities.

Laurin denounced the article in the National Assembly as "false, distorted, and vicious", Lévesque attacked what he called "a sort of common form in some media . . . where practically anything goes against the Quebec government", and the controversy dominated the front pages for days. Lévesque's anger was all the greater because he wanted to focus attention on the economy, not culture: he had asked Denis Vaugeois to downplay some of the sweeping elements in the White Paper.

The nature of the controversy was abruptly transformed with the publication of a long interview with Laurin in the separatist monthly *Ici Québec*. Laurin confirmed many of Thomas's points, making it clear that he wanted an interventionist strategy. Calling the Quebec government "the only capitalist we have", he said: "We are going to proceed in two ways: by helping what is French in the cultural area, and by regulating the rest."

The government's embarrassment was increased by the fact that *Ici Québec* was clearly anti-Semitic: the same issue included an article that called Zionism "the cancer of the world", and accused the Israelis of injecting mercury in their own oranges.

The whole incident added to the government's appearance of defensiveness and clumsiness, and helped to undermine the credibility of its global approach to planning and development. It seemed like a symptom of this weakening under pressure when Robert Burns was admitted to hospital on May 19, after suffering a serious heart attack. He was forty-one.

These incidents, coinciding with the Liberal leadership campaign, had an impact on public opinion. In February the PQ was trailing the Liberals by 38.5 per cent to 40 per cent and observers began to remember that almost 60 per cent had voted against it in 1976. Claude Ryan looked like the next premier.

AFTER THIS DISASTROUS WINTER, JACQUES PARIZEAU TRANSFORMED the morale of the government and the party with a single gesture. In one stroke, he undermined Jean Chrétien as federal finance minister, and arrested the government's slide in popularity. He also created an enemy in Chrétien, who would conclude, once and for all, that the PQ could not be trusted, dealt with, or taken into account in dealings with the other provinces.

In the late winter and early spring of 1978, economic problems were not confined to Quebec. There had been virtually no growth in the U.S. economy in the first quarter; the Canadian dollar was in decline, floating below 85 cents U.S., and kept from dropping lower by massive support from the Bank of Canada. In Ottawa, an election seemed imminent. The Liberals had been in power four years — the traditional length of a parliamentary mandate—and there were signs of preparations, with sudden appointments to commissions and the judiciary. There was some debate inside the government as to whether there should be a spring budget. But the decision was made, and Chrétien began preparing one for April 10.

In addition to the pre-election desire to please, Chrétien wanted to produce a stimulative measure that would help get the economy moving. An across-the-board income-tax cut would mean a small cut for individuals and a massive loss of revenue for the government. A tax cut would have more impact on the economy if it were directly applied to people who bought things. In other words, a sales-tax cut. However, sales taxes were in provincial jurisdiction.

Chrétien had been named minister of finance in September 1977, and this was the first budget that was really his. As the first French Canadian to hold the job, he wanted to do something innovative. He was prepared to undertake what would be virtually a federal-provincial budget. So, in spite of the tradition of budget secrecy, he embarked on a series of careful consultations with his provincial colleagues to see if they would agree to cut sales taxes by three per cent over six months, with the federal government compensating them for two-thirds of the lost revenue.

Ontario was very enthusiastic; the Atlantic provinces were particularly agreeable, since Ottawa offered to pay the full three per cent in their case. Saskatchewan preferred the idea of a two per cent cut for nine months instead of three per cent for six months, since it was expecting to have an election in the fall and did not want to have the sales tax raised again just before the election. Alberta had no sales tax.

The one problem was with Quebec. Parizeau was consulted several times, and he refused to commit himself. As one federal official put it later, "He wouldn't say yes, he wouldn't say no, and he wouldn't return his phone calls." Finally, on March 30, just before the Easter weekend, Chrétien and the Ontario treasurer, Darcy McKeough, met Parizeau at the Hotel Bonaventure in Montreal to discuss the proposal. Parizeau came alone; the three men ate together. Both Chrétien and McKeough came away from the dinner convinced that Parizeau would agree to the proposal. Before Chrétien headed off to Shawinigan for the weekend, he told an aide, "We've got him — he's basically agreed."

Chrétien then had to get back to the other provincial finance ministers to notify them of the final decision, since the discussions, because of budget secrecy, had been hypothetical. But again Parizeau began to be non-committal and hard to reach. Two nights before the budget, he said, "I can't give you an answer." As one federal official recalled later, with some bitterness, "He never said no. And he never came to us with an alternative idea."

Finally, Chrétien couldn't wait any more and decided to go ahead without a firm reply from Parizeau.

On April 10, he brought down his budget, announcing the

sales-tax offer in a budget with a $11.5 billion deficit, tax deductions for research and development, and tax incentives for the development of the heavy-oil reserves and the tar sands.

For what many assumed was a pre-election budget, it was conservative, staying away from what one business reporter called "big vote-catching concessions". But politically it seemed a success. At the traditional finance minister's luncheon for journalists, Chrétien was given an ovation; Geoffrey Stevens wrote admiringly that he was "a splash of bright colour in a cabinet peopled by grey cardboard figures". But the aura of success was to be short-lived.

Quebec had still not responded, but it seemed as if Chrétien had Parizeau in an impossible position. If he agreed to the sales-tax cut, he would be accepting federal direction on a question of purely Quebec jurisdiction; if he refused, he would be sacrificing $226 million in federal compensation.

The night Chrétien presented his budget, Rodrigue Tremblay, the Quebec minister of industry and commerce, called his deputy minister, Claude Descoteaux, at home to suggest that he call his counterpart in the Finance Department, Michel Caron, to inquire about the impact of a selective tax cut. Tremblay had been arguing for some time in cabinet that the sales tax should be taken off building materials; Guy Joron, the minister of energy, had been arguing that this would have little impact — that a focus on Quebec industry was needed.

The next morning, April 11, there was a special cabinet meeting, and on the way in Lévesque told reporters that the Chrétien plan was "rape" and "truly odious trickery", and that Quebec would reject the plan. However, there was no hint as to how. In cabinet, the debate was inconclusive, and the civil servants were asked to review the options. The government looked a little silly, and there still seemed no escape from the dilemma.

That night, a small group met with Parizeau in his office: some of his staff, Michel Caron, Michel Gauvin, the deputy minister of revenue, and Michel Grignon, assistant deputy minister of finance in charge of taxation. Their options were now reduced. With Lévesque's casual remark, they now had to produce something very different.

Grignon suddenly spoke up. "What would happen if we made some vertical reductions of the sales tax on certain products, to a total of $226 million — and not a penny more?" he asked.

Parizeau gave a start. "That's an idea!"

The files were pulled, and the costs of various tax cuts were studied. The problem was reaching $226 million. They tried different combinations. Clothing, shoes, and furniture wouldn't reach $226 million; building materials would exceed it. Then someone remembered that the budget had already cut the sales tax on hotel rooms to help the tourist industry. That made exactly $226 million: clothing, textiles, shoes, furniture, and hotel rooms. It was only then that someone realized the strategic importance of these areas. For they were the weakest sectors of the Quebec economy.

Parizeau brought the plan to cabinet the next morning, where it was accepted immediately. That afternoon, he notified Chrétien and the opposition leaders and then told the National Assembly, where the news was greeted with a wild ovation. The gesture was pure theatre, and seemed both good politics and clever economics. It would give a boost to Quebec's weakest industrial sectors, creating an estimated eight thousand jobs in the clothing industry alone. The heat was then on Ottawa to come across with the $226 million in promised compensation.

The move seemed canny, and brilliantly timed. Parizeau looked like a superb technician and a shrewd economist; Chrétien looked naive and foolish. Parizeau won applause from almost all quarters in Quebec. The ensuing confusion both weakened Chrétien's political credibility, and helped swing the scales against the idea of a federal election in the spring of 1978. Parizeau was carried around the hall on the shoulders of the crowd at the next PQ Conseil National. In those halycon days, before the bills came in, he seemed like a fiscal magician.

JACQUES PARIZEAU HAD ONE BIG ADVANTAGE, WHICH HE CAREFULLY cultivated. He looked like a finance minister. Large, round, exuding the confidence of a nineteenth-century banker, he had a weight and a presence that were imposing to colleagues and dazzling to financial amateurs. He was superbly articulate, and his provincial colleagues looked to him for advice with something approaching awe; Darcy McKeough called him "the only professional finance minister in Canada". Parizeau looked right-wing, and sometimes sounded right-wing. But this was deceptive. In the 1940s, he had delivered tracts for Montreal Communist Fred Rose. It was a gesture that he explained with a smile as a mixture of youthful rebellion and interest in a girl.

"I am centre-left; socialist, no," Parizeau said shortly after his election. *"Barron's* [the Wall Street weekly] can say I am a socialist in English, because there is no French Canadian who reads it. But it's laughable. Me, a socialist? I am not right-wing, either. I am a progressive."

Parizeau's impact was reinforced by his sense of drama. After the presentation of the 1981 budget to cabinet, Lise Payette walked over to him and put down two dollars on the cabinet table, the climax of a running joke that she couldn't sit through such a show for free.

Nearly all his budget presentations were full of sparkling, witty turns of phrase and sweeping insights. They were superb lectures, with a mixture of overview and pungent details, delivered with pleasure by a man fascinated by the intricacy of the state financial system, who led his listeners through the economy with the arcane delight of a tour guide at Chartres Cathedral.

The professorial style was deeply rooted. He was fond of saying, "I was born a teacher, I will die a teacher, and everything in between is simply accident." But he could also be impulsive and passionate. In the early 1960s, he was driving to an appointment when he got trapped in a traffic jam; in a rage, he leapt from the car, tore up his driver's licence, and set off on foot. He has not driven since.

Once, a new member of Lévesque's staff heard that Parizeau was threatening to resign, and burst into a meeting with the news. There was an explosion of laughter, and the embarrassed newcomer realized that the threat was not made for the first time.

Parizeau's colleagues also saw a streak of paranoia in him. "If Parizeau went to a football game, and saw the team in a huddle, he would be convinced they were talking about him," one former colleague said wryly. He kept a network of contacts in the party and the federal government, and a system of personal sources of information in the financial community.

But he prided himself on his loyalty. When he hired staff, he would lecture them on the need for complete loyalty to Lévesque, and tell them formally that he would never challenge Lévesque's leadership. He was, he said, a good soldier. The ritual phrase was not a form of political hypocrisy: it reflected Parizeau's personal code of honour, his sense of the rules of the game in a parliamentary democracy. It was equally a reflection of his sense of propriety.

Lévesque once said, "Most of us are one or two generations from the farm; Parizeau has been in Outremont for seven generations, and is proud of it." Not quite; Parizeau's immigrant ancestor was a soldier in the Carignan-Salières regiment, demobilized in Montreal in the late seventeenth century, who opened a shop on the rue Saint-Paul. But by the end of the nineteenth century, the Parizeaus were prominent in Montreal. One grandfather was president of the Chambre des Notaires, the other was Dean of Medicine at the Université de Montréal. His father, Gérard Parizeau, was president of an insurance company, and also an author, historian, and teacher.

For three generations, the men had studied in Europe; it was a family which was, in a word, bourgeois. "I was born into the bourgeoisie internationale," Parizeau enjoyed saying. "I was aware of the quarrel between Reynaud's mistress and Daladier's mistress in France and its influence on French national defence before knowing who was prime minister of Canada. Long before."

This worldly view was reinforced at school. He was one of the first pupils at the Collège Stanislas, a French lycée established in the 1930s. "It was a family reaction against the so-called 'classical' colleges of the period," Parizeau said later. "For the first time, one could study algebra without counting rosary beads or communion wafers. Stanislas was the first college where you could pass your baccalaureate without having all your courses taught by priests. Obviously, Stanislas was considered to be in league with the Devil, and my parents were viewed as adventurous unbelievers."

Then, Parizeau went to the École des Hautes Études Commerciales (HEC) and then to Paris. In the early 1950s, there were no scholarships for study in Europe because Duplessis disapproved. To get around this, the HEC hired promising students and paid them a salary while they were in Europe.

In Paris, Parizeau studied first with the demographer Alfred Sauvy, and then with a man who was to have a major influence on his thinking, the economist François Perroux. As a result, he came to question classical market theory, and learned that the market does not consist of pure and perfect competition, but that there are dominating effects, industries, and economic sectors; that the economy is not symmetrical, but asymmetrical.

Then he went to the London School of Economics, where he

did his doctorate under James Meade, writing his thesis on
the terms of exchange. He acquired a set of British phrases
and mannerisms that he was to keep and cultivate, from his
taste in tailoring to his English expletives like "By Jove".

"I went there mainly because my father pushed hard for me
to go," he said. "Only much later I understood why. For me it
was the discovery that life is something that can be astonish-
ingly balanced, extraordinarily open to knowledge that doesn't
necessarily lead to anything. I won't deny that I almost didn't
come back."

He did come back, to teach at the HEC and do some consulting.
Salaries had not risen since 1931, and he was paid $2,500
in 1956. In addition, he was involved in the publication of
L'Actualité économique, the review published by the HEC. It
was the second-largest economic journal in Canada after the
Canadian Journal of Economics and Political Science, but
never managed to have any impact in English Canada. There
were more subscriptions in Poland than in Ontario, and, to
Parizeau's intense frustration, the McGill University Library
would not take it, even when he offered it to them free.

In 1956, Parizeau married Alycia Poznanska, a Polish writer
who had come to Canada because she wanted to see the Arctic.
A vibrant person, she became a journalist and a novelist; when
Parizeau's reputation made her work as a journalist difficult,
she specialized in criminology and youth protection.

Not long after his marriage, Parizeau went to Ottawa and
became a researcher for the Bank of Canada and the Porter
Royal Commission on the banking and financial system. But
after the 1960 election, he returned to the HEC. In 1961, he got
a phone call on a Sunday from René Lévesque, asking him if
the private electricity companies could be nationalized.

"I don't know, I would have to see the file," Parizeau said.

"Look," Lévesque replied, "I live three or four streets away—
come on by and I'll show you the file. I have it at home."

So Parizeau dropped by, and Lévesque dropped a huge pile of
papers on the table, saying, "There's the file."

Startled, Parizeau said, "How much time do I have to look at
it?"

"Take the time that you want," Lévesque replied.

"What does that mean?"

"Oh, four or five days."

That conversation began Parizeau's career as a government

consultant and adviser. He concluded that Quebec could acquire the companies for $600 million. Armed with this, Lévesque made his pitch at Lac-à-l'Épaule in 1962.

Parizeau worked on the nationalization after the 1962 election with Douglas Fullerton and Michel Bélanger, and then advised the Ministry of Youth on the financing of school boards, the Parent Commission on education, the Ministry of Finance on the first issue of Quebec savings bonds, and the Conseil d'Orientation Économique on the creation of the Caisse de Dépôt.

However, he lost favour with Lesage when he attacked the bond syndicates: the system under which the Quebec government always used the same banks and brokerage houses to sell their bonds and securities. But that changed when Eric Kierans, the former president of the Montreal Stock Exchange, joined the Lesage government as revenue minister after a by-election in September 1963. Kierans made the same case and saw that the syndicate was widened; Lesage relented, and Parizeau began to be called upon more and more.

When he found himself working in Quebec City five days a week, Lesage urged him to come to work full-time. So in 1965, Parizeau went to work in Lesage's office as an economic adviser and trouble-shooter—spending a day at Finance, a day at Education, a day with Lévesque, a day with the Comité d'Orientations Économiques.

He was part of the key group that provided the ideas to the Quiet Revolution. It would meet at the Comité d'Orientations Économiques and then lunch at the Georges V restaurant in the basement of the Château Laurier hotel on the Grande Allée. There, plans would be kicked around a table; if an idea took shape and needed clearance, someone would walk across the street to the legislature building to see Lévesque or Gérin-Lajoie. It was an era when all brainwaves seemed possible, when there seemed to be no limits to what could be achieved. "For all intents and purposes, the Quiet Revolution consisted of three or four ministers, twenty civil servants and consultants —and fifty chansonniers," Parizeau said with a chuckle.

When Parizeau came to work in Quebec, he already had a clearly defined nationalist position that saw a much larger role for Quebec than fitted easily into federalist assumptions. He already saw an economic shift provoked by post-war prosperity and the explosion of demands for social services, education, urban transport, housing, and city planning: all areas in provincial jurisdiction.

By 1964, Parizeau felt the result would be either the imposition of economic policies on the weaker governments by the stronger governments, or a half-baked compromise between divergent economic approaches developed by different provinces. In addition, he thought that Quebec policy must inevitably lean to the left, because of the lack of French Canadians in the private sector.

In June 1964, Parizeau presented these arguments at a conference in Charlottetown. He suggested that provinces must be involved in commercial policy, and that the board of the Bank of Canada might be composed of appointees of the federal government and the provinces: an idea that would emerge three years later in Lévesque's proposal for sovereignty-association. Some of his listeners saw the implications immediately. Marc Lalonde, then at the Université de Montréal, felt that Parizeau's nationalism could "swing just as well to the right as to the left". Scott Gordon, an economist at Carleton, found Parizeau's paper "very disturbing but . . . very skilful" and pointed out that it implied "a nation whose degree of cohesion would be considerably below, say, that of the European Economic Community as a political community". He shrewdly observed that Parizeau's position was "a stump from which an agile cat can jump in many directions".

Prescient words. Jacques Parizeau was nothing if not an agile cat.

In those years as an economic adviser, Parizeau became identified with two major accomplishments which made an indelible mark on the Quebec state: the creation of the Caisse de Dépôt, the Quebec pension fund, and the creation of the Common Front of public-sector unions. One would be a crucial economic instrument during his years as finance minister, the other an albatross around his neck.

When Lesage rose in the legislature to introduce the bill creating the Caisse with a speech that Parizeau had written, he was at pains to stress the independence of the Caisse from government interference, and to underline its primary role as a pension-fund administrator.

When Parizeau became finance minister, he assured the financial community that the original goals of the Caisse would be maintained. However, as the fund grew, reaching total assets of $6.5 billion by the end of 1977, it became only a matter of time before the Caisse's conservatism would be undermined, and its full potential as a tool for the government and the state would be used. The price of its virginity would become simply too high.

Already, in 1978, the government was calling on the Caisse to absorb part of its borrowing requirements to give it some manoeuvring room. The conflict between the government's needs and the Caisse's standards was to blow open in 1979-80. It was Alberta's decision to lend money from the better-known but smaller Heritage Fund at uniform rates to the provinces that sparked the conflict. Parizeau found it unacceptable that the Quebec government was being offered better rates by the Heritage Fund than by the Caisse.

For in 1979 the government was using the pension fund as a credit card when it tried to buy off the public-sector unions in a pre-referendum settlement. The refusal of the Caisse to give the government preferred rates precipitated a transformation of its approach which would reshape the role of the Quebec state in the economy.

If Parizeau could pride himself on being an author of the Caisse de Dépôt, he had less reason to boast about the paternity of the idea of centralizing negotiations with the public-sector unions. In 1966, he had been given the job, first by Lesage and then by Johnson, of rationalizing government salaries. He was appalled at what he discovered. Three weeks before a threatened public-sector strike, the government did not know how many employees it had, how much it was paying them, or how many hours a week they worked. On further investigation, Parizeau learned that the state was paying nine hundred different pay rates for teachers, and twenty-seven different pay scales for cooks. The result was a decisive move towards the most centralized collective-bargaining system in North America.

In 1970, Parizeau hoped that the Common Front would be the beginning of union involvement in government decision-making, of a new co-operative era of participation that would break down the traditional negotiating relationship. "If the experiment succeeds," he told a teachers' union conference, "it will perhaps be, socially speaking, the beginning of something profoundly revolutionary in Quebec."

The revolution he envisaged, in which the union movement

would share in government decision-making, budgetary direction, and social choices, didn't happen. Union demands remained traditional and confrontational.

In 1972, there was a violent clash with the Bourassa government, a general strike, and an emergence of Marxist rhetoric and analysis which would shape the language of labour relations for another decade.

As the 1979 negotiations approached, the union leadership denounced Parizeau as a reactionary conservative, a defender of the bourgeois state. This was an error that led them to misread his values and his bargaining offers. As a negotiator, Parizeau was motivated by both idealism and cynicism: idealism in his hopes for the Common Front, and cynicism in his desire to keep union support in the referendum. The result, in 1979, was a costly mistake: an extravagant pre-referendum Common Front settlement.

In 1968, Parizeau had been invited to give a speech at Banff on Canadian federalism. He decided that he would take the Canadian Pacific train "The Canadian", and spend the three-day trip relaxing with his wife away from the telephone, writing his speech.

"When I left Windsor Station, I was a federalist," he would recount later. "When I arrived in Banff I was a separatist."

Moving from the decentralist vision he had expressed in Charlottetown four years earlier, he concluded that the powers Quebec had won during the sixties had created a situation in which there were two national governments for Quebec, locked in conflict. "It was as if we had a piece of paper torn halfway," he said. "Either you patch it back together, or you keep on tearing."

Parizeau concluded that patching it back together—in other words, having Quebec give up the powers it had won — was unthinkable. The only alternative, he concluded, was for Quebec to have all the powers necessary to govern. Sovereignty. Independence.

He was then chairman of a government study of financial institutions, and remained politically neutral until the report was completed and published. But in 1969 he joined the Parti Québécois, and was a candidate in Crémazie in 1970.

In 1973, after the crushing election defeat, Parizeau resigned from the PQ executive. Although he had been opposed to the idea, he had been responsible for the Budget de l'An 1, took the responsibility for its failure, and quit.

Although he played little part in fighting the referendum proposal at the 1974 convention, he was never enthusiastic about the idea, arguing that the rules of the game in a parliamentary democracy meant that parliament was supreme. However, he rallied.

In the years following the 1973 defeat, he was heavily involved in the day-to-day tightrope existence of *Le Jour*, the tabloid launched with PQ support after the election. It was an elaborate financial sleight-of-hand operation: Parizeau deducted income tax from *Le Jour* employees at source — but delayed sending it on.

"For pretty long periods of time we didn't send in the money," Parizeau conceded later. "The tax people got excited until we paid, and then we didn't pay again for a while." He managed to scrape together the money to allow the paper to fold without going into bankruptcy, and there were rumours, which he refused to confirm, that he mortgaged his own house. However, several journalists were haunted with tax problems for years afterwards, some of them by the Quebec Ministry of Revenue — headed by the man who had caused them the problems in the first place.

WHEN JACQUES PARIZEAU PRODUCED HIS SLEIGHT OF HAND OF $226 million in selective sales-tax cuts on April 12, 1978, Jean Chrétien and the federal finance officials were, in the words of one federal civil servant, "stunned and shocked". And furious. Parizeau had reshaped an across-the-board sales-tax reduction into the elimination of tax in areas that would only help Quebec industry, and was now insisting on his full share of compensation. They felt they had been suckered and betrayed: humiliated and made to look foolish in the worst way.

Chrétien was a proud man; he had been mocked too often for his small-town manners, his Canadianism, and his bad French. From now on, he was determined to play tough: to by-pass the Quebec government, and send $85 to each taxpayer as an income-tax rebate.

The two governments settled into a siege on the sales-tax issue, and pressure began to increase on the federal government to hand over the money to the Quebec government. On April 30, Lévesque threatened to have the PQ participate in the federal election if the federal government didn't back down. On May 2, Trudeau promised that Quebecers would get the cash — somehow.

The Quebec federal Liberal caucus was beginning to feel the heat; only one Quebec MP favoured Chrétien's plan. Chrétien began to feel more and more isolated; colleagues would duck into doorways to avoid talking to him in the corridors. But he was determined not to budge. The issue became obscured as people leapt to the pages of *Le Devoir* to suggest compromise solutions and face-saving devices.

On May 15, Chrétien introduced his bill to send an income-tax rebate to Quebec taxpayers. On May 16, the National Assembly passed a unanimous motion urging MPs to reject Chrétien's approach. The debate dragged on, with Senator Maurice Lamontagne, Robert Bourassa, and Claude Ryan separately putting forward proposals. The respective deputy ministers met; there were long conversations and discussions — which ultimately broke down.

Finally, Parizeau cracked, and, in an astonishing throwaway remark, said, "Let them send the cheques." In August, every Quebec taxpayer received a cheque for $85. Parizeau promptly taxed it back at the first opportunity.

The whole incident acquired a mythological quality which had very little to do with the nature of the tax policy at stake; despite Parizeau's final concession and Chrétien's $85 cheques, it retained its original political significance of a "victory" for Parizeau and a "humiliating defeat" for Chrétien.

But it was a Pyrrhic victory. It made a permanent fixture of a tax cut that had been intended as a temporary incentive, thus reducing its impact as a stimulus and causing a permanent loss of revenue. It transformed Jean Chrétien from a minister willing to deal openly with Quebec into one who was determined not to. In the years ahead, a Jean Chrétien who felt he had been stabbed in the back was to prove a dangerous adversary, who had learned that he could hang tough, stick to his guns against pressure even from his own caucus, and win without being forced to compromise.

But this was not recognized at the time. The PQ and the Quebec public continued to see it as a brilliant stroke by a superb economist and tactician. The image of victory remained triumphant over reality.

PARIZEAU'S REPUTATION FOR TECHNICAL EXPERTISE WAS ENHANCED in many quarters by his April budget in 1978. After the "banker's budget" of 1977, which, in Parizeau's phrase, "whistled the end of recess", the 1978 budget was expansionary. The budgetary deficit, which had dropped in 1977 to less than $500 million, was projected at a billion dollars for 1977-8. The tax burden was shifted towards those earning more than $30,000; the first steps were taken towards a reform of municipal taxation; there was a cut in personal income tax of $313 million for 1978-9, and an estimated cut of $500 million promised for 1979—all part of what Parizeau called "the expansionary character of the government's policies".

It was a gamble: a gamble that the American economy, stalled for a year after Carter's election, would pick up steam; a gamble that the tax cuts would stimulate investment; a gamble that the business slump in 1977 after the PQ victory was a temporary phenomenon; a gamble that the increased deficit could be stimulative.

In retrospect, this was the beginning of a cycle of increased borrowing, increased deficits, and diminishing economic vitality in Quebec, as the recession hit and the economy failed to achieve the vigour that Parizeau was counting on.

At the same time, Parizeau began to shift the tax burden from low- and middle-income earners to those earning over $30,000. The result was a virulent emotional reaction that Parizeau would refer to sarcastically as "the revolt of the rich".

His response, a year later, was to challenge high-income earners to invest in Quebec stocks, and thus obtain a tax deduction. While this was a success, it did not soothe high-income earners' resentment. They never felt Parizeau understood the emotional basis to business decision-making over high taxes, and the degree to which the tax differential with Ontario was encouraging businesses and professionals to leave the province.

Parizeau did understand, but he also understood that Ontario—most often compared with Quebec—had what he considered "the most regressive tax structure in Canada: its workers pay the highest taxes, and its millionaires the lowest." He adopted a heavily ironic tone in 1980, when he reviewed the impact of the investment incentive.

"We will recall that [high taxes on those earning over $30,000] caused quite a stir," he said. "How could a social-democratic government have the gall to implement a fiscal policy that corresponds to its ideology? . . . For the poor to be less heavily taxed was all fine and dandy. But for the rich to be more heavily taxed! What a scandal!"

In addition to his classic Keynesian gamble on being able to stimulate the economy with an expansionist budget, there was another bigger gamble. The PQ had linked "good government" to the referendum, arguing that if they governed the province well they could convince the electorate they could manage a country. In the minds of the new men in power, men who were planners and intellectuals with roots in the public sector, good government was inevitably more government. In addition, in the desire to build an independent state in waiting, the PQ cabinet proved to be, in the words of one former civil servant, "terribly undisciplined". Each minister argued that his pet project was crucial to the success of the referendum. Parizeau had held the purse-strings tight the first year, but relented. Each subsequent year, he wagered that he could stimulate and expand, cajoling the system to respond. Politically he seemed omnipotent; financially, he was getting into ever deeper trouble. Like a gambler on a losing streak, he kept betting double or nothing. The result was a continuous growth in Quebec's deficit.

ELEVEN

The
Hesitation Waltz

*Delays have
dangerous ends.*
William Shakespeare

In April 1978, René Lévesque referred to "the waltzes, the hesitations, 'one step forward, one step back'", of the federal government as Pierre Trudeau hesitated over whether to call an election in 1978, or whether to extend into the legal but unusual fifth year of his mandate. But Lévesque had his own hesitation waltz to dance. He had repeatedly stated that he would not hold the referendum at the same time as a federal election; convinced that Trudeau would be defeated, he wanted to wait him out. "There could be nothing more confusing than mixing up a federal election with the discussions of the future of a people," he said in August 1978. "We don't want it to be screwed up by the mess of a federal election."

The major reforms of the first mandate had become law, and the problem of the referendum now remained. In one sense, it lay behind every piece of legislation in some form or other, because of the "good government" strategy. But, except for the referendum law, there had been no action on the national question for almost two years. Both sides were quietly preparing their positions during 1978, and little of substance was discussed or debated.

Throughout 1978, the leaders were waiting—Pierre Trudeau for the right time to call an election, Claude Ryan for the right time to run for the National Assembly, and René Lévesque for the right time to begin preparations for the referendum campaign. And by late fall the parties were growing impatient. Liberal impatience was directed at Ryan. For three months, there had been television in the National Assembly, and Liberal activists began to chafe at the fact that the leader was not on television every night. Government members seemed more telegenic, better prepared, better organized for the new rules of the game; the opposition seemed almost a generation out of step.

On the PQ side, the impatience was for the referendum question to come to the fore. But, before launching the campaign, Lévesque was determined to limit and pacify the indépendantiste elements in the party, and further define sovereignty-association as a firmly welded double objective: not simply sovereignty with a mandate to negotiate economic association, but sovereignty-association clearly defined and simultaneously achieved.

This required a careful process of adjusting and amending the PQ program, and preparing the referendum arguments. It began in the fall of 1978, with a statement that Lévesque read to the National Assembly on October 10; it was to continue through ensuing National Council meetings, the party's February statement on sovereignty-association, *D'égal à égal*, (*Between Equals*), the party convention in June 1979, and the White Paper on Sovereignty-Association in the fall of 1979. The whole laborious process reached a climax with the announcement of the referendum question in December 1979. Throughout this year, René Lévesque rode the two horses of government and party.

Although he had founded it, René Lévesque never lost his wariness of the Parti Québécois and its militants, and remained distrustful. Those who clashed with him at party meetings, usually on the left, usually veterans of the RIN, ruefully reminded each other that Lévesque had never been a party man, even when he was a Liberal. The more cynical were convinced that he distrusted any loyalty in the party that was not to him: loyalty to the party, the program, or the independence of Quebec.

Lévesque's personal goal remained the complex, ambiguous idea he had developed in 1967: political sovereignty and economic association with the rest of Canada. Much of the party and the program was indépendantiste; however, bit by bit, convention by convention, Lévesque had brought the party back, nearer to his original conception.

In 1973, the party policy was very clear: a PQ government would set to work immediately to try to achieve independence. But step by step, aided by Claude Morin's arguments, Lévesque had led the party through the process of sugaring what he saw as the pill of independence. And, in each case, he unilaterally weakened the position a little more afterwards, getting the next convention to confirm, retroactively, the new position he had taken.

First, in 1974, there was the introduction of the idea of a referendum — but only if negotiations to achieve independence reached an impasse. This became, during the 1976 campaign (as it had, in the last days of the 1973 campaign), a commitment to seek a mandate in a referendum first, and then begin negotiations. This was endorsed at the 1977 convention. Then, on October 10, 1978, René Lévesque rose in the National Assembly to announce a crucial new wrinkle in the ideology of sovereignty-association.

"We have no intention of first obtaining sovereignty and then negotiating an association," he said. "We do not want to end, but rather to radically transform, our union with the rest of Canada, so that, in the future, our relations will be based on full and complete equality."

As Claude Morin put it a few days later, "Sovereignty-association is a single word." This became known instantly as the "hyphen strategy"; it was a significant step backwards from all the previous positions the party had taken. Economic association had become a precondition for independence; thus, Quebec sovereignty would depend, not on the will of Quebec voters, but on the success of negotiations with the rest of Canada.

The October 10 statement caused considerable unhappiness inside the PQ, but the expected confrontation between Lévesque and the party at the December National Council meeting did not happen. The Montreal Centre region of the party tried unsuccessfully to get the meeting to pass a resolution making independence an absolute priority, and economic association only a desirable one. But it was no contest. Louise Harel, the president of the region, was violently attacked when she defended the existing party program; Lévesque's remarks were greeted by an absolute, reverent silence.

"Luckily, Lévesque didn't bring along his vat of Kool-Aid," quipped a Montreal activist bitterly, alluding to the Jonestown mass suicide. "They all would have drunk it!"

With her husband, construction union president Michel Bourdon, Harel was a symbol of everything Lévesque disliked and feared most about the left of the party. A thirty-two-year-old lawyer, she had first clashed with him in 1970 when she had organized the party headquarters staff into a union.

Since the PQ had taken power and she had become a regional president, National Council meetings had been marked by her soft-voiced dissent. During this meeting, Bourdon, a bulky, witty man with deceptively sleepy eyes and a wry drawl, had been strolling on the periphery, buttonholing ministers and upbraiding them on the direction that he saw the government taking, and its refusal to crack down on police harassment of striking unions.

When Louise Harel came to the December 2-3 meeting, she had taken a decision: she would run for the vice-presidency of the party. Quietly, she came up to Lévesque at the executive table, and informed him of her decision. From then on, it would be up to Lévesque to decide whether or not to try to block her candidacy.

ON JANUARY 25, 1979, JEAN-LUC PEPIN AND JOHN ROBARTS SUBMITTED the report of the Task Force on Canadian Unity to Prime Minister Trudeau. To the surprise of many, the report was positive, innovative, and substantial. Like the Laurendeau-Dunton commission, the Pepin-Robarts task force saw Canada in terms of duality, and wrote that it was crucial "to come to terms with modern Quebec".

The report said formally that Quebec should have the right to self-determination, and that the constitution should recognize Quebec's distinctiveness and the historic partnership between English- and French-speaking Canadians. It recommended that the provinces be given the right to control language policy, and urged a greater decentralization of power to the provinces in social and cultural matters, but called for a counterbalancing increase in economic integration in Canada.

But Trudeau dismissed the report on the basis of its recommendation that language policy should be left to the provinces. "They are dead wrong," he said flatly.

A few days later, on February 5, 1979, a first ministers' conference on the constitution opened in Ottawa. The federal-provincial constitutional discussions that had stopped in 1976 had begun again, in October 1978, after the federal government withdrew its 1978 constitutional bill, C-60. The conferences, while they ended in failure, can be seen in retrospect as important steps in a process that was to end, three years, two federal elections, and a referendum later, in the amendment and patriation of the British North America Act.

For the officials and strategists in the PCO, the conference had a political as well as a constitutional purpose. The federal government wanted to show flexibility, and offer Lévesque a choice between agreeing to something reasonable, and weakening his position, or refusing to agree — and weakening his position.

"In a sense, we were trying to do what Claude Morin was such an artist at doing — facing us with a no-win situation," Gordon Robertson said later. "We were trying to face Lévesque with a no-win situation."

But, strategically, the Pepin-Robarts report complicated that strategy. Going to Ottawa, Lévesque was quite concerned about the impact Pepin-Robarts would have, for it would have created a whole new ball game. But when he raised it at the governor general's reception on Sunday night, there was very little response from his provincial colleagues.

This was Trudeau's last chance in a dying mandate to achieve constitutional reform, and he was to go further in offering concessions to the provinces than he had ever gone before. Ottawa was prepared to restrict its spending power in areas of provincial jurisdiction, to grant the provinces control over family law, to make significant concessions in the question of ownership of natural resources, and to make some concessions in the area of control over fisheries. It also proposed a reform of the Senate, with half the members named by the provinces. In exchange, it wanted consent to a Charter of Rights enshrined in the constitution, and agreement on patriation of the constitution.

But Trudeau would not accept Pepin-Robarts, which had a coherent position that went further than he was prepared to go. Pepin-Robarts suggested permitting the federal government to spend in areas of provincial jurisdiction only on condition of full financial compensation for those provinces opposed; obligatory provincial consent for the use of federal declaratory powers; fewer conditions on provincial power over indirect taxation; a clear rejection of the idea of enshrining a federal Charter of Rights in the constitution; larger Quebec representation on the Supreme Court; a purely provincially appointed Senate that would play a key role in federal-provincial relations; and a regional veto for all constitutional amendments.

Pepin-Robarts had little impact; the process was too far along for a new approach to be taken into account, and not far enough along to succeed. The provinces (except for Quebec) had no co-ordinated approach; the premiers responded suspiciously to Trudeau's package, convinced that if they accepted it they would simply be helping his chances for re-election, and if they didn't, they would get more from Joe Clark.

The premiers could sense Trudeau's weakness and fatigue; they were not prepared to budge when they felt they could win substantially more by waiting.

During the conference, Trudeau complained that he had "given away the shop" in his attempt to make a deal. Almost three years later, on December 5, 1981, when he did reach an agreement with all the provinces but Quebec, he would literally laugh aloud at how little he had conceded in comparison with what he had been prepared to concede in 1979.

"Trudeau has never, before or since, been so forthcoming," Gordon Robertson said later. "We were reaching just as far as we could reach. I knew perfectly well the PM was quite uneasy about some of it."

Near the end of his mandate and low in the polls, Trudeau was too weak to win a deal; when he returned, almost exactly a year later, he would be too strong to need the offer he made then.

Lévesque called the progress at the conference "microscopic", which suited him perfectly. Provincial distrust of Trudeau had enabled him to avoid the federal no-win scenario, and he was able to point to Pepin-Robarts without actually having to endorse it.

RENÉ LÉVESQUE HAS ALWAYS BEEN NOTORIOUS FOR DISLIKING protocol. The February visit of the French prime minister, Raymond Barre, gave him another reason; it was the first in a series of embarrassments for him.

His first gaffe was at the state banquet for Barre at the Musée du Québec on Sunday night, February 11. He rose to give the toast and, slightly giggly, rambled on for sixteen minutes as the embarrassed guests listened. It was an extraordinary performance, in which he made jibes at Trudeau and Bourassa, and even a lame joke at Barre's expense.

It was stunning in its gaucheness and awkwardness. Reporters who were listening to the speech over a loudspeaker at a nearby hotel could hardly believe it. Lévesque's aides argued that there had been distortion in the sound transmission, that Lévesque had made some good-humoured jokes and the reporters should not misinterpret them.

Protocol remained correct on Monday, as a reciprocal treaty for social services was signed, and Barre spoke to the National Assembly, stressing that France would continue its policy of non-interference and non-indifference (Giscard d'Estaing's adroit formula for France-Quebec relations).

But Tuesday was a diplomatic disaster. On a balcony at Place Desjardins in downtown Montreal, Lévesque made an incredibly crude attempt to pressure Barre into repeating the de Gaulle line, "Vive le Québec libre." Pointing out that they were on a balcony, he handed Barre the microphone.

Twice, Barre did not take the hint; twice Lévesque whispered to him. Finally, Barre said, "Mr. Lévesque, who always makes suggestions, asks me whether, from this balcony, I would not want to cry Vive something. Well, then, I ask you to cry with me. Vive les Français du Québec."

That was not what Lévesque had in mind; he made wiping-out gestures with his hands, making it clear that he didn't want the crowd to shout. There were a few boos.

The departure scene crowned the ill-fated visit, making the federal-provincial arm-wrestling obvious. Ottawa insisted on presiding over the departure ceremonies, and Lévesque became a simple member of the "Canadian delegation" at Mirabel Airport. Furious, he made no attempt to hide his rage, standing with a cigarette behind his back during "La Marseillaise" and, after flicking the butt into a flowerpot, standing with his arms crossed during "O Canada".

"Poor Mr. Lévesque. He must be suffering from a persecution complex," said Marc Lalonde, the federal minister responsible for federal-provincial relations, who had presided over Barre's rather embarrassed departure. "It might be desirable that he go for a rest cure and treatment."

In France, the diplomatic stumbles made little impact; the press was largely won over to Lévesque's cause. The press congratulated Barre for adroitly picking his way between the two governments. As *Le Nouvel Observateur* put it in its cover story, "The French prime minister succeeded in not making too many gaffes between Ottawa and Quebec. And the francophones pursue their quiet advance towards independence."

On March 26, 1979, Pierre Trudeau called the long-awaited election for May 22. This was the day after the weekend scheduled for the PQ convention, and party organizers were worried that Trudeau would be able to use it, as he had used the St. Jean Baptiste riot in 1968, to his electoral advantage. "We had a choice," quipped an organizer. "We could have got the whole convention to stand and sing 'O Canada' waving red maple-leaf flags, or we could change the date. We changed the date."

It soon became clear that it was an uphill struggle for Trudeau, and that the election was Clark's to lose. Realizing this, Clark avoided major centres, hopping from one small town to another across Canada, visible, as much as possible, only on the TV news.

ON THURSDAY, APRIL 12, LÉVESQUE GOT MARRIED. IT TOOK PEOPLE BY surprise; his relationship with Corinne Côté had become public knowledge with the accident in February 1977, but it was discreet.

They had met in 1968, at an Italian restaurant in Quebec, after an MSA meeting. Lévesque had been married for over twenty years, but he had a notorious eye for women; as one associate said later, "It was *un titre d'honneur* to have said 'no' to Lévesque."

Corinne Côté was then twenty-four, and stunningly attractive, with high cheekbones and dark hair. Born and raised in Alma, near Chicoutimi, she was the youngest of six, with one sister and four brothers. Her father, Roméo Côté, worked for Price Paper for thirty-eight years. A fervent Union Nationale supporter, he had lived through a period when it was impossible to become even a foreman without speaking English, even in Alma. It was something Corinne, who did not speak English, never forgot.

She had an independent streak, and after teaching school in Alma for a few years, between 1962 and 1966, she moved to Quebec to get a degree. Then she met Lévesque. Shortly afterwards, she went to work in his office at the National Assembly and, after his defeat in 1970, moved to Montreal. In the spring of 1970, Lévesque left his wife; his election defeat in April meant the end of three nights a week in Quebec City, and exposed the difference that had grown between them. In the fall of 1970, during the October Crisis, he moved in with Corinne in an apartment on avenue des Pins.

The wedding was a quiet civil ceremony at the Palais de Justice. Claude Ryan was appalled: the premier was getting married on Maundy Thursday, the day before Good Friday. He felt it was an insult to the religious traditions of Quebec, and proof that Lévesque was basically tasteless.

The Lévesques flew to France for their honeymoon; in Paris they stayed at Quebec House. There, they were faced with an embarrassment. While they were still there, *Le Devoir* revealed that the Quebec delegate-general in Paris, Jean Deschamps, would be replaced by an old friend of Lévesque's, Yves Michaud.

THROUGHOUT APRIL, CLAUDE RYAN WAS CRISSCROSSING THE SPRAWLing riding of Argenteuil, campaigning. He went at it with the same dogged determination with which he had tackled the leadership, visiting old-age homes, city halls, and Liberal loyalists at home in all the little villages in the valleys that twisted up from the flat plain of the Ottawa River valley, west of Mirabel Airport.

It had not been an easy year for Claude Ryan. Largely invisible to the public, he had maintained an exhausting pace, trying to rebuild the party to the image of the enlightened voluntarism that he was trying to achieve. In September, he was saddled with a phrase that never passed his lips when he talked about his faith in response to a question by Roy Bonisteel, who asked if he felt he was guided by "the hand of God". The phrase immediately became part of Quebec's political language.

Later that fall, with television in the National Assembly, pressure began to mount on Ryan to get a seat. "People don't know what they're supposed to be doing in the Assembly because he hasn't told us where he stands on the legislation we're dealing with," one Liberal MNA complained. "We go in front of the camera and we look terrible. This must be the only place where they've brought TV into the House, and it's benefiting the government."

The bitterness was increased by Ryan's failure to observe some of the hypocrisies of political etiquette: he did not attend the funeral of Raymond Garneau's mother in early December; in the close, sentimental world of Quebec City Liberal politics, Garneau's friends were outraged.

A more pressing problem was the fact that no sitting member wanted to give up his seat to make room for the leader. It was not until mid-December that, under considerable pressure, Dr. Zoël Saindon, a Lachute physician and MNA for Argenteuil since 1966, resigned to make way for Ryan. Five days later, Raymond Garneau resigned his Quebec City seat of Jean-Talon.

The April 30 by-election in Argenteuil was obviously a crucial step for Ryan in consolidating his leadership and preparing for the referendum and the subsequent election. But Jean-Talon was an almost equally important test for the government: a kind of showcase for the "good government" strategy. The PQ candidate was Louise Beaudoin, then thirty-three, who had lost to Garneau by only two thousand votes in 1976, and had worked as Claude Morin's executive assistant. The daughter of a judge, she had grown up and gone to school in the riding: she was bright, attractive, and articulate.

She had had particular responsibilities for Quebec-France relations — and had largely been responsible for cultivating the French so that the fall-out from the embarrassments of the Barre visit was minimal. Direct, forceful—but with a reputation for intrigue—she was a powerful force in the government and in the party.

The government was mobilized; cabinet ministers canvassed, their limousines waiting discreetly down the block, and the emphasis was placed on the achievements of the government, with as little discussion as possible of the referendum or the goal of sovereignty-association.

Louise Beaudoin was well matched; the Liberal candidate was Jean-Claude Rivest, a Liberal aide and former adviser to Robert Bourassa. At thirty-six, Rivest was bright, witty, and shrewd — and campaigned on the PQ's style of government and the national question, making the by-election a trial run for the referendum campaign.

"There's the whole sequence," he would say. "Sovereignty, semicolon, exclamation mark, question mark, hyphen—who knows any more? They are going to run out of punctuation marks soon." Then he would zero in on a major contradiction in Parti Québécois rhetoric.

"[They] maintain, on the one hand, that Quebec is a society that is colonized, oppressed, brutalized, diminished, weakened, depressed—René Lévesque has this remarkable vocabulary . . . — and so we must get out of federalism," Rivest said. "At the same time, in the same breath, they say Quebec is terrific. We're a modern society, a developed society, a competent society, we do remarkable things, our artistic creations are wonderful, our workers are competent, our natural resources are rich, we've got a high standard of living, *on est capable, le Québec c'est faisable* . . . so we must get out of federalism. That poses a serious question about the seriousness and credibility of their option."

On April 30, Ryan won a sweeping victory with a 9,118-vote margin; more significantly, Rivest got 14,684 votes — 350 more than Garneau had — while Louise Beaudoin's vote dropped from 11,532 to 8,936. Almost 2,500 people who had voted PQ in 1976 simply didn't vote at all. For indépendantistes in the Parti Québécois, that was the most disturbing sign of all.

On May 9, Claude Ryan and Jean-Claude Rivest were sworn in as members of the National Assembly, to the applause of a gallery full of excited, expectant Liberals.

That night, in Toronto, Pierre Trudeau made one of his major campaign speeches. Over his advisers' objections, he insisted on speaking on the constitution and national unity — vowing to recall Parliament to discuss a resolution to patriate the constitution, to meet with premiers to work on a new one, and, in the case of a failure to reach an agreement, have a national referendum. "We will have a Canadian constitution, made by Canadians for Canadians, and we will do it together."

It was ironic that, in the campaign that Trudeau was bound to lose, he talked constantly about national unity and the constitution. Ten months later, in an election he was likely to win, he talked about it very little. The 1979 campaign expressed Trudeau's constitutional goals following the 1980 election. The listless crowd in Maple Leaf Gardens that spring evening had had a glimpse of the agenda for the future. But their very torpor was an indication of how little that vision captured their imagination.

On May 10, ten days after the two by-elections, Guy Bisaillon wrote down some of his worries about the attitudes he saw in the government. It was a stinging criticism, and a plea to Lévesque from the left of the party. Bisaillon saw the defeats in Jean-Talon and Argenteuil as a symptom of the malaise caused by the whole "good-government" strategy, which he said "has been shown to be false and debilitating". For the polls showed no increase in support for independence. In Bisaillon's eyes, the desire to win over the undecided voters was crippling the government. "Through fear of displeasing, we are beginning to make laws that are neither fish nor fowl, to take serpentine directions, to freeze, paralysed by the fear of disturbing possible enemies. . . . Everything has happened as if Quebecers were led by people who do not want independence."

The obsession with administration, he thought, had depoliticized the PQ, and deprived the party of a serious political debate about independence, and what it would mean. What infuriated him was Lévesque's distrust of the left wing; in his mind, it was the left that was providing the party's only intellectual vitality.

He concluded with a plea for projects that would mobilize people's idealism and imagination in the cause of independence. "One doesn't become independent to change a constitution," he wrote impatiently. "One becomes independent to be able to do things that only an autonomous collectivity can do."

Bisaillon called for a five-year plan that would give some content and meaning to independence, and a purpose to the sacrifices that would be required. "Finally," he wrote, "it is essential to give again to the party its openness of spirit, its dynamism, so that all together, each in our own way, we can guide Quebecers towards a clear and convincing YES in the referendum."

It was the voice of the progressive tradition in the PQ: idealistic, open, collectivist, often provocative, populist, and optimistic. When Bisaillon spoke to Lévesque about his paper, he said, "Wait until after the convention."

ON MAY 17, 1979, *LE JOURNAL DE MONTRÉAL* COLUMNIST NORMAND Girard broke the story that Robert Burns had decided to quit politics. It was shocking news; Burns was a symbol of the left-wing energy in the party.

But worse; once Girard had published his scoop, Frank Mackey of Canadian Press decided that the embargo was lifted on an interview that he had had earlier with Burns, in which he had predicted that the government would lose the referendum and the next election. Burns had given the interview on condition it be held until his resignation was public. Now, the interview ran on the CP wires.

It was a year almost to the day since Burns had suffered a heart attack, on May 19, 1978. He had been replaced as House leader—first on an interim basis, and then permanently—by Claude Charron. In addition to the pain and sense of mortality that the heart attack had brought, he was wounded in other ways. During the weeks that he was recuperating, Lévesque had never got in touch. He had not visited, phoned, or written a note. Despite their tensions over the years, Burns was taken aback. He was also hurt when Charron moved immediately into his seat in the National Assembly beside Lévesque, while Burns was still recuperating.

He felt Lévesque was incapable of working as part of a team, that things were sliding to the right, that there was no point in fighting on at considerable risk to his own health. It wasn't fun any more.

The story's timing could not have been much worse. It was only a few days before the federal election, and two weeks before the PQ convention, which was supposed to start the mobilization for the referendum. Even worse, it put Lévesque on the spot.

Visibly embarrassed, Lévesque confirmed in the National Assembly that he had talked to Burns, who had decided after the Argenteuil by-election that he could not continue for reasons of health. He also confirmed Burns's remark about the referendum — adding his own particular interpretation: "It is true, we would lose it, because, for two years, we had a job to do which was to be as much as possible what we had committed ourselves to try to be — that is to say, a good government," he said. ". . . We have largely, if not to say practically totally, put our political perspective for the future on the back burner."

When they began to explain "our vision of the future," he said, "I am sure that we will win the referendum."

It was a complete reversal. After saying for years that the PQ would win referendum support by providing good government, he was saying that it would lose the referendum because it had spent all its time being a good government.

There was obedient applause from the government benches, but it was clear that Burns had revealed the tension that the cautious prudence of the referendum strategy had created.

Chatting with reporters, Burns tried to play down his sense of disappointment. "Look, I am a socialist, and the Parti Québécois is not always socialist," he said. Only once was there a hint of the bitterness he felt, when he was asked if he found the experience of being in politics similar to being a union militant.

Burns, who had been chuckling and joking, was suddenly serious. "It's a lot tougher in politics," he said. "In the union movement, your friends remain your friends. Friendships are a lot more temporary in politics than in the union movement. In the union movement, I've got friends who last forever, and I have no fear of turning my back and getting knifed. It's not like that in politics."

ON MAY 22, 1979, THE MOMENT LÉVESQUE HAD BEEN WAITING FOR finally arrived. The Trudeau era seemed over at last; Joe Clark was elected prime minister of a minority Progressive Conservative government, with virtually no support in Quebec.

It was exactly the result Lévesque had wanted. He had publicly expressed his admiration for Fabien Roy, who had resigned as an independent MNA to assume the leadership of the federal Social Credit Party, and while he claimed that the PQ was remaining neutral, it was an open secret that in several ridings, PQ organizers were working for and even running as candidates for the Créditistes. It was part of what Lévesque's staff hoped could be "a bridge to the right" that would enable them to reach out to the traditional conservative nationalist constituency during the referendum campaign.

Now, for the first time, Lévesque felt that he could plan for the referendum unobstructed by Quebec's loyalties to a favourite-son prime minister. He began to focus on what he felt were the political realities in Canada: power in the hands of the English-Canadian majority, with French-speaking Quebecers in opposition.

On the weekend of June 1, 1979, the Parti Québécois held its biennial convention at Laval University. The party had to establish a consensus for the referendum, and enshrine the changes in Lévesque's October 10 statement and the February policy document, *D'égal à égal.*

This was done smoothly and easily. The party had begun to change its complexion after almost three years in power. It had many of its spiritual roots in the gritty streets of east-end Montreal. But after the election, it had been virtually decapitated: most of the executive was in the cabinet, and many of the most active and vigorous party organizers went to work for the new ministers.

Gradually, the government began to absorb the energies of the party, and Quebec City began to shape the attitudes of the party leadership. Little by little, the party began to acquire a higher civil servant's view of the world — and of Montreal.

Lévesque's opening speech to the convention was a lengthy

account of what the government had achieved, and a vigorous attack on critics in the party "who feel charged exclusively to underline the weaknesses, to underline the smallest mistakes, and even sometimes make them up if necessary". He described them as either "worriers by nature" or having "an opposition temperament". It was his answer to Guy Bisaillon and Louise Harel.

As Lévesque had hoped, any reference to the unilateral proclamation of independence was deleted from the program, and a commitment to a second "consultation" should negotiations fail after a successful first referendum was introduced. The Canadian dollar was established as the currency of an independent Quebec. A member of the executive, Pierre Harvey, joked that no-one cared whether the Queen was on the dollar or Maurice Richard.

However, the delegates refused to give Lévesque everything he wanted. Having conceded him his changes in the party program, they were determined to show some autonomy. Lévesque had supported the former PQ treasurer, Pierre Renaud, against Louise Harel for the vice-presidency. To his considerable annoyance, she won handily.

As she walked on stage to the ovation of the packed arena, she said quietly to Lévesque, "Do we kiss?" "We'll pretend," he said shortly. In his speech, he made lengthy mention of Renaud's work as treasurer, and no reference to the woman who had just defeated him.

Previously, the vice-president of the party was the chairman of the executive, and ran the national office. But the following week, the party staff was told "business as usual". Lévesque had a majority on the executive, and Philippe Bernard, the new treasurer, was elected chairman. Harel was effectively isolated; she was not even given an office at party headquarters.

Not long afterwards, Bisaillon went to see Lévesque about the recommendations in his paper. Lévesque looked surprised. "But the convention took care of all that, didn't it?" he asked.

POLITICAL ACTIVITY CONTINUED THROUGH THE SUMMER, WITH THE jockeying for by-election candidates in Prévost, to fill the seat left by the late Jean-Guy Cardinal, and in Beauce-Sud, to fill Fabien Roy's seat.

In August, Marc Lavallée, the new president of Montreal Centre, had a three-hour meeting with Lévesque to discuss

Pierre Bourgault's possible candidacy in Prévost. He came away deeply depressed, convinced that Lévesque had become isolated. Part of his worry came from the very environment of the premier's office — the fortress-like building known as the Bunker, with labyrinthine carpeted halls, soft indirect lighting, and a constant hum of air conditioning — but part came from the feeling that Lévesque was depending too much on the advice of a small group of advisers.

Some, like his chief of staff, Jean-Roch Boivin, and special advisers Yves Michaud and Yves Gauthier, were men he had known since the early days of the Quiet Revolution: men who were congenial, sardonic, and shrewd, but not of the intellectual calibre of the people he had attracted to work for him when he had first become a cabinet minister.

The younger ones, like Michel Carpentier, Claude Malette, and Martine Tremblay, were intensely loyal, very competent technicians, organizers, and strategists who had worked for Lévesque for years.

Whatever the cause, the result of the fatigue and isolation was a sense of indecision and procrastination. Lévesque was increasingly postponing decisions that did not have to be made. The referendum, the by-elections, the selection of candidates, the cabinet shuffle — each in its turn was postponed; the wording of the referendum question still remained to be tackled.

Lévesque hated cabinet shuffles. They forced uncomfortable face-to-face confrontations. But by the third week in September he had made the decision: he would drop the communications minister, Louis O'Neill, and the industry and commerce minister, Rodrigue Tremblay. O'Neill, while shocked and hurt, took the bitter news with grace.

But Tremblay was another matter. Although a competent economist, he was stubborn, arrogant, tactless, and sometimes stunningly conceited. ("I have an IQ of 172! There aren't four people in Quebec with my intelligence!") What ultimately did him in was his total inability to work with his colleagues, or to hide his contempt for their lack of training in economics. Since his nomination, he had been locked in a bitter rivalry with the minister of state for economic development, Bernard Landry, whom he accused of trying to sabotage his projects.

On Thursday, September 20, Tremblay had heard rumours of his impending departure. When he was summoned to see the premier Friday morning, he sat down with his wife to write a five-page letter of resignation. It was a mixture of self-defence, self-aggrandizement, and prescient warning.

"The situation [under the Liberals] has only got worse under the current finance minister, who has accentuated the bad in addition to going to Tokyo and to Zurich to borrow at real rates of interest of more than 20 per cent, taking into account the depreciation of the Canadian dollar against the yen and the Swiss franc," he wrote.

He ended on a flamboyant note. "I leave, wishing you well in strengthening our moral leadership and, for the good of Quebec, not contenting yourself with the flattering advice of fawning 'yes-men'. And I thank you for having given me the opportunity to write you this letter and to remind you of the words of Cyrano de Bergerac, 'to grovel to be a minister — never.' "

On Friday morning, he gave Lévesque the letter, and, brushing away Lévesque's urgings to keep it private, called a sudden press conference at which he dramatically attacked "the rumour campaign from the premier's office designed to destroy me morally, professionally, and politically."

When a minister saw Lévesque leaving the National Assembly buildings at 4 p.m. Friday afternoon, he couldn't help being struck by the relief in his face.

That night, Lévesque drove with Corinne in the limousine to Chicoutimi for a National Council meeting. The weekend provided a study in the contrasts and contradictory reflexes in Lévesque's personality and governing style.

For, despite his fatigue, he went on the road, honing and developing his referendum speech. Part of Lévesque's mastery as a politician came from his recuperative power and his ability to derive strength and energy from meeting people. At the same time, it was possible to see his frustration in dealing with his own party.

For on Saturday morning, the party faithful got a taste of his bitterness. His dislike of Louise Harel was so intense he actually bumped into someone to avoid eye contact, and in his speech, he complained petulantly about party politicking, and how he had been disturbed on his holidays by daily phone calls about the possibility of Pierre Bourgault's being a candidate.

But that night, he gave a nationalist group in Alma a deeply moving referendum speech on Quebec's social progress from the backwardness and corruption of the past, the fears, insecurities, and complexes of insecurity.

There was a similar contradiction in his governing style. On the one hand, he had done more than any other premier to encourage a structure of rational decision-making. On the other hand, he was becoming increasingly elusive and unpredictable.

Feeling the need for a smaller group than the priorities committee, a group he could be completely at ease with, he set up a kind of inner circle of people he had known for years, who would balance the different sides of his own reflexes and instincts. The result was a group that called itself the Gang of Four: Jean-Roch Boivin, Lévesque's chief of staff; Michel Carpentier, Boivin's deputy; Marc-André Bédard, the taciturn, cautious minister of justice, and Pierre Marois, the voluble, emotional minister of state for social development.

However, it was characteristic of Lévesque to short-circuit his own system. The moment he began to feel a group of that kind had begun to take on a life of its own, he would avoid it, or undermine it, or invite someone different.

He hated to feel that his own room to manoeuvre was being eaten away by meetings or committees, or jurisdictions. Thus, spontaneously, he could change his mind, change his course, drop an apparently casual remark killing a minister's pet project. "He has always been a *marmiton* [a soup-taster, or meddler]," remarked one cabinet minister ruefully.

But the speaking-tour magic, the extraordinary recuperative power, the mercurial elusiveness — none of it could mask the problems the government had to face, and the fatigue it was showing after three whirlwind years in power.

The most pressing problem in the fall of 1979 was with the public-sector negotiations with the Common Front. Over the years, they had grown to a kind of monstrous confrontation; the system which Jacques Parizeau had hoped would be the beginning of a new era of union participation in government decision-making had degenerated into a grappling of Byzantine complexity.

However, this negotiation was taking place just before the referendum debate, and the government was determined to resolve the situation as quickly as possible; it made concessions in five major areas.

It was an indication of how poisoned labour relations in the public sector had become that this caused consternation in the ranks of the union leadership. But it was also an indication of the strategic problems that the government had. For the generous concessions did little to stop the union machine, geared up and moving for a series of rotating strikes and illegal work stoppages.

"We had hoped to make labour our partner," complained Gérald Godin. "But it's been no use. The public service unions want lifelong security, they want clauses that limit their work mobility to a radius of fifty kilometres, and their appetite for money has no limit. There would be nothing left for social programs, nothing for day-care centres, nothing for home care for the aged, nothing for the handicapped." They not only wanted all that — they got it. And Godin spelled out the consequences all too clearly.

In the weeks leading up to the three by-elections in Maisonneuve, Prévost, and Beauce-Sud, there was a transit strike in Montreal and some rotating strikes in hospitals. On Sunday, November 13, on the eve of the by-elections, in the midst of the sporadic strikes, Lévesque made a television appearance to appeal to the population. It was a spur-of-the-moment thing; on Saturday night, Lisette Lapointe, Pierre Marois's press secretary, had phoned the head of TVA, the private French-language network, at home during the hockey game. He had agreed to bump a game show — and Marois persuaded Lévesque, against the wishes of his own staff, to do the show. The result, in the proprietary world of political staffs, was a virtual kidnapping of a premier from his own advisers, and a sudden, day-long rush to prepare for the half-hour solo broadcast.

Despite his mastery of the medium, Lévesque looked tense and nervous at first — and, although he hit his stride, he could not shake the fatigue. Part of his charm comes from his air of modesty; at his weakest and most vulnerable he finds his greatest political strength. Thus, he conceded his errors in the negotiations, saying, "probably the worst was an error of confidence." This was absolutely true. The government had shown it had very little idea how to negotiate, and established a pattern that would be hard to break.

The performance was not enough. On November 14, the Liberals swept all three by-elections. Lévesque's chosen candidates, Pierre Harvey and Jacques Desmarais, were defeated by Solange Chaput-Rolland and Georges Lalande; Raymond Boisvert, an industrialist in the Beauce, was defeated by Hermann Mathieu.

Before November 14, none of the seats had been Liberal; afterwards, all of them were. The hardest blow was Maisonneuve. It had been a Parti Québécois seat since 1970; it had withstood the Liberal tide of 1973, and now it was a Liberal seat. One cabinet minister was so shocked by the result that he spent the night vomiting.

A week later, to no-one's surprise or shock, a Liberal, Herbert Marx, won the by-election in D'Arcy-McGee to fill the vacancy left by Dr. Victor Goldbloom—with over ninety per cent of the vote.

Only six weeks from the end of session, when Lévesque promised the referendum question would be announced, the government seemed to be at rock bottom.

3
The
Referendum

TWELVE

The Question

"When I use a word,"
Humpty Dumpty said in a
rather scornful tone,
"it means just what I choose
it to mean — neither more
nor less."

"The question is," said
Alice, "whether you can
make words mean different
things."

"The question is," said
Humpty Dumpty, "which
is to be master — that's all."
Lewis Carroll

Even though the final question was not his, the whole refer-
endum process was firmly and inescapably identified with
one man: Claude Morin. For months, Morin had been sketch-
ing out possible questions, trying them out on people, testing
them against public-opinion polls, and preparing for the intensive discussions. Those began in earnest in the spring and
summer of 1979, when the PQ convention was over.

The process reached a climax with the cabinet meeting on
December 19, 1979, a night-long session with lawyers afterwards, and Lévesque's announcement of the question the next
day in the National Assembly. The ultimate synthesis had
been made by Lévesque, sitting in his office, while a nervous
and exhausted group of aides waited in a nearby anteroom.
But the man who was the symbol of the whole process was the
tall, fifty-year-old strategist with the carefully combed side-
burns: Claude Morin.

The étapiste. Someone who proceeds gradually, carefully, step by step. Claude Morin wore the label like a tattoo. For federalists and indépendantistes, his role as the author of the referendum idea, his background as a senior civil servant, and his air of all-knowing mystery as minister of intergovernmental affairs and master strategist in the Parti Québécois government all combined to give him a Machiavellian air of deceit. As a result, the very word étapiste had acquired a kind of pejorative connotation.

On the eve of the referendum campaign, Morin was nothing if not sensitive to the negative vibration the word created. And he resented it, all the more since he had never used it. "The origin was after the 1973 election [when the Liberals won 102 out of 110 seats]," he said. There were a number of post-election analyses, and Michel Roy of *Le Devoir* had telephoned him to talk about the election. Morin told him he felt that the PQ should proceed in a different fashion — "Instead of having an election which would involve at the same time a change of government and a change of political régime, perhaps it would be necessary to distinguish, and proceed by stages." He suggested that there should be an election to change the government first, and a popular consultation on changing the régime afterwards.

"The story appeared saying, 'Claude Morin believes we can achieve sovereignty by stages [par étapes].' It was accurate, but taken out of context. And from that moment on, it entered the language. But I never used the phrase. . . . I never meant that sovereignty would be achieved without people knowing it. I never meant that. I don't like the word 'étape'. I never used it myself. Never never. I talked about GBS — gros bon sens [common sense] — but I never never never used the word étapiste."

The litany of never-never was an indication of his unease at what was under way. For it seemed clear then that, if the referendum was a failure, he would be the scapegoat, as Parizeau had been the focus (unfairly) of resentment in the party after the failure of the Budget de l'An 1 in 1973. With a Yes vote, he would supervise the next step: negotiations with the rest of Canada. With a No vote, it seemed certain he would take the blame.

MUCH OF CLAUDE MORIN'S LIFE HAS REFLECTED THE MIXTURE OF canny strategist and stubborn, cautious conservative that his public role as negotiator and referendum strategist has dictated. For, despite his apparent sophistication, Morin remained a profoundly rooted man, uneasy away from home for more than a few days, who—except for two years in graduate school—has lived in only two houses all his life.

The son of a Montmorency doctor, he was born on May 16, 1929, in the small town a few miles east of Quebec, and, like most of the middle-class children of his generation, was educated at classical college: first Collège Saint-Grégoire in Montmorency, and then the Séminaire du Québec. From there, Morin went to Laval, where he studied economics at the École des Sciences Sociales, studying under Father Georges-Henri Lévesque, Maurice Lamontagne, Léon Dion, and Doris Lussier.

"It was Maurice Lamontagne who introduced me to economics," Morin recalled, not bothering to underline the irony of the fact that Lamontagne had launched a virulent critique of the economic assumptions of sovereignty-association.

The Laval faculty was one of the most vigorous intellectual environments of the 1950s, and Morin was part of a group of the brightest minds of the society. Fernand Dumont, Yves Martin (a former senior civil servant now head of the Université de Sherbrooke), and Michel Bélanger (now president of the Banque Nationale) were close friends. Gilles Vigneault was at Laval at the same time. It was a time of ferment.

But Morin showed a characteristic caution. Spotting a scholarship announcement for Columbia University for graduate work in social welfare, he investigated and found that if he took it there would probably be a job waiting for him at Laval when he got back. So he went to New York for two years, and got a master's degree in social welfare.

While in the United States he met Mary Lynch, a very musical Philadelphia girl who had been born in France and lived there until 1941. Within a few months they were married, and in 1956 he brought his bride back to his parents' home in Montmorency.

For several years, the couple lived in an apartment in Dr. Morin's home — an arrangement that worked well when the first two children were born. But when Mary Morin gave birth to twins in 1960, it was clear that they had to move.

By then, Laval University was about to move from the Quartier Latin — the fabled centuries-old city inside the walls — to suburban Sainte-Foy. So the young professor had a bungalow built not far away. It was the first house built in that part of the now sprawling suburb.

Since then the jobs have changed, but the preoccupations have remained strikingly similar—and every night, or as near to it as he can manage, Morin has returned along the Chemin Sainte-Foy to his wife and five children, the suburban street and the suburban bungalow, where he spent—and still spends—his free time puttering away at furniture-making and carpentry, or retreating to his book-lined study in the basement.

His stability and caution are deeply ingrained. As a minister, he carefully calculated all his expenses and debts — not in terms of the $60,000 he was making in 1980, but in terms of the $45,000 or $50,000 he would have been making if he had remained a university professor. He kept a careful schedule, and was very upset if it was suddenly thrown awry. Some see this carefully ordered stability as characteristic of Quebec City.

"There are no challenges in Quebec City — everybody has job security," observed Morin's executive assistant, Louise Beaudoin, with a wry smile. "That's why some people in the party from Montreal don't understand Claude Morin. But without him, we wouldn't have won very much."

Morin calls himself *un casanier* — a homebody — and a colleague said with a chuckle, "He's the most boring man I have ever known." (When that remark was published, he asked me whether the colleague had said "ennuyant"—which suggests "unvaried" or "monotonous" — or "ennuyeux" — which implies "irritatingly tedious". "It must have been 'ennuyant'," he said firmly.)

Not long after he moved to Sainte-Foy, Morin became a crucial part of the adventure of the Quiet Revolution. While teaching, he had been busy as a consultant, working on everything from briefs to governmental commissions to charity drives. A Liberal, he got to know a man who was to have a profound influence on him: Jean Lesage. Impressed by the young academic, Lesage hired him as an adviser in 1961. Soon, Morin was Lesage's right-hand man, writing speeches, doing research, advising on strategy. He wrote all Lesage's budget speeches.

In 1962, he travelled with Lesage throughout the election campaign that was fought on the acquisition of the private hydro-electric companies. Shortly after that election victory, Lesage asked Morin to become the first deputy minister of intergovernmental affairs or, as it was first called, federal-provincial affairs. As deputy minister, Morin acquired his reputation as a master strategist and key negotiator in the dealings with the federal government that were such a spectacular part of Quebec's emergence as a political force in the 1960s — especially those that surrounded the introduction of the Canada Pension Plan and the creation of the Quebec Régie des Rentes and the Caisse de Dépôt.

In the spring of 1966, on the night the Lesage government was defeated, Morin received a call from Ottawa at two o'clock in the morning, offering him a senior civil-service job. He had no interest in going to Ottawa, but he was thinking of leaving the civil service to return to teaching. Even as a deputy minister he had kept up one course which he half-jokingly called "unemployment insurance". However, Lesage persuaded him to stay, saying that the achievement he was proudest of was the creation of a competent civil service, and that it would be severely weakened if Morin and his senior colleagues were to leave.

Morin stayed on — and was to play an even stronger role in Daniel Johnson's struggles to win more powers for Quebec from Ottawa. When Robert Bourassa became premier in 1970, there was federal pressure on the young Liberal leader to get rid of him. But Morin was, in fact, a closer friend of the new premier than he had been of his predecessors. However, in September 1971, not long after conducting the negotiations that culminated in the rejection of the Victoria Charter, he left the government, saying that he needed time to reflect and consider. Returning to teaching, he taught at the École Nationale d'Administration Publique, and wrote *Le Pouvoir québécois* and *Le Combat québécois*, in which he argued that Quebec had lost badly on every front over a decade of federal-provincial relations. During this period, he spoke out with increasing bitterness at what he considered the weakness of the Bourassa government in dealing with Ottawa.

In May 1972, he announced he was joining the PQ. In a statement published in *Le Devoir* on May 23, he said that he had come to the conclusion that the federal system resulted, inevitably, in the dissolution of Quebec power. Describing his decision as "the result of a long and sometimes difficult evolution", he laid out the themes he was to repeat in the National Assembly in his speech in the debate on the referendum question: how he had believed in federalism, and how he had come to be disillusioned.

Morin came to the PQ with the determination that the party should win power. A year after the defeat of 1973, he prepared a working document for the national executive, published in *La Presse* on September 26, 1974. In it, he stressed his insistence on caution: "The achievement of independence cannot be instantaneous, or swift, still less abrupt." Later, the image he would use was more graphic: "You don't make a flower grow faster by pulling on the stem."

Morin had one convert: René Lévesque. However, the indépendantistes in the leadership of the party and many in the rank and file — who were suspicious of this senior civil servant's conversion on the road to Damascus — were opposed. A compromise was worked out to avoid a major split in the party: Gilbert Paquette, a member of the executive, worked out a compromise clause which proposed that the referendum be introduced as a measure to be used in case no agreement was reached on Quebec sovereignty in negotiations with Ottawa. A resolution to this effect was passed at the November 1974 party congress, but for the following year debate raged inside the party as to whether Morin's resolution had diluted its goal.

Morin's position was that "there is no question of having independence if the people don't want it." However, the Montreal Centre executive denounced Morin's position, saying that "to dissociate taking power from the necessity of having independence is to abandon the global project of changing Quebec society."

As the 1976 election campaign got under way, it was clear that Morin had won and the militants had lost. After taking power, the new government gave the referendum strategy, in effect, to Morin and, despite periodic grumblings that the étapes would stretch on to infinity, Morin set the tone, style, and approach to the referendum strategy.

ON NOVEMBER 1, 1979, THE WHITE PAPER ON SOVEREIGNTY-ASSOCIATION was tabled in the National Assembly: a booklet of 118 pages in French—*La nouvelle entente Québec-Canada*—and 109 pages in the English translation, entitled *Quebec-Canada: A New Deal. The Quebec government proposal for a new partnership between equals: sovereignty-association.*

The day was disrupted by a walk-out of 2,500 angry civil

servants, who decided to use the occasion for an embarrassing labour demonstration. Singing songs and hurling paper in the air for the TV cameras, they delayed the distribution of the document to the three hundred journalists who had gathered, and forced the cancellation of the planned closed-door press briefing, but Lévesque was able to give a full-dress press conference in the Salon Rouge, the old Legislative Council chamber. "This will have enabled you to see that there is something quite different from a police state atmosphere in Quebec," Lévesque quipped to reporters. "It seems there weren't even enough [police]."

René Lévesque had established the indivisibility of sovereignty and association a year earlier: to the cabinet at a two-day meeting in September in Montebello, and to the public with the October 10 statement. It had become party doctrine with the *D'égal à égal* statement in February and the convention in June.

Despite the amount of work that had gone into the formulation of the party policy, the White Paper was not produced easily. To begin with, everyone wanted to have a hand in its preparation — and at times it seemed as if practically everybody did. One of Lévesque's political advisers, Claude Malette, was the principal co-ordinator, but other aides, like Daniel Latouche and Evelyn Dumas, were involved at different stages; Camille Laurin, Denis Vaugeois, and Gérald Godin contributed to the historical chapters; Jacques-Yvan Morin contributed a text on constitutional law; Gilbert Paquette and Jean-Pierre Charbonneau, who had written *L'Option*, a telephone-book-sized tome on sovereignty-association in 1978, contributed drafts. Claude Morin was responsible for the chapter on the institutions of sovereignty-association.

The versions would shift and change as they were discussed at cabinet. Latouche had written a draft in May, which was rejected. Malette then submitted a preliminary draft in mid-July, a first draft in mid-August, a second in early September, and a third on September 24. It was decided that one person should rewrite the whole thing to have consistency of style — and when Pierre Maheu, a veteran indépendantiste, was killed in an automobile accident, the job went to a historian at Laval, André Vachon. However, there were final discussions over changes right up to the last minute. In October, at the composing room, above Ben's restaurant in Montreal, Malette was juggling calls from Morin, and double-checking with Lévesque.

The result was an awkward document, with the terse, didactic tone of a high-school civics text. The central part was not an appeal for liberty and independence, but a list of the Alice-in-Wonderland world of joint institutions that would be proposed as the agencies of sovereignty-association to be operated by Quebec and Canada: a community council, made up of ministers "acting on instructions from their respective governments"; a commission of experts to act as a general secretariat and "responsible for establishing technical liaison with the international bodies concerned in matters of custom and trade"; a court of justice with "exclusive jurisdiction over the interpretation and implementation of the treaty of association"; and a central monetary authority "chaired alternately by a governor named by each government; the number of seats allocated to each party on the board of directors will be proportional to the relative size of each economy."

Thus, Quebec was to be politically sovereign, with citizenship, passports, and membership in NATO, NORAD, and the United Nations—and, oddly, the White Paper added, "While developing its relations and its co-operation with francophone countries, Quebec will consider remaining a member of the British Commonwealth."

At the same time, Quebec would propose to have common currency, a customs union, free circulation of goods and people—and an elaborate system of agencies with joint Quebec-Canada representation.

Two years later, in an interview with *Barron's*, Lévesque was to dismiss the common currency casually, as an idea that had been put there for political expediency. That may be so—but it was something that he had clung to for thirteen years as a principle. As a result, he was proposing a country that would have a seat at the United Nations — but not its own money; would collect all its own taxes, but not be able to control interest rates; pass all its own laws, but be unable to control the foreign-exchange value of the dollar.

The White Paper defined sovereignty as "the power to make decisions autonomously, without being subject in law to any superior or exterior power". However, it continued, "the sovereign state may . . . agree to limit its scope or delegate part of it in certain specific fields."

Then the document proceeded to argue that negotiation was

inevitable, regardless of what English-Canadian politicians were saying, virtually suggesting that Quebecers should maintain the inevitability of negotiations as an article of faith.

"Many English-Canadian personalities, politicians, and others tell anyone who will listen that they will categorically refuse to negotiate," it said. "This is quite fair, though rather crude. We must not be taken in by it but must, on the contrary, convince ourselves that if the majority of Quebecers say YES in the Referendum, Ottawa and the rest of Canada, though they will be disappointed, will have no choice: they will negotiate."

To back this up, it quoted a survey of Canadian decision-makers carried out by researchers at York University suggesting that the process of bargaining and compromise might be more flexible than official rhetoric would suggest, and quoted remarks by David Crombie, the health and welfare minister, Pierre Trudeau, Jean-Luc Pepin, and Joe Clark — all to the effect that negotiations would have to take place if there were a Yes vote.

When the White Paper was tabled, there were a number of accusations — as there were when the question was tabled — that there was something devious and unclear about the proposal. In fact, it was almost naive in its clarity. Lévesque, with help from Claude Morin, had returned to the simplicity of *Option-Québec*, the manifesto he had written in 1967. He had fine-tuned it, and developed the arguments somewhat — but the architecture of the idea remained exactly the same.

Lévesque and Morin had been reinforced in their caution by the polls the party took constantly, every month, and by additional polls commissioned by the government. Morin had published one major poll in September 1979 which had confirmed Yvon Deschamps's 1977 joke: "Quebecers want an independent Quebec — in a strong Canada."

That poll, prepared by the Centre de Recherches sur l'Opinion Publique (CROP) and supervised by the Université de Montréal political scientist Édouard Cloutier, revealed all the ambiguity that surrounded public desires — and the confusion that still shrouded the concept of sovereignty-association.

Of those polled, 54 per cent said that they would vote to give the government a mandate to negotiate sovereignty-association. But when they were asked if they would vote to have Quebec become "a distinct country", the proportion voting Yes dropped to 41.3 per cent.

A clear majority said that they wanted Quebec to have more powers than other provinces in the field of culture (57 per cent) and economics (50 per cent)—but only 37 per cent wanted it to have more powers than other provinces in international affairs.

The understanding of sovereignty-association was clearly limited: 46 per cent thought it meant that Quebec would not be a country "distinct from Canada"; the same proportion thought that it would not mean a Quebec army; 31 per cent thought that Quebec would continue to elect federal MPs; and 29 per cent thought it would mean a separate Quebec currency.

Fully 73 per cent of those polled said that they didn't want Quebec to become a country distinct from Canada, and 66 per cent said that there were more advantages than disadvantages in being part of Canada.

The poll — like several of the polls before it — established a very coherent position. A strong majority wanted Quebec to have more powers, and looked to the Quebec government as their principal government — but did not want an independent Quebec. To the extent that they felt that the referendum and the ensuing negotiations would give Quebec more power inside Confederation, they were prepared to vote Yes; to the extent that they thought that it would result in an independent Quebec without an organic political link with the rest of Canada, they were not.

As the Laval political scientist Vincent Lemieux summarized the findings, "The collective opinions expressed in the poll are coherent if one assumes that a majority of Quebecers hold to the following four political principles:

"1. Two governments are better than one, even if the Quebec government is more valued than the Canadian government;

"2. These two governments ought to succeed in negotiating a new constitutional structure that would be federal in nature, but with more powers for Quebec;

"3. To achieve that, it is a good thing to give the Quebec government its chance to go and negotiate with Ottawa from its starting position: sovereignty-association;

"4. However, it is essential that this be only an opening position which would allow the achievement of a new federal system."

IN QUESTION PERIOD, AFTER THE TABLING OF THE WHITE PAPER, THE Liberal House leader, Gérard-D. Lévesque, asked the premier if he agreed with Louis O'Neill—who had been dropped from the cabinet by Lévesque six weeks earlier — that sovereignty-association meant the same thing as independence.

In the visitors' gallery, O'Neill's wife tensed. A long-time indépendantiste, she was afraid that the White Paper would water down the party program. But to her surprise, and enormous relief, Lévesque said — with the inevitable qualification that this is an interdependent world and the policy called for economic association with the rest of Canada — "The answer is yes."

The general relief in the PQ caucus was palpable; the referendum was one large step closer. As Lévesque gave a press conference, surrounded by his cabinet, the backbenchers who stayed in the Assembly autographed each other's copies of the document like students at graduation.

Later, as the ministers went off to an upstairs room at Le Continental, a restaurant in Old Quebec, for a celebratory drink, O'Neill and his wife ended up at the Aquarium, the traditional late-night restaurant down the hill from the Château Frontenac, where reporters and politicians usually head after moments of political excitement—Michèle O'Neill joking that they were celebrating the fact that the Parti Québécois had become indépendantiste.

But the initial reactions to the White Paper were, while predictable, less than graceful. The four Western premiers, understandably, issued a statement on November 7 saying that they would not negotiate sovereignty-association. Unfortunately, they gave little indication they had actually read the document.

The Ontario premier, William Davis, went further, calling the White Paper a reflection of "a self-imposed ghetto mentality surely beneath the dignity of the French-Canadian people" and saying that sovereignty-association "would be the ultimate denial of the inner strength, cultural depth, and vigour of a civilization which has withstood many threats to its ultimate survival through strength of character and conviction." Coming from a man who had consistently resisted official bilingualism for Ontario, the speech was pompous and appallingly condescending.

Nobody looked good that week. René Lévesque looked cheap and shoddy when he told the National Assembly on November 12 that the Western premiers were acting like a band of terrorists, when they were only repeating what they'd been saying publicly for the previous three years. (Although Lougheed had told Lévesque and Morin privately at the premiers' conference at Pointe-au-Pic in August 1979 that "When the negotiations get going, we want to be there.")

Claude Ryan looked slippery when he tried to wriggle out of Lévesque's accusation that he had lied when he said in English that the White Paper meant that the government would proceed immediately to establish a sovereign state if it won the referendum.

The only public figures who looked calm and rational were Prime Minister Joe Clark and his federal-provincial relations minister, Bill Jarvis. Ever since, after meeting Claude Ryan on October 6, Clark had said that since he was not a resident of Quebec he "naturally" would not be participating in a provincial referendum campaign, some observers began to wonder if he wasn't being too calm.

ALTHOUGH THE REFERENDUM HAD BEEN IN THE WORKS FOR YEARS, the actual question itself had never been worked out. In the summer of 1978, Claude Morin had worked out a piece of draft legislation which would have redesigned the division of powers as laid out in the British North America Act, and divided them up according to the principles of sovereignty-association. Then, the question on the referendum would have been something along the lines of "Do you endorse Bill So-and-so?"

However, this idea was never pursued—and one reason was the consistent findings of the polls, which were beginning to make a distinction between support for sovereignty-association (whether understood or not) and support for *a mandate to negotiate* sovereignty-association. In other words, for sovereignty-association as a bargaining position rather than as an object in itself.

The first public poll after the PQ victory to ask about a mandate was a CROP poll conducted for *Reader's Digest* in August 1977—and it found fifty per cent support for it. After that, the idea of a mandate to negotiate became part of the floating debate.

In the spring of 1979, Daniel Latouche summarized the state of the question in a memo for Lévesque and his staff. Latouche had gone to work for Lévesque in the fall of 1978 as an adviser. Then thirty-three, he was a professor of political science in

McGill's French Canada Studies Program. Bright, funny, irre-
verent, Latouche was a former student politician (he had been
a member of the executive of the Union Générale des Étudiants
du Québec in 1965-6), and a well-known commentator. In addition to teaching, he had been an editorialist at *Montréal-Matin*
before its collapse.

Latouche was an unusual addition to Lévesque's staff in a
number of ways. He was an outsider — one of the few people to
join the staff without a strong background of loyalty to
Lévesque and the party, and one of the few well-known intellectuals to go to work on Lévesque's staff. Apart from Evelyn
Dumas, a former *Montreal Star* reporter, and the short-lived
Beverley Smith, he was also the only person to work for
Lévesque who had strong personal links to English Canada; he
was virtually unique in senior government circles in having
done his doctorate at the University of British Columbia.

Whether from impatience, personality conflict with some of
the veteran members of the staff, or incompatibility with the
intuitive, unstructured style of Lévesque's office, Latouche
was never really successful in making the transition from
independent intellectual to political adviser. He kept expecting the premier's office to function like an American football
team — with huddles, strategies, and plays; instead, it functioned like a Canadian hockey team: spontaneous, unplanned,
and improvised. Nevertheless, he was to play a key role in the
formulating of the referendum question.

In December 1978, he wrote a 133-page paper, summarizing
the situation, analysing the public-opinion polls, and suggesting a question: "Accordez-vous au gouvernement du Québec le
mandat de négocier avec le reste du Canada une nouvelle entente politique fondée sur les principes de la souveraineté-
association et l'égalité entre les deux peuples du Canada?"
("Do you give the Quebec government a mandate to negotiate
with the rest of Canada a new political agreement based on the
principles of sovereignty-association and equality between the
two peoples of Canada?")

In April 1979, he again recommended posing a referendum
question that would ask people to give the government a mandate to negotiate. He tried out a variety of formulations, concluding a little gloomily, "At the rate things are going, a Yes
victory to a question on the basic object won't happen tomorrow morning, even if we have made progress in a year. The
difference between a question on the basic object or on a man-

date seems constant over the last ten years: ten to twelve per cent more for the Yes. We need a question that brings people together, not one that divides people."

However, by the middle of December there still had been no discussion of the question at cabinet. There was a meeting of the organization of francophone co-operation in Africa in mid-December, and, after some hesitation, Claude Morin left to attend, saying that he would return to draw up a proposal for a question for the Wednesday cabinet meeting.

The next day, Thursday, December 13, in the middle of the legislative "sprint", which creates a mad rush in the National Assembly for the month of June and the month of December, the Supreme Court of Canada announced two major decisions. One declared the clauses of Bill 101 limiting the use of English in the courts and the legislature to be unconstitutional; the other made the same judgment of the Official Language Act of Manitoba, which, in 1890, had declared English to be the only official language — and which had now been challenged over a unilingual traffic ticket by a Franco-Manitoban, Georges Forest.

When Lévesque heard the opinion of Ministry of Justice officials that the decision applied to all government decisions — and not simply the 250-odd laws passed in French only by the Assembly since Bill 101, but all by-laws, regulations, and even municipal decisions since 1867 — he was furious, saying the decision "maintained, or rather re-established, the exorbitant privileges of a minority that has dominated for two centuries, and has been dangerously assimilationist".

Speaking to reporters, Lévesque snapped angrily, "English is being made not only coercive again — but of more coercive use than ever before." (Later, the officials' opinion was shown to be too hasty; the judgment applied only to provincial laws.)

That day, the cabinet quickly drew up emergency legislation to render the 250 laws operative — and the National Assembly went into an overnight debate, punctuated by speeches of bitter rage from the Parti Québécois members, who argued that after Manitoba wiped out the French language it took the courts ninety years to react, but when the Quebec government acted to protect French — with greater institutional-services guarantees for English than existed in any English-speaking province for French — the Supreme Court moved with lightning speed.

That night in Ottawa, the Clark government fell. Six votes

short on a vote of non-confidence in the Crosbie budget, with Fabien Roy's Créditistes not voting, the government was defeated. An election was inevitable.

Lévesque was visibly stunned. This was one possibility he had never taken into account. The timing of the referendum had seemed perfect — the federal election campaign of 1979 was over; Trudeau was out of office and had announced that he would shortly retire from politics. Now, there was not only another federal election, but a possibility of Trudeau's returning.

No-one was prepared. Morin was at the francophone conference in Africa; Daniel Latouche, who had been working with Morin on strategy questions, had left for his place in Magog; Lévesque and the rest of the cabinet were exhausted by the emergency legislation, which had been finally voted on at 6.38 a.m.

The next day, in Question Period, without having consulted anyone, Lévesque replied to questions from Claude Ryan and Rodrigue Biron in unequivocal terms: there would be no change in the referendum timetable — either for tabling the question at the end of the following week, or for holding the referendum in the spring.

Morin, who came rushing back from Africa, was appalled. The whole justification for delaying so long was tossed out the window. If the intention had been not to have a federal election mixed up with the referendum, that argument still applied. Lévesque had just brushed it away.

On Tuesday morning, over breakfast at the cafeteria in the "H" building, Claude Morin fumed. He hadn't been consulted on a key strategic decision, it was outrageous, and, he said, he was going to resign.

Later, waiting in Lévesque's office, a whole group of ministers and aides muttered angrily. What good was it drawing up strategy if Lévesque was going to shoot from the hip like that? Then Lévesque came in, and with an embarrassed shrug said, "I think I made a mistake, announcing that like that on Friday. I'll look silly, but, if you like, I will swallow my words and reverse myself."

"No no no," everybody said in chorus — and at least one person in the room is convinced he saw a twinkle in Lévesque's eye. "He didn't come out and say 'Ha, ha, gotcha,' or actually wink — but I am sure I saw him smile inside."

ON TUESDAY NIGHT, DECEMBER 18, CLAUDE MORIN, LOUIS BERNARD, and Daniel Latouche drew up a draft question for cabinet:

"Le gouvernement du Québec a fait connaître sa proposition de négocier avec les représentants du reste du Canada une nouvelle entente fondée sur l'égalité de droit des partenaires.

"Une telle entente permettrait au Québec d'atteindre en même temps un double objectif: acquérir la souveraineté politique et maintenir des liens étroits d'association économique et monetaire avec le reste du Canada. Les résultats des négotiations . . . seraient soumis à la population par voie de référendum."

("The Quebec government has made known its proposal to negotiate with the representatives of the rest of Canada a new agreement founded on the equality in law of the partners.

("Such an agreement would permit Quebec to achieve at the same time a double objective: to acquire political sovereignty, and maintain close economic and monetary ties with the rest of Canada. The results of the negotiations . . . would be submitted to the population through a referendum.")

On Wednesday afternoon, the cabinet began to discuss the referendum question. First, Lévesque took Morin totally by surprise by reading a quite different question — which no-one liked much. Then the whole cabinet set to work, each one with a pad and paper, suggesting changes in wording. "We were obsessed by the wording," one participant recalled ruefully later.

"I don't believe my eyes or ears," Lise Payette wrote later. "I am incapable of taking the thing seriously. We are being manipulated. We're being made fun of. Either the question is already written and so one should have only to circulate it. Or else it is true that it is not written and we look like a bunch of amateurs in the middle of writing the history of Quebec." She speculated who was in on the secret: "Difficult to say. Parizeau is too furiously trying to get his point across to be in on it. Bédard is too quiet not to be." Then she left in disgust.

Marc-André Bédard, the close-mouthed minister of justice, had become, along with Claude Charron, an increasingly trusted adviser to Lévesque, who never liked to have his hands tied by committees of advisers. The next day, kidded by reporters about the complexity of the question, Bédard knew it by heart.

Since the government was seeking a mandate to negotiate, Lévesque wanted the question to include a promise to hold a second referendum before the status of Quebec actually changed. Jacques Parizeau was opposed to the idea—but, knowing Lévesque's mood and the futility of attacking it directly, he tried to do so sideways, arguing that by promising a second referendum the government would reduce the impact of the first one. It would be better not to promise it, but just to do it, he argued.

Claude Morin felt that it was unnecessary to put the whole definition of sovereignty-association in the question, but that view did not prevail. Periodically, Lévesque would say, "How does this sound?" and read aloud a version—each one marked by his inimitable, looping sentence structure.

Finally, about midnight, when the question was reaching its final form, Denis Vaugeois—who had wondered aloud whether this was a question or a book—asked, "Is it legal?" It was a good point—for the preamble was written in affirmative statements. Was it legally a question? What, in fact, was a question in law? Would the legality be challenged by the opposition? After some discussion, the cabinet meeting broke up—and Lévesque left the problem with Jean-Roch Boivin and Daniel Latouche.

At 1 a.m., Boivin and Latouche summoned the government's top legal minds: the deputy minister of justice, René Dussault; the assistant deputy minister, Daniel Jacoby; Jules Brière; Bédard's chief of staff, Jean-Claude Scraire. Boivin left — and the discussions went on until 5 a.m., when they reached a consensus that the question was, in fact, legal, if formulated as a single sentence.

Too excited to go to bed, Latouche waited in his office for Lévesque to come in and agree on the final wording. As morning came, people gathered in his office, as if it were a hospital waiting room: members of Lévesque's staff, ministers, deputy ministers—waiting as Lévesque made his final decision. Louis Bernard, calm and relaxed, said to Latouche, "Stop being edgy — you'll have the question."

Lévesque came out with the final wording of the question, and headed across to the National Assembly to tell the caucus. Then he rose in the Assembly at 3.07 to make his announcement.

Calling the question "clear and frank and . . . stripped of all disguise" (limpide et franc et . . . dépouillé de tout déguisement) — the Liberals coughed a lot during that part — he said that there would be no change in Quebec's political status before the population had had a chance to approve the change in a referendum.

After saying that the ballots would be printed in French and in English and, where appropriate, in Amerindian languages or Inuit, he concluded: "If the National Assembly approves it during the debate expected at the resumption of the session, it will read as follows:

" 'Le Gouvernement du Québec a fait connaître sa proposition d'en arriver, avec le reste du Canada, à une nouvelle entente fondée sur le principe de l'égalité des peuples;

" 'cette entente permettrait au Québec d'acquérir le pouvoir exclusif de faire ses lois, de percevoir ses impôts et d'établir ses relations extérieures, ce qui est la souveraineté — et, en même temps, de maintenir avec le Canada une association économique comportant l'utilisation de la même monnaie;

" 'tout changement de statut politique résultant de ces négociations sera soumis à la population par référendum;

" 'EN CONSÉQUENCE, ACCORDEZ-VOUS AU GOUVERNEMENT DU QUÉBEC LE MANDAT DE NÉGOCIER L'ENTENTE PROPOSÉE ENTRE LE QUÉBEC ET LE CANADA?' "

(The Government of Quebec has made public its proposal to negotiate a new agreement with the rest of Canada, based on the equality of nations;

(this agreement would enable Quebec to acquire the exclusive power to make its laws, administer its taxes and establish relations abroad — in other words, sovereignty — and at the same time, to maintain with Canada an economic association including a common currency;

(any change in political status resulting from these negotiations will be submitted to the people through a referendum;

(ON THESE TERMS, DO YOU AGREE TO GIVE THE GOVERNMENT OF QUEBEC THE MANDATE TO NEGOTIATE THE PROPOSED AGREEMENT BETWEEN QUEBEC AND CANADA?)

As the government benches rose to give Lévesque a standing ovation, Parizeau gave a theatrical hint of dissent — waiting in his seat for what was probably only ten seconds, but seemed like hours, before rising to join in the applause.

THIRTEEN

The
Divided Elite

*No-one hates like him who
has once been a friend.*
Sam Slick (T. C. Haliburton)

One of the fascinating aspects of the referendum was the
mystery at the heart of the division that it represented. The
generation that had reached adulthood after the Depression
and World War II had been united in the 1950s by its opposition to the Duplessis régime, and united in the early 1960s in
its support of the Lesage régime.

But in the mid-1960s, that generation—which had become a
political élite — divided over the national question. Part of it
rejected nationalism and felt that the pendulum had swung
too far towards Quebec City in the federal-provincial struggle:
men like Pierre Trudeau, Jean Marchand, Gérard Pelletier,
Marc Lalonde, Pierre Juneau, Charles Lussier, Raymond and
Albert Breton, Maurice Pinard (all of whom had written for
Cité libre); the key event in the formation of this group was
the decision by Marchand, Pelletier, and Trudeau to join the
Liberal Party and be candidates for the House of Commons
in 1965.

The other group, whose nationalism developed into a hope of
sovereign status for Quebec, included René Lévesque, Camille
Laurin, Jacques Parizeau, Jacques-Yvan Morin, Doris Lussier,
Pierre Perreault, Marc Brière, Denis Lazure, Fernand Dumont,
Marcel Rioux, Pierre Vadeboncoeur. Their key event was
Lévesque's departure from the Liberal Party and the creation
of the Mouvement Souveraineté-Association.

In the middle and late 1960s, there were still many who tried
to maintain a middle course between the two: criticizing
Trudeau's federalism, which they found too rigid, and rejecting separatism. Instead, they opted for some form of special

status for Quebec: Claude Ryan, Léon Dion, Paul Gérin-Lajoie, Claude Morin, Robert Bourassa, Claude Castonguay, Solange Chaput-Rolland, Michel Bélanger. However, the referendum forced them to choose sides, to opt for one group or the other.

What was it that pushed an individual into one group or another? What combination of interests, reflexes, background, class, or psychology? Why did one opt for a sovereign Quebec, and another — a colleague, a friend, even a brother or sister — choose a Quebec that was part of Canada?

Pierre Dansereau suggests that the optimists were sovereignists, and the pessimists federalists. As a young man, he broke with a nationalist group because he felt an independent Quebec could not survive. Over forty years later, he felt he had become more optimistic and accepted what he rejected then.

In contrast, the sociologist Guy Rocher thinks the reverse: the optimists, who feel that French Canada can survive in a federal Canada, are federalists; the pessimists feel that French Canada is doomed without the powers of a national state, and are sovereignists.

There remains no clear answer that is not vulnerable to immediate contradiction — for the élite is too interwoven, the friendships are too close, the common values and instincts too numerous to allow any simple explanation.

One factor is humiliation. Many of those who became major figures in the Parti Québécois had had, in some way or another, a personally wounding contact with English Canada; an experience that had ultimately broken their confidence in the good faith of the English-speaking majority. But this explanation is insufficient — if only because it was an experience suffered by federalist Quebecers who, despite all the language legislation, found it no easier to be served in French in Ottawa in the 1970s than it had been in Montreal in the 1950s; who found a quiet resentment of bilingualism, and an inability on the part of most English Canadians to converse with them in French with the same ease as they had in English. In fact, the strongest residual anti-English reflex was — and is — often to be found among Quebec federalists; they were determined to make French a fully accepted Canadian language, and resented each slight much more than indépendantistes, who had given up that fight.

But the common experience and common background shaped both fragments of the political élite, and shaped the political agenda in both Quebec City and Ottawa. For if one subtracted the "national question", the ideas they had in common were much more numerous than the ideas that divided them. The two groups were united by an intellectual vigour, a reformist determination, a belief in interventionism, and both were strongly committed to the survival and growth of French Canada. It was the means to those ends that divided them.

Each group had, in effect, taken over or created a political party, and had then captured a government. From their different vantage points, they were seeking the allegiance of Quebec society as a whole. The referendum was their battleground. But in many ways, it only highlighted their interwoven pasts.

In an interview before the referendum began, the seventy-seven-year-old Father Georges-Henri Lévesque, who had profoundly influenced so many of the leading figures on both sides, was asked if the division bothered him. "No," he said with a grin. "On the contrary, I am happy. I am happy because each one is carrying his own stone. And what is going to happen? I don't know. Each one has to work for his own position."

IN HIS 1979 BOOK *LA NOUVELLE CLASSE ET L'AVENIR DU QUÉBEC*, Jacques Grand'maison described the "new class" as "the graduates of the Quiet Revolution and its enormous bureaucratization": "They massively entered the public sector without a lot of competition. They quickly acquired job security with relatively easy possibilities of advancement. Unionized in the higher grades, they won a very advanced system of conditions and advantages, often disproportionately to their counterparts in the private sector. As professionals, they were able to establish a prosperous group status thanks to the thousand and one regulations of the bureaucratic state, thanks to the public resources to which the private practice of yesteryear had little access. As managers, they benefited from union victories in money and security; they did not suffer from the individual sanctions of the private sector; they were not publicly accountable for their management or their expenses."

Graduating from university in the late fifties and sixties, they were part of the demographic boom that the Quiet Revolution had been designed for. Over twenty years, they had built a state; a state-in-waiting, with more ministries and administrative tools than were necessary to manage a province, on the assumption that they would be needed when Quebec acquired more powers.

That expanded state — described by a group of academics as *L'État du Québec en devenir* — shaped and developed the assumptions and expectations of the generation that it employed and nurtured. Necessarily, that expanded state became an instrument and an environment for the protection and development of the French language.

All these factors combined to ensure support for the Yes option among the New Class of public-sector employees, and those whose livelihood depended upon the use of French: intellectuals, teachers, artists, journalists, broadcasters.

In their poll on the referendum, Maurice Pinard and Richard Hamilton found that among francophones the highest support for the Yes option — 67 per cent — was among intellectuals, whom they defined as "creators and diffusers of culture, . . . teachers, academics, scientists, artists, authors, journalists, etc." Of these, 47 per cent were souverainistes.

However, this group's solid support for the government was known and virtually taken for granted; to win the mandate it was seeking, the government had to reach out to those whose support could not be counted on: the aged, women, those in the private sector, those in small business.

Ironically, the government's option — which necessarily involved some risk — had greatest appeal to those who lived in the risk-free environment of job security and tenure in the public sector and the universities. Those whose lives were more intimately and daily involved in taking risks — in the marketplace, or simply in the uncertainties of living on a fixed income — were least inclined to endorse what seemed like an adventurous step into the unknown.

Lévesque and the referendum strategists were well aware of this. As a result, they tried to emphasize initiatives and innovations in the private sector, and the new entrepreneurial zeal to be found in Quebec.

For there was a growing enthusiasm for the private sector. Growth had virtually stopped in the public sector, and jobs had dried up; the francization of large companies in Montreal had created a new demand for francophone managers; there seemed to be a new vigour in the regional economies in areas like the Beauce and Lac-Saint-Jean; the phrase "le miracle de la Beauce" was becoming a political cliché, but there were more jobs being created in small businesses outside Montreal than there were in Montreal.

This new energy had been developing for several years. Fully one-third of the business-school students in Canada were in Quebec; in 1978, ninety per cent of the graduates of l'École des Hautes Études Commerciales at the Université de Montréal found jobs, and the other ten per cent were pursuing further studies. That year, the HEC had to turn away 1,150 applicants. A year later, the figure rose to 2,000.

One of the driving forces behind this phenomenon was, ironically, Camille Laurin's younger brother, Pierre Laurin, the dean of the HEC. Inspired himself by Laurent Picard, the former president of the CBC who was head of the school of business at McGill, Laurin was engaged in a double promotion campaign: selling business education to francophone students, and selling his graduates to employers. He was succeeding at both.

As traditional English business seemed to be moving out of Montreal, it looked as if there were dynamic regional entrepreneurs who were gathering the energy and the capital to fill the gap they had left. Thus, in 1979, a Lac-Saint-Jean trucking-company owner named Alfred Hamel bought Québecair, the regional airline, and had plans to acquire Nordair. In the same region, there was a financial investment network known as the Caisses d'Entr'aide Économique, which was growing fast.

Lévesque began to refer to this regional dynamism in his speeches; they became as much a part of his referendum speech as Hydro-Québec, as he talked about the inventive, fix-it tradition in Quebec. Thus, in his letter at the end of the White Paper, he wrote of those who had made fun of "Desjardins and the pioneers of the co-operative movement; that didn't stop them from growing to their present size. As more recently they made fun of those Caisses d'Entr'aide, whose daring is now as proverbial as their growth."

It was a rhetorical attempt, expressed in the government's economic document *Bâtir le Québec* (Building Quebec) and repeated throughout the referendum campaign, to reach out to Quebecers outside the public sector, and to expand beyond the appeal of the Parti Québécois to a broader base that would include the more conservative, the more entrepreneurial, the more traditional — and, at the same time, the generation that was moving to the private sector and away from the traditional mainstay jobs of the generation of the Quiet Revolution.

ONE MAN WHO SEEMED A KIND OF SYMBOL OF THE NEW TRANSITION of focus from the public to the private sector was a man who had been a key Quebec civil servant throughout the 1960s and the early 1970s, and was now one of the most visible francophones in the financial community. It was possible to think that, regardless of the result, Michel Bélanger would be a key figure in the Quebec that emerged from the referendum.

In 1960, after six years in the Department of Finance in Ottawa, he had been hired by René Lévesque to work on the economics of acquiring Hydro-Québec; one of his closest collaborators was Jacques Parizeau; one of the aides in Lévesque's office was Bernard Landry; one of his close colleagues was Claude Morin. Lévesque remembers him as "a one-man think-tank", and once said that the young economist taught him everything he knew about administration; he was one of the crucial figures in the Quiet Revolution.

Bélanger was to move up and on — from the acquisition of Hydro to the development of Hamilton Falls in Labrador and the creation of the Quebec-owned steel company, SIDBEC. In 1963 he became assistant deputy minister of natural resources; in 1965, Blair Fraser observed in *Maclean's* that Bélanger was "generally regarded as the most brilliant of all the bright young men in the Lesage government's brain trust".

In 1971, he was given one of the two top jobs in government. After five years as a deputy minister, he was made secretary of the Treasury Board. A year later, he became president of the Montreal Stock Exchange: the first francophone ever to have been offered the job. At this time the MSE was still an anglophone bastion. When he left, four years later, it was a predominantly French-speaking organization.

In 1976, Léo Lavoie, the president of the Banque Provinciale, was reaching retirement age, and urgently looking for a successor. He asked Bélanger to take over his job. Bélanger accepted. Then, in May 1979, he was approached by the president of the bank's major competitor, the Banque Canadienne Nationale, who suggested a merger.

Thus, as his former colleagues were campaigning for referendum support, Bélanger was struggling to make the merger work. The struggle both symbolized and accelerated the shift of talent from the public to the private sector. Raymond Garneau, a former minister of finance, was vice-chairman of the Montreal and District Savings Bank; Pierre Goyette, former deputy minister of finance, was vice-president of finance at Consolidated Bathurst; André Saumier, former deputy minister of natural resources, was a senior investment analyst in Montreal. Bélanger himself had drawn on the senior ranks of government, hiring the former secretary of the Treasury Board, Jean-Claude Lebel; Yvon Marcoux, an assistant deputy minister; and, from Ottawa, a former minister in the Clark government, Robert de Cotret. They looked like the basis for a new, post-referendum Quiet Revolution: this one in business.

Months after the referendum, Michel Bélanger mused about the process, sitting in his office on the rue Saint-Jacques in Montreal.

"What I find tragic," he said, "is that a whole group of intelligent people have spent this crazy amount of energy for at least four years — all focused on a referendum."

He paused. "You know, there is one thing that I never managed to say at the time. If one thinks of all the energy, all the intelligence, all the creativity which was poured into that—if a tenth had been put into discussing real problems, complex, boring, difficult problems of the evolution of Quebec society, the evolution of government, all the myths that plague us . . ."

He paused again, uncharacteristically groping for the right tone to strike.

"I have hesitated to say this, because it sounds contemptuous, but if all that intelligence had been put into something concrete, dammit! Just think of what we could have done to show the rest of the world!"

FOURTEEN
The Campaign

*It is a mistake to count
with too much assurance
on the help and support of
the multitude in a perilous
enterprise.*
Machiavelli

Quebec is a society in which language, in every sense of the word, is of enormous importance. Its survival has, obviously, been welded to the survival of the French language. But, more than that, it is a more intensely oral society than most of the rest of North America. A surprising number of the most popular entertainers simply talk. They are not comedians, but monologuistes: Yvon Deschamps, Jean Lapointe, Clémence Desrochers, Sol. The artists who shaped and marked the Quiet Revolution most significantly were not just singers, but chansonniers, like Gilles Vigneault and Félix Leclerc, who sang their own poems.

It is no accident that the political leaders who dominated the referendum all had superb command of language. René Lévesque, Pierre Trudeau, Claude Ryan — all had spent their lives dealing with words. In fact, one only has to listen to the major English-speaking politicians, in Canada or in the United States, to realize what high oratorical standards are expected — and reached — in Quebec politics. This is partly because of the historical restriction of the French-Canadian élite to the professions: the Church, the law, medicine, the notariat. Moreover, they were educated in a rigorous classical-college system — an intense private, usually boarding-school education comparable to the public schools in England. Given a well-educated élite with very limited access to corporate power, politics and government, law and the universities, journalism and literature attracted almost exclusively the best energies and minds of the society.

AS 1979 ENDED AND THE REFERENDUM YEAR WAS ABOUT TO BEGIN, Claude Ryan looked as if he was in a position of unshakable strength. Since he had taken over the leadership, the Liberals had won seven successive by-elections by decisive margins, and looked strong in the polls. More importantly, the Union Nationale, whose surprise showing in 1976 had given the PQ its majority of seats, had collapsed. On the eve of the publication of his long-awaited constitutional document, Ryan looked not so much probably as inevitably the next premier of Quebec.

After two years in politics, the continuities in his life remained more important than the changes. "Today, I haven't changed since I was a journalist," he said in an interview in late December 1979, sitting in an armchair in his book-lined study at home on Saint-Joseph Boulevard. "I have the same kind of life, the same way of working. For, as I have said, when I entered politics I did so at an age when one does not change easily."

But he was not unchanged by politics. One of the fascinating things over the previous two years had been to watch the transformation of a careful, measured, at times even tediously scrupulous analyst into a non-stop flesh-pressing campaigner and a mercilessly slashing partisan. Claude Ryan had become a politician.

"The major observation I have made in politics is that you've got to say things clearly," he said. "There is no place for nuance. When I was at *Le Devoir*, I could say 'Yes, we could approve of that if this, or this, or this.' I had a lot of space, and I had a public which wanted nuance. If I did not deal in nuance, the readers of *Le Devoir* were unhappy. But in politics you can't do that—for two reasons. First of all, your adversary will grab the part that serves his purpose, take it out of context, and use it against you, jumbled and twisted. He will use the least appearance of concession to say 'Even our adversaries . . .'

"And secondly, your supporters don't tolerate any collaboration or appearance of collaboration with the enemy."

So, after spending his first year as leader getting to know the party, reorganizing and rebuilding at the level of the riding, the region, and the party headquarters, Ryan came to learn that it was no longer his job to weigh, consider, evaluate, and judge — but to attack. So he did.

He constantly attacked the referendum question as dishonest, and sovereignty-association as a disguise for separation. His denunciation of the referendum question as "a real fraud" was what he called later "a reaction that was harsher and a bit simpler than it would have been in the past".

The transition had been gradual. But at the end of six months in the Assembly and two years in politics, Ryan could rouse a crowd and provide a good thirty-second clip. He had begun to realize the importance of television in the National Assembly.

He campaigned relentlessly, as if the election had been announced. Anyone taking Air Canada Flight 532, the late flight to Quebec from Dorval on a Sunday or Monday, could catch him in action, "working the plane" — going up and down the aisles, shaking hands, or waiting for people as they came off and shaking hands.

As part of the political toughening, Ryan had developed a strong hostility for René Lévesque. But, privately, he was even more resentful of the federal Liberals. He had met with Trudeau over the summer, and urged him not to name Jean Chrétien federal-provincial relations critic, because he had no respect for him. Trudeau went right ahead. Ryan could not bring himself to support Clark, because he thought he was too weak to be prime minister — but he remembered each slight from the Trudeau Liberals. He had never forgotten Marc Lalonde's snowboots. One could sense that, if Ryan became premier, as everyone then assumed he would, federal Liberals would have to take off their boots — if not their shoes — when they entered his office.

ON WEDNESDAY, FEBRUARY 27, ABOUT 5 P.M., ALL THE MINISTERIAL staffs gathered in a large room at the civil servants' recreation centre for referendum-strategy briefing. There were some 150 aides present.

Things were looking up. Lévesque and his advisers had now reconciled themselves to the idea that Trudeau would be re-elected, and decided that this would, after all, be better for the PQ. Clark was too vague, and hard to attack; it was like punching a pillow.

Better still, Claude Ryan seemed to be losing his air of invincibility. He had published his constitutional document, the Beige Paper, on January 9 — earlier than planned because of an embarrassing leak — and his decentralist vision had received only lukewarm support in English Canada. Suddenly, the PQ had a target; it was immediately dubbed the "drab paper", and attacked constantly.

Claude Charron began the meeting by telling the roomful of political advisers that during the debate on the referendum question ministers must be constantly present in the Assembly, their speeches had to be carefully prepared and timed to the minute, and "preferably remarkable"; each minister would receive an indication of the topic he should focus on. Nothing was to be left to chance; this was to be a crucial debate.

There would be several themes: arguments for the economic advantages of sovereignty-association, a sustained critique of federalism, a historical statement (what Charron jocularly called "le trip SSJB" — or the Société Saint-Jean-Baptiste trip) — and an appeal for solidarity. But the most important, he said, was the economic argument. "We have to take the bull by the horns, and talk about the Quebec potential that is wasted in federalism," he said, adding that this was the other side of the coin of what he called "the Liberals and the fear of freezing" — referring to Liberal arguments about energy supply.

Then Michel Carpentier spoke. "We have to make the referendum debate non-partisan," he said; the Comité National du Oui would be non-Péquiste as much as possible. However, the campaign committee would be restricted to people with election-campaign experience.

But the first step in the process was the televised debate in the National Assembly. The Parti Québécois members had responded to Charron's demands, and had prepared scrupulously for what they considered the most important speech in their lives. Men who had not written or researched a speech in years painstakingly practised delivering them to their wives in basement rec rooms to get the timing and delivery perfect. During Question Period on March 4, Lévesque went through his own speech, scribbling changes, mouthing the phrases to judge the effect, altering and improving to the last minute.

Charron, as House leader, coached, co-ordinated, and marshalled the speakers, controlling the flow of debate and stressing first one theme and then another. As PQ members spoke, Lévesque would slip out of his seat to be out of camera range, so as not to be a distraction; Charron would pace the floor, just outside the camera's vision, looking for all the world like a hockey coach or a TV floor director, greeting members coming into the Assembly before their speeches with a slap on the shoulder or a hug, watching the delivery carefully, and flashing his fingers in a countdown to show how much of the allotted time remained. As each speaker finished, the members would gather around him, applauding and shaking his hand. Posed, planned — but effective.

The Liberals, on the other hand, looked as if they had only started thinking about the debate the day before it started. Until then, they had been preoccupied with the Beige Paper, which was discussed at a two-day policy convention that ended the day before the debate began. Assuming that the debate would keep to the wording of the question, their single strategy was to attack it as dishonest. There had been no thought about the impact of television, and they were unprepared for the PQ's addressing the broad questions of the flaws of federalism and the arguments for sovereignty-association. Soon the Liberal accusations of dishonesty sounded carping and repetitive. And, in contrast with Lévesque, Ryan seemed totally unconscious of the camera—staying at his desk throughout, and, more than once, unconsciously stealing the scene from a colleague by yawning and scratching.

The television impact seemed to be enormous. Sewing classes broke up early so that people could be home in time to watch. Taverns turned the dial to the evening coverage. Some people adjusted their factory shifts so as to see it.

What they saw was the marshalling and presentation of the case for sovereignty-association — with all the arguments that each PQ MNA had been developing over the years — and a constant, but often sloppy, Liberal attack on the question as a dishonest trick to obtain a mandate for separation. Only sporadically did the Liberals muster effective replies. All observers, federalists and indépéndantistes alike, concluded that the Parti Québécois had won the debate decisively.

ON MARCH 5, THE NEW TRUDEAU CABINET WAS SWORN IN, AND JEAN Chrétien became minister of justice and minister responsible for federal-provincial relations. That day, he was shown a Decima poll commissioned by the Clark government, which showed a very slim victory for the No side. After some hesitation, he decided to show the results to Ryan. In addition, he was given an advance look (as was the PQ) at the Radio-Canada poll to be released on March 7. It showed a 52 per cent No vote, and a 41 per cent Yes vote—but more francophones voting Yes than No (48 per cent to 46 per cent).

On March 6, Chrétien travelled to Montreal to meet Ryan at Liberal headquarters and, saying he hadn't had a chance to read the Decima poll yet, offered it to Ryan as a gesture of co-operation. Ryan's response was that, because the poll had been done under the Clark government, he could not blame Chrétien, but he didn't want polls, he didn't believe in polls, and because his party was close to the people he didn't need polls. (The federal government did weekly polls from then on, and simply didn't tell Ryan, but passed the information on to his chief organizer, Pierre Bibeau, and his analyst, Yvan Allaire.)

That day, Ryan and Chrétien had lunch at Ryan's house and then walked back to Liberal headquarters. Ryan shook the hand of every passer-by they met. Chrétien said privately later he had never been so embarrassed in his life.

It was an inauspicious beginning. It was the end of the first week of the debate in the National Assembly, and a week since the Liberal policy convention that had approved the Beige Paper. Momentum seemed clearly with the Quebec government. In addition to disliking the Beige Paper, federal Liberals began to worry that Ryan might blow it. Ryan, for his part, was uneasy about a federal take-over of the referendum campaign.

These fears grew when over the weekend the Institut Québécois d'Opinion Publique (IQOP) published a telephone poll that had been done at the end of the first week of the debate in the Assembly. The Yes support had jumped to 47 per cent of those polled, with 44 per cent voting No—a lead that widened dramatically among francophones to 55 per cent Yes against 35 per cent No. As Michel Roy observed in *Le Devoir*, either Quebec was witnessing a shift of exceptional proportions in support of the government—or it was another poll war. Either way, federal Liberals began to fear a bandwagon effect for the Yes campaign.

Three weeks later, on March 27, the first meeting of the 22-member referendum-strategy committee for the No side was held at the Bonaventure Hotel. Pierre Bibeau had a large organization chart on the wall—a detailed organizational chart, but with very few names. He acknowledged that the referendum strategy was a little behind.

There was a discussion about Pierre Trudeau's participation, and a consensus that he should intervene in the campaign soon. But Ryan's suspicion of federal involvement lingered. Federal Liberals were unhappy with the Quebec Liberal slogan, "Mon non est Québécois," and Jean Chrétien had had buttons made up in Ottawa saying "La séparation, non merci." But Ryan did not want to use this, and the compromise was a simple "Non merci."

The day after the strategy meeting, there was a meeting between Chrétien and Ryan, and Richard Dicerni of the Canadian Unity Information Office was introduced as a possible help on communications. "I am sure that Ryan to this day doesn't know that almost the totality of brochures and themes and advertising and whatever else was done by the federal people," one federal official said later. "We'd give it to Ryan's people and they would show it to Ryan and say, 'Look what we've done.'"

For at the staff level it was quietly recognized that Ryan would veto anything that he knew came from Ottawa. Thus, material was fed to Bibeau, Allaire, and the communications official Jacques DuSault from Dicerni, who had, as the federal officials would put it, "the resources of a government behind him".

However, Ryan was furious when the federal advertising became too heavy-handed: when Health and Welfare advertisements began using "Non merci" as part of an anti-alcohol campaign. He wanted a direct, person-to-person, handshaking and speaking campaign with as little media promotion as possible. Thus, the No campaign consisted of days spent shaking hands in shopping centres, and climaxing with long evenings of long speeches that took no account of television or newspaper deadlines. Ryan brushed off criticisms and complaints, saying that his campaign was aimed at the people, not at the television cameras. He was determined to win on his terms.

ON APRIL 7, THE MONTREAL FORUM WAS FILLED WITH FIFTEEN thousand women from across Quebec, cheering one woman speaker after another — for the No side. It was an unprecedented political coup. It was the phenomenon of Les Yvettes.

Lise Payette had been struggling to present the feminist point of view in the cabinet — with limited success. Jacques-Yvan Morin, the minister of education, told her once that he had difficulty understanding the phrase "equality of women"; he thought it would be better to talk of "complementarity of women".

On March 9, at a meeting organized by the Montreal Centre region of the Parti Québécois, Payette read an excerpt from a primary text being used in Morin's school system.

> Guy is active in sports: swimming, gymnastics, tennis, boxing, diving. His ambition is to be a champion and win lots of trophies. Yvette, his little sister, is happy and nice. She always finds a way to make her parents happy. Yesterday, at mealtime, she cut the bread, poured water on the tea in the teapot, she carried in the sugar bowl, the butter dish, the pitcher of milk. She also helped to serve the roast chicken. After breakfast, she happily dried the dishes and swept the rug. Yvette is a very helpful little girl.

She went on to say that she was an Yvette, that all the women there were, because of their upbringing. But women should not be afraid, like the English, and vote No. Then she added that Claude Ryan was the kind of man that she hated, the kind of man who wanted Quebec full of Yvettes. Then — "blunder of blunders", as she said later — she added, "Moreover, he's married to an Yvette."

Renée Rowan reported her remarks in *Le Devoir* the next day and Lise Bissonnette got angry. Bissonnette, whose pen could peel a peach at a stroke, wrote an editorial of such stinging sarcasm and controlled rage that she single-handedly transformed the remark into an incident. It echoed across Quebec as nothing had since Pierre Trudeau called Robert Bourassa a hot-dog eater.

"One seemed to have misread," she wrote. "The minister who is responsible for advancing the status of women in Quebec, the one who claims to have a key role to play in the political education of her sisters, is ready to descend to the depths of sexism for the Yes?"

After a few scathing remarks about Payette's "hatred" for Ryan reaching the point that she felt the need to attack his wife, Bissonnette drew breath.

"Before attacking Madeleine Ryan through her husband, Mrs. Payette might have informed herself a tiny bit. Just a little. She would have learned that while she was illustrating the equality of women in Quebec with such verve by playing goalie for Les Canadiens [one of her publicity stunts as a TV talkshow host], in launching a male beauty contest, and interviewing everyone served up to her camera to draw out their intimate secrets, Mrs. Ryan was, for example, a member of the Superior Council of Education, where she chaired the Adult Education Commission and the Secondary Education Commission."

And on she went, detailing Madeleine Ryan's activities in social, community, church, and international activities. It was a devastating critique. On March 12, Payette got up in the Assembly to apologize, saying she had had no intention of hurting anyone, including Ryan's wife. But the damage was done.

Three weeks later, on March 30, a group of Quebec City women active in the No campaign and the Liberal Party organized the "Brunch des Yvettes" at the Château Frontenac. A seed of an idea was planted that would virtually destroy Payette's political career. The Yvette movement, spearheaded by Liberal activists, became the triumph of the No campaign. What was portrayed as a spontaneous movement of housewives, or, alternatively, as a reactionary revival comparable to the anti-ERA movement in the United States, was actually an extremely efficient operation organized by Louise Robic, later elected president of the Quebec Liberal Party. Speakers at the Forum rally on April 7 included Monique Bégin, the federal minister of health and welfare, Thérèse Casgrain, who had organized the campaign to win women the right to vote in Quebec provincial elections forty years before, and Sheila Finestone, a former president of the Quebec Federation of Women.

This was a phenomenon filled with terrible ironies for the Parti Québécois. Since 1976, the women in the party had been the most militant, and in Quebec as a whole the women's movement was virtually the only progressive interest group which did not subside into silence after the election of the PQ. The women in the party had organized a campaign to mark the fortieth anniversary of women's obtaining the right to vote; it was completely overshadowed by the Yvettes.

Lise Payette's gaffe had sparked a reaction that managed to combine an appeal to the traditional values of family and child-rearing, feeding anti-feminist indignation, and, at the same time, gather together federalist feminists who were able to use the rhetoric of solidarity among women and attack Payette for her intolerance.

Only a few days before, federal strategists in Ottawa had

mused that what was really needed was something that would fill the Forum. It had happened, with an impact that was more than anyone had calculated. The episode provided exactly the note of solidarity and indignation that the No campaigners had been looking for, and, until then, had been unable to find.

AT FIRST THE YES CAMPAIGN WAS SMOOTH, ALMOST LEISURELY. AS Michel Carpentier had put it at a strategy meeting on April 11, "It's a low-profile, fun, quiet campaign. We don't want to assault anyone."

The gimmick of the campaign was the Regroupements — groups of taxi-drivers, families, employees in factories, economists, scientists — which declared for the Yes side and were awarded certificates, often by Lévesque himself, usually to the accompaniment of the campaign theme song, a jingle that began: "Oui, c'est parti, c'est parti pour le Oui."

Pierre Dansereau announced that he would be voting Yes as part of the Regroupement des Scientistes pour le Oui. A few days later, he was shopping at a specialty store in Outremont, and bumped into Marc Lalonde. "Pierre is very disappointed," Lalonde said severely.

PIERRE TRUDEAU MADE ONLY FOUR SPEECHES DURING THE REFerendum campaign: well spaced, well timed, and devastatingly effective. He did not tour, he was not on the Ryan caravan — but he managed to crystallize the referendum debate with his four speeches: on April 15 in Ottawa, on May 2 in Montreal, on May 7 in Quebec, and on May 14 at Paul Sauvé Arena in Montreal.

The first was his speech in the House of Commons on the address in reply to the speech from the throne. Coolly, he dissected the logic of sovereignty-association. They were inseparable, according to the White Paper — but neither he nor the English-Canadian premiers would negotiate an economic association with a sovereign Quebec. Ergo, no association. And the referendum would give Lévesque no mandate for independence. Besides, Quebec had just elected seventy-four Liberal MPs (out of seventy-five) to exercise, as he put it, "sovereignty for the entire country".

As Robert Sheppard and Michael Valpy put it in their book on the constitution, "It was a majestic performance, incisive, riveting (even for his opponents), demonstrating to everyone that Trudeau was back and in control. *He* was setting the agenda."

Then, in Montreal, Trudeau spoke to the Chambre de Commerce on May 2. He began with no introduction, no warm-up jokes — simply plunging into the heart of the argument. He talked about the challenge of constitutional change and the origins of the independence movement, saying that no-one should be surprised that those who had spent the last twenty years supporting independence or separation wanted to propose the question, "Do you want to stop being Canadians, yes or no? Do you want to live in an independent Quebec, yes or no?"

Then, shrewdly, he expressed his respect for those who had been his adversaries twenty years earlier in developing this mistaken but powerful ideal of independence: Marcel Chaput, Pierre Bourgault, André d'Allemagne, all leaders of the RIN. They were wrong, but they were idealists, with "a sense of honour more highly developed than their sense of reality".

"Where are they now, these prophets?" he asked. "Where are these intellectuals, these artists, these publicists, these academics who were contemptuous of those who had chosen the Canadian option, the federalist option, saying that it was an option that lacked courage, an option that did not dare to face the destiny of Quebec, an option built from a certain number of compromises to live with others in a large country? Where are these valiant knights of independence, of the Quebec nation, these valorous champions of separation, of sovereignty?

"From being separatists, they became indépendantistes. From indépendantistes, they turned into sovereignists. But, fearing that the option was still a little too clear, they moved to sovereignty-association. Then, they hastened to assure us . . . that they wouldn't do one without the other — they begged us to believe that they only wanted a mandate to negotiate them, not to do them, because to do it, they would have a second referendum."

He paused. "You've got to admit that, for courage of conviction, for nobility of ideal, for spirit of decision, we've seen better!"

It was classic Trudeau: scathing, sardonic, combative. As he always did, he managed to insinuate more than he said, contrasting Quebec's circuitous mandate-to-negotiate with the direct approach used in Ireland, Algeria, and Zimbabwe — comparisons calculated to infuriate Lévesque.

He went on to poke at the logical hole in the Yes campaign argument that English Canada would accept the result of the referendum and negotiate, through a sense of fair play and respect for democracy. The question would democratically obligate those who asked it.

"But can it obligate others?" he asked. "Suppose Cuba, or suppose Haiti would like to make an association, a common market with Canada; it likes Canadian prosperity, likes the Canadian countryside, likes Canadian women, likes the economic level of Canadians, etc. They want to have an economic union with us, a kind of common market, they take a vote. Massively, the Cubans or the Haitians say 'YES, we want union with Canada.'

"In the name of democracy, would we be obliged to form that union? In the name of fair play, would we be obliged to say, 'Well, yes, they voted unanimously, we can't say anything.'"

There was a long burst of laughter and applause. Skilfully, without making any specific accusations, Trudeau had not only struck at one of the logical flaws in the Parti Québécois argument, and at Lévesque's failure as negotiator—but he had subtly compared an independent Quebec to Cuba and Haiti. He went on to accuse the PQ of risking the humiliation of the Quebec people by embarking on a process when there was no indication of a positive response, and, at the same time, planted an invidious comparison between Lévesque and Castro or Duvalier.

"Mr. Castro or Mr. Duvalier would have at least sent up some trial balloons, would have at least had some prior negotiations, would have at least sounded Canadian opinion before saying 'We want to associate with Canada' for fear, precisely, that Canada should say 'Take off, eh?'—which is pretty humiliating for a people."

The phrase in French, "allez vous faire voir", is tough, rude slang—"take off, get lost, take a walk"—and there was a surprised chortle of glee in the audience. The spectre of humiliation was clearly evoked.

After the speech, Trudeau went up to a suite in the hotel, and waited for Ryan. He waited ten, fifteen, twenty minutes. Finally, an aide came to the suite to say that Ryan would not be coming up; he felt it would be more valuable to spend the time shaking hands in the lobby.

However, the most memorable speech, the speech that was to echo through the campaign and immediately become part of the mythology of the referendum and part of the language of public discussion, was the speech in the Paul Sauvé Arena on May 14.

A few days earlier, Lévesque had made the error of telling a group of Mexican journalists that the referendum was showing Trudeau's "Elliott side". It was a stupid, ethnocentric remark, and it infuriated Trudeau, spurring him to his scathing rhetorical best.

"Well, that's contempt for you, my friends, to say that there are different kinds of Quebecers, to say that the Quebecers of the No are not as good Quebecers, and have perhaps a little bit of foreign blood, while the Yes people have pure blood in their veins. That is what contempt is, and that is the division that has been created in a people, and that is what we are saying No to! . . .

"Let me tell you how ridiculous this kind of contemptuous argument is that Mr. Lévesque has fallen into, when he describes my name. Mr. Pierre Marc Johnson is a minister, no less. Is Johnson a French name, or an English name? And Louis O'Neill . . . and Robert Burns, and Daniel Johnson — are they Quebecers, yes or no?"

But the most important part of the speech, the part that marked the campaign the most, and was most open to misinterpretation later, was the vow that "a No will be interpreted as a mandate to change the Constitution, to renew federalism."

"I know because I spoke to the [Liberal] MPs this morning, I know that I can make the most solemn commitment that following a No, we will start immediately the mechanism of renewing the Constitution, and we will not stop until it is done," Trudeau said. "We are staking our heads, we Quebec MPs, because we are telling Quebecers to vote No, and we are saying to you in other provinces that we will not accept having a No interpreted as an indication that everything is fine, and everything can stay as it was before. We want change, we are staking our seats to have change."

Those were the sentences that were to be interpreted by many as a turning point in the campaign. (The polls indicate that they weren't, but no matter: they were certainly the emotional turning point.) When people talk about the "promise to Quebec" in the referendum campaign, they mean that commitment to change made at Paul Sauvé Arena on May 14, 1980.

But what change? Quebec's so-called "traditional demands" for more powers inside Confederation, that Trudeau had always rejected? The propositions in Pepin-Robarts? Or the Beige Paper? Many people assumed that there was some commitment to concessions in Trudeau's statement — but when, on May 2, Trudeau had referred to specific proposals for constitutional change, he had included the 1978 federal White Paper, *A Time for Action*, in the list.

Claude Ryan had been persuaded by Trudeau the previous summer not to campaign on the Beige Paper in the referendum for the sake of federalist unity. Ryan was gambling that, if he kept control of the referendum campaign and won, Trudeau would wait until after the following provincial election before negotiating constitutional change, and that the Beige Paper would necessarily be on the agenda. It was a fatal strategic error; Trudeau made no such commitment on May 14.

Joe Clark was to claim almost three years later that Trudeau had lied during the referendum campaign, and many Quebecers who voted No were to argue that they felt they had been deceived when Trudeau began unilateral patriation — which led to the constitutional agreement being reached without Quebec. Ryan was to feel personally betrayed.

But there is no evidence to suggest that Trudeau had committed himself to anything but "change" — and change, in his terms, had always meant patriation of the British North America Act and a Charter of Rights.

Several days before the Paul Sauvé speech, the Yes strategists had learned, from a highly placed source, that Trudeau would make such a commitment. Some of them pressed Lévesque to defuse the impact in some way, or upstage it by saying he would resign if the referendum were defeated. But this idea was rejected.

FOR THE FEDERAL LIBERALS, THE RESPECTIVE STRATEGIES GOING INTO the campaign seemed pretty obvious and straightforward. "I think we knew what their strategy was, just as they knew what our strategy was," one federal strategist said. "They were going to go after younger voters, consolidate the separatists, and their determination was that they couldn't win on independence, so they would play up the negotiations and the mandate. We knew that. And we had to show there would be an impasse [after a Yes vote], show [sovereignty-association] wouldn't work, and we had to appeal to people's sense of their standard of living. They knew we were going to do that."

And thus the No campaigners hammered away on the question, its complexity, and what they said its real meaning was. "They want a mandate," Jean Chrétien told audiences. "To do what? To make us lose our Canadian passport, to make us lose our Canadian citizenship, to make Pierre Trudeau the last French-Canadian prime minister of Canada, to make us lose the riches that have always belonged to us, a mandate to make a little country in a world that is more and more interdependent."

Chrétien had always had a kind of personal resentment of the Montreal élite of Paris-educated Outremont intellectuals who made fun of his French and his federalism; in the referendum campaign, he took pleasure in laying it on with a trowel.

Night after night, he would go through a comparison of the cost of a Chevrolet's eighteen-gallon "tank du gaz" — sarcastically adding the proper French, "ou réservoir d'essence, comme dirait M. Landry": $21 or $22 in Quebec, $31 or $32 in the United States, and, at the international price, $70.70 in France.

"I'm not giving you the price in Italy, it's worse," he would say. Then, after reviewing Canada's oil and gas deposits in the tar sands, the Beaufort Sea, Alberta and Saskatchewan, and offshore, he would say, "The Péquistes are telling us to let all that go so that we can have our bourgeois friend Claude Morin as Quebec's ambassador in some country in a big Cadillac with the province's flag on the hood!" — in his intentionally fractured French, "dans un gros Cadillac avec le flag de la province dans le hood!"

Other Liberal ministers kept up the attack. Marc Lalonde said that an independent Quebec would have an energy deficit of $16.6 billion; Monique Bégin argued that a sovereign Quebec would not be able to pay the same pensions and welfare payments without substantially increasing taxes; André Ouellet repeated the same theme for social services.

Against these arguments, the Yes campaigners would argue that nothing would happen after the referendum, that it was a vote for negotiations, not a vote for action, that there would be a second referendum on the result of the negotiations, and that there was absolutely no risk in voting Yes. But it was the argument of a campaign on the defensive.

Claude Ryan insisted, as he told an audience in Beaconsfield, that the referendum was "not a war of slogans. It must be a reflective experience." He campaigned on his positive vision of Canada, and attacked the negative vision portrayed by the

PQ, which he called "so narrow, so distasteful". Saying that in the eyes of the PQ the relations between French and English were a failure, Ryan said he was "convinced that the positive aspects of our past experience are more substantial than the negative aspects. We're far more advanced than we were twenty-five years ago."

Ryan told that audience that the co-operation between the federal Liberals and the provincial Liberals was a model of the kind of co-operation and trust he believed was possible between Ottawa and Quebec. "I would have refused to enter into a written agreement [with the federal Liberals]. We were able to reach a measure of mutual trust. That's the stuff of which true politics is made."

Then he added the kind of personal profession of faith that made him such an awkwardly naive politician at times: "I would rather be betrayed by someone I trusted than reproach myself for having lacked trust in someone who was sincere."

ON MAY 5, ERIC KIERANS SUDDENLY RESIGNED FROM THE BOARD OF directors of the Caisse de Dépôt, claiming that the huge pension fund was being misused — with pressures being exerted on the fund by the government to increase its investment in Hydro-Québec, and to lend to the government at preferential interest rates.

Coming only two weeks before the referendum, the gesture infuriated the government, which insisted that it was a cheap political trick, timed for the greatest possible impact on the referendum. (For years afterward, the incident would be used as an argument inside the Quebec cabinet against naming anglophones to government bodies.) But Kierans insisted that this was not the case; he had been slow to grasp the shift in policy.

Kierans's sudden, noisy resignation had its origin, strangely enough, in a decision by Peter Lougheed concerning the Alberta Heritage Fund. For Alberta had faced a dilemma: if it gave different rates for its loans to different provinces, it would end up favouring Ontario and the traditional industrial strength of Central Canada at the expense of, for example, Newfoundland. So, in 1979, Lougheed decided that the Heritage Fund would lend money at the same rate across Canada.

As a result, Quebec could borrow more cheaply from the Heritage Fund than from its own Caisse de Dépôt. Jacques Parizeau was not amused at the paradox. Thus, on December

10, 1979, Michel Caron, the deputy minister of finance, wrote the president of the Caisse, Marcel Cazavan, asking the Caisse to charge Quebec and Hydro the best interest rate in Canada—the rate that Ontario received and that the Heritage Fund was giving.

On January 22, Cazavan resigned. Jean Campeau, an assistant deputy minister of finance, was in Japan, on a borrowing mission, when he received a call from Parizeau. Would he agree to be on the short list? Campeau tentatively agreed—but only gave a firm commitment after returning to Quebec and checking the annual report. He found what he wanted: the board was already committed in principle to a more active, interventionist role.

On March 17, the Caisse agreed to increase its lending to the government and Hydro from $1.2 billion to $1.5 billion. Kierans left that meeting before the question was raised, and was furious when he discovered what had happened. At the next meeting, on April 21, he was outvoted.

Despite Kierans's opposition, the board agreed to lend to the province and to Hydro at the rate that Caron had suggested: the rate that Ontario could get, with a better credit rating — about a quarter of a percentage point less. Kierans decided to quit. "The Caisse is a pension fund!" he complained later. "It exists to get a good deal for pensioners, not for the government."

The Caisse de Dépôt then managed a fund worth $11 billion; considerably more than the Heritage Fund. It had been designed by Jacques Parizeau when he was an adviser to Jean Lesage in 1965; ever since, it had been a key instrument in Quebec's financial activities. But with its creator as minister of finance, it underwent some quiet changes. A number of indepéndantistes were named to the board: men like Pierre Peladeau, the newspaper publisher; Fernand Paré, head of La Solidarité life insurance and chairman of the official Yes committee; and Louis Laberge of the Quebec Federation of Labour.

On the eve of the referendum, this change in direction was highlighted; in the years to come, it was to be of ever greater significance, and shape the expansion of the power of the state in Quebec.

IT WAS A HAPPY CROWD. SOME FIVE THOUSAND PEOPLE HAD COME TO the Petit Colisée de Québec on May 15 for their last chance to cheer the Yes campaign, five days before the vote. Lévesque was putting on his last, desperate drive to reach out to voters, and, night after night, was speaking in large arenas. Like the crowds in Montreal North, Sherbrooke, Drummondville, and Verdun, the crowd in Quebec seized every opportunity to cheer — chanting OUI! OUI! OUI! or the chant of the recently formed student organization Méoui, "Mais Oui! Mais Oui! Mais Oui!" or the old chant of the RIN, "Le Québec aux Québécois! Le Québec aux Québécois!" — as the loudspeaker poured out chansonniers' songs at top volume.

When René Lévesque came on stage, the arena erupted in a sea of sound. He stood there, clearly tired, but without the desperate, end-of-his-rope exhaustion that had marked him in some earlier campaigns, and sometimes seemed to overtake him during the referendum campaign. He waited for the crowd to subside. It didn't.

He wiped the sweat off his forehead, sighed. "Whew, il fait chaud," he breathed, and, only a few feet away, you could see his lips move, but not hear a sound.

Standing very still, moving his hands only slightly, he tried to bring the crowd down. It is a particular, patented gesture that he has used for years in front of screaming crowds, recoiling slightly in a gesture that is part false modesty, part genuine unease at the power of a mass rally.

"Mes chers amis . . ." he began — and, instead of diminishing, the noise picked up, as if the crowd was determined not to be deprived of the sensual pleasure of a full, flat-out, voice-cracking, exhausting ovation as if, like Joshua's army, they could bring down the walls of federalist Jericho by sheer noise.

"Écoutez . . ." Lévesque began again, and again the crowd shouted louder. Finally, losing patience, he snapped "Franchement!" (literally, "Frankly", but in this context "Come on!") and the noise dropped enough for him to start his speech before he was interrupted again with a spontaneous rendering of the chorus of Gilles Vigneault's birthday anthem, "Gens du pays" — and yet another ovation, which brought a barely audible "Maudit!"

It was one of Lévesque's last calls for solidarity at the end of the thirty-five-day campaign that had led him the length and breadth of Quebec, giving his hour-long speech as often as five times a day in a flat-out, final sprint.

Solidarity was the theme of that final week. Not independence, or sovereignty, or sovereignty-association — but pride and solidarity. He had been sharing platforms that week with Rodrigue Biron, the former Union Nationale leader, Kevin Drummond ("Mon cher Kevin, c'est à ton tour . . .", the crowd had sung in Sherbrooke) and Jean-Paul L'Allier, both former Liberal cabinet ministers, and former Union Nationale ministers like Dr. Fernand Lizotte and Albert Rioux.

At first, the campaign had seemed to be based on the assumption that the great majority gathering of Quebecers had already happened, and that all that Lévesque had to do was hold on to his lead. Thus, he moved carefully from one small friendly gathering to another, handing out certificates to the "regroupements". It was a reassuring series of inconsequential events of the kind that television cameramen and photographers call "photo opportunities" — and which have more to do with organizing appropriate TV backgrounds and projecting an image than with issues.

But now it was clear that it was at best a dead-heat contest — and, while Ryan was grinding it out to large audiences night after night, Lévesque seemed to be merely cruising. Two weeks before the vote, the organizers realized that the strategy of reassuring and wooing the undecided voters through a soft media campaign was not working.

So, in the last ten days, the Yes campaign changed gears. Lévesque began to increase the tempo, and make his appeal to large, enthusiastic rallies. He was reaching into his last reserves of energy to deliver the latest version of a speech that, in one form or another, he had been delivering for thirteen years, his hands working like a mechanic's grabbing at invisible levers as he shouted out new turns of phrase in his long monologue of persuasion, urging, cajoling, encouraging, and challenging Quebecers to take a step towards a new future.

When he was tired, the speech ran longer. In Sherbrooke, he was exhausted, near the end of his rope, and rambled on, groping for a place to interrupt himself and bring the speech to a close. The next day in Trois-Rivières, he seemed almost miraculously fresh, having found new energy to rebound and go at it again, as if he could give mouth-to-mouth resuscitation to the dream.

He didn't have much time left.

That night in Quebec, Lévesque told the crowd that the majority of francophone voters had been won over, but that the non-French-speaking minorities in Quebec — "and it is understandable, and it is their perfect right" — identified more with the federal government than with the Quebec government.

"But, you know, seventeen years ago, the Laurendeau-Dunton report put its finger on the crisis in Canada: it lies in two majorities, on one side French Quebec, and on the other side English Canada." English Quebecers, he said, particularly unilingual English Quebecers, had an "instinctive solidarity" on the referendum question, a solidarity that was virtually impenetrable because of the English "establishment" and the "infernal propaganda" of the English media, controlled and run from Toronto, which prevented a truly democratic debate from taking place.

It was a desperate appeal for French-speaking Quebecers to pull together, and a skilful pitch, enabling Lévesque to argue that Yes voters should blame the English media rather than the English-speaking voter should a majority of francophones vote Yes, but not in sufficient numbers to win an overall majority.

But offstage and backstage, PQ organizers and strategists admitted that it was an uphill struggle. They calculated that with only eight to ten per cent of the non-francophone vote supporting the Yes option, it would require over 62 per cent of the francophones to get an overall majority. That seemed a long way off: much of Lévesque's last rush was to try desperately to get a face-saving francophone majority.

The party polls showed a slide: at the end of March, Yes was at 51 per cent and No at 49 per cent; in mid-April, Yes 48 per cent and No 52 per cent; at the end of April, Yes 45 per cent, No 55 per cent. Only a small group had seen the party polls, and realized how bad the slippage had been; the official word, even to campaign organizers, was that it was neck and neck. In the last weeks, they felt they were gaining—and the guess was one percentage point per week.

But even without the party polls, many of those campaigning could tell it was not working. As people still filed in to the Petit Colisée, Denis de Belleval mused that a defeat might, in fact, be better over the long run for Quebec independence — since it would then be up to the federalists to prove that they could achieve a renewal of federalism.

MAY 20 WAS A BEAUTIFUL SPRING DAY AND THE TURNOUT AT THE POLLS was massive: 85.6 per cent. Claude Ryan left the house shortly after 9.15, and walked to the poll at his church, two blocks away. Two hours later, Pierre Trudeau dropped by the house before going to vote himself in the Town of Mount Royal. About 12.30, René Lévesque voted at St. Patrick's Church on Dorchester Boulevard. For the rest of the day, they waited.

Once the polls closed at 7, the results were not long in coming. From the beginning, the pattern was clear — and remained clear all night: a No total that never dropped below 58 per cent, and a Yes vote that never rose above 42 per cent. Within an hour, Radio-Canada projected a No victory.

There were only a few hundred No supporters in Verdun Auditorium to cheer the victory, but over five thousand had gathered at Paul Sauvé Arena, to sing and chant and weep together. Pauline Julien — who had won renown for her indépendantiste convictions in 1964 when she refused to sing for the Queen, and who was jailed during the October Crisis — came on stage.

"I feel like a woman, I feel like a Quebecer, and I feel like an optimist," she called out cheerily. "What we need now is a song for healing."

And as eyes clouded, lips were bitten, and throats caught in grief, the red-haired spirit of Quebec nationalism gave a ringing version of Gilles Vigneault's foot-stamping jig, "La Danse à Saint-Dilon".

At 9.31, René Lévesque came on stage, alone. A few minutes before, the Yes campaign had formally conceded defeat. Several paces behind, in a dark dress, Corinne Côté followed, and stood, blinking, holding a single rose. Beside her, dressed in black, stood Lise Payette.

The arena erupted in an ovation that continued for well over five minutes as if, in a final shout of emotion, the crowd could turn back the sea of No votes. After seven long minutes, when Lévesque began to try more seriously to bring down the crowd, there was a spontaneous chorus: "Mon cher René, c'est à ton tour."

"If I have understood you properly, you are saying 'Wait until next time,'" Lévesque said, and the arena lit up with joy again. "Well, in the meantime, with the same serenity, we have to swallow this one. It's not easy."

He told them that the ball was now in the federal court. "It is clear that the people of Quebec want to give the federal system another chance," he said. "Now it is up to the federal government and Mr. Trudeau himself to put some content in the promises they have made for the past thirty-five days."

He promised that until the next election the government would be vigilant to make sure that Quebec's present powers were not eroded, and that its traditional demands would be respected, and told the audience that people must remember that they still had to live together. One of the few negative notes that he struck was to reiterate his campaign attacks on the federal campaign, which he accused of being "scandalous and immoral". "Trudeau vendu!" shouted the crowd.

Lévesque told them not to give up the dream of sovereignty. "It will come, and we will be there for it. But I confess I am not in a position this evening to say when or how."

Then, his voice cracking with hoarseness, fatigue, and emotion, unable to find the right key to the song that had been sung to him so often, he led the crowd in "Gens du pays". And, as the last notes died out, he said simply, "A la prochaine." Until next time.

Several miles away, at his committee headquarters in Saint-Jacques in east-end Montreal, Claude Charron felt a pang of guilt. He should have been there. In the careful plans for the evening, a variety of speakers, including Charron, had been slated to speak if there was a victory, and to stand silently behind Lévesque if there was a defeat. But as the numbers rolled in, Charron decided to go to his committee rooms. On the drive down, he decided that if, after ten years of work, he was not able to carry his riding for sovereignty-association, he would quit politics. But by the time he got there, it was clear that Yes would win Saint-Jacques. It was one of only fourteen ridings in the province that the Yes won. The others were Lévesque's riding of Taillon, Marc-André Bédard's Chicoutimi, Parizeau's l'Assomption, Claude Morin's Louis-Hébert, Bisaillon's Sainte-Marie, Abitibi-Est, Dubuc, Duplessis, Lac-Saint-Jean, Rivière-du-Loup, and Saguenay — and two Liberal ridings, Roberval and Maisonneuve. The final vote: No, 59.56 per cent; Yes, 40.44 per cent.

At 10, Ryan spoke. He had just come from an intense argument backstage with Jean Chrétien, and it shaped his speech. He spoke as if the campaign had not ended — boasting how they had won in every section of the province, listing off the cities, towns, and communities where the No had won, his finger jabbing harshly. After Lévesque's performance, and the moving sight on television of people weeping at Paul Sauvé, it sounded grating, harsh, and graceless.

Later that evening, Pierre Trudeau appeared on television. In contrast with Ryan, he was conciliatory — praising Lévesque and his supporters for their faith in democracy.

There was healing to be done, and Lévesque recognized it as well as Pauline Julien and Pierre Trudeau. That night, after leaving Paul Sauvé Arena and returning to the Yes campaign headquarters on Saint-Denis, he broke with his usual custom and, instead of gathering only with his closest associates, he went to the home of Bertrand Bélanger, a long-time organizer who was giving a post-referendum party for the activists of Montreal Centre.

Montreal Centre, one of the regional sections of the party, has traditionally been a base for critics of Lévesque: those who have grumbled that he has diluted the goals of the party and cut off decision-making from the base. It was from Montreal Centre that PQ members criticized the linking of sovereignty and association, and argued against the idea of a second referendum. Usually, Lévesque responded with bitter anger, attacking his critics publicly or undermining them in subtle but effective ways.

But in the early hours of Wednesday morning, he sought them out, to listen, to talk, to consult. His instinct—characteristic of all his gestures since becoming premier—was caution: no hasty decisions, no snap judgements. And, above all, no scapegoats.

The very margin of the defeat made it impossible for anyone to be singled out, since no region of the province (with the exception of Saguenay–Lac-Saint-Jean) had done well. But bitter reprisals often know no logic, and Lévesque—a proud man, supersensitive to slight and given to hard-eyed, graceless vindictiveness against his critics—moved skilfully to assuage and consult those whom he had often treated shoddily in the past.

On Wednesday, he met with the cabinet, and on Thursday with the caucus. Only one person urged him to call an election: Guy Bisaillon. Everyone else urged him to stay on, and fight for Quebec's interests in the negotiations that Trudeau had promised.

But Louise Harel, the party vice-president, captured best the sense of shock. "We are like someone who just got out of a car accident — we are till touching ourselves to see we haven't broken any bones," she told a *Gazette* reporter, Michel C. Auger. "It will take some time before we are able to decide anything."

WHAT DID THE REFERENDUM MEAN? AT ONE LEVEL, VERY LITTLE. Nothing happened. No legal decisions were made. Two weeks later, the National Assembly resumed as before. Claude Ryan had said before the referendum that it was less important than the next election; René Lévesque, without actually saying so, acted on the same assumption.

By deciding not to resign, Lévesque had committed himself and his government to the process of constitutional negotiations which began almost immediately, and resulted in summer-long discussions between ministers across the country. The referendum was what made those talks — and the ultimate result, the amendment and patriation of the constitution — possible.

At its simplest level, the referendum had been a vote on change. Some 40 per cent had voted in favour of a mandate for change; the same percentage that voted for the Parti Québécois in 1976. Some 60 per cent had voted against. The same number of voters that had produced a sweeping parliamentary victory made for a profound referendum defeat.

By early summer, Lévesque had recovered some of his energy, but his ministers were profoundly depressed. The Parti Québécois was in a state of shock; in June and September, the National Council meetings were quiet and uneventful. No-one complained, no-one blamed, no-one criticized, no-one (except Pierre Bourgault, from outside the party, which confirmed the rule) said "I told you so."

Outside the party, there were a variety of interpretations. Daniel Latouche — who had left Lévesque's staff before the referendum campaign had begun — wrote a stinging analysis in *Le Devoir* on June 14, saying that the referendum was "more than a simple election defeat, it was a rout". He called for a recognition that Quebecers had rejected sovereignty and accepted federalism, and argued that the PQ should change its approach and definition of sovereignty, and work for it inside Confederation.

Michel Morin, co-author of *Le Territoire imaginaire de la culture*, argued that the referendum represented a massive defeat for the "national culture", which was the fruit of a whole intellectual class. "Not just poets and chansonniers, but also sociologists, politicians, historians and others tried to develop a new 'collective vision' of Quebec society," he wrote. "Without denying that works of value were produced in the wake of this 'national culture', it must be said that the idea itself, its concept, is bankrupt even as I write."

Certainly, the major figures in that national culture interpreted the result as a personal defeat. Gilles Vigneault was profoundly shaken, and only spoke publicly about how the referendum had affected him two years later.

"One can be disappointed that Quebecers did not feel solid and adult enough to take charge of their own affairs and decided to let themselves be managed by others. But this isn't a decision that's up to you alone," he said. "I can't say that it is so-and-so's fault, or somebody's else's. There weren't enough people who thought as I do. I didn't convince enough people. I didn't write the good songs that had to be written. I wasn't convincing enough to advance my idea in people's minds.

"One withdraws, and one analyses oneself, one looks at oneself and one says: if it happened like that, it is not only the fault of those gentlemen who came to help us betray ourselves. It is because we really wanted to betray ourselves."

Other major nationalist figures were less tolerant. François-Albert Angers, an aging economist and senior figure of the Société Saint-Jean-Baptiste, wrote a three-part series in *Le Devoir*, arguing that the fundamental error was in abandoning the identity of French Canadians in favour of the idea of a "Quebec" identity — when the "people" whose self-determination was being debated was the French-Canadian people. As a result, he argued, the error was in allowing non-French Canadians to vote in the referendum.

Despite the attempts to minimize its importance, the referendum was a crucial event. It gave the newly re-elected Pierre Trudeau a double mandate: an authority with respect to Quebec that no federal prime minister had ever had before.

For English Canada, the question seemed settled. This was an attitude perhaps most clearly revealed when New Brunswick Premier Richard Hatfield appeared on a Montreal television program with Daniel Latouche during the summer constitutional discussions. Latouche was talking about Quebec's positions and Quebec's demands when Hatfield brusquely cut him off. "We don't have to listen to this any more—this is over," he said. "There was a referendum which settled all that."

Pierre Trudeau now had an unequalled opportunity to use the referendum momentum to do what he had never succeeded in doing before: amending and patriating the British North America Act.

But in Quebec, the referendum had another effect. It transformed the Parti Québécois from a national movement into a provincial political party. It transformed René Lévesque from a national leader into a provincial premier.

As a national leader, he had been a figure of moderation, and a symbol of pride. As a provincial premier, he was to prove to be rigid, bitter, and weak. As a national leader, he had brought a coalition of dissent together and forged a progressive nationalist party, winning power in a surprisingly short time, and introducing a range of reforms. As a provincial premier, he failed to do what every preceding premier had managed to do since the Second World War: he failed to keep Quebec's political powers intact. The state which he leaves his successor will be weaker than the state which he inherited from Robert Bourassa.

For René Lévesque, that was and remains the most humiliating result of the referendum defeat.

4
The Politics of Humiliation

FIFTEEN

A Provincial Premier

*La mélancolie n'est que
la ferveur retombée.*
André Gide

It's nine o'clock in the morning, Thursday, November 6, 1980.
A dark-blue 1978 Buick Electra limousine pulls up in front of
91 rue d'Auteuil, a narrow street just inside the walls in Old
Quebec, and waits with the engine running. Two tall men sit in
the front seat, Gilles Lévesque and Marcel Drouin. They are
security agents with the Quebec Provincial Police.

René Lévesque comes downstairs, and the car pulls away,
turns left, and heads up the Grande Allée towards the National
Assembly. Then it turns left again, to the austere modern for-
tress with the slit windows: "Administrative Building J" in
the language of the bureaucracy, but known to everyone in the
city as "the Bunker". At 9.06, Lévesque walks through the
door, arriving at the same time as his chief of staff, Jean-Roch
Boivin. The day begins. A day in the life of the premier. It is the
beginning of the post-referendum session. Yesterday Lévesque
delivered the inaugural address, beginning with a sober and
formal denunciation of Trudeau's announced plan to patriate
the constitution unilaterally. He said that Quebec would withdraw from federal-provincial conferences, and the National
Assembly would reaffirm its rights.

THE FOYER IN THE BUNKER IS LARGE, WITH BENCHES; BEFORE HE GOT
the equipment to transmit his material to Montreal, Ralph
Noseworthy of CFCF-TV got into the habit of waiting for ministers going into weekly cabinet meetings so that he could send
his film before noon. The idea caught on when Noseworthy
began breaking stories — and the foyer regularly fills up with
reporters.

As he comes in, Lévesque nods and says good morning to Danièle Tremblay, the receptionist at the desk who signs in visitors, and walks to the elevator. He looks tired, grimaces a bit self-mockingly at how crummy he feels in the morning, and mutters, "I'm beat." It is an unspoken rule among those who work with him that in the morning he has little patience for long conversations until he has settled into the day, had a few cups of black coffee, and read the newspapers.

Last night he put the finishing touches on a cabinet shuffle: a fairly wide-ranging rejigging of the cabinet, involving ten existing members and two promotions. Then, after seeing Clément Richard, the speaker, and settling the final version of the new cabinet, he returned to the apartment for supper with his wife. The minister of industry and commerce, Yves Duhaime, recently rented an apartment in the same building, and Corinne Lévesque and Lise Duhaime have become friends. An after-dinner drink became a longer evening than he had planned.

Coming into his office, Lévesque hangs up his coat, and, lighting a cigarette, moves to the couch where the morning papers are laid out on the coffee table: *Le Journal de Québec*, *Le Devoir*, *Le Monde*, *La Presse*, the *Gazette*, and the *Globe and Mail*.

The office is a corner suite, with a private office where Lévesque makes his phone calls, studies and signs documents, and reads his newspapers, and an adjoining salon with a long refectory table, couches, chairs, and a fold-out bar. The salon remains tidy: a place where Lévesque meets with people, and writes undisturbed. The office is a clutter. Every piece of desk space is piled high with papers and books, and Lévesque gestures at the mess with a shrug: "Once a month we try, but Christ . . ."

The office is a strange mixture of the strikingly beautiful — a Jean-Paul Lemieux painting, from the collection of the Musée de Québec, has recently been hung facing Lévesque's desk — and odds and ends. On Lévesque's right, along the wall, there is a multicoloured orange and brown wall-hanging, against which are propped a framed quotation from Félix Leclerc on the referendum, a colour photo of Lévesque and Corinne, and, incongruously, photos of the Toronto Metro Library and the Ontario Science Centre. To his left, through the narrow windows, he can see the Old City, the Château Frontenac, and, beyond, the St. Lawrence and the Île d'Orléans.

As he sits down, his secretary, Mariette Saindon, arrives with a cup of black coffee. He thanks her, and proceeds to read through the papers, starting with Normand Girard, the often acerbic, often gossipy, extremely well-informed columnist for the *Journal de Montréal* and the *Journal de Québec*. More than any other journalist, Girard gets under Lévesque's skin.

He glances at the front page, where Girard has got a partial scoop on the new cabinet. Then he turns to the editorial page of *Le Devoir* and reads Michel Roy's editorial on the inaugural address.

This is one of the few fixed, constant elements in Lévesque's days: the time he has alone to read the papers in the morning. If he is disturbed, it is only very briefly. Jean-Roch Boivin sticks his head in to say that a colleague has called and will telephone Lévesque. Lévesque asks what it was about, but Boivin shrugs and says he doesn't know.

Tall, silver-haired, and shaggy, Boivin is a lawyer who was part of the small group who worked on Lévesque's manifesto to the Liberal Party in 1967 and who, when it was rejected, left the party with him and worked with him to build the Mouvement Souveraineté-Association and then the Parti Québécois.

He is a rough-hewn, drawling man, whose gruff exterior disguises a taste for contemporary French fiction. Like Lévesque, he is a night person — and sometimes plays the role of court jester to him. He ran for the Parti Québécois in 1973 and was defeated, and in 1976 flew with Lévesque on the campaign trail. After the election, he joined Lévesque's staff as a special adviser and trouble-shooter. Although he became chief of staff in 1977, he kept his trouble-shooting style: much of the day-to-day administration is handled by his assistant, a permanent civil servant from the Ministry of Justice, Gilles Tremblay.

A few minutes later, the phone rings and Lévesque answers. It is Louise Cuerrier, a deputy speaker who had hoped to be named speaker. Lévesque listens politely, but says simply that the final decision has been taken, and it is too late to change now.

This morning, the time for the papers is cut short. There is to be a swearing-in of the new cabinet members at ten, to be followed by a press conference, a speech to the Chambre de Commerce at noon, and the first regular sitting of the National Assembly in the new session. With a little "hmmm" of interest at Michel Roy's comment on the inaugural address, he gets up from the couch and heads into the salon to sit down at the end of the table. He has to start thinking about his speech.

At 9.45, Gratia O'Leary, Lévesque's press secretary, comes into the room with the list of the new cabinet. She is a plump, cheerful woman of thirty-nine who has been working with him since 1973, first at the party headquarters and then, after the election, as press secretary. Calm, relaxed, and good-humoured, she is one of the few people in Lévesque's entourage who are veterans of the RIN. She hands him the list and says, "That has been verified by Louis Bernard: the titles are correct."

In fact there has been an error. In one draft, the alphabetical order of the ministries was wrong, and in retyping it a secretary typed in Denis Vaugeois as minister of communications — one of his portfolios until that morning, in addition to Cultural Affairs — and neglected to type in Clément Richard's name. It is a minor slip, but it is to contribute to the confusion in the afternoon.

AT TEN, LOUIS BERNARD ARRIVES TO ACCOMPANY LÉVESQUE TO THE swearing-in at the lieutenant-governor's suite. Accompanied by O'Leary, the two men move to the elevator. Lévesque sees Michel Carpentier in the hall. "Salut," he says. In his denims, long black hair down to his collar, and open-necked shirt, Carpentier looks like a glimpse of storefront politics in the air-conditioned world of the Bunker. But it is an illusion. At thirty-five, Carpentier is as discreet as Bernard, and a more seasoned veteran of the Parti Québécois. He started in 1969 as director of the fledgling party's documentation and research at $25 a week, and by 1973 was the director of the party organization. From 1974 to 1976 he was Lévesque's executive assistant, was the director of the election and referendum campaigns, and, from the time of the 1976 election on, had been deputy chief of staff and the man in charge of Lévesque's relations with the party.

Bernard, Boivin, and Carpentier are the three key senior advisers; no others have such influence and easy access. Below them, there is a second rung that consists of O'Leary, Martine Tremblay, and Claude Malette. Their access is less frequent, their role more passive. Then there are others: floating advisers who work on specific subjects. But in this operation there is very little organization or hierarchy; consultations occur and decisions are made with the apparent spontaneity and almost haphazard flexibility of a hockey or basketball passing sequence.

Carpentier looks at Lévesque, smiles, and nods. "Another one," he says, referring to the cabinet shuffle.

Lévesque shrugs slightly. "It will make a round of musical chairs."

The elevator doors open, and Lévesque, Bernard, and O'Leary, joined by Marcel Drouin, the bodyguard, head down to the tunnels linking the government buildings: across the Grande Allée to the National Assembly, west and then north, then west again, around a corner and up a ramp. Halfway there, Lévesque is getting twitchy, and says, "Look, we're coming back by the Grande Allée."

He goes into the lieutenant-governor's suite, on the ground floor of the André Laurendeau Building, behind the National Assembly. The ministers trail in. Outside the door, the reporters wait and speculate. Inside, the ministers chat and, one by one, take the oath of office, sign the book, and shake hands with the premier. Lise Payette, who was moved from Financial Institutions a year ago to the Ministry of State for the Status of Women, jokes that she has had lots of practice. As she shakes hands with Lévesque, she smiles and says, "Merci, Boss."

Clément Richard, who has made no secret of his impatience for a cabinet job after four years as speaker, blurts "Enfin!" — "At last!" — as he shakes Lévesque's hand. Lévesque does a double take, laughing.

At 10.25 Lévesque walks across the street to the "B" Building, adjoining the Assembly, where there is a formal press-conference room. The reporters follow in a throng. As Lévesque enters the room, Mychel St-Louis, the president of the press gallery, says, "Congratulations! You're three minutes early — I think that's a record."

The reporters take their seats, and Lévesque begins by saying, "There are those among you who think that I hesitate before making changes." It is true; he has become notorious for dithering over cabinet shuffles. In this case, rumours have been flying for weeks, since the resignations of Guy Joron, the minister of consumers, co-operatives, and financial institutions, and the immigration minister, Jacques Couture. Both, in their own way, were idealists, not career politicians; neither wanted to continue after the referendum. In addition, it was known that Jacques-Yvan Morin was unhappy with Education, and there was a rash of speculation about the backbenchers that might be named to the cabinet.

Lévesque tells the reporters that the resignations of Couture and Joron were both "an opportunity and a constraint" — and jokes that Joron came to the swearing-in "to be absolutely certain that it happened". There are chuckles at that; Joron's attendance at the ceremony had provoked speculation that he had been persuaded to change his mind.

He then proceeds through the list, beginning with Guy Tardif, who has become minister of state for planning with responsibility for housing, and saying that this is the first step towards the creation of a Ministry of Housing. As he goes through his description of those he has moved, references to hard work recur: he refers to Tardif as "unkillable" (Tardif is notorious for his ferocious work habits, telephoning civil servants in the middle of the night and recalculating statistics with his pocket calculator) and Camille Laurin, the new minister of education, as "tireless".

As he is talking, Gratia O'Leary distributes the list of new appointments, and the new cabinet, complete with biographies. The error has been caught and corrected. However, some uncorrected copies were sent out, one of which was delivered to Claude Ryan.

When Lévesque finishes his statement, there are questions. It is a shorter period than usual, because Lévesque hasn't finished making notes for his noon speech. Normand Girard asks the first question, asking if it isn't dangerous to have Jacques-Yvan Morin replaced by someone as radical as Camille Laurin on the question of subsidies to private schools.

This is an allusion to one of the sacred cows of Quebec political life: the private schools, which receive massive government subsidies. Quebec is one of the few provinces in Canada to subsidize private schools. ("Conservative" Ontario, with a tradition of public education that is 130 years older, doesn't do it.) The Parti Québécois has always opposed these subsidies, but Jacques-Yvan Morin continued them.

Lévesque says no — that Laurin and Morin have worked together closely over the last four years.

Most of the questions that follow focus on the status of the ministries of state, since Laurin, Marois, and Léonard have all moved to ministries on the administrative firing line.

At 10.50, Bernard Chabot, a TV reporter chairing the press conference, says that the time for questions in French is up; it is time for questions in English. This is explicitly for the English-language radio and TV reporters, who need tape of comments in English; the English-language newspaper reporters, who will translate, usually ask their questions in French.

However, although most of the questions, and answers, will be the same as the exchanges that occurred in French, nobody gets up to leave. Lévesque sometimes says something more bluntly, more concisely, or more colourfully in English than he did the first time in French and, if someone pops an unexpected question at him, he will always answer it and often produce a fresh new story.

The press conference ends, and Lévesque walks back to his office, walking outside. Back in the office by eleven, he asks Mrs. Saindon to hold all calls, as he hasn't finished working on his speech. He goes into the salon and sits at the end of the table, with a foolscap pad and a black felt pen. He is one of the few politicians who write their own speeches. He often works from notes prepared by someone else — usually Claude Malette — with facts, details, examples, and sometimes a basic structure — but he invariably reworks the material. He hardly ever has a prepared text as such, but speaks from longhand notes. Thus he is doing what virtually no other senior decision-maker would allow himself to do: he has given himself a free hour and a half in a busy day already filled with other things, so that he can compose the speech himself.

His notes completed by 11.56, he leaves the office and heads briskly for the elevator and the waiting limousine with Gratia O'Leary. On an ordinary day, Mariette Saindon makes a bowl of soup in the kitchenette nearby, which he drinks in the salon as he goes through files.

TWO WEEKS BEFORE, PIERRE TRUDEAU ADDRESSED THE CHAMBRE DE Commerce, launching his constitutional campaign, and the Charter of Rights; now it is Lévesque's turn. As the limousine pulls up at the Château Frontenac, he is whisked in for a drink with the head-table party, and then they all move into the banquet hall.

At 1.30, the president rises to introduce the premier with a flowery introduction. Lévesque speaks for forty-five minutes, using the occasion to continue the campaign against the plan to amend and patriate the constitution unilaterally, calling it Trudeau's attempt "to make us swallow a project that is terribly personal, individual, a personal obsession".

This is a campaign speech; thus, it is not new: he goes over much of the ground he has covered talking to the party, in a special television speech, and in the inaugural address. But he adds new wrinkles. He accuses Trudeau specifically of lying, referring to a federal proposal to the provinces on July 8 which would have imposed bilingualism on Ontario and New Brunswick, and quoting Trudeau as denying that it has been changed. He concludes by repeating the hope that was central to his inaugural address yesterday: that the Assembly can succeed in reaching a unanimous position opposing the Trudeau gesture. He finishes the speech with the words: "So I say simply this — for all the reasons I have given, for people who have some self-respect and care about their real fundamental interests, there is only one slogan possible—if we must live with slogans. It is that this must not pass, and it shall not pass. I thank you very much."

Then, as briskly as he can, Lévesque moves through the crowd to the door. His bodyguards are waiting in the lobby. The eight-man security detail has done a careful advance job on the hotel, as they do on every site of every public appearance, and are working with the hotel security. All the security men wear a little lapel badge of the same colour, so that they can recognize each other instantly. The badge is the shape of the map of Quebec and, on this day, it is black and yellow.

But today, for once, there is a slip-up. The guards spot Jean-Roch Boivin, and assume the premier is with him. But Lévesque has moved ahead and, hurrying to get back to the Assembly and caught up in the throng, he moves right past the bodyguards without being seen. As a result, his car is not waiting. Impatiently, Lévesque flags another government car and, with Gratia O'Leary, jumps in. "A good thing you were here, Mr. Richard," he says to the driver.

He is pleased at the way the speech went; "the food wasn't so bad, you know," he says. The car takes him to the side door of the Assembly, and he heads straight in, turning down the hall, and, walking briskly, steps through the ornate wooden carved door. But instead of going straight into the chamber, he turns right. There, behind the speaker's chair and off to the side, is a lounge for government members: Room 186. (On the other side is the opposition lounge.) At the far end of the room is a sign saying "Strictement privé — Bureau du premier ministre." Through this door is a small office with a simple antique pine desk and chair, and a chair for visitors. Here, Martine Tremblay gives Lévesque his briefing before Question Period. She is a short, slim woman in her mid-thirties, who has worked with Lévesque since 1973; quiet, intelligent, loyal, and intensely partisan. She is expecting a child in February. Every day the Assembly sits, she briefs Lévesque. With their experience, they can do the job quickly, in few words. She hands him short briefing pages, and points to key passages.

"Ah, economic expansion. That's it, isn't it?" asks Lévesque.

"Yes," Tremblay replies, and Lévesque underlines a phrase here, ticks a paragraph there.

"Now, on the Sulpician lands — here is the opinion we have on that," she says, referring to a development issue in Montreal, where a developer plans to build a condominium complex on a patch of green space on Sherbrooke Street that used to belong to the Sulpician monastery. There are protests, and an attempt to get the provincial government to intervene.

"Ah yes." Lévesque marks a paragraph. "The issue the English environmentalists care so much about. Phyllis Lambert's issue," he continues, referring to a Montreal architect who has been very active in the fight to protect old buildings in Montreal."You know she lives right across the street?"

"The minister of justice is absent today," Tremblay reminds Lévesque, as he takes out a cigarette and offers her one. She hesitates — and then takes it. "I only smoke one a day now," she says.

Lévesque nods sardonically, and teases her. "Oh yeah. *He* smokes, *he* drinks . . ."

Then she runs through the routine for the new cabinet ministers, indicating areas in which he may be questioned, since the ministers have been named only this morning. Then, the routine for naming a new speaker. "The scenario is there — and Mr. Ryan is aware."

The parliamentary ritual is for the prime minister and the leader of the opposition to hold on to the person being named speaker, who is supposed to struggle and resist — a symbolic holdover from the early parliaments in England, when the speaker of the Commons might be the target of the king's wrath.

But while Martine Tremblay is briefing Lévesque, Claude Charron is meeting Claude Ryan on the floor of the Assembly, to give him a similar briefing.

"You know, Mr. Charron, I was never consulted," Ryan says. Charron stiffens and winces — for another part of the parliamentary tradition is that the premier is to consult the leader of the opposition before nominating the speaker—and Lévesque forgot.

Still unaware of this, Tremblay leaves the premier's office at 2.34, and Lévesque writes some notes on what he is going to say on the motion to name Claude Vaillancourt speaker. A cigarette is still burning in the ashtray, and he reaches absent-mindedly for another pack of Player's Light while he finishes jotting his notes. He moves to another page, and finally sticks the cigarette in his mouth.

AT 2.43, MNAS, AIDES, AND WIVES ARE MILLING AROUND IN THE LOUNGE. Corinne Côté-Lévesque, looking strikingly beautiful in a white blouse and black velvet slacks, has come to watch the TV in the lounge, as have a number of political aides. Access to Room 186 is theoretically restricted to MNAs and seventeen aides from the premier's, Claude Charron's, and Marc-André Bédard's offices—but nobody is enforcing the rule today. Charron strides into the room: the mace is being carried out into the Assembly, and the show is about to begin. But Lévesque has not emerged from his private office.

"Quickly, quickly!" implores Charron, beckoning furiously. "The secretary-general has gone in!"

Gratia O'Leary shrugs. "He's in the bathroom. He has a right."

Lévesque emerges at 2.44, and he and Charron walk quickly into the National Assembly chamber. As there is no speaker yet, René Blondin, secretary-general of the Assembly, presides. After calling for order and a moment's silence, he reads Clément Richard's letter of resignation. "As a result, the position of speaker is empty," Blondin says. "Mr. Premier."

But Lévesque has only got one word out when Gérard-D. Lévesque, the Liberals' House leader, rises to complain that the opposition was not consulted, and that this is an abuse of parliamentary procedure.

This plunges the Assembly into three-quarters of an hour of partisan — but basically good-humoured — stick-handling on procedure and rules of order. Lévesque is caught: he had simply forgotten to phone Ryan, and no-one reminded him during the morning.

It is a display of vintage Gérard-D. Lévesque; he is a superb parliamentarian. In the government members' lounge, the aides watch: partly irritated, partly amused, partly admiring. At one point, he accuses the government of having planned the cabinet shuffle to overshadow Claude Ryan's reply to the inaugural address, and there is an admiring laugh in the lounge. "C'est bon, ça," chuckles Martine Tremblay, conceding the debating point.

Gérard-D. refers to the "unilateral" choice of a speaker — as the PQ campaign against Trudeau's constitutional plans has made this a term of abuse, the point wins him laughter and applause from his colleagues and sheepish grins from the government — and suggests adjournment until next Tuesday.

René Lévesque apologizes for the omission, saying that the decision was taken the night before, "and I should tell you — it's an explanation, it's not an excuse — that I have had to endure a hellish pace this morning that put it out of my mind; it's as simple as that."

The sitting is suspended for a few minutes, and there is some milling about and rapid back-and-forth consultation with Gérard-D. Lévesque. The sitting resumes; Lévesque apologizes again, there is some further fencing on the rules, and the Assembly adjourns until Tuesday afternoon.

Then Lévesque quickly consults with Charron and Louis Bernard, and sets about reorganizing the rest of his day. He had planned to spend the afternoon listening to Ryan's speech in reply to the inaugural address. ("He toughed out my speech, I have to tough out his.") Suddenly, the afternoon has opened up.

AT FOUR, LÉVESQUE MEETS IN HIS PRIVATE OFFICE OFF ROOM 186 WITH Ryan and Michel LeMoignan, the Gaspé priest who is interim leader of the Union Nationale. They agree that Vaillancourt will be the speaker, that Ryan will give his speech on Tuesday afternoon followed by LeMoignan, and that the debate on the special resolution on the constitution will begin on Wednesday.

At 4.10, Lévesque walks through the chamber to the small room used for quick impromptu press conferences. He reiterates some of the things he said about Trudeau at the Chambre de Commerce luncheon, and says that he simply forgot to consult Ryan about the speaker because he had too many things to do that morning, adding that he hopes the extra time will give the Liberals time to reflect on the importance of the constitutional resolution. As the reporters are putting away their tape recorders, and moving towards the door, they chat briefly with Lévesque. Bernard St. Laurent, of the English Montreal radio station CJAD, points out that there are some tensions in the Liberal caucus over the question.

"That's a good point," Lévesque says, and walks back through the Assembly chamber. Beside Room 186, there is a private elevator which takes him down to the executive tunnel, which leads him directly over to the Bunker. As he is walking back, he muses aloud to O'Leary on what St. Laurent has said. "Maybe the delay is all for the best," he says. Back on the third floor by 4.40, he sticks his head into Boivin's office and repeats this idea. Then he walks into his office, reaches for the phone, and calls Louis Bernard.

"How could you let that happen to me?" he blusters—but he is laughing, and cannot even feign annoyance. The joke over, he says, "Look, I've just spoken to Jean-Roch about this: it may be just as well. I get the feeling that part of the reason for this was that they want to use the time and get more agreement."

Lévesque is right: the Liberals have no strategy about how to respond to the resolution, which places them firmly on the horns of a dilemma. But rather than working in Lévesque's favour, the delay will work against him. For it will enable the Liberals to find a way out. It is just one price that he pays for the disorganization of his office routine; with all the people working for the premier, there is no-one with the job of functioning as an executive secretary, to ensure that this kind of lapse does not occur. He has never allowed the people around him to become structured and organized. He prefers free-flowing spontaneity. Whenever someone tries to organize the office he short-circuits it in some way — often by giving what one person calls "corridor mandates" — wandering down the corridor and sticking his head into someone's office and saying, "Would you mind looking into such-and-such for me?"—even if looking into whatever it is just happens to be somebody else's job. The result is that there is no effective delegated authority inside the premier's office—and no accumulation of power other than with him.

AT 5 P.M., LÉVESQUE WALKS INTO THE SECRETARY'S OFFICE. ESTHER Turgeon has come in for the night shift, replacing Mariette Saindon.

"Excuse me, but would you mind phoning Angus Maclean of P.E.I. and Gérald Godin?" Then, as the secretary is placing the calls, Lévesque goes back to "the red book": the red leather folder in which Jean-Roch Boivin and his staff have placed the key documents that they feel Lévesque should see: letters, memos, pieces of draft legislation. The staff has learned over the years to keep a copy of everything they give Lévesque — partly because he may lose it, or leave it in the other office or in the car — and partly because his reflex action after having dealt with a piece of paper is to tear it in half and dump it in the wastebasket. The next hour or so is punctuated by a series of rrrrrips.

The secretary comes in at 5.10 to say that Godin is on the line. Lévesque picks up the phone and says mischievously, "I was just phoning to check up on you and see if you were at work!" Then he says he has just gone through a statement on demographics by the departing immigration minister, Jacques Couture, and it seems that there is a debate on demographics that Godin should take a look at; he will send over a copy. Then he suggests Godin call him the next day in Montreal about something else. "One second, I'll get it," he says, gets up from his desk, walks into the secretary's room, and comes back with the Montreal phone number of the premier's office.

At 5.20, the secretary comes in to say that Angus Maclean is on the line. Lévesque is calling to bring him up to date on the possibility of Hydro-Québec power transmissions to Prince Edward Island. They chat briefly — Maclean is an older man, with a kind of avuncular wisdom, and he is one of the few premiers that Lévesque has grown fond of — and agree to be in touch again on the subject the following week.

Corinne comes into the office at 5.35. "Salut, I won't be too much longer," Lévesque says, and she picks up a few magazines and walks into the salon. A few minutes later, she is joined by Gratia O'Leary, and she gets drinks for Lévesque, O'Leary, and herself. Lévesque has said they will leave for Montreal at 5.45. Periodically, he says, "I'll be another fifteen minutes or so" — but the time stretches on.

In a nearby room, an ad hoc government-party committee on the constitution chaired by the deputy minister of intergovernmental affairs, Robert Normand, is sitting. The group includes Claude Morin, Claude Charron, Boivin, and Carpentier;

they are discussing constitutional strategy and the options for the government if it succeeds — or doesn't succeed — in getting unanimous support for the resolution.

Lévesque drops in on the committee for a few minutes, comes back to the office, places a call to Marc-André Bédard who is meeting with his provincial colleagues in Victoria on the constitutional challenge in the courts, learns from him what has happened, brings him up to date, and chats with him about party business and the by-elections. The next day, he is to campaign in Brome-Missisquoi.

He also gets a call from Jocelyne Ouellette, the minister of public works, who is preparing a letter to her federal counterpart, Paul Cosgrove, and has phoned to let Lévesque know that she is planning a very tough response.

"Check with Claude [Morin] on the details," Lévesque suggests. "Of course the tone is up to you. You might talk to Jacques Parizeau about some of the figures on that case."

At 6.10, Lévesque is sitting at the end of the refectory table in the salon, going through a draft that cultural adviser Alain Pontaut has prepared at the request of a newspaper in France as a comment on the tenth anniversary of the death of Charles de Gaulle.

O'Leary and Corinne Lévesque are chatting, and O'Leary turns on the television to try to catch the news. Radio-Canada is on strike and the TVA evening news is at 6.30; they spin the dial looking for some Quebec news, and come across a film clip of Ronald Reagan, elected president a week before. Lévesque looks up from his work, sees Reagan, and asks what he has said. Hearing, he goes back to the text.

Finally, he is done. He shows O'Leary the text with his notations. "Ah, but Pontaut is good at this!" he says with satisfaction. It is a rare compliment, and Pontaut is not there to hear it. Lévesque's staff observe that those who wait for praise — or even acknowledgement — from him have to wait a long time. The key reason one person decided he no longer wanted to work on the staff was that when he continued working on an interprovincial conference after his girl-friend was fatally injured in an auto accident, there was never any acknowledgement or thanks from Lévesque.

Pontaut has found a quotation from de Gaulle which refers to the dangers of intervention by foreign governments in a way that seems to apply to unilateral patriation of the constitution. The subtlety and the mischievousness of it appeal to Lévesque, and he giggles.

At seven it is done, the last piece of work for the day. Lévesque does the last paper-tearing, finding a few bits of paper with scribbles of earlier versions of the cabinet shuffle.

"OK — done," he says, and shoves the documents into a folder for the evening's work. Corinne notes with a wry smile that they are not doing too badly, leaving only an hour and a quarter later than planned, and they head for the elevators and down to the waiting limousines: one for Lévesque and his wife, while Gratia O'Leary gets into the car behind — an insurance car in case one breaks down. The day is over: the cars pull onto the Grande Allée and head west for Montreal.

The next day, there will be a morning's work at the Hydro-Québec office in Montreal, and then an afternoon and evening touring the riding of Brome-Missisquoi for the by-election campaign. But that is another day.

SIXTEEN

Slump and
Recovery

*There is a tide
in the affairs of men
Which, taken at the flood,
leads on to fortune.*
William Shakespeare

In the late fall of 1980, it seemed as if the Parti Québécois government was doomed to defeat. The cabinet — as bright and competent a group as any parliamentary democracy could hope for — was tired and despondent, even with the new additions. The referendum defeat seemed to have broken its spirit. No-one in the party laid any blame, everyone accepted responsibility for the strategy, and everyone seemed, as a result, to take the referendum loss as a personal defeat.

René Lévesque seemed the exception; despite the profound sense of loss, he set to work to buoy up his cabinet colleagues and defend Quebec's interests. The referendum transformed him from a national leader into a provincial premier, and, having failed to expand Quebec's position and horizon, he reverted to the traditional stance adopted by his predecessors.

The federal government had immediately begun talks on constitutional reform after the referendum, and the summer of negotiations across Canada led to a five-day first ministers' conference in Ottawa in September. But the chemistry wasn't there for agreement. To Lévesque's obvious relief, the premiers stuck together on a common position.

Pierre Trudeau's response was not long in coming: on October 2, he announced that he was going to proceed with unilateral patriation. More than that, he would be asking the British Parliament to amend the BNA Act by approving a Charter of Rights.

Lévesque's strategy after the formation of the loose Common Front of provinces determined to fight the Trudeau plan was to seek unanimity in the National Assembly for a motion of censure — and when the Assembly resumed it looked as if he might get it. But his failure to consult Claude Ryan on the nomination of Claude Vaillancourt as speaker gave the Liberals the breathing-room they needed to reach a consensus.

The result was an intense effort by the government to draw up a resolution that the Liberals would feel compelled to support. On November 12, Lévesque presented it:

> The Quebec National Assembly categorically opposes the steps taken by the federal government, unilaterally and despite the opposition of a majority of provinces, with a view to having the Canadian constitution modified by the British Parliament instead of seeking renewal here by means of negotiations.
>
> Since this constitution has defined, since 1867, the rights of Quebec as a founding member state of the Canadian federation, the National Assembly asks the members of the Parliament of Canada and of the Parliament of the United Kingdom not to accede to this unilateral proceeding which is contrary to the very nature of the federal system and to the well-established rule that the consent of the provinces is necessary.

It had been tailored to fit Claude Ryan's views of federalism. Back on October 6, Ryan had told a Liberal audience that the federal proposal "breaks the equilibrium in which our two levels of government have been equals until now, [in which they] have functioned in a complementary fashion which is the very essence of federalism."

However, Ryan had taken a strong position the day before in his reply to the inaugural address, calling the government illegitimate after the referendum defeat, and its participation in the constitutional debate "purely tactical". He now proposed an amendment which would have had the motion begin, "Faithful to the will of the majority of citizens of Quebec which has expressed its attachment to Canadian federalism in rejecting the option of sovereignty-association in the referendum of May 20 1980 and conscious of the advantages of Canadian federalism . . ."

The Liberals had resolved their dilemma by deciding to put the screws on the government before accepting any appeal for unanimity.

On November 17, in the midst of the debate, the Liberals won four by-elections, caused by the resignation of three Union Nationale members almost a year earlier, and André Raynauld in June: Outremont, Johnson, Mégantic-Compton, and Brome-Missisquoi. Liberal canvassers had got strong reactions to the debate in the National Assembly as they went door to door during these campaigns. If the Liberals supported a PQ motion, many traditional Liberal voters had been saying, they would stay home on by-election day. That night, in the Outremont committee rooms, a veteran Liberal organizer said, "If we had voted to support the government motion, we would have lost Johnson and we would have lost Mégantic-Compton. People do not make subtle distinctions. For them, it is very simple. Are we in bed with the PQ or are we not? Trudeau is a myth in Quebec, and we cannot touch a myth."

The debate reached a climax on November 19, after the Liberals offered a sub-amendment, softening "faithful" to "respectful". In the late afternoon, on the floor of the Assembly, Lévesque made a personal appeal to Ryan for a final compromise. It was an extraordinary sight: for several moments, it seemed as if there were no-one else in the Assembly but these two, talking with the kind of negotiating intensity that one only expects to hear in a hotel room in the middle of the night. Lévesque was prepared to accept a reference to the referendum results, and called on Ryan for a final effort to reach a text they could agree on. As the Assembly adjourned, Ryan seemed willing to try.

In the lounge of the press gallery, a group of visiting British correspondents watched Lévesque on television with incredulous fascination. "My God, he's begging," one said softly. (The next morning, the headline on Normand Girard's column was, in fact, "Lévesque goes on his knees before Ryan.")

For Lévesque knew that Quebec's position would be strengthened immeasurably in Westminster when the time came to lobby against the federal package if the vote of censure in the National Assembly were unanimous. And now that the by-elections were over — and in spite of the divisions in the Liberal caucus, where some shared Pierre Trudeau's vision of Canada and some Claude Ryan's — it seemed there was a chance of agreement.

But chance intervened. On the way out of the Assembly, Ryan gave an interview to a cluster of radio reporters, reiterating his bargaining position that Lévesque had to agree to a permanent recognition of the advantages of federalism.

Back in his office, Ryan told associates that he had to do something to accommodate Lévesque, given the courage he had shown in the Assembly. So Gérard-D. Lévesque got in touch with the premier's office to offer a concession: the Liberals would drop their final condition.

But it was too late. The PQ whip, Guy Chevrette, had walked past the scrum and, hearing a snatch of the interview, had got Bernard St. Laurent to play back Ryan's comment that he wanted a recognition of the advantages of federalism. The word spread quickly through the caucus and, by the time it met the next morning, the PQ MNAs, many of whom had been stunned by the concessions Lévesque had been prepared to make in order to get unanimity, were outraged. By the time the contact had occurred between Gérard-D. Lévesque and Claude Charron, the final compromise was withdrawn and the chance was lost. And, in a flurry of mutual recriminations and bitterness, the deal was off.

Before the vote on November 21, Lévesque conceded that he had "humiliated" himself in his attempt to get Ryan's support. The final motion, which included parts of Ryan's amendment and an additional amendment by Morin, was passed by a 63-21 vote.

But in the eleven-day debate on the issue, it became clear that the government was in a weakened state. Léon Dion was to call the day of the vote "a day of mourning", saying, "It is the whole Quebec people who will suffer the consequences of this objective and subjective betrayal by the Liberal MNAs." Robert Décary, who, like Dion, had worked for the Pepin-Robarts Commission, accused Ryan of voting against the government motion out of vengeance.

The government was weakened; so was Quebec's traditional autonomist position, which the PQ was now claiming it could defend. Although the PQ had in fact improved its position in the four ridings, the by-elections seemed to show that the referendum polarization had endured.

Perhaps more revealing was a repeated opposition Freudian slip. One Liberal member after another, spontaneously and unconsciously, referred to René Lévesque as leader of the opposition. Power seemed to have slid across the floor of the Assembly.

AT THE SAME TIME, THE MINISTER RESPONSIBLE FOR HOUSING, GUY Tardif, was trying without success to explain away the messy irregularities in a renovation project for the Quebec Housing Corporation. Contracts had been given without tender to Luc Cyr, an old friend of the PQ who promptly set about hiring his relatives.

Tardif, a man with little patience for bureaucratic niceties, had insisted on quick action; his aides had acted unwisely. It was a shabby, all too familiar story of government looking out for political friends, and a trail was left which the Liberals succeeded in following to Lévesque's staff, where Jean-Roch Boivin had first recommended that Cyr be hired. While it would be months before all the details emerged, it added to the impression of a government in decline.

The first signs of a financial problem also began to emerge in the fall. At the lieutenant-governor's reception after the inaugural address, a reporter greeted Jacques Parizeau with an impudent joke.

"Mr. Parizeau, I hope you've made an application to Chargex — to pay for all those measures just announced."

Parizeau smiled indulgently and shook his head. "No no, not Chargex." He paused for dramatic effect. "Diner's Club."

It was classic Parizeau: quick, funny, and apparently brutally frank. For four years, he had been disarming his critics by beating them to the punch, summing up the problems of the economy in more vivid, more devastating prose than his critics were capable of. Six months before, in the pre-referendum budget, he had revealed the $500 million hole in the Ministry of Education budget — and, by revealing it and denouncing it, managed to deflate the short-term effects of the criticisms.

Now it was becoming clear that the provincial deficit was soaring towards the $3 billion mark. In answer to a question from Rodrigue Tremblay on November 28, Parizeau conceded that he had been borrowing to pay current expenses. He immediately qualified the admission, saying that it was the first year it had happened, and that one had to realize that some of these current expenditures covered capital expenditures on public works and contributions to crown corporations, and that one also had to take into account the current funds used to stimulate the economy through grants to business.

No matter. The admission was made, and the damage was

done. It was Parizeau's first public recognition of the financial crisis which would gradually overtake the government.

In a flood of statistics, Tremblay accused him of being the "champion of deficits and the champion of taxes" — an ironic echo of the 1976 election campaign, when René Lévesque's stock line was that the Bourassa government had won the triple crown: the championship for debt, unemployment, and taxes.

Four years later, Lévesque, in choosing to wait until spring before calling an election, was leaving Parizeau with the problem of simultaneously trying to tighten the government's belt — and he was making ferocious cuts in education — and to make the cuts as painless as possible in preparation for an election. It was hardly an easy combination.

OVER CHRISTMAS, AND IN EARLY JANUARY, THE MONTHLY PARTI Québécois polls began to show a shift. The months of attacking the federal plan of unilateral patriation of the constitution as a "coup de force" were beginning to have an effect. From the polls, Michel Carpentier could read a pattern: opposition to the federal plan, affection for Lévesque, dislike for Ryan, satisfaction with the government, concern about the economy.

In fact, one of the paradoxes of the referendum defeat had been the continued popularity of Lévesque, the high level of satisfaction with the government, and Ryan's unpopularity.

The change began to be felt inside the Parti Québécois. In early February, Louis O'Neill was caustic about the low state of morale in the party. "People talk about a revival in the party," he said. "I can't see it. It's just not there." He paused and added, "Do you know that there are four vacant positions on the executive of the National Capital region [the PQ title for the Quebec City region] of the party? Four. No-one wants the jobs."

Three weeks later, at a National Council meeting on the weekend of February 21-2, O'Neill was saying enthusiastically, "You know, we might win. No, really — I had a full house for the opening of the financing campaign, and the polls show my riding is one of the strongest in the region. Don't forget that Daniel Johnson won in 1966 with only 42 per cent of the popular vote and Lesage had 46 per cent." (Despite the change he felt, O'Neill decided not to run again, saying that his primary political commitment was to Quebec independence.)

In the summer and fall of 1980, the leaderless remnants of the Union Nationale had tried to persuade Jean Drapeau to lead the party — a flattering but Quixotic campaign which the mayor flirted with for months before finally refusing. Then, in early January, Roch LaSalle became the new leader of the old party. LaSalle, an old-fashioned lightweight from Joliette, was the only Quebec Conservative elected to the House of Commons in February 1980. As a result, he had acquired a certain celebrity which made his decision to take over the Union Nationale seem more significant than it was. Rumours began to circulate of opinion polls showing the UN with eight per cent of the popular vote and rising. Even that sliver of support could pull away enough Liberal votes to give the PQ a narrow victory.

In the last week of January, Sir Anthony Kershaw, chairman of the foreign affairs committee of the British House of Commons, issued a report which recommended against granting the Canadian government's request to amend and patriate the British North America Act. Back in October, after the tabling of the federal plan, External Affairs had presented the British with the federal government's view of what their job was. In a word, minimal. They should keep quiet and vote. Or, as Trudeau put it, "hold their noses and send it back".

The External Affairs terminology was a bit more refined, but not much. "The British Parliament or government *may not look behind any federal request* for patriation of the Canadian constitution," the paper said. "Whatever role the Canadian provinces might play in constitutional amendments is a matter of *no consequence as far as the U.K. government and Parliament is concerned.*"

Sir Anthony italicized those passages in his committee's report as a sign of annoyance. Meticulously, he and his colleagues held the statement up to the light and proceeded to examine the precedents.

In 1907, Winston Churchill told the House of Commons that "in deference to the representations of British Columbia", the phrasing of an amendment to the BNA Act was changed. In 1930, the Imperial Conference concluded that "it was necessary to provide an opportunity for His Majesty's Government in Canada to take such action as might be appropriate to enable the Provinces to present their views" before altering the constitutional status of the dominion. It was after this was done, at a federal-provincial conference in April 1931, that there was unanimous agreement by the provinces that the British Parliament should maintain the amending role laid out in the BNA Act.

And in the White Paper on constitutional amendment published by Guy Favreau as minister of justice in March 1965 (which External Affairs had referred to offhandedly as "a booklet" and "a pamphlet"), it was stated that "the Canadian Parliament will not request an amendment directly affecting federal-provincial relationships without prior consultation and agreement with the provinces."

Sir Anthony concluded his analysis of the precedents with the cutting remark that "the established constitutional position is not correctly stated in the Canadian Department of External Affairs background paper 'Patriation of the British North America Act' of 2 October 1980."

The report provided Lévesque with the unanimity he had failed to get in November; all three party leaders in Quebec applauded Kershaw. It seemed as if Quebec's fight against the federal plan was gaining momentum.

At the February National Council meeting, Lévesque observed that "something has depolarized," referring to the "unhappy polarization" of the referendum, and added, "It would have been morbid if it had remained that way."

He gave the delegates a careful, written statement of the party's constitution policy for the election: having lost the referendum, the PQ would fight "to defend and promote the rights and autonomy of Quebec inside the federal régime" and promised that there would be no referendum on sovereignty-association in the next mandate. He got a standing ovation.

So did Lise Payette, who gave her farewell speech to the party (having announced in the fall that she would not run again), saying that the PQ must not lose sight of the reason for which it was founded: "the independence of Quebec". As Louis O'Neill remarked wryly, "There is a profound ambiguity in this party."

But the ambiguity was based on an understanding of political realities. The government had decided in January on the election date, and was able to orchestrate a series of events to convey a sense of strength and coherence. Lévesque and his strategists had realized that their great weakness in the referendum campaign had been that they had been on the defensive, trying to explain that the vote was simply on a mandate to negotiate.

The Quebec electorate had voted clearly against change, and Lévesque and his advisers had understood. They began to design a campaign to respond to a desire for reassurance.

The National Assembly resumed its session on March 10 for the presentation of Jacques Parizeau's fifth budget — but the government had been visibly moving every piece into place for the election for over a month. First there had been the televised hearings of the National Assembly standing committee on the constitution in early February, which showed one group after another coming forward to attack the federal Charter of Rights. At the committee, the government succeeded in winning what Lévesque had pleaded for unsuccessfully in November: an effective all-party consensus opposing the federal proposals.

Then, as a precursor to the budget, the National Assembly had televised hearings on Hydro-Québec's $55.5 billion development plan. This simultaneously gave a showcase to Hydro-Québec, a symbol of technological competence, and a forum to announce that Hydro-Québec profits were too high. A few days later, Parizeau announced that Hydro would have to pay royalties to the government.

When the Assembly resumed, the pre-race tension was almost tangible, with the buoyant good humour of a high-school class just before the holidays. The sitting was called, in large part, to present a budget and launch the election campaign.

In his $20 billion budget, Parizeau announced a $2.97 billion deficit — acknowledging that spending had increased 16 per cent the year before instead of the 13 per cent he had predicted. The sales taxes on refrigerators and stoves were dropped, personal exemptions were increased, and income-tax cuts of 1.5 per cent announced, with a promise of another 2 per cent cut in 1982: what Parizeau called "the fourth systematic attempt to reduce the tax burden of Quebecers".

But behind the pre-election candy, there were gloomy signs: a billion dollars was cut from social spending, and the deficit was still hovering near $3 billion. Parizeau tried to explain it away. "A good part of this deficit is due to the reductions in income and other taxes made by the present government," he said. "Imagine if we had kept the tax structure we inherited from the previous government and had not carried out the reform of municipal taxation. Just think what our deficit would be today! Somewhere in the vicinity of one billion dollars, almost the same level as four years ago, since which time prices have risen 40 per cent!"

Similarly, Parizeau revived his debate with Tremblay, and argued that public-sector investments continued to exceed borrowings. "In short, so far we have not borrowed to pay current expenditures."

That night, at the traditional finance minister's reception following the budget, Parizeau had a kind of serenity. It was the end of a cycle; he had presented a fifth budget. He didn't look as if he thought the government would be re-elected, but he was looking calmly ahead. As the party ended, staff members, secretaries, and parliamentary restaurant waitresses came to bid him farewell, obviously feeling an era was ending.

Earlier in the evening, he was beaming and chuckling at what he felt was a delicious paradox: that the social-democratic Parti Québécois government had presented a budget resulting in the lowest corporation taxes in the country.

Business leaders immediately retorted that this was more than offset by the increase in employer contributions to health services — the kind of hidden tax increase that Parizeau excelled in — but PQ backbenchers were already preparing to sell the economic benefits they saw in the budget: no projected increase in the deficit over the fall, and a tax cut. Sober responsibility. Sound management. In contrast, they argued, the Liberals were promising to increase services and cut taxes.

But the Liberals could hardly wait to campaign against the Parizeau budget. For Ryan, the important figure was not the almost-but-not-quite $3 billion deficit projected for the coming year—but the fact that the accumulated deficit that Parizeau had run up totalled $10 billion — making a grand total of $15 billion. "In the first 110 years of Confederation, Quebec accumulated a $5 billion deficit," he said. "In only five years, the Parti Québécois has tripled that."

The next night, Wednesday, March 11, Lévesque met his caucus and told them he would call an April 13 election the next day. However, reporters waiting outside the caucus meeting overheard his speech — and the "confidential" announcement made headlines across Quebec the next morning. As Lévesque observed grumpily to reporters the next day, it killed the suspense.

On Thursday, just after Bernard Landry had finished his speech on the budget, Lévesque slipped into the Assembly and announced that he had seen the lieutenant-governor, and the election would be held on April 13. After Speaker Claude Vaillancourt told the Assembly that the thirty-first legislature was dissolved, Lévesque and Ryan moved to the table in front of the speaker's chair and shook hands. Then, like hockey players after a Stanley Cup final game, the other MNAs milled past one another, shaking hands.

Even then, few people thought the PQ could win. Denis de Belleval cheerfully predicted it would win between seventy and eighty seats — but did so knowing that few believed him, even in the PQ. The party polls were available only to a very select few around Lévesque.

THE 1981 PARTI QUÉBÉCOIS CAMPAIGN WAS A TEXTBOOK EXAMPLE OF a well-organized, well-structured, well-marketed campaign. Carpentier and the other strategists had learned from the referendum defeat: this time, there was to be no challenge to the electorate, no sense of risk, no defensiveness. The government was safe from challenges from the left — thus, it could move to the centre-right and be as reassuring and conservative as it wished.

In 1976 and in the referendum in 1980, the PQ had campaigned for a mandate for fundamental change, social or constitutional — and had obtained forty per cent of the vote. Now, the polls indicated that there was no hunger for change — but rather for protection.

A useful criterion for evaluating social-democratic governments is the extent to which they succeed in — or in fact attempt — taking power away from those who have it, such as large private interests and the well-to-do, and giving it to those who don't: ordinary people. It is a crude measure of progressive political parties and governments, but generally an effective one. Who benefits? Who gets (or keeps) power? To answer those questions effectively, a political party has to define who its clientele is, and whom it is trying to serve.

The 1981 campaign marked a shift in Lévesque's approach, his rhetoric, and his target. At times, the party line seemed to be moving perceptibly to the right. But Lévesque remained ambiguous.

On Friday, March 13, at his opening news conference, broadcast live on French-language radio across the province, it was clear that he was setting the stage for a nasty bit of Anglo-bashing. The PQ was governing on behalf of the French-speaking majority, the Liberals were acting on behalf of les autres; the PQ had its heart and soul rooted in Quebec, the Liberals identified with les autres; the PQ used the criterion of what was good for Quebec while for the Liberals "the criterion of what is good or bad for Quebecers is les autres." The list went on and on.

It was a refrain that was reminiscent of the slogan Duplessis used to use: "Les Libéraux donnent aux étrangers, Duplessis donne à sa province." As Robert McKenzie pointed out in the *Toronto Star* the next day, "The meaning was clear. Les autres inescapably are les anglais, although the Parti Québécois premier rarely uses the blunter term. They are The English, either within Quebec itself, or in the rest of Canada."

At the press conference, when Lévesque was asked to give examples of how the government had taken measures to transfer power from private interests to ordinary people, he bristled and attacked the questioner by name, saying that the question was an example of propaganda.

However, on Sunday in the working-class Montreal riding of Saint-Henri, his message was different—more reminiscent of the 1976 campaign. The emphasis had shifted from the ominous, shadowy foreigners, les autres, to specific, namable, powerful interests.

Telling the crowd that the Liberal slogan for the campaign was "Pour du vrai progrès au Québec", Lévesque asked the question that two days before he had implied was leftist propaganda: progress for whom? And then he ran through the interests that the Liberals had defended in opposition: speculators unhappy about agricultural zoning, employers unhappy about the minimum wage, insurance agents unhappy with the automobile-insurance plan, people earning over $30,000 unhappy about the income-tax changes, and, of course, anglophones unhappy about the language restrictions of Bill 101.

The PQ slogan was "Faut rester forts au Québec" (roughly translatable as "We gotta stay strong in Quebec")—and Lévesque's main campaign speech was about confidence in Quebec. The PQ had it, the Liberals didn't. As he put it in Saint-Hyacinthe on March 16, "There are those on our side who believe in Quebec, who believe in Quebecers, whose belief is as hard as iron that we can get through our problems and find the solutions ourselves. And there are those who perhaps pretend to believe that, but all of whose actions and attitudes show that, on the contrary, they give mere lip service to the belief, or they pretend."

He then went through the government's legislation, citing the achievements as examples of confidence in Quebec, and the election as revolving on this question of confidence and strength.

The Liberals, on the other hand, were not merely opponents and adversaries, but insidious, almost treacherous threats to Quebec.

"I can say one thing, though. Those who pretend to believe in Quebecers, but continually belittle our efforts, don't even realize that they humiliate in their own nasty way, undermine the resources and the capacities of Quebec, these people who give lip service to believing in Quebec, these people are dangerous because they can weaken Quebec which, on the contrary, always needs to be reinforced."

Then he went through the list of laws the Liberals had opposed — "the reforms that their own negligence made necessary — it was their Old Guard that put us in the hole until 1976, and it is still there in large part, I still see them every day when we are in the Assembly, they are the same, it is the same people who by their negligence and very often by their collusion in the corridors with the interests that contributed to the election slush fund made these reforms urgent, more than just necessary."

Then Lévesque moved to the language question. Just before the campaign had begun, the Liberals had opted for the "Canada clause" — which would restrict English schools to the children of those who were educated in English in Canada — and defeated the position Ryan preferred, which would have given access to English schools to all English-speaking children.

"You have Free Choice extremists who are Liberal candidates, and have never been overruled by their leader, like Mrs. Dougherty and Mr. Ciaccia — who want Quebec to be a 'wide-open' society, as they say in English." The way he said "une société *wide-open*" made it sound both vulnerable and obscenely promiscuous, "Wide-open to assimilation: any time, anywhere, anyhow. Those are the Liberals who want to bring us back to the most humiliating period in our past, when we let ourselves be walked over.

"Mr. Ryan would prefer what he calls the 'universal clause'.

What does that mean? That someone can come from Hong Kong and say he is of English-speaking origin, from Hong Kong, from South Africa, from anywhere in the United States, from ... from ... from England, obviously, and these people would have the automatic right, when they got here, to toss their children into English school."

Harshly biting into his words, making the sound "Hong Kong" ring like a bell, Lévesque was striking at one of the oldest fears in French Canada: the fear of assimilation through immigration. Neatly avoiding the fact that the Liberals had adopted the policy that he himself had wanted in 1977, and that the editors of *Le Jour* had publicly called for, he hammered at the minority positions in the party.

"That's the 'real progress' which is promised us: progress for exploiters, any time; they are all on their side, those who have always exploited us. Progress for the assimilators, no problem, it is not French Quebec that will be a priority on that side."

What Lévesque knew — and, in an emotional way, sometimes felt himself — was how Quebec's language legislation flowed from the fears that are among the profoundest elements in Quebec history: fear of assimilation, fear of humiliation, fear of loss of control of society and loss of identity. It was not long since those fears had been religious, and linked to a fear of loss of faith: now, they were identified with language.

What was at stake, in the minds of many, was the last rampart against the flood. And it was in just that kind of apocalyptic language that the government attacked the federal Charter of Rights, which would overrule Bill 101. The fear was, in some ways, a fear of bilingualism: bilingualism as the slippery slope to assimilation, a menacing whisper that was not the racist chestnut, "Would you want your daughter to marry one?" —but a much more menacing "Would you want your daughter to *become* one?"

When relaxed and sure of himself, Lévesque has a cosmopolitan, urbane comfort with diversity; when he feels threatened, his voice can conjure up a harshness that implies, without ever actually saying, that Hong Kong and the Philippines threaten Quebec's identity.

Warning of the danger to Quebec of having Liberals in Quebec and Liberals in Ottawa, and accusing the Liberals of being controlled from outside Quebec, he concluded:

"I have nothing against our English-speaking friends. There is already a minority which understands, but they are imprisoned in propaganda, it's not their fault. But one thing is certain: it is French Quebec which is the majority, and which will decide the election. And on that side, I have more and more confidence."

It was a shrewd appeal to some of the more conservative instincts in a still-conservative society. The party knew it would lose seats in Montreal, and it aimed to replace those losses by gains in the small industrial towns up and down the St. Lawrence valley: the traditional conservative hinterland of the Union Nationale. Lévesque was saying, in effect, that the major reforms were now in effect, and were threatened by the Liberals. The themes he used had been part of nationalist political rhetoric since Duplessis: identifying the Liberals with the federal government, foreign influences, and exploitation.

The government had identified the groups it felt it had lost in the referendum — women, the aged, and rural voters — and developed a set of promises for the family, farmers, and small business. At the same time, they hammered away at what they knew was the greatest Liberal weakness: Claude Ryan's lack of personal appeal. The themes were worthy of the Union Nationale: autonomy for Quebec, economic development, and the family. The promises were equally conservative: more subsidies to industry for modernization, loans to young farmers, and a scheme to entice women to stay home and have more babies — and qualify for a $10,000 home-ownership grant.

The government seemed to be designing a stick-and-carrot approach to push women out of the workplace and back to the maternity ward. The carrot was the $10,000 forgivable loan for families of three children; the stick was a proposed tax adjustment in the name of "fairness". Parizeau had said in his budget speech that it wasn't fair that working mothers had a $2,000 child-care deduction unavailable to mothers at home. So it was abolished in favour of a $400 lump-sum grant, sliding to $600 and $700 with two and three children.

Then, in the campaign, Lévesque began saying that the tax system should be changed "to help the family". The contrast to the referendum campaign could not have been greater. In 1980, Lise Payette made her insulting remark about Madeleine Ryan; in 1981, Corinne Côté-Lévesque was talking about how housewives felt devalued and undermined. As if to atone for

Payette's gaffe, the PQ was preparing an extra tax burden for working mothers, and Lévesque was telling rural audiences that it was unfair that a head of family earning $30,000 was taxed more than two working parents whose income totalled $30,000. Shortly afterwards, Lévesque promised a ten per cent tax cut for single-income families.

Many of the promises stressed the economy: a new emphasis on exports, an action plan for research and development in high-technology areas and $28 million for R&D in manufacturing, more jobs for young people and women with a $3,000 "employment bond".

Other promises included a commitment to increase the number of non-francophones hired in the public sector, the decentralization of school administration, and an improvement of negotiation mechanisms in public-sector negotiations rather than abolition of the right to strike.

Ryan responded with a promise of baby bonuses to pregnant women — which, while based on federal studies of the nutritional needs of women during pregnancy, was attacked as another form of promoting a higher birthrate — interest-free loans of up to $5,000 for would-be homeowners, an increase of $74 a month in pensions to single people over sixty living alone, the creation of an arbitration board for agricultural zoning, and the creation of a fund for agricultural research.

In this competition, Roch LaSalle and the Union Nationale candidates were out of their depth. LaSalle opened his campaign saying that if he were elected he would make the wearing of seatbelts optional — and, once the chuckles had subsided, there was very little left to his campaign. He attacked Ryan, saying that his party was infiltrated by people from Ottawa, and said that people were tired of state intervention, but as he made his way around the province it soon became clear that he would have little or no impact on the election result.

IF LÉVESQUE HAD LEARNED A GREAT DEAL FROM HIS REFERENDUM defeat, Claude Ryan had learned nothing from his referendum victory. Just as he had come to the referendum debate tired from the Beige Paper discussions inside the party, he came to the election from a divisive debate in which the party had rejected the language position he wanted—access to English schools for all English-speaking children — in favour of a narrower "Canada clause".

Ryan was, as an aide admitted, a terribly undisciplined campaigner. He made needless gaffes — saying that Louise Cuerrier was incompetent as deputy speaker, but that because she was a woman the Liberals hadn't complained. At times he was on the defensive — as in Saguenay–Lac-Saint-Jean, trying to explain his remark that the riding had voted Yes in the referendum because it was cut off from the mainstream. He spent too much time reaching too few voters in villages and small towns. He made long speeches, so crammed with information that the reporters following his campaign had a choice among six possible stories—and he was so disdainful of media deadlines that sometimes none of them would make the television news. He refused to do any polling. He wasted energy in ceaseless campaigning.

"He likes to think he's a superman," an aide said. "We told him to stop saying he never takes holidays—that scares people. People like holidays!"

It was enormously frustrating for his aides. Some had seen danger signs in the results of the by-elections in November 1980, when the PQ had done better than before — but Ryan dismissed their fears. They had won them, hadn't they? Just as they had won the referendum. The result was that there was nothing to check the errors in approach he had made during the referendum campaign. So he plunged on, shaking hands constantly, diving into crowds at shopping centres, kissing women, with the tic of saying the same words twice: "Formidable! formidable! Très bien, très bien! Ça me fait plaisir, fait plaisir!"

Ryan had begun the campaign with a global critique of the government: its policies, its legislation, its financial management, and the expensive promises it had been making in the campaign. However, in the second week, he was persuaded to be more positive, and make some promises himself. This effectively wiped out a substantial part of his criticism.

In the referendum, it was the Yes campaign that had a confused, often contradictory message, while the message of the No campaign could not have been clearer. In the election, the situation was reversed. Lévesque was running on a platform of "no change", and Ryan was delivering confused, contradictory messages. Identified in the public mind as too close to Trudeau, he defended the content of the Charter of Rights, but was critical of the federal government for imposing it.

After attacking Bill 101 for four years, he was now talking about Quebec as "frankly French — but respectful of other cultures".

Similarly, out of a sense of public responsibility, he offered a complex and realistic set of policies which accepted the bulk of the reforms enacted by the PQ, like agricultural zoning and automobile insurance. On the eve of the election campaign, he pulled together all his energy to make the reply to the Parizeau budget himself. Not only did this tire him just before the campaign, it highlighted his lack of a finance critic. What was planned as a team effort emerged sounding like a one-man band. What was intended as responsible nuance emerged, in the overheated simplification of an election campaign, as contradiction and indecision.

Ironically, the Liberals campaigned on their weakest card. Ryan was known to be less popular than the party, yet there was little effort to present the "team" that he had carefully put together. Since before the referendum, the polls had indicated very clearly that he had a popularity problem. But he was contemptuous of image politics, feeling that this had been the curse of the Bourassa administration, and a fundamental part of the dishonesty of the Parti Québécois government.

There was, as a result, no strategy on how to improve Ryan's popularity, as the Liberal communications specialist, the former adman Jacques DuSault, admitted to Lysiane Gagnon during the campaign. "Personally, I have given some pieces of advice which have not necessarily been followed, because Mr. Ryan is very reticent on that question," he said. "I respect his attitude. I knew what to expect when I went to work for him during the leadership campaign. Mr. Ryan didn't want to hear about image or communications strategy. As for me, I had just sold my company, I was no longer interested in doing image-building."

Then, on Saturday, March 28, going into the last two weeks of the campaign, two polls were published that came as a shock to all but the small group of PQ strategists who had been following the party polls.

La Presse published a CROP poll which showed 41 per cent for the PQ, 32 for the Liberals, 3 per cent UN, and 21 per cent undecided. The *Gazette* and *Le Soleil* jointly published a SORECOM poll which showed 44 per cent PQ, 38 per cent Liberal, 5 per cent Union Nationale, and 12 per cent undecided. Maurice Pinard, the McGill sociologist who supervised the

Minister of State for Cultural Development Camille Laurin in 1977. Laurin, a psychiatrist, is the chief architect of Quebec's language policy. (Jacques Nadeau)

Jean-Roch Boivin, Lévesque's chief of staff, before a National Assembly committee. (Jacques Nadeau)

The unlikely politician: Claude Ryan at the Quebec Liberal leadership convention, April 15, 1978 (top), and at his swearing-in as a member of the National Assembly in May 1979. (Jacques Nadeau)

Lévesque during the 1980 referendum campaign. (Jacques Nadeau)

Claude Ryan, Pierre Trudeau, and former Quebec premier Jean Lesage appear at a No rally during the referendum campaign. (Canapress Photo Service)

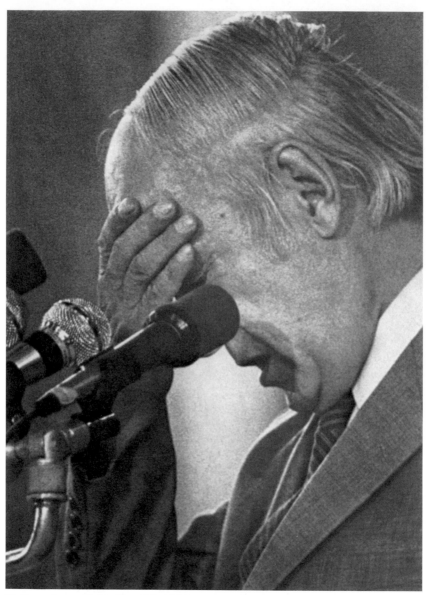

Referendum night, May 20, 1980: an emotional moment as Lévesque concedes defeat. (Canapress Photo Service)

Trudeau and Lévesque shake hands at the First Ministers Conference on the Constitution, in Ottawa, November 2, 1981. Quebec was excluded from an all-night meeting, during which an agreement was reached between Ottawa and the nine premiers, which Lévesque refused to sign. (Canapress Photo Service)

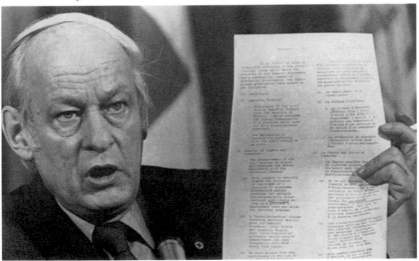

Lévesque holds up the agreement signed by the nine premiers and Trudeau. (Canapress Photo Service)

Lévesque at a caucus meeting in December 1981 after announcing that his future as leader will depend on the results of an internal PQ referendum. (Jacques Nadeau)

Lévesque with the leaders and negotiators of the Common Front during the 1982–3 conflict. (Jacques Nadeau)

Common Front demonstrators march on the National Assembly, with effigies of Lévesque, Laurin, and Parizeau, November 1982. (Jacques Nadeau)

Lévesque with Justice Minister Marc-André Bédard at a cabinet meeting in September 1982. (Jacques Nadeau)

Lévesque with his wife, Corinne Côté-Lévesque, during the cabinet meeting on economic recovery, at Mont Ste-Anne, Spring 1983. (Jacques Nadeau)

SORECOM poll, figured that the PQ would win seventy-five seats.

The effect was like an earthquake. Shortly after the papers hit the streets, Liberals who had assumed they would do nothing more demanding than organize a few coffee parties in Westmount were telephoned and called into service for heavy-duty door-to-door canvassing in ridings crucial to a Liberal victory. Liberal advisers persuaded Ryan to change his old-fashioned two-tone glasses for a more stylish, nearly aviator look.

And suddenly Lévesque began to radiate a kind of calm confidence; the harsh, raspy attacks on Ryan almost faded away.

Ryan now returned to the referendum themes. It was necessary to finish the job begun on May 20. The economy would only improve when the constitutional question had been settled by defeating the PQ. Voters were worried about the economy and not the constitution, and it was only in the last weeks that Ryan found this way of linking the two issues. It was too late.

ON ELECTION DAY, RENÉ LÉVESQUE ROSE AT NINE A.M. — AND NEARLY went back to bed. The night before, it had been his second wedding anniversary, and he and Corinne had dined at home on champagne and lobsters and smoked salmon that he had bought himself, standing in line at Waldman's on Saturday with the limousine waiting outside.

It was over. He was confident of victory; everthing had gone as planned. After a breakfast of orange juice and coffee, he spent a long time on the phone with officials in Quebec City, preparing for the premiers' meeting in Ottawa three days later, before heading off to tour the riding, and encourage the campaign workers who were getting out the vote.

He voted shortly after one o'clock at the Erskine and American United Church on Sherbrooke Street, a block or so from his condominium at 1250 Pine Avenue. The stale joke of the day was that he voted for Ryan — Pierre Ryan, the PQ candidate in Saint-Louis.

In the afternoon, driving around the riding, urging on the volunteers and telling them to ignore the polls, Lévesque muttered to himself in the limousine, "Provided we don't end up with eighty members—that would mean a lot of people to sort out."

Claude Ryan voted at ten sharp, and then drove out to Lachute and, like Lévesque, spent the day touring the riding. He remained, despite all the polls, confident of victory. He had screened out the negative indications, he was still sure that the network of canvassers with marked lists were more accurate than any polls.

Ryan had already prepared two speeches—one for a victory, the other for a defeat. But he had little doubt of the outcome. "In the eighteen east-end [Montreal] ridings, our vote has come out twice as strongly as the PQ's," he told journalist Benoît Aubin at five o'clock. The only worry at the six o'clock meeting of advisers was how they could get away from the supporters in the riding soon enough to get to the victory celebration planned at the CEGEP du Vieux Montréal. And, as the polls closed, Ryan and his advisers were confident that the vote had turned out.

The first hour of television coverage was disastrous. Both CBC networks were on strike, and the computer for the French private network TVA showed the PQ leading, but the Union Nationale close behind. For almost an hour, guest commentators swallowed their disbelief, and talked about the surprising resurgence of conservatism, and the astonishing strength of Roch Lasalle's team.

The computer was wrong. Finally, in considerable embarrassment, the network switched to CTV's computer. The Parti Québécois was sweeping to an overwhelming victory: 80 seats, and over 49 per cent of the votes. The Liberals were trailing with 42 seats, but 46 per cent of the popular vote—only three percentage points behind. The Union Nationale, with 4 per cent of the vote, was a distant third.

After watching the results in a suite at the hotel La Barre 500 in his riding on the South Shore, Lévesque went first to a packed brasserie for the celebration of riding workers. He told the crowd of hundreds of supporters that he had confidence that the victory "will become rooted and become permanent". Sensing the allusion to sovereignty, the crowd began to chant "On veut un pays!" ("We want a country!") An hour later, at Paul Sauvé Arena, Lévesque pulled back from that inference: it was the "values" of integrity and the defence of Quebec that he hoped would become rooted and permanent.

As Lévesque was making his way to Paul Sauvé, Claude Ryan made his concession speech at the CEGEP de Vieux Montréal. It was an incredible scene, which showed the disarray of the Liberals as clearly as the results. The hall, where two thousand had been expected, was almost empty.

Ryan found a grace in defeat that had escaped him in victory the year before. Conceding defeat, he congratulated Lévesque and his party, and wished him a fruitful mandate, promising to fulfil the role of leader of the opposition. He congratulated the elected members and expressed regret for those who were defeated, and gratitude to the thousands of volunteers.

He referred to what he called the four themes of the Liberal campaign — a logical follow-up to the referendum, an economic revival, a greater emphasis on personal liberties, and greater openness to minorities — adding, "The people have chosen instead the program of the Parti Québécois. We accept and we respect this choice without a second thought." It was a glimpse of Ryan at his best: courageous and dignified.

At Paul Sauvé Arena, a crowd estimated at twelve thousand had gathered: in and outside the arena. Inside, the hall exploded with ecstasy. Lévesque talked of continuity and responsibility, praised Ryan, vowed that all the election promises would be kept, and, in an unprecedented gesture in front of a partisan PQ audience, spoke English — thanking those in the English and ethnic communities who had supported the PQ and "joined in the mainstream of Quebec support which has given us this second mandate". While it sounds like nothing more than an obvious courtesy, it would have been unthinkable in 1976, unthinkable on referendum night. It was possible to believe that the PQ was moving to a new tolerance, a new openness.

It had been a sweeping victory. Lévesque had got the eighty members he had feared — making for hard cabinet choices. Only one minister, Jocelyne Ouellette in Hull, had been defeated. Rodrigue Biron, the former Union Nationale leader, had been elected as a PQ member. The PQ had won or kept virtually every small industrial town up and down the St. Lawrence: Sorel, Saint-Hyacinthe, Sherbrooke, Drummondville, Victoriaville, Lévis, Rimouski, Rivière du Loup, Sept Îles, all but one riding in Quebec City, Trois Rivières, Shawinigan, Joliette, Sainte-Thérèse.

This shifted the heart of the party — away from the gritty

east-end streets of Montreal to small-town Quebec. This shift from the urban left to the small-town centre and centre-right was not immediately clear; Robert Dean, the director of the United Auto Workers, had been elected, as had Louise Harel, who had won back Maisonneuve for the Parti Québécois. However, they were psychologically outnumbered by former Union Nationale newcomers like Rodrigue Biron and Raynald Fréchette — both of whom were immediately named to the cabinet.

The Liberals were now confined to Montreal, the Eastern Townships, one riding in the Beauce, one in Quebec City, one south-east of Quebec City, and the Ottawa Valley. Worse, for Claude Ryan's future, most of the francophone candidates closest to his thinking — Solange Chaput-Rolland, René Dussault, Marcellin Tremblay, Alain Cousineau — had been defeated. The best new members of the caucus were English-speaking, like Richard French, Clifford Lincoln, or Christos Sirros. The Liberals had failed in the crucial test of a party seeking to govern in Quebec: they had failed to win the confidence of the French-speaking majority.

It had been a clear choice, and a massive defeat. As André Bernard and Bernard Descôteaux put it in their book on the election, "Contrary to other elections in which only the actions and gestures of the outgoing government are at stake, the electorate this time chose, in Claude Ryan's own terms, between two conceptions of Quebec society (federalism vs. indépendantisme, free enterprise vs. state interventionism, personal liberties vs. collective liberties) defended by two parties, incarnated by two teams and two programs.

"The defeat of the Liberals seems more than the failure of a party; it is a social program that seems to have been rejected . . . unless it is the real absence of such a program that has been condemned."

For Lévesque, the victory was complete. He had exactly the mandate he sought to defend Quebec's interests in the constitutional negotiations. He could remake the cabinet as he wished. He had a free hand.

SEVENTEEN

The Constitution

*It should be borne in
mind that there is nothing
more difficult to arrange,
more doubtful of success,
and more dangerous to carry
through than initiating
changes in a state's
constitution.*

Machiavelli
as quoted in the Kirby Memo,
August 30, 1980

On election night, Lévesque had told the crowd "Tonight we
celebrate and tomorrow we work" — and he was not simply
being rhetorical, The next day, the cabinet met in the government offices in Place Desjardins in Montreal, and Lévesque
presented them with his plans to go to Ottawa for the premiers'
meeting, Afterwards, some ministers would regret not having
spoken up against the idea — but they had not followed the
discussions, and, moreover, those who had countered Lévesque
in the past had found the experience so unpleasant that they
stopped. (One minister who had not restrained himself was
Denis de Belleval. In the fall of 1980 he had had an argument
with Lévesque of an intensity that stunned his colleagues. The
April 14 cabinet meeting was his last; in the next cabinet
shuffle he was dropped, along with Denis Vaugeois.)

The constitutional struggle had intensified through the winter and spring. In January and February, the federal government had become increasingly testy in its dealings with Britain,
and the U.K. high commissioner, Sir John Ford, had got into

trouble by explaining his government's position to an NDP member at the governor general's skating party.

In March, the constitutional debate had reached its final stages in the House of Commons, and the eight dissident provinces (all, that is except Ontario and New Brunswick) were worried that the project would be through, complete, passed, and in London before the snow melted. At the beginning of March, Claude Morin had met with his colleagues from the dissident provinces in Winnipeg, and, leaving to fight the election, told them that his deputy minister, Robert Normand, would keep in touch as they worked on developing a common position.

The Alberta minister of federal and intergovernmental affairs, Dick Johnston, had been particularly insistent that what became known as "the Gang of Eight" should develop a counter-proposal to the federal plan. "We've got to be positive, we've got to be constructive," he kept telling his colleagues.

Alberta had proposed what was known as the "Vancouver formula" (because it was discussed at the meeting of ministers in Vancouver) for amending the constitution. By this formula, any amendment to the patriated constitution would have to be passed by Parliament and the legislatures of at least seven provinces containing at least half the population of Canada. This would prevent any province from having a veto — but would allow for "opting out".

This was the alternative to the "Victoria formula", which would have required the consent of Parliament, Ontario, Quebec, two Atlantic provinces constituting half the population of the region, and two Western provinces constituting half that region. This was objectionable to Lougheed and Bennett, since it relegated their provinces to a subordinate position, below Ontario and Quebec. On the other hand, the Vancouver formula was unacceptable to the federal government because it provided for opting out.

In mid-March, Normand phoned Morin. He saw two problems: the dissident provinces wanted to stiffen the conditions for opting out to require a two-thirds vote of the legislature, and they did not want to include financial compensation. Morin told Normand this was unacceptable. However, by agreement, neither Morin nor Lévesque saw the text so that, if the proposal leaked during the campaign, they would be able to say honestly that they hadn't seen it. Unwillingly, the group working on the document inserted financial compensation — but stuck with the two-thirds vote for opting out.

On March 30, in the middle of the election campaign, the eight premiers held a telephone conference, and discussed the tentative agreement they were reaching on a common position. However, the other seven did not realize how strong Lévesque's opposition was to the two-thirds vote.

As the consensus was being worked on, the premiers agreed not to announce the state of their discussions until after the Quebec election.

"If we threw that [out] in public — and I agreed with them, and it didn't have anything exclusively to do with the Quebec election — throwing that [out] in public would be, to say the least, premature, with things more confused than ever at the federal level, in the House of Commons and the courts and elsewhere," Lévesque said later.

They decided that whatever government was elected April 13 would have a mandate to deal with the situation, and reach a final agreement, if it could be done.

The premiers originally wanted to meet on April 14, but Lévesque killed that idea. "For the love of God — you guys know what an election is—give us a couple of days to breathe." So April 16 was agreed upon.

On March 31 the Newfoundland Court of Appeal ruled that the federal proposals were illegal. It was a decision that the federal government was prepared for, and it immediately agreed to have the matter referred to the Supreme Court.

Throughout this period, Joe Clark and the Conservatives had been fighting the Canada Bill in the House of Commons, and tying up Parliament on procedure. The Newfoundland decision, and the federal referral to the Supreme Court, led to an agreement to put off the final vote until after the Supreme Court decision.

On April 15, Lévesque flew to Ottawa to meet with the other seven premiers. But he was uneasy. On the one hand, he was suspicious of the durability and reliability of the Gang of Eight. He neither liked nor trusted Allan Blakeney, and particularly resented the way he had come to Quebec during the referendum campaign and promised change if there was a No vote. On the other hand, he was determined to stop the federal bill with its Charter of Rights that would reduce Quebec's powers.

If the alliance collapsed, he was convinced, as was Claude

Morin, that Trudeau's plan would be passed quickly. But if it stuck together, he was sure that they could beat Ottawa in London. Gilles Loiselle, Quebec's delegate general there, had done a superb job of lobbying.

But while the other premiers and their ministers wanted to design a proposal that Trudeau could accept, Lévesque was determined not to accept something that would make opting out difficult. He had already succeeded in getting the principle of financial compensation accepted; now he was determined to have the opting out decided on by a majority, not two-thirds. Otherwise, he argued, the opposition would make the decision. The other premiers were appalled: this wiped out the whole thrust of their effort to make a proposition that might be acceptable to Trudeau.

Bargaining went on in Sterling Lyon's suite until 2.30 in the morning, as Lévesque told his fellow-premiers that a veto was Quebec's birthright. Quebec had been prepared to sacrifice it only in exchange for the commitment to financial compensation; but, even then, the symbolic price for this concession was high, and it worried Lévesque. He wanted to delay; if he signed an agreement, he was determined to sign something with an opting-out right that could be exercised.

Blakeney and Bennett pressured him — but he stood firm: he didn't care if the room had been reserved and the photographers notified — if the two-thirds rule wasn't removed, he wouldn't sign. Finally, they gave in.

In exchange, Bennett insisted that Lévesque sign a full-page newspaper advertisement, acknowledging support for patriation, and the terms of the proposal, under a large Maple Leaf flag.

Lévesque was very reluctant. It would be a much more public signature than the official signing the next day, and he didn't like the ad. It was, as Claude Morin was to observe later, "pas seulement très fédéraliste, mais très *Canadian*". At last, somewhat resentfully, Lévesque scrawled his signature, and bopped Bennett over the head with a pile of papers in mock anger. "There. I've signed your damn ad."

His signature was to be there, with the others, in newspaper ads across the country, endorsing patriation. It was the first time a Quebec premier had ever publicly endorsed the idea of patriation of the constitution without previous agreement on a new division of powers.

The next day, the premiers had a formal signing ceremony to mark the agreement. They all made short mutually congratulatory statements; Lévesque called it "an amending formula which perfectly protects the rights and powers of Quebec, and also includes a flexibility and a dynamism which will make it possible to adapt to contemporary reality." He quickly added: "It's clear that this participation on the part of Quebec in the interprovincial accord before us today in no way affects the inalienable rights of Quebecers to decide democratically, by themselves, on their future." And, after saying that it was "an honest and sincere effort and we worked hard to find a compromise which would be honourable for everybody," he concluded, "It's now up to the prime minister to show good sense and come back to the bargaining table."

Lévesque was gambling on two possibilities: either that the Gang of Eight would hold, and Quebec would have won financial compensation for opting out; or that, if it didn't, it would be impossible for Trudeau to rebuild a consensus.

He had used his newly won electoral strength to bargain, not with Ottawa, but with his fellow-premiers. He had become simply another player around the table. In the process, he became the only premier in Quebec's history to concede what was considered a sacred part of Quebec's partnership in Confederation: its veto.

As it turned out, on December 6, 1982, the Supreme Court ruled that Quebec had not, in fact, ever really had a veto. But for generations governments had thought it had. And Lévesque thought he was giving it up in exchange for financial compensation for opting out of future constitutional changes.

His decision to sign the accord proved to be a fatal error — not because of the substance of the exchange, but because of the exposed position it left him in. As Roy Romanow was to tell Claude Morin months later, "The alliance of the eight dissident provinces was first and foremost a defensive alliance against the unilateral action of the federal government. . . . In this strategy of common defense, the Accord of April 16 was decisive. . . . But we established clearly at the time and several times since that Saskatchewan didn't consider itself to be limited to this single document." In other words, the April Accord was a bargaining position: a counter-offer.

Lévesque, on the other hand, *was* limited. For him it was not a bargaining position, but a final position. Once negotiations resumed, he had nowhere to go. It was characteristic. On Bill 101, on sovereignty-association, on the expropriation of Asbestos, in negotiations with labour, Lévesque was no bargainer, no negotiator. He and his government developed a position with careful, Cartesian logic, based on a set of principles from which the argument flowed. The result was a closed logical circle, a final offer with no bargaining room, no fall-back position.

This was something the other premiers never understood. They and their ministers kept saying to Lévesque and Morin, "You guys aren't going to stick to this." They had some grounds for their scepticism. As they kept reminding the Quebec representatives, Lesage had supported the Fulton-Favreau formula — and then dropped it in 1965; Bourassa had supported the Victoria Charter in 1971, and then, after returning to Quebec, had renounced it. But Morin and Lévesque kept insisting they would stick to this agreement, "In our culture," Morin would say, "when one has signed something, one sticks to it."

He meant it. It was a crucial misunderstanding, which would create an enormous personal breach between Lévesque and Morin and their counterparts in the other provinces when the latter abandoned the Accord in the middle of the night on November 5. The depth of Lévesque's and Morin's bitterness was never really grasped or understood in the rest of Canada. Because, while the April Accord was a bargaining position for the other premiers, for Lévesque it was the only design of a new Canadian constitution he could accept. He had signed, and considered the Accord as binding as a contract. He was prepared to fight to the end for it.

But once negotiating of any kind began, he was stuck. He had given up whatever manoeuvring room he had. As so often before, he had placed himself in a situation where he could only play the cards he had — and then win or lose. This time he lost.

ON SEPTEMBER 28, A SMALL GROUP OF CABINET MINISTERS AND aides joined Lévesque in the salon outside his office to watch the Supreme Court judgment on the federal constitutional proposals. The group included Claude Charron, Marc-André Bédard, and Jacques-Yvan Morin. (Claude Morin was in Ottawa.) They would send out for chicken for lunch as they watched and prepared strategy.

There had been months of speculation about how the Supreme Court would deal with the court challenges that had been part of the strategy of the opposing provinces: to question the courts on the validity of the approach in Manitoba, Quebec, and Newfoundland. And, at the same time, there had been some strategic speculation inside the government about how to respond. Even before the decision was rendered, Quebec had begun a publicity campaign of brochures and billboards showing a hand reaching out from a vague Union Jack background, and scrunching up a piece of paper. Another hand was grabbing the first hand's wrist, and the caption read "Minute, Ottawa!" It was a harsh, crude image with some fascinating implications. With its Union Jack background, it looked almost like an anti-conscription poster. The hand scrunching up the piece of paper (perhaps Bill 101?) was reminiscent of the Félix Leclerc line quoted so often during the referendum —about the fat foreign fingers going through the family papers.

The men in Lévesque's salon had developed a range of responses, depending on the degree to which the Supreme Court endorsed the federal package — ranging from an extreme position of rejection if the package was fully endorsed to a more moderate position in case of a split judgment.

For one possibility — which Claude Morin expected — was that the Supreme Court would find that the federal proposal was legal, but not legitimate, since it broke with the conventions that had prevailed in federal-provincial relations. Then a great deal would depend on whether the federal government was determined to proceed. Claude Charron felt that, in this case, outright defiance would be inappropriate, and that Quebec should work out some response with the other dissenting provinces.

One possibility was to seek what Lévesque had told the British high commissioner, Lord Moran, in August that he would accept: "patriation, pure and simple". But there were other factors to consider. There were signs of unease in the Parti Québécois, and the biennial convention was coming up in December. Ten days ago the riding association in La Peltrie, a suburban riding west of Quebec City, had passed a resolution calling for a unilateral declaration of independence should the Supreme Court support the federal proposals.

Thus, Lévesque had to walk carefully; after the referendum defeat, the party's tolerance for negotiating federalism was not high. On Friday, September 25, while discounting the importance of the La Peltrie resolution, Lévesque had announced that the party executive's proposal to the party congress in December would be that the next election would be fought on the issue of sovereignty-association.

The televised Supreme Court announcement was an unintelligible disappointment. One of the judges had accidentally pulled out a microphone cord — and Chief Justice Bora Laskin suddenly seemed to be mumbling inaudibly as he read the judgment aloud.

The judges had to decide on the questions that had been referred to the Supreme Court from Manitoba, Quebec (where the court had found in favour of the federal government), and Newfoundland (where the court had ruled narrowly against the federal government). Posed in slightly different fashion in each province, the questions basically asked if the amendments to the constitution would affect provincial powers, if it was a constitutional convention that the federal government should not request constitutional amendments without agreement of the provinces, and if agreement of the provinces was constitutionally required for amendment of the constitution.

The answers themselves were terse. Would provincial powers be affected? Yes, 9-0. Is it a constitutional convention for the federal government to get the consent of the provinces before seeking amendments to the BNA Act? Yes, 6-3. Is the agreement of the provinces required for amendment? As a matter of constitutional convention, yes, 6-3. As a matter of law, no, 7-2.

This, as Robert Sheppard of the *Globe and Mail* put it the next day, was "both a smashing legal victory and a stern rebuke on propriety for the Trudeau government's constitutional initiatives." For in its explanation of the decision, the court had decided that the federal amendments would create a different federation, "made different at the insistence of a majority in the House of the federal Parliament acting alone. It is this process itself which offends the federal principle." But the court also decided that constitutional conventions are not legally enforceable, and that the federal government had legal authority to carry out its plan.

The judges' views on constitutional conventions were clear and strongly expressed. "It should be borne in mind, however, that while they are not laws, some conventions may be more important than laws," they wrote, in a phrase that Lévesque was to quote more than once in the weeks ahead."That is why it is perfectly appropriate to say that to violate a convention is to do something which is unconstitutional although it entails no direct legal consequence." And later: "Furthermore, and to repeat, whatever the result, the process offends the federal principle." And in conclusion:

> "We have reached the conclusion that the agreement of the provinces of Canada, no views being expressed as to its quantification, is constitutionally required for the passing of the 'Proposed Resolution for a joint Address to Her Majesty respecting the Constitution of Canada,' and that the passing of this Resolution would be unconstitutional in the conventional sense."

Unconstitutional in the conventional sense! That became the key phrase of the judgment. And what did the judgment mean? In his office, Jean Chrétien had turned to his deputy minister, Roger Tassé, after the 7-2 verdict had been announced, and said, "We won." Tassé answered, "Yes."

Coming down the steps of the Supreme Court building, Michel Robert, one of the key federal lawyers, made some finer distinctions, "It means that we won on a legal level. On the political level, it remains to be discussed."

In the Bunker in Quebec City, the phrase "unconstitutional in the conventional sense" provoked a collective moan. The legal-but-not-legitimate possibility had been part of their planning, but they had not been prepared for this particular hair-split.

"Another word to explain!" muttered Claude Charron. He felt that he had spent the last year explaining the word "unilateral" to working-class Quebecers, and was proud of the fact that by the end of the year they were phoning open-line shows to complain about Ottawa's "unilateral action".

Chrétien was firm at his noon press conference. After talking briefly with Pierre Trudeau, who was in South Korea, he made it clear that what mattered was legality.

"When you respect the constitution and you're acting legally, you cannot make a distinction about other things—you know, the legitimacy of this and that. They [the provinces] took us to court because they claimed we were acting illegally, and we're acting legally."

For almost twelve months since Pierre Trudeau had announced his plan to amend and unilaterally patriate the constitution, Lévesque and his ministers had been hammering away constantly at it with the powerful phrase "coup de force". Now, they watched as Jean Chrétien banged away on camera with *his* word: "legal". The constitutional package was legal, he was happy that the plan was legal, the federal government had won because it was legal legal legal.

Then Lévesque and his colleagues spent three hours studying the decision in detail — copies had been sent to Quebec by jet from Ottawa that morning. During that time, Lévesque had a conference call with six of the seven other premiers opposing the federal plan. (Peter Lougheed was in West Germany, supporting Calgary's bid for the 1988 Winter Olympic Games.)

In the conversation, Lévesque told his colleagues that "on the French side of things" he felt he had to respond to Chrétien. Everyone agreed that he should — so what would seem like a breaking of ranks had in fact been discussed and approved by his fellow-premiers.

Later, at a press conference, Lévesque was very critical of Chrétien's apparent determination to push ahead, and vowed to use "all legitimate means of resistance" to stop the federal plan. He was scathing about Chrétien's remark that the federal government had to pass the package quickly and get on to the problems of energy and the economy, accusing the federal government of "incompetence" and "leading us to the abyss".

"Mr. Chrétien's words on that score were a bit like a guy who would set fire to a credit union after stealing everything," he said. "When people come up and say 'We want to arrest you for theft,' the guy answers, 'Well, don't bother about that; what is urgent is to stop the fire.' What we say is that we want to stop both: the fire, economically, everybody should get together to stop. But it is very important also to stop the thieves, especially since those thieves want to rob us of much more than what is in the Caisse Populaire funds . . . It means robbing us of our rights, our basic rights."

That night, about ten o'clock, Chrétien tracked down Roy Romanow at his hotel. "We won," he said. "You owe me a bottle of Scotch." The liquor stores were closed, but Romanow, accompanied by the Ontario attorney general, Roy McMurtry, dropped over to Chrétien's house, and the three sat drinking beer, discussing how the process could develop from there. Chrétien and McMurtry urged Romanow to isolate Lévesque, saying that Quebec was controlling the Gang of Eight, and that no agreement was possible as long as that situation continued.

A few days later, the ministers met in Montreal, at the Dorval Hilton. Morin buttonholed Romanow. Was it true that he had met Chrétien to discuss ways of reaching an agreement? Romanow insisted they had met only to discuss the appointment of federal judges in Saskatchewan. It was a lie Morin never forgave.

The premiers began a process of public bargaining with Trudeau over dates for a last-chance meeting to negotiate. But already Lévesque and Morin could feel the will to resist ebbing out of the dissident premiers. Lévesque kept telling his colleagues how they could beat the Trudeau plan in London, and getting vague, evasive replies like "Yeah, if it goes that far."

And in Toronto, at a meeting at the Harbour Castle in October, Claude Morin told the other ministers how he had personally staked his career on the April Accord. "It this were to collapse, I would also collapse," he said.

For the English-Canadian ministers, it seemed like posturing; Robert Sheppard and Michael Valpy, in recounting Morin's appeal, described him as "Metternich-like to the end" since he had planned to leave politics after the referendum and had only agreed to stay on because of the constitutional negotiations.

But Morin was staking his reputation on a Common Front of provinces. It was ironic; back in 1976, a few weeks after his election, he had argued that provincial Common Fronts were doomed to failure — and, if they succeeded, would do so at Quebec's expense. Then, he had been convinced that the other provinces fundamentally wished to see power centralized on Ottawa. Now, whether through miscalculation or lack of choice, he found himself inextricably committed to an instrument that he instinctively distrusted.

In the days leading up to the November conference, Morin became increasingly worried. At one point, he told a reporter privately that he thought Ottawa was trying to bring about the worst scenario of all: the isolation of Quebec by all the others. He quickly added that he was sure that this worst-case scenario would not happen. It did.

ON SEPTEMBER 29, THE DAY AFTER THE JUDGMENT, LÉVESQUE announced that he was calling the National Assembly into special session to debate a special resolution calling on the federal government to renounce unilateralism. Despite the ill-will generated a year earlier, Ryan was prepared to collaborate this time; the final motion was drawn up in consultation among Lévesque, Charron, Ryan, and Gérard-D. Lévesque, with checks with both caucuses. It consisted in large part of phrases taken word for word from the motion passed at the Liberals' general council meeting ten days earlier.

The result was unwieldy, but not unclear:

> The Supreme Court of Canada having decided that the federal proposals respecting the constitution of Canada decrease the powers of the National Assembly of Quebec and that unilateral action by the federal government , although legal, is unconstitutional, being contrary to the conventions,
>   this assembly demands that the federal government renounce its unilateral course of action,
>   is opposed to any action that could impair its rights and affect its powers without its consent,
>   and requests the federal and provincial governments to resume negotiations immediately with full respect for the principles and conventions that must apply to any modification of the federal system.

Lévesque made it clear that the government would defy the proposed Charter of Rights, telling the Assembly that every Quebec government had complained of Quebec's weakness and that no Quebec government could allow the powers it had to be reduced. The motion was to throw the Liberal caucus into agonizing confusion.

Only ten days before, Claude Ryan had delivered a lengthy analysis of the reasons for the Liberal defeat and had concluded that the party had lost — and had to regain — the confidence of the francophone majority. When there was a choice between the interests of the federal Liberal Party and the interests of Quebec, he said, the party had to choose the interests of Quebec. It was as clear and detached an analysis as any he had made at *Le Devoir*. It also angered and alienated a substantial part of his caucus.

In the Assembly, Ryan called for a "strong and unanimous vote" on the motion, saying, "What is at stake is the defence of Quebec's legislative powers." But for some in the caucus, the choice was harrowing. In many cases, they had to choose between their leader — whom many of them disliked — and their hatred of the Parti Québécois. At one point, it seemed as if as many as half the caucus might break. But Michel Pagé, the whip —a Garneau supporter in 1978 —and Michel Gratton were the only Liberals not to rise to give Ryan a standing ovation after his speech.

During the day of October 1, the day before the vote, the number of dissidents was estimated as high as fourteen, a third of the caucus. But by evening, after considerable pressure by Gérard-D. Lévesque, the number who were still unwilling to vote for the motion had dropped to fewer than ten — the number that had been established as crucial for the survival of Ryan's leadership.

Pagé had been persuaded to come on side, as had three hard-line federalist Liberals from the Eastern Townships, Pierre Paradis, Fabien Bélanger, and Yvon Vallières. Lise Bacon, a strong supporter of Trudeau and a former president of the Quebec Liberal Party, bent for reasons of party solidarity only; in her speech, she went out of her way to praise Trudeau.

Reed Scowen and Herbert Marx, the members for Notre-Dame-de-Grâce and D'Arcy-McGee, never doubted how they would vote. Scowen, as a former research director for the Pepin-Robarts Task Force on Canadian Unity, had spontaneously called the Trudeau unilateral plan "a betrayal of the principles of federalism" when he had first learned of it exactly a year earlier. Marx, a professor of constitutional law, felt the same way.

One Liberal who found the vote enormously difficult was the MNA for Westmount, Richard French. "Intellectually, I can accept the motion and I want desperately for the interests of the party to vote for it," he said the night before. "But emotionally, I find it very difficult because the rights of the National Assembly have been used to erode the privileges of the people I represent."

After dinner in the parliamentary restaurant, he went up to his office to telephone some of his key supporters to tell them he had decided to vote for the motion. They told him flatly that if he voted with the PQ they would get another candidate. He toyed with resigning and seeking re-election, but decided that his primary obligation was to the people who had turned over their kitchens and basement rec rooms for the campaign to get him the nomination, and had then elected him.

The morning of the vote, there was a strange emotional

solidarity among the Liberals. As they went to their seats, Jean-Claude Rivest went over to Joan Dougherty, and quietly squeezed her hand. After the vote, as Reed Scowen and Richard French passed each other in the corridor, Scowen gave French an affectionate punch in the shoulder, a wordless acknowledgement of what they had both gone through.

Nine Liberals had broken ranks. Gratton, Dougherty, French, John O'Gallagher, John Ciaccia, Clifford Lincoln, Cosmo Maciocia, William Cusano, and Lucien Caron. But for many, especially those who had voted with the party and against their conscience, the incident was the end of their tolerance for Claude Ryan. He had forfeited their loyalty and support.

In his austere way, Ryan saw the vote as a matter of conscience, and had little notion of the need his members felt to be reassured or personally inspired. At least two of the dissidents were to say later that if Ryan had personally asked them for their help and support on the vote, they could not have refused. But those who had been pressured, and had given in, felt resentful. It would be another ten months before he resigned, but this was the beginning of the end of Ryan's leadership of the Quebec Liberal Party.

AS THE PREMIERS, MINISTERS, AND AIDES GATHERED IN OTTAWA, THERE was a strong sense that this was the last chance to reach an agreement. If the September 1980 conference had been a high point in publicly stating the divergent visions of Canada, the November 1981 conference had to be either a breakthrough or a failure. There was no middle ground, no room for "progress", or, as premiers always told reporters after unproductive meetings, for "understanding each other's position better". Their positions were all clear, rock-hard, and understood. The question was whether they would move from them.

Nevertheless, the conferences had begun to take on certain ritual qualities. The Quebec delegation stays across the river in Hull, at the Plaza de la Chaudière; other provincial delegations stay at different Ottawa hotels, but most of them reserve suites at the Château Laurier, across the road from the conference centre—what was once the central hall of Union Station: a magnificent, high-vaulted room where it is almost impossible to hear without using earphones.

On the upper floors, there are smaller meeting rooms, where the premiers adjourn for private sessions. Off the main hall are television studios, and a large press room, full of typewriters, where reporters wait, gossip, and drink coffee and — the only gesture towards nutrition in an otherwise uniformly unhealthy environment — apple juice that is wheeled in regularly. Across the corridor: a press-conference room.

The four days during which the deal was put together, in fits and starts, was filled with little events which became part of the anecdotal lore of English-Canadian journalism; the long night of negotiations while the Quebec delegation slept became part of the Quebec nationalist discourse on the betrayal of Quebec.

Sunday night, November 1, the eight dissident premiers met to discuss strategy. At the same time, Premier William Davis met Pierre Trudeau and told him he would withdraw his demand that Ontario keep a veto. This moved the negotiating a step towards the Vancouver formula.

On Monday, November 2, the conference opened, with a series of formal statements by all the participants. Trudeau began by identifying the three areas to be discussed: the patriation of the British North America Act, an amending formula, and a Charter of Rights. His tone was conciliatory — but he made his objections to the dissenting provincial position clear.

"The Vancouver formula proposed by eight provinces — well, our objection to it is that it solves the problem of consensus by saying that there cannot be one. It really denies the existence of a national will. It says in reality that if 95 per cent of Canadians from nine provinces agree to something, one province can still say, Well, that is not the national will. One province can pick up its marbles and opt out."

After Trudeau, Davis made his concession: that Ontario would be prepared to accept an amending formula in which Ontario did not have a veto. And, a little later, Hatfield proposed a plan to defer parts of the Charter of Rights. All three statements had been carefully planned as part of the federal position — to lay out the concessions through Davis and Hatfield, and see if the Gang of Eight could be undermined. But the dissident premiers seemed to be holding firm.

Lévesque, who followed Davis, made a strong speech, saying that Trudeau had no mandate to patriate and modify the constitution unilaterally — and challenging him to call an election on the issue. The other premiers made similarly strong statements to the effect that the federal government had lost at the

Supreme Court, and that unilateral patriation violated federalism — although Blakeney and Bennett both indicated a willingness to find a compromise. This was, in fact, Quebec's greatest worry — that Blakeney and Bennett would be cut away from the Gang of Eight.

On Tuesday, November 3, Davis began to feel out the idea of what he called "a straight swap" — if Trudeau would accept the Vancouver amending formula, the provinces would accept the Charter. However, in the process of being discussed, this became an offer of what federal officials contemptuously called "a gutted charter".

However, Tuesday night, a chain of events was set in motion which blew apart the Gang of Eight, and made the final deal possible. It began when Trudeau held a special cabinet meeting to brief his colleagues on the state of the negotiations. He and Jean Chrétien told them that they would be prepared to accept a straight swap — provided it was for a full Charter of Rights. However, this had already been rejected by the Eight, who had come forward with other alternatives.

Then Trudeau told the cabinet what he would propose to the premiers in the morning: patriation with a moratorium on the Charter followed by a referendum on the Charter and the two amending formulas. This was proposed as a strategic gesture — but also, more importantly, to overcome the Supreme Court's argument that "substantial" support of the provinces was needed. If substantial support were won from the citizens, it would make it harder to argue that support from their provincial governments was necessary.

On Wednesday, the deadlock broke. At 8.30 a.m., the Eight met for their daily breakfast at the Château Laurier, and Allan Blakeney surprised his fellow-premiers with his own new amending formula. He was proposing that the formula be that amendment would require the consent of the federal government and any seven provinces. This was accompanied by a thirty-page document distributed to the premiers. At 9.15, they had it photocopied and distributed to their delegations.

The Quebec delegation was furious, and senior officials stormed out into the corridor by the press room to say so. "Blakeney has screwed us!" ("Blakeney nous a chié entre les mains") raged one ordinarily unflappable senior official.

For Blakeney had proposed something they found totally unacceptable: Quebec would lose its veto and not receive opting out — let alone compensation — in return. Moreover, the Quebecers began to be concerned that the titular provincial chairman, British Columbia's William Bennett, was slipping in his determination to stay with the group. For Bennett was preparing his own proposal — a concession to Trudeau's language rights. Thus, when the premiers began to gather with Trudeau on the fourth floor of the conference centre, Lévesque and his delegation were worried that the Gang of Eight was falling apart.

The first ministers began by discussing Blakeney's proposal. His reasoning was based on Trudeau's insistence on an amending formula that required approval by regions, a proposal that angered the Western and Atlantic provinces, since they would be counted as single units. He set out to break the logjam with a counter-proposal that would treat each province separately, taking away vetoes and the right to opt out.

Then Trudeau told the premiers of his fall-back proposal to solve the deadlock: patriation, with a moratorium on the amending formula and the Charter of Rights; if no agreement were reached after two years, there would be a national referendum.

At first, all the premiers, including Lévesque, were very dubious. None of the English-Canadian premiers liked the idea of a referendum; they saw it as foreign to the parliamentary system. (In fact, many of them thought that a Charter of Rights was foreign to the parliamentary system — and had said so at length in September 1980 — but they increasingly felt they had to come to terms with Trudeau's determination to have one.) But only one premier immediately saw Trudeau's purpose in proposing a referendum.

"He's trying to conventionalize the charter," Blakeney said. The Supreme Court had said that substantial provincial support was necessary; presumably that would be outweighed by popular support in a referendum.

Then Trudeau began to bait Lévesque, personally taunting him in French. You're the great democrat, the great believer in referendums — are you afraid to take me on? Provoked, Lévesque responded to the dare. Sure, he wasn't afraid of a referendum.

Trudeau and his officials were delighted. They had hoped, but hadn't dared expect, that they could trap Lévesque and hive him off from his allies. Lévesque was accompanied by Claude Morin and Louis Bernard, secretary of the Executive

Council, and they felt this was a chance. The Gang of Eight seemed to be dissolving, with Blakeney coming out of nowhere with his proposal and Bennett looking as if he was about to jump. They figured the other premiers, perhaps Buchanan of Nova Scotia or Maclean of P.E.I., might slide.

"If Mr. Trudeau picked himself up six provinces, the job would be much harder for the four who were left to make an alliance of some kind with the federal Conservatives and go to London to fight the plan," one Quebec official said. "It was the lesser of two evils. In two years, perhaps the situation would be better, and perhaps it would be better to take a free game in the future than a possible immediate loss."

Trudeau emerged from the meeting with a mischievous smile, saying, "The cat is among the pigeons," and referring to an "alliance" with Quebec. Lévesque called it a spectacular opening, very interesting, and worthy of consideration: "an honourable way out if there is no other way out". Claude Charron said enthusiastically that the idea was, in fact, from Quebec. "Claude Ryan suggested a referendum a couple of weeks ago in an interview, and Mr. Lévesque opened the conference challenging Mr. Trudeau to go to the people. How can we be opposed?"

The Western premiers were opposed — partly because they didn't like its being run on a regional basis, partly because they were uncomfortable with the idea of campaigning against a Charter of Rights. But when the premiers went back to meet Trudeau in the afternoon, more details began to emerge about the proposal, and another document began to be circulated. It called for the legislation to be passed and sent to Westminster; there would be a referendum only if all provinces wanted one.

Lévesque backed away furiously. "What Mr. Trudeau said," he told reporters afterwards, "was very simple. But later, when we saw it written down, it became very complicated and perhaps even bizarre and worrisome. . . . It was almost as if it were written in Chinese."

But his "alliance" of several hours had blown what remained of the Gang of Eight apart. As he headed back to the hotel to brief his delegation, chances of an agreement seemed slight. The delegation met briefly, and then went for dinner in the ornate hotel restaurant. During dinner Louis Bernard was called to the phone; a B.C. official wanted to remind him that there would be a breakfast meeting the following morning.

Next day, Lévesque went to breakfast with the premiers at

the Château Laurier. As he arrived, almost half an hour late, Brian Peckford said simply, "We have a new proposal, René. It's there by your plate."

Through the night, the English-speaking premiers had put together a new package — leaving Quebec out of the final deal, and dropping the provision that Lévesque had forced his dissident colleagues to agree to in April: financial compensation for opting out.

The arrangement had begun with notes exchanged between Chrétien, Romanow, and McMurtry at 5 p.m. the day before, in the kitchen off the meeting room on the fifth floor of the conference centre — thereafter known as "the kitchen consensus". In essence, it used the Vancouver amending formula, but dropped financial compensation, and adopted the override, or "notwithstanding" clause, on the second part of the Charter of Rights.

Gradually, through the night, it became modified as the consensus broadened and agreement was reached. In the morning, it was formally proposed by Brian Peckford: a Tory, a hard-line provincial-rights man, and the premier of the most recent province to join Confederation.

Lévesque was stunned. In the remaining few hours before the premiers went before the cameras, he alternated between anger and disillusioned withdrawal. His formal reasons for refusing to sign were threefold: he objected to the removal of the financial-compensation clause in the amending formula, which had been his condition for giving up the traditional Quebec veto when he agreed to sign the April Accord; he objected to the mobility clauses, which he argued would endanger Quebec job-creation programs and construction-labour regulation; most of all, he objected to the minority-language rights clause in the Charter of Rights, which would override Bill 101.

He had fought an election campaign only seven months earlier, mentioning the language provisions of Bill 101 in every speech. Now, the criteria for admission to English schools were no longer to be established by the National Assembly in its legislation, they were to be imposed by Ottawa and by provincial premiers who had never given their francophone minorities as many services as even the Parti Québécois, with Bill 101, was providing for its English-speaking minority.

But the policies were one thing. The compensation question

could be debated (it was later modified to provide for compensation in education and culture), and it would be politically difficult to penalize Quebec for opting out; the mobility clause was modified by a proviso Newfoundland had insisted on, allowing provinces with higher-than-average unemployment to disregard it. Even the language provisions, if closely examined, came down to a question of how quickly the English minority in Quebec would decline.

Worse than any one of these policy questions was the sheer humiliation. His career had been devoted to trying to strengthen Quebec, and it was now weaker; he had sought more powers for Quebec, and now he had lost some of the powers Quebec had had. In the referendum campaign, he had said that a No vote would weaken Quebec. He had been proved right in the worst way. No-one had even phoned. The worst-case scenario had happened. They had left him out.

Ironically, back in Quebec City, a rumour had reached the Executive Council offices to the effect that a deal had been reached *with* Quebec. The reaction was pure visceral elation: cheers, hugs, shouts of joy. One senior civil servant who had once been a Parti Québécois official watched with a wry sense of discovery: even there, even at the heart of the government's planning secretariat, the deep-rooted, fundamental desire was not for rupture and liberation from Canada — but for reconciliation. He had never seen the emotion expressed so openly before. The elation at the inaccurate rumour only emphasized the subsequent rage, resentment, and humiliation at the final result.

As the premiers had their final meeting, word began to filter down to the floor of the conference centre that an agreement had been reached which Quebec would not accept. Aides and civil servants were giving impromptu briefings as the word spread and reporters clustered around.

Then, after the signing, the premiers came into the room, elated. Lévesque came last — looking resigned and dejected. Trudeau spoke first, saying that he was happy to report that a consensus had been reached.

"I have one regret," he said. "I put it on the record. I will not return to it. I have the regret that we have not kept in the amending formula a reference to the ultimate sovereignty of the people as could be tested in a referendum."

Then William Davis, in his orotund way, said that it was an

emotional moment, and that to say so was an understatement. He said that the compromise was proof that Canadian political leaders could show ingenuity, flexibility, and stubbornness. He praised Trudeau for his flexibility and his willingness to compromise. He didn't mention Quebec.

Lévesque spoke, softly and bitterly, fatigue and anger showing in his voice on occasion, but more often the sound of defeat. "I must say that I sincerely regret that Quebec now finds itself today in a position which has become one of the fundamental traditions of the Canadian federal régime: Quebec finds itself alone. It will be up to the Quebec people, and to them alone, to draw their conclusions."

After running over Quebec's objections to the final version, he said that the joy and self-congratulations would change when the premiers realized the consequences of isolating Quebec. "The straitjacket which the federal régime represents is being tightened again for us. There is absolutely no question of accepting that; we will never capitulate, and we will use all the means that remain to prevent it."

Then, as the conference broke up, he repeated his remarks at a press conference, saying, with his lip curling around the phrase, that the result had been "the Canadian Way".

When, shortly afterwards, he boarded the government F-27 jet at the Gatineau airport, across the river in Quebec, he looked like a beaten man. Tears welled in his eyes as, slumped in his seat, he flew back to Quebec.

For the humiliation could not have been much greater. He had been trapped by Trudeau and tricked by his fellow-premiers. The result was the end of an era that had begun in 1960, with Lesage. Since then, Quebec's role in Canada had been to build a state: a state that was energetic and expanding, and seeking more power.

It was assumed by everyone associated with government in Quebec, federalist or indépendantiste, that it would get more power, inside Confederation or out. Now, the game had fundamentally and dramatically changed. Quebec was not to have more powers, but fewer powers. Not a lot fewer powers — but fewer than it had. Minority-language education, which had been a political question for over a decade, making and breaking governments, was now being settled by imposition.

The Charter of Rights was not simply a setback or an embarrassment, but the overturning of a policy that Lévesque had fought and won an election on. The defeat he felt was much deeper than the referendum defeat. For it was a defeat of everything he — and every Quebec premier since the Second World War — had fought for.

Long before the PQ, Quebec had been seeking to expand its jurisdiction: to get exclusive responsibility over communications, cultural affairs, agriculture, social affairs, adult education. Now the prospect of that, or anything resembling that, was over. Not more, less.

For if sovereignty-association had been defeated in the referendum, special status for Quebec seemed to have been killed by the constitutional settlement. From then on, it would be in or out. The whole perspective of an expanded responsibility for Quebec was now closed. Lévesque had lost.

THE NEXT DAY, LÉVESQUE, CLAUDE MORIN, AND MARC-ANDRÉ BÉDARD gave the caucus a briefing on what had happened: a summary of the year's history of collaboration and alliance with the seven other premiers, and the events of the previous days.

Lévesque went over it all — how he had insisted on financial compensation for opting out back in April as the exchange for dropping Quebec's historic veto — and how the premiers had dropped this in the late-night deal; how he had been stunned to have the final agreement "shoved under my nose at breakfast" on Thursday morning. Worse, he said, he had been drawn away from the Gang of Eight himself in the confusion of the meeting on Wednesday.

When the account was finished, the members of caucus spoke out: indignant at the betrayal, but cautious about the implication in Lévesque's remarks at the conference that there should be a referendum or an election. "Canada has withdrawn from Quebec," Élie Fallu said. "The other provinces have behaved with incredible dishonesty and tossed Quebec away like a dirty dish-rag."

That afternoon, in his office, Claude Morin wrote a letter to all his colleagues in the Gang of Eight. He said how much he had appreciated the work they had put into fighting the unilateral plan, and went over how much Quebec had hesitated before signing the April Accord.

"So it was with growing unease that I realized at the beginning of October, after the Supreme Court decision, that some of you were beginning to question the content of our April

Accord, and were saying you were ready to look at other solutions to accommodate Ottawa better.

"This unease turned to consternation and disappointment as I saw more and more clearly that the Accord of April 16 no longer had the importance for everybody that it still had for Quebec."

Then, after reviewing the events that led to the signing of the deal, he pointed out that Quebec now faced a situation in which a federal government with an English-speaking majority and nine English-speaking provinces were about to ask another English-speaking government "to reduce, without its consent, the integrity and competence of the only French-speaking government in North America!

"For eighteen years now, in one way or another, I have been directly involved in the constitutional debate. At no moment have I ever thought we would get to such a deplorable and painful situation as Quebec is now living through."

He concluded, "I thought I should let you know my feelings, in the hope that you will understand how much we in Quebec, and I personally, are affected by the turn of events."

Only his secretary sensed the full significance of the letter, and commented: "I think that letter is serious." For it was his farewell. Morin felt that he had been lied to, and could not face those men again. Ten days later, he submitted his resignation.

EIGHTEEN

Morbid Symptoms

*The ancien régime is dying,
while the new one does not
know how to give birth to
itself; during this interregnum, a wide diversity of
morbid symptoms emerge.*
Antonio Gramsci

When Lévesque returned from Ottawa, his rage and humil-iation could not be contained, and he exploded in a month-long venting of spleen. No word was too strong or too coarse to describe the constitutional settlement: it was "a stab in the back", "a night of long knives", "a shameful betrayal", "treachery", "contemptible", "banditry", "contempt for Quebec".

He said he was "screwed left and right" by Blakeney, Bennett, and Peckford; the Liberals were "political sluts"; he would not allow Quebec to get involved in "cleaning up the dirty sheets" of this despicable deal. He blamed "anglophone mandarins", and left a threat hanging in the inaugural address on November 9, warning English Quebecers that if they were to receive similar treatment to that received by francophones in other provinces it would be a serious loss for them.

As so often happens, Lévesque's anger was echoed and am-plified in the National Assembly. One PQ member after another used the debate on the inaugural address to elaborate the rage and humiliation. One of the more sweeping images came from a backbencher, Yves Blais, who compared Pierre Trudeau and the nine premiers to General Wolfe, "who, in 1760 [*sic*], climbed the banks of the St. Lawrence in the middle of the night to attack Montcalm and his sleeping soldiers". The continuing display of rage was to prove self-defeating. For Lévesque's spitting anger was heard, absorbed—and misunderstood—in the Parti Québécois.

Since summer, the party had been working on the resolutions for the December convention—a process in which resolutions slowly worked their way up from riding meetings to regional meetings to the national executive, and then to the convention. The process had begun with a working document, produced by a party committee chaired by Pierre Harvey. It called for the next election to be on sovereignty. "A general election which would not exclude sovereignty as one of the stakes, even among other questions, would have the value of a referendum and would thus be in perfect conformity with the democratic ideals that the party wants to respect in this matter, since sovereignty constitutes the first article of the program."

Harvey, an economist at the École des Hautes Études Commerciales, was nothing if not a Lévesque loyalist: he had responded to Lévesque's request to run in Outremont in 1976 against André Raynauld—an unwinnable contest—and against Solange Chaput-Rolland in 1979. He was the program adviser on the executive, and generally considered to be an unconditional Lévesque supporter who helped carry out what Lévesque wanted done on the executive.

Thus, when Harvey brought out the report, the party assumed that Lévesque had accepted the end of the pure referendum principle of a majority vote, and had agreed that a parliamentary majority, whether the result of more than half the popular vote or not, would be enough to begin the process of negotiating independence.

Months had gone by since the referendum, and the party had never gone through the emotional catharsis of expressing its rage and frustration at the defeat. But in the fall of 1981, the indications became clearer that the party was going to sweep away the étapiste strategy which had resulted in the tortuously phrased referendum question, and make a clear, unequivocal commitment to Quebec independence.

The dilemma which Lévesque had wrestled with since he conceived the party in 1968 was how to balance the ardour of the party militants with the demands of electoral pragmatism. But the referendum defeat had altered the equilibrium: Lévesque knew that he had to toughen the party policy.

With the recommendation that the next election should be on sovereignty, he and his advisers were confident that this would be sufficient to keep a broad consensus in the party. However, at the riding and regional meetings, the whole idea of sovereignty-association was being questioned.

At the Quebec City regional meeting in October, Louise Beaudoin took many people by surprise by her sweeping endorsement of unhyphenated independence. It was a double surprise, since Beaudoin had worked for Claude Morin throughout the pre-referendum period, and she was now a senior civil servant.

In November, the National Council endorsed the idea of an election on sovereignty — and Lévesque gave a strange description of what he claimed he had always meant by sovereignty-association.

"In my mind, there has never been a hyphen [between the two words]," he said, "since we have never intended to isolate ourselves, but first and above all, we have to discuss sovereignty." In fact, he added, if the party asked him to drop the idea of association completely, "That wouldn't be the end of the world."

No hyphen? In its news coverage of the meeting, Radio-Canada ran a clip of Lévesque saying "What hyphen?"—along with a cut of him speaking to the National Assembly on October 10, 1978, saying, "There can be no question, in our mind, of first achieving sovereignty and then of negotiating association afterwards. . . . Since these two concepts of sovereignty and of association complete each other, we must define what we mean by the first and the second, with the hyphen that we put between the two."

Under the circumstances, it was understandable that PQ members should conclude that Lévesque's position had changed: that he had moved from a commitment to sovereignty-association to a belief in independence, and that the party would make a historic shift back to a clearer commitment to Quebec independence, unrestricted by an obligation to negotiate an economic association with the rest of Canada.

But that was not what Lévesque intended.

AS THE PARTI QUÉBÉCOIS CONVENTION DREW NEARER, THERE WAS little indication that Lévesque, the members of his staff, or cabinet ministers recognized the misunderstanding that was developing. Lévesque continued to rage, the members continued to vote tough indépendantiste resolutions, and few sensed the gathering storm.

In his speech at the opening of the convention, on December 4, Lévesque reached the climax of his rage against Ottawa. "It's over, the game where the dice are always loaded," he said, and was answered by a standing ovation from the 2,100 delegates, who chanted the street slogan of the separatist demonstrations of the 1960s: "Le Québec aux Québécois" — "Quebec for Quebecers".

There were some subtle notes of caution: the constitutional deal was the fault, not of the English-Canadian premiers, but of "two eminent Quebecers named Trudeau and Chrétien" who had acted "on the orders of the English-speaking mandarins who seek the gradual death of our minorities" (the francophones in the other provinces). There should be no hasty moves, however. "We have to get through the economic crisis to arrive at Quebec sovereignty. It is the deepest and most serious crisis that we've seen in fifty years, and it affects the budget of each family, as it affects the finances of the government."

In other words, blame Trudeau and the federal bureaucrats, not English Canada. And no snap election. Nevertheless, the speech was one of Lévesque's strongest on independence — using the phrase "genocide" to describe federal policies (even though he was quoting the title of a recent book by Pierre Vadeboncoeur), and committing himself to action.

"What remains now is to build ourselves a country," he said. "As a party activist and as party president, allow me to say that nothing else should motivate us. And as a member of the National Assembly and as premier, I commit myself to do everything so that we can deserve this confidence, for this confidence [in the PQ government] will be an essential part of the historical decision that should not be long in coming."

He concluded with the slogan of the convention — a pun meaning both "It's about time" and "It's time for sovereignty": "C'est souverainement le temps."

Lévesque's gamble was that he could ride the party's rage: direct it, channel it, and control it. He was wrong. The next day, December 5, the first indication of the mood and the determination of the delegates came in the workshops. For the first time, the convention had all the morning workshops studying the same thing: the resolutions on sovereignty. The result was that the leadership of the party could not concentrate their arguments in one workshop, as they had done in the past.

There was a feisty mood in the classrooms at the Université de Montréal, where the workshops were held; chairmen were angrily overruled by the delegates, and, one after another, the groups voted to scratch out the word "association", and the hyphen linking it to "sovereignty".

But it was equally clear that Lévesque clung to the idea with as much determination as ever. In his workshop, he said that it would be "suicidal" to delete from the party program references to economic association with the rest of Canada.

And later, when the workshop came to a resolution that talked about "an economic community", Lévesque, acting as if he were an ordinary delegate, moved to change "community" to "association". In a classroom workshop, Lévesque's authority passed the amendment. But it would not stay there long.

That night, as the delegates gathered for the plenary session at the Claude Robillard Arena, it became clear what had been happening all day in the workshops . For the resolutions all emerged from the workshops collated and prepared for voting. The delegates, unaware that Lévesque himself had put forward the amendment changing "community" to "association", promptly defeated it. It was the beginning of a long night.

A Parti Québécois convention is an extraordinary sight: 122 delegations on the floor of a large, increasingly smoky, arena, each delegate and alternate poring over the "cahier" of resolutions, and listening to the chairman leading them through. There was little or no action in the coffee shops or corridors that Saturday night; everyone was scrupulously following each resolution, and over 2,000 pages would turn in unison.

It was an extraordinarily complicated process. A steering committee of the party executive had sent out copies of a book of resolutions proposing changes to the party program. Each riding and regional meeting had passed amendments to these resolutions.

These amendments had been voted on, and often amended, in the workshops — producing four "cahiers" of amendments to be voted on at the plenary session. The result was a process of mind-numbing complexity, with delegates flipping back and forth from one thick book to another.

In the centre of the arena, facing the podium, were three standing microphones: "le micro pour", for those supporting resolutions, "le micro contre", for those opposing, and "le micro du centre" in between, for those raising the often lengthy questions of procedure.

It was there, at the micro du centre, that a key question was established — a question that made the long Saturday night to Sunday morning necessary, and doomed the convention to spending the whole weekend wrestling with the nature of independence. Pierre Cloutier, a lawyer and a member of the executive for Montreal Centre, spotted the fact that the existing party program would remain intact if resolutions criticizing association were not voted on. He challenged the chair's ruling and succeeded in winning the support of the convention for staying on the issue instead of moving on to the next subject as the agenda proposed and the regular procedure required.

The first question that dealt with association head-on was a series of amendments that would have deleted references to association in the preamble of the party program. The anger at the idea of dealing with the rest of Canada, so soon after the constitutional climax, became clear. "After the low blow we just suffered, people will think we are real dummies if we keep on talking about association," one Montreal delegate said.

Then, as he had done so often in the past when conventions threatened to undermine principles he felt were crucial to his definition of the party, René Lévesque came to the microphone. "I want to say that the party's future will be at stake, just a little bit, on this question," he said quietly.

He talked about how the government had wedded association to sovereignty with a hyphen, arguing that the two things would happen simultaneously. "Everybody agrees we should take [the hyphen] away," he said. "We paid dearly for it. During the referendum, people like Hatfield and Davis came here and said they would never negotiate association." But he urged party members to recognize that ordinary people live in a day-to-day world where they know how interdependent Quebec is with the rest of Canada.

At the microphone ten yards away, le micro contre, stood Michel Bourdon, the large, bear-like union organizer, a delegate from Maisonneuve. "The night is still young," he rumbled.

Bourdon was followed by Jean-François Bertrand, the communications minister and a strong supporter of association, who said that he and others had gone halfway in accepting the emphasis on sovereignty and making it the theme of the next election — and that the indépendantistes should go halfway as well.

The deletion was rejected as Lévesque and Bertrand wanted

— and, about 11 p.m., it looked as if Lévesque would emerge with a satisfactory consensus. But that was only the preamble and, as Bourdon had said, the night was young. The key amendment was still to come.

This spelled out that a sovereign Quebec would propose an economic association with the rest of Canada which would include a common currency, free flow of goods and services, and a common market. Lévesque was getting worried. He told the people around him that if that amendment was defeated, he would quit.

"I am not going to stay if the party becomes the RIN," he said bitterly. "I'll hand my job over to somebody else." The rumour made its way around the hall as the motion came to the floor. And what Lévesque was saying privately, Jean-Pierre Charbonneau, a backbench MNA, said publicly.

"If we have worked for thirteen years for sovereignty-association, it is because it is the best way to do it," he said. "That's why we scuttled the RIN. That's why we formed the Mouvement Souveraineté-Association. That's why we created the Parti Québécois. If we defeat this motion, we are going back to the RIN, and we're saying that we never should have created the Parti Québécois."

He was booed — and the next delegate said: "We'll get independence first, and then we'll see. It would be masochistic, even obscene, to suggest an association now, after what happened in Ottawa."

Again, Lévesque went to the microphone to say which motion he preferred, and that he accepted the amendment that association "could" include various elements. But he warned that, if the motion were rejected, "certain people would die laughing — and I am talking about people in Ottawa."

Again, Bertrand came to the microphone to plead for flexibility. There were twenty delegates lined up at the opposing microphone. But then there was a collective intake of breath. For at the head of the line was Jacques Parizeau.

A minute or so earlier, the head of Parizeau's riding association, Ernest Boudreau, had hustled to Parizeau's side and said urgently, "If you don't intervene now, it is all over." They went to the line, and discreetly, those waiting gave up their places.

There was a sudden ovation as about a third of the hall rose, ecstatic. It seemed that after thirteen years of hedged, rounded compromises, there would be a sudden, dramatic confrontation, and Jacques Parizeau, indépendantiste, would oppose René Lévesque directly on sovereignty-association.

But, as Boudreau recounted later, "One second before he opened his mouth, René Lévesque rose from his seat, stared fixedly at him for one long second, and sat down." Parizeau asked the chair if the motion now said that association "could" include a common currency and so on. Yes, he was told, it did. Apparently reassured, he told the delegates that this would not tie the hands of a sovereign government, and he supported the resolution.

"Despite the ovation that people were nice enough to give me, I was at the wrong microphone," he said—and was given an ovation by a different third of the hall.

He returned to his seat with the delegates of L'Assomption, who eyed him angrily — and voted against the resolution. Parizeau was the only one at his table to raise his hand in support. Boudreau would never really trust him again.

Parizeau's strange gesture was a tactical disaster. Those who agreed with Lévesque were furious, convinced that Parizeau had been determined to oppose the motion, had panicked at the ovation, and had lost his nerve. "If it hadn't been for Parizeau, we would have won," spat Michel Carpentier angrily. "He's finished, finished!"

But those who had opposed the resolution were equally annoyed, feeling that Parizeau had tried to manipulate the delegates and have it both ways: show he was opposed to association but loyal to Lévesque.

The resolution was rejected by a decisive show of hands. The Parti Québécois had rejected sovereignty-association in favour of independence — wiping away thirteen years of work by Lévesque and bringing the party back to the separatist position of the RIN. Lévesque was furious. And, as the delegates left the arena, there was a sense of foreboding and, in an odd way, disappointment for those who had expected more from Parizeau.

"Parizeau missed a good chance to emerge with his stature increased," muttered Bourdon as he left the arena. Parizeau himself left saying, "I should have kept my mouth shut."

THE NEXT DAY, IT WAS AS IF A DAM HAD BROKEN THE NIGHT BEFORE. THE debates were short and to the point. It was as if a heavy rock had been laboriously pushed to the top of the mountain the night before; now, it was gathering momentum as it bounded down the other side. The convention systematically wiped almost all references to association from the program, like so many stains and bitter memories of the referendum defeat.

Lévesque had suffered what the veteran *Toronto Star* correspondent Robert McKenzie called "a rare humiliation". The only shred left was a suggestion in the new program that a sovereign Quebec could "if it considers it appropriate to do so" offer Canada some kind of economic association. But even this was qualified, for the article stressed that this must not limit Quebec's "right to associate with other countries", and insisted that the Parti Québécois, as a party, no longer "promote the idea of association which is already inscribed in the economic and political reality of the countries of North America".

Another motion that passed the convention said that independence could be achieved by a government which had a parliamentary majority — but not necessarily a majority of votes. Lévesque had defended this position a decade earlier — but had abandoned it.

But Lévesque was not there for the debates. He spent the morning away from the convention, and the afternoon in the "operations room", watching the convention on television, preparing his final remarks. Fifteen minutes before he was scheduled to speak came the most dramatic emotional display of all.

It had become clear that all the resolutions dealing with matters other than sovereignty would not be dealt with before the convention ended, and that there would have to be a continuation of the convention at a later date. But some of the resolutions that had been passed in workshops were brought forward for emergency debate.

One of these was a motion asking the federal government to transfer the imprisoned former members of the FLQ from federal to Quebec jurisdiction.

The man who went to the microphone to propose and defend the motion was Jacques Rose, who had been convicted as an accessory after the fact in the 1970 kidnapping of Pierre Laporte, and whose brother Paul was still in prison serving a life sentence for Laporte's murder. Rose, his long red hair tied back in a pigtail, was given a longer time than most to speak, finally being called apologetically to order by the chairman, who said, "I know that where you've been you haven't had a right to speak, but we are running out of time."

As Lévesque watched in horror from the operations centre, Rose got a standing ovation and a burst of wild rhetoric in his support from several delegates — one of whom shouted, "These are our pioneers for the liberation of Quebec!"

This was the climax of a process which had been quietly developing through the 1970s: the consecration of the Rose family as a kind of symbol of virtue in Quebec nationalist circles. Even journalists who had become highly critical of Lévesque, the Parti Québécois, and the Société Saint-Jean-Baptiste became almost maudlin in writing about Rosa Rose, the mother of the two Rose brothers, who had fought for years to have them released on parole.

Lévesque was appalled. It was his worst nightmare about the Parti Québécois come true. He had wept that night in 1970 when he heard that Pierre Laporte's body had been found; he had absolutely no sympathy for the sentimental ovation for those convicted for his kidnapping and murder.

When he came to the microphone to make his closing remarks, his anger flashed. By turns sarcastic, bitter, and sad, he said that in its present form he would have trouble voting for the PQ himself — and that he would take a few days to reflect before deciding whether or not to resign. Then he walked off stage, leaving a stunned convention to dissolve.

The Parti Québécois convention was one of a series of events that followed the constitutional agreement of November 1981 which stand as a testimony, not only to the rage and humiliation that seemed to be felt by the whole nationalist community in Quebec, but to its loss of judgement, restraint, and equilibrium — personal and collective.

On the eve of the PQ convention, the Société Saint-Jean-Baptiste published and sold a poster listing and denouncing the seventy-four Liberal MPs from Quebec as traitors. On the Monday after the convention, Lévesque darkly accused the sparkplugs of the movement that had defeated his positions as infiltrators and "agents provocateurs".

In the days that followed, the PQ caucus, the cabinet, riding-association executives, all issued pleas to Lévesque to stay on as president. He finally announced that there would be an internal party referendum — immortally christened the "rené-rendum" by the *Gazette* columnist L. Ian MacDonald. There was a distasteful grovelling to the whole process — and all the more so since the ballots were numbered, and even cabinet ministers were convinced that their loyalty to the leader would be double-checked by the party's computer.

Gilbert Paquette, an MNA and member of the executive, drew up an eleven-page statement that accompanied the ballot, narrowing the gap between the positions adopted by the convention and the positions insisted upon by Lévesque. The question was every bit as convoluted as the referendum question:

> Do you accept as fundamental principles of our activity:
> 1. That Quebec's accession to sovereignty should occur through democratic methods, of which the key element must be the majority agreement of our citizens;
> 2. That our program, while eliminating the obligatory link between the two, still combines sovereignty with a concrete offer of a mutually advantageous economic association with Canada;
> 3. That the party reaffirms its respect and openness toward all Quebecers, regardless of their ethnic or cultural origin, and especially the recognition of the right of the English-speaking minority to its essential institutions, educational and other?

In late December, when the question was announced, there began to be a slight squirming of embarrassment inside the party. The mainstream remained clearly behind Lévesque, and, although two riding presidents and one regional president resigned, it was clear that the dissidents remained a tiny fraction of the party. The most caustic critique of the process came from the former minister, Louis O'Neill.

"After surrendering Quebec's constitutional veto right, René Lévesque has decided to impose a veto on his own party," he told Robert McKenzie. "After being the victim of a coup de force by Trudeau, he's perpetrating a coup de force on his own supporters."

O'Neill said he didn't know whether Lévesque really wanted independence — and that, in any case, he had become an obstacle in achieving it.

"The referendum in the party isn't a referendum, it's a plebiscite. And the real question is, 'Do you love René Lévesque?' While 135,000 young people between the ages of eighteen and twenty-five are out of work, while we face one of the hardest winters economically in a long time, 300,000 people are being mobilized for two months to decide whether they love René Lévesque."

He predicted that if Lévesque stayed on, the party would be finished as a dynamic force in Quebec. "Quebecers are polite people, you know. The most critical minds in the party will simply stay at home. They won't resign, they'll simply find different pretexts to fade out of sight. The aging process will set in. That's how political parties die.

"There are so many good ordinary people in the party who adore Lévesque. They have a blind faith that he can lead them through the fog, that he has a vision, a grand design. I am a practising Christian, and I am more critical than that about the Pope.

"Lévesque is leading them nowhere. It's sad, but the real choice is 'René Lévesque or independence'."

The question was sent out by mail to 292,888 members of the party; 142,954 voted — a 48.8 per cent turnout — and 95 per cent voted Yes.

It had been an embarrassing display of personal blackmail by the leader — reminiscent of the Egyptian president Gamal Nasser's tactic of resigning as a way of overpowering his opposition and then returning to power even stronger than before.

On February 13-14, the second half of the convention was held, and a delicate operation was undertaken to heal the wounds of the December convention and the renérendum. On Saturday morning, the delegates voted overwhelmingly to endorse a new statement of the PQ's goal of sovereignty.

The key figure in this compromise was Gilbert Paquette. Although he occasionally suffered from a reputation as an opportunist (he abstained on a back-to-work law during the Common Front strike in the fall of 1979, and was one of the architects of the Alice-in-Wonderland structures of sovereignty-association with his book *L'Option*) he had maintained solid contacts with the nationalist left. In addition, he was a prolific writer, and adept at pulling together a consensus. Over the Christmas holidays, he had sat down with a transcript of the December convention and the text of the Lévesque referendum question and set to work to build a consensus.

He began with the assumption that everything that the December convention had voted on that was not specifically rejected by the party referendum question would remain party policy. That meant, as far as he was concerned, that economic association would no longer be a condition for Quebec sovereignty, and that the next election would be fought on sovereignty. However, a majority of votes would be required before independence could be achieved, and an offer of economic association would have to be made to the rest of Canada.

With these principles, he was able to win the agreement of key people on both sides: Michel Bourdon and Pierre Cloutier, who had played important roles at the December convention, and Pierre Harvey, the major Lévesque loyalist on the party executive.

The next step came at the closed meeting of the National Council, on the eve of the February convention. Lévesque came as close as he is capable of to apologizing. "La colère est mauvaise conseillère" — "Anger is a poor adviser" — he said, quoting Bismarck. His concern about infiltrators had been taken out of context, he said; he had no doubts about the sincerity of 99.9 per cent of the delegates, and he would not make a habit of party referendums.

In response, on the floor of the convention the next day, the black sheep came back to the fold. Michel Bourdon said he would be supporting the "synthesis resolution" because he felt it was perfectly consistent with what the convention had agreed on in December.

And on Sunday, when there was a motion of censure against Lévesque, one of the people who urged its defeat in a spirit of reconciliation was André Boulerice, the president of the Montreal Centre region, who had danced for joy on the convention floor in December when some of the offending resolutions had been passed. Listening, Gérald Godin grinned sardonically. "Ah, Boulerice has come around," he said. "You know, we are going to change the name of the street outside the Claude Robillard Arena. We are going to rename it the Road to Damascus."

Lévesque had won his victory — but the party was never to be quite the same.

IN THE MONTHS FOLLOWING THE ACCORD OF NOVEMBER 1981, IT SEEMED that the feelings of rage and humiliation had not only shaped both political rhetoric and the mood of the Parti Québécois but had become part of a wider public mood.

One symptom of injured pride and collective hurt was the storm of outrage that greeted remarks by Ted Tilden, the president of the car rental company. On February 2, 1982, Tilden was the guest speaker at the French-speaking businessmen's club, the Chambre de Commerce de Montréal. "We thought

[he] was a good example of that [ability] to live in perfect harmony," explained Serge Saucier, president of the Chambre.

With the title "A surviving anglophone's view of Montreal", he gave what, in retrospect, was a fairly predictable summary of the English Montreal business community's feelings of frustration and anger towards the Quebec government. In fact, most of the speech consisted of the same kind of complaints about excessive bureaucracy, high taxes, and Quebec City's insensitivity to Montreal which had characterized Jean Paré's editorials in *L'Actualité* and speeches by Pierre Laurin, both as director of the École des Hautes Études Commerciales and as vice-president of Alcan, by Pierre Lortie, president of the Montreal Stock Exchange, and by a variety of other francophone business spokesmen.

But Tilden was making the speech in English; he said out loud, in public, in English, before a French-speaking audience, what thousands of English Montrealers had been saying in private or to English-speaking audiences. And not only could he not give a speech in French in the city where he was born, he gave no indication that he understood any of the pressures, fears, and insecurities that had made language legislation a political necessity, or that he realized how much pride and satisfaction the law had created.

One paragraph particularly caught people's attention. "I frankly think that the kind of damn-fool language legislation we have in this province had to be written by those who weren't thinking clearly. Strong words, you say? Who pays taxes? People and companies — there aren't many other sources of tax revenue! Laws that unduly scare away people and companies are therefore likely to be foolish laws. How better could you scare off a six-million-dollar investor than by establishing insulting language laws that require, among other things, the setting up of language committees inside your company so that workers on your assembly line can report to the government that the boss or owner is not using quite as much French as he should in his day-to-day business, or in his internal memos, or in his effort to translate certain manuals relating to the production-line efforts? If you were an investor from Illinois or Ohio or Amsterdam or Osaka, Japan, or Stuttgart, Germany, would you put up with such garbage?"

The reception at the luncheon was cool. "At least he could

have had the competence to make [the speech] in French," muttered a businessman as he left. Serge Saucier phoned *La Presse* personally to dissociate the Chambre from Tilden's remarks.

The public reaction was extraordinary. No direct government action was taken against Tilden—although Yves Bérubé, the president of the Treasury Board, said that civil servants who rented from his company "will have to have bloody good reasons". Since Tilden had got almost $800,000 in business from the government over the preceding two years, this was no idle threat. But mainly the government relied on what Camille Laurin called "the spontaneous reactions of citizens whose pride and dignity have been wounded".

These "spontaneous reactions" were not long in coming. The teachers' union federation, the CEQ, cancelled its contract; the Quebec government's senior managers' association asked its 1,700 members to turn in their Tilden credit cards. Tilden business in Quebec dropped fifty per cent in the following week.

Tilden was obliged to meet with twenty-nine franchise holders and issue a statement saying that he had been speaking as a private individual, and that he was sorry he upset people. The volcanic eruption, with its shower of torn-up credit cards, was a quick, unnerving demonstration of just how frayed nerves and tempers in Quebec had become after the constitutional fight.

ON JANUARY 30, 1982, ABOUT THREE O'CLOCK, CLAUDE CHARRON AND his companion Jean-Luc Gauthier walked into Eaton's in downtown Montreal and browsed in the men's boutique "Timothy E.". Charron tried on one jacket, and slipped another jacket under his coat. His friend, similarly hiding a jacket under his coat, was intercepted by a security guard, who had been watching them both surreptitiously.

Spotting the woman calling for support on her walkie-talkie, Charron shouted to Gauthier, who quickly replaced the coat. Still clutching the jacket, Charron bolted for the door. As he wrote somewhat melodramatically, "Like a criminal I fled from the place where I had just tried to kill myself."

He and Gauthier ran through the adjoining shopping complex, Les Terrasses. The security guard gave chase and caught up with them on McGill Street. Identifying herself as a security agent, she asked Charron to follow her to her office.

Gauthier began shouting at her that it was unfair — and Charron bolted again, across St. Catherine Street, down Cathcart, up the stairs and across Place Ville Marie, and across Dorchester Boulevard, dodging cars. A security guard finally tackled Charron, only to discover, to his embarrassment, who he was. Immediately he began to brush the snow off Charron's coat.

Charron was escorted back to Eaton's, questioned, and released. According to Charron, he was told he would not be prosecuted. But almost a month later, on February 23, the bailiffs arrived at his door and notified him that Eaton's had decided to take him to court on charges of theft under $200. By that night, the rumour had reached the newspapers, but no-one would confirm it. The next day, Charron spoke to Lévesque, and to the Parti Québécois caucus, resigned from the cabinet, and held a press conference.

The incident was bizarre enough, but even stranger was the extraordinary bitterness that erupted in Quebec — not towards Charron, but against Eaton's for pressing charges. "France had its Dreyfus, we have our Charron," was one reaction. Others saw this as vengeance for Bill 101 and part of the tradition of Eaton's insensitivity to French-speaking Quebec. Charron himself complained at his press conference that Eaton's had "decided to execute me".

This was the second of three incidents that would lead Charron to resign from the National Assembly, thus ending — for the time being, at least — a brilliant political career. He had bounded to prominence in 1968 as a student leader during the occupations. Small, slight in build, with frizzy hair and a startling resemblance to Ringo Starr, Charron was an electrifying speaker. He was from modest background, the son of a school-bus driver and former horse trainer.

He was one of the first members of the Mouvement Souveraineté-Association. He had watched René Lévesque leave the Liberal Party at the Château Frontenac in October 1968, and had come up to him afterwards and given him a slip of paper with his name and address on it. To his surprise, he was called and invited to the founding meeting of the MSA at the Dominican monastery. (He almost missed the meeting; he had been arrested the day before at a Vietnam demonstration at the American consulate.) Elected to the PQ executive in 1969, he became a star candidate in 1969, defeating the Union Nationale labour minister, Jean Cournoyer. In the National Assembly, he proved to be a brilliant debater, and an intimidating orator, with a kind of electric sensuality. He was like a political Mick Jagger: extravagant, theatrical, sexy. And, like Jagger, he took enormous risks in his personal life. As he acknowledged later, he is a homosexual: a fact that led to whispered rumours of risky encounters.

In 1976, he was publicly critical of Lévesque's leadership, which made Lévesque reluctant to include him in the cabinet. But he did, and Charron proved so adept at working with his civil servants that Lévesque named him to succeed Robert Burns as House leader. In this role he was extremely successful. In addition, he accompanied Claude Morin on the cross-country constitutional discussions in the summer of 1980.

The first blow came on November 19, 1981, when Bernard Chabot of TVA broadcast a report saying that a member of Charron's staff was involved in a ring making pornographic films on National Assembly equipment. The report, which had its origins in a rumour from the staff of the Liberal whip, Michel Pagé, proved to be untrue. In fact, a police investigation showed that all that had happened was that on three occasions a few people watched pornographic films in the Assembly on the equipment used to televise debates and, once, in September 1978, one copy of a pornographic film was made on the equipment.

But Charron was devastated. His name had been falsely identified with a so-called sex scandal that was in the news for weeks, spawning a phrase (Pornobec), endless jokes, and an actual pornographic film based on what people thought had happened. The linking of his name with an event that had never occurred made him feel even more helpless and vulnerable, as a homosexual in public life who had never discussed his sexual affiliation publicly.

Charron had always felt an outsider. He was obsessed with dates; he always knew, to the day, how long he had been a member of the National Assembly, and with unfailing ritual, he would not only celebrate the April 29 anniversary of his election, but every month he would drink a glass of cognac on the 29th. During the summer of 1982, in Paris, he met two psychologists, and began to reflect on the significance of this insistence on marking off the months with this "sacred anniversary": "After ten years, and 120 cognacs had been drained, I only saw this date as a mark of my own perseverance, patience, persistence," he wrote later. "But even deeper, you have to go still deeper, what I was celebrating was that the impossible was still surviving. That the bridge stood. That my vulnerable armour had not been pierced. That my feet of clay had not been discovered."

Despite the shoplifting incident, Charron had been such a good House leader, skilful conciliator, and first-rate parliamentarian that many thought he would return to the cabinet after a period on the backbenches. But in August 1982, driving back to his apartment in Old Quebec after the speaker's annual golf tournament, he hit a fire hydrant, and was charged with drunk driving. It was the last straw. Ruefully, he resigned his seat.

DURING THE MONTHS THAT FOLLOWED THE CONSTITUTIONAL ACCORD, René Lévesque became the target of a strange anonymous whispering campaign. There were two separate waves: each one was characterized by people telephoning newspapers and radio stations saying that there were legal documents on file which "proved" what they had heard: the Lévesque marriage was in trouble.

The first wave came in the late fall of 1981. According to the different versions, Corinne Côté-Lévesque was leaving Lévesque, had already left him, was being paid to appear in public with him. Variously, she had set a deadline for him to leave politics that he had not respected, or she was fed up with his interest in other women, or he was being treated for some disease that made him impossible to live with. None of them were true, though many politicians' spouses might testify that politics is, in fact, a disease that renders its victims impossible to live with.

Then, in 1982, a new twist on the rumour: Lévesque was said to be involved in some way with his wife's younger sister. One version had it that Lévesque's father-in-law had pressed charges of corrupting a minor. When one particularly convincing caller telephoned the *Gazette* in the fall of 1982, Lewis Harris travelled to Chicoutimi, Alma, and Roberval to check out the rumour. Corinne Côté was furious, and phoned Harris to complain.

"It's been a year now that the rumours have been circulating," she said a few weeks later. "Finally, my mother phones me, extremely upset. She is seventy-eight, and she has a heart condition. A journalist from the *Gazette* had just phoned her to say that my father had supposedly laid a charge against Réne for corrupting a minor."

Corinne Côté-Lévesque has no younger sister. That there may have been — and, for that matter, may still be — tensions in the Lévesque marriage is one thing. Lévesque was under constant strain, often irritable, intensely pressured, working incredibly long hours, and had always been attracted by and attractive to women. In fact, he had always been more at ease in the company of women than of men; he would sometimes startle formal dinners by directing all his attention to a junior official's wife and completely ignoring everyone else. His wife was only working part-time, writing book reviews, until the fall of 1983, when she began to work as a co-host on a Montreal radio program. It would have been extraordinary had there been no tension in the marriage after the personal humiliation of the November Accord.

But the rumours were all far more precise than that, and all untrue. Still, they were plausible. When Corinne Côté-Lévesque agreed to speak about them publicly, however, the whispers suddenly vanished — as abruptly and mysteriously as they had begun.

Lévesque's staff become convinced that the premier and his wife were victims of an insidious black propaganda campaign — all the more effective because of Lévesque's reputation as a womanizer. Whether or not this was the case, the obsessive persistence of the rumours until Corinne Lévesque spoke about them publicly was testimony to the almost pathological sensitivities that were evident in the months following the constitutional settlement. They showed themselves in different ways: in the absurdity of Claude Charron's behaviour in Eaton's, in the frenzied reaction to an impolitic businessman's speech, in the intensity of the backfence gossip about the premier's private life. Each incident was a symptom of how many Quebecers felt reduced, diminished, and undermined by the constitutional accord.

NINETEEN

Crisis
Politics

*"Politics is the skilled
use of blunt instruments."*
Lester B. Pearson

In August 1982, René Lévesque turned sixty. He had been in politics for twenty-two years, and he told his staff that this was the worst of them: the constitution, the convention, the Charron incident, the economy. He began to show signs of the toll it had taken. By turns he was impatient, indecisive, impulsive, tough, teasing.

During the early years, it had seemed as if Lévesque's real voice was heard through Pierre Marois, then minister of state for social development: a voice of spontaneity and compassion. Now, it was heard more often through the raspy tough talk of his chief of staff, Jean-Roch Boivin: impatient with nuance, tough, calculating, cynical.

The ministers were now a little afraid of Lévesque and his moods. He would interrupt ministers at cabinet meetings and cut them short, making little effort to hide his impatience. Men who, before 1976, had referred to Lévesque somewhat contemptuously as "le vieux" (the old man) were now nervous about calling him anything but "Monsieur Lévesque" — even in the most intimate privacy.

Part of his bad temper was simply caused by fatigue: one colleague calculated in December 1981 that Lévesque had taken only two days off in four months. But the result was a kind of autocratic impatience, a shrewd elusiveness, an unpredictable shifting from encouragement to bullying that made more and more people compare him to the aging Maurice Duplessis. Both had created new parties, which they controlled completely; both had a mischievous charm; both had succeeded in dominating the reformers in their parties. The comparison amused Lévesque. "I think it's rather funny. Maybe it's because I'm a bit like him. Maybe people find I'm a bit too long-living as a politician."

By the spring of 1982, he had succeeded in a number of important things. With the 1981 election, he had shifted the electoral base of the party to the more conservative roots of small-town Quebec. With the party referendum, he had re-established his unquestioned control over the party. He had begun to introduce the co-operative tripartite rhetoric of "la concertation": business, government, and labour working together to plan economic development. And he had extended the role of the state in the Quebec economy.

Increasingly, the crown corporations like Hydro-Québec, the Caisse de Dépôt, SOQUIP (the oil and gas crown corporation), and the Societé Générale de Financement were flexing their muscles in the economy. With the help of the Caisse de Dépôt, SOQUIP acquired control of Gaz Métropolitain and began speeding up the distribution of natural gas in order to permit the export of Hydro surpluses. The Caisse acquired major indirect interests in Noranda and Domtar, two large resource corporations.

Worker-management relations remained unchanged with state involvement. However, francophones benefited. Whether through direct state participation or indirectly because of the language legislation, more and more francophones were entering corporate board-rooms.

But Lévesque also had an economic crisis to deal with. Canada was in an economic recession for the second half of 1981 and in 1982; the gross national product was dropping, interest rates were climbing, the Canadian dollar was dropping, and unemployment was serious. Quebec was hit extremely hard by the recession, with a staggering forty-four per cent of the jobs lost in Canada. Quebec's loss of 219,000 jobs, recorded in August 1982, cancelled out the total increase in jobs since December 1977.

Jacques Parizeau had gambled in 1978 that he could stimulate the economy with an expansionist budget; not only did he lose the gamble, but the losses became cumulatively greater each year as the deficit climbed to $3 billion. He was a masterly political performer, with a knack for creating the illusion of being in control of every situation. But his stock inside the government was shaken. Lévesque took away the presidency of the Treasury Board in the cabinet shuffle after the 1981 election, and gave it to Yves Bérubé. Then, in September 1981, at the annual caucus retreat, Lévesque casually said that the spring budget before the election had been prepared "en catastrophe". Parizeau was shattered at first, but rallied. "He has created a precedent by showing no confidence in his minister of finance," he told a former associate. "I will create a precedent by not resigning."

However, in November 1981, Parizeau had to increase taxes, doubling gasoline taxes and making them a percentage of the gas price so that they would increase automatically. At the same time, Yves Bérubé was imposing cutbacks in government services.

One politician saw what was coming. When the Liberal MNA Claude Forget resigned his seat on November 16, he told reporters that "technically speaking, I think the government of Quebec can be said to be in a state of bankruptcy." He blamed the generous pay increases that the government had given the civil service in the pre-referendum Common Front settlement in 1979.

There was another analyst who saw clearly how badly things were going, but could not say so publicly: Marcel Gilbert, the general co-ordinator of negotiations for the CSN. In June 1981, he wrote an analysis of the previous Common Front negotiations, and concluded that things were in bad shape and would get much worse. He argued that the unions should rethink their traditional negotiating approach. But neither the unions nor the government could break the pattern.

In December, Lévesque called on the unions to give up their "enrichment" clause in the existing contract, which would have saved the government $100 million. The FTQ and the CEQ both said no immediately; Gilbert urged Norbert Rodrigue of the CSN to agree — in exchange for a prolongation of the existing contract for two years. But the confederation would not agree to this, and the CSN joined the others in saying no. In his analysis of the negotiations afterwards, Jean-François Munn, the co-ordinator of public-sector negotiations for the CSN, pinpointed this as the first of a series of missed chances. It was the beginning of a process that would end in a massive defeat for the unions, and a Pyrrhic victory for the government. Every opportunity to break the cycle of confrontation was missed.

At an economic summit in Quebec from April 5 to 7, Lévesque said that there was a gap of $700 million in the government's finances, and that there were three choices: cut programs by $700 million, raise taxes, or freeze public-sector salaries from July 1, 1982. But the way the government presented its case made it clear that some form of salary freeze was coming.

At that same summit, Louis Laberge of the FTQ, after some careful and quiet consultation with senior government officials, proposed a crash program to build fifty thousand houses. In June, this emerged as Corvée-Habitation — roughly translatable as Housing Bee, or House Raising—an exercise in business-labour-government co-operation with the creation of a non-profit corporation to administer the construction of low-cost houses with below-market mortgage rates. Throughout the long year of labour strife, this was to remain one of the government's carrots to compensate for its big stick.

In the budget speech on May 25, Parizeau froze medical fees and senior civil-service salaries, and increased sales taxes from eight to nine per cent for ten months and the tobacco tax from forty-five to fifty per cent.

Since the previous fall, the cabinet had been divided. There was a consensus that something had to be done, but disagreement on exactly what. Some, like the civil-service minister, Denise Leblanc-Bantey, argued that the government should simply refuse to pay the last increase in the contract, and decree a salary freeze. But others, like Jacques Parizeau, argued that the government's credibility would be destroyed if it did not respect its signed word. The solution, announced by Parizeau, was tricky: what they gave between July and December, they would take back between January and March with a twenty-per-cent salary roll-back. This would reduce expenditures by $521 million. Freezing automatic raises saved another $122 million. Bérubé introduced the legislation to do this: Bill 70.

This financial sleight-of-hand trick was the last straw for Guy Bisaillon. On June 22 he resigned from the Parti Québécois caucus to sit as an independent, and, as an additional mischievous touch, remained a member of the party. Bisaillon—along with Louise Harel, the only member of caucus to vote against Bill 70 — saw that the bill was an exercise in bluff and threat. With the threat of a salary roll-back hanging over their heads, the government thought, the unions would not dare stick to a tough bargaining position. The government was wrong.

FOR A LONG TIME AFTER THE 1981 ELECTION, CLAUDE RYAN REMAINED unaware of how seriously his support was deteriorating in the caucus. Wounded by the defeat, he further alienated part of the caucus and the party in September 1981 by his nationalist prescription for the rebuilding of the party's fortunes, and he was unable to survive the strains created by the constitutional debate.

By the spring of 1982, the Liberal MNAs were feeling enormous pressure from their constituents and the public. In late May, one spent a week on a fishing trip, and saw eight people; six of them mentioned the Liberal leadership. Another was sitting on his front porch catching his breath after jogging, and people walking past called out, "You've got to get rid of Ryan!" Later that day, in the supermarket, little old ladies came up to him to volunteer that Mr. Ryan didn't come across well on television.

For months, Ryan insisted that he had the support of the grassroots and that over the long haul he would keep the support of the party. He was wrong. In August, he made a final appraisal of the situation, and on August 4, met with a group of diehard loyalists at the Bonaventure Hotel. It was a group of people who had gathered together in June to see if Ryan would be able to win the mandatory vote on the party leadership at the policy convention in the fall. The news was not good. Guy Saint-Pierre, the chairman of the Ryan leadership campaign in 1978, had tried to get people like Claude Castonguay, André Raynauld, and Claude Forget, all of whom had supported Ryan in 1978, to sign a petition urging him to stay on. They all refused. Only six members of caucus would sign: Thérèse Lavoie-Roux, Pierre Fortier, Reed Scowen, Herbert Marx, Christos Sirros, and Daniel Johnson.

On Saturday, August 7, Michel Ray had an exclusive story in *La Presse* that Ryan had decided to resign; on Tuesday, August 10, Ryan made it official and turned over the interim leadership to Gérard-D. Lévesque. The adventure in layman's action in the Quebec Liberal Party was over, and the party would turn from spiritual amateurism, intellectual rigour, and goodwill to a professional.

OVER THE SUMMER OF 1982, LÉVESQUE BEGAN TO HESITATE AND DELAY a cabinet shuffle; some ministers began to wonder if his heart was still in the job. The PQ was down to twenty-eight per cent in the polls, and ministers were getting restless.

In early September, aware that he would probably be dropped from the cabinet, Lucien Lessard resigned. Marcel Léger, the environment minister, disregarded the rumours, and Lévesque asked him to resign. The next day, September 9, Lévesque announced his cabinet changes. He dropped Louis Bernard's major innovation of the first term: the new cabinet structure, with its ministers of state, who had become figureheads after the reforms of the first few years. The time had come for more conservative moves, and gestures to ease irritations. Businessmen had been getting uneasy about plans for the redrafting of the Labour Code; suddenly the labour minister was not Pierre Marois, the social democrat, but Raynald Fréchette, a conservative small-town lawyer and former Union Nationale member.

Pig farmers had been complaining about being harassed by environment inspectors; suddenly the minister was not the voluble Marcel Léger, but Adrien Ouellette, a clumsy, self-effacing member from a riding with one of the highest concentrations of pig farmers in the province.

Quebec exporters were complaining about a lack of support from the government, and a lack of understanding of the demands of high-technology industries. Lévesque gave the aggressive and ambitious Bernard Landry, who had been growing impatient after almost six years as minister of state for economic development, the new job of minister of external trade. (In doing so, he created a conflict between Landry and the intergovernmental affairs minister, Jacques-Yvan Morin, who had been trying to redefine his ministry in terms of external trade.) At the same time, he made Gilbert Paquette the minister responsible for science and technology. Finally, he took responsibility for Bill 101 (except for the educational provisions) away from the minister of education, Camille Laurin, and gave it to Gérald Godin: a move aimed at soothing the unhappy minority communities. The shuffle set the tone for the second term: self-protective and conservative.

As the ministers filed into the conference room at the Manoir Richelieu on September 16 for a cabinet retreat, they were astonished to find a photocopy in front of every chair. That morning, *Le Devoir* had published a story based on a private poll which suggested that Lévesque's personal popularity had dropped. The headline read "Lévesque n'est plus l'homme de la situation" — "Lévesque is no longer the man for the times." Lévesque had had it distributed, as if to say, "If anybody has a problem with my leadership, raise it here and now." No-one mentioned it, and more than one minister was struck at how brisk and determined he seemed, and how he had taken charge again.

During the summer, the government members had been shocked at how badly the recession was hitting their constituents. The Corvée-Habitation program had been a public-relations success, but the impact remained limited, and there were only a few hundred houses under construction. But it provided an example of what could be done, and "la concertation" became reinforced in the vocabulary of the government and the party. Ministers and party executive members travelled to Austria and returned full of enthusiasm for the idea of tripartite co-operation.

In September, Denis de Belleval, the former transport minister, wrote a twenty-page paper which described the process in some detail. De Belleval suggested the creation of what he called a "solidarity fund" — a $750-million development fund created and administered jointly by business, labour, and the state for investment in firms unable to find necessary financing, thus stimulating the economy.

Lévesque seemed impressed, and there was speculation that de Belleval might return to the cabinet. But it never happened, and de Belleval resigned to become a vice-president of the engineering firm Lavalin. The idea emerged six months later as a proposal from the FTQ.

THE PARTY HAD ITS REMINDER THAT RENÉ LÉVESQUE WAS IN CHARGE at the end of October. On the weekend of October 30-1, 1982, the National Council was supposed to ratify a motion to create a federal wing of the party.

The idea had begun to take shape after the 1981 election, when a number of activists were struck by the apparent contradiction that Quebec ridings that voted PQ provincially voted Liberal federally. If the PQ seriously intended to work for independence, they began to argue, it had to offer federal voters an alternative. After the constitutional accord, this feeling became stronger: Michel Lepage did a PQ poll which showed that forty-five per cent of voters would vote PQ federally. This would produce between thirty-five and forty seats. Marcel Léger, the major proponent of the idea, tried unsuccessfully to raise it at the December convention, but the anti-Ottawa mood was too strong.

But in June 1982 a compromise motion was passed which endorsed the principle of federal "participation" and left the party executive to report back on how this would happen. Over the summer, it seemed that a consensus was building on the need for the creation of a federal wing. The executive brought forward a resolution to this effect.

Even Lévesque, who had always opposed the idea in the past, seemed to be supporting it. Michel Carpentier had been working on it for months, with Lévesque's knowledge. But suddenly, at the cabinet meeting on October 27, Lévesque reversed himself—but vowed, "If that gets out of here, and I find out from whom, I'm killing him." Carpentier had four days before the National Council meeting to undo the consensus he had been working on for months. Totally loyal to Lévesque, and defining himself as a political civil servant, he set to work —but he was furious.

The vote was taken: the commitment to form a federal wing of the PQ was deleted, the decision was postponed, and, partly as a consolation prize for having been dropped from the cabinet, Marcel Léger was made responsible for a committee on the subject. Michel Carpentier took a scrap of paper, and wrote, "Mission accomplished; you've turned on a dime. But don't ever ask me to do that again." He wrapped a ten-cent piece in the note and gave it to Lévesque. From then on, "Carpentier's dime" was part of the vocabulary of party officials.

Lévesque had outfoxed the party again. But Léger, a former professional parish fund-raiser, was not prepared to lie down. He worked incessantly among his colleagues, wringing commitments here and there, and talking to any journalist who would listen. Polls now showed that the Parti Québécois would get between twenty-five and thirty per cent of the vote federally, which would produce between twelve and twenty seats: more than enough for official party status. An indépendantiste party in Ottawa, much more sophisticated than the group of twenty-six Créditistes elected in 1962, undermining the Liberal base in Quebec, began to seem distinctly possible.

BY NOVEMBER, IT BECAME CLEAR THAT THE BLUFF OF BILL 70 HAD NOT worked. Far from encouraging a new kind of negotiation, it was viewed as straight provocation. The government was now in a bind caused by its own manoeuvre: unless there was an agreement to change the law, the public servants would lose

$641 million — and, even taking into account the lost income taxes, the Quebec government would get back the $521 million it had spent in pay increases. Worse, the government realized that the nature of the roll-backs laid out in Bill 70 would hurt the lowest-paid employees worst of all.

Unfortunately, the law was not simply a bargaining position, but part of the budget. To alter it would require dismantling the government's financial projections. And, ironically, Bill 70 showed that the government not only misunderstood union negotiating, it also misunderstood the credit-evaluation system. Some veterans of Wall Street credit rating from outside Quebec argued convincingly that Bill 70 was responsible, single-handedly, for Quebec's loss of its AA credit rating. Wall Street, the argument went, disliked instability, and unilaterally taking back salary increases was asking for trouble. Since the whole purpose of the exercise was to keep Quebec's deficit fixed at the arbitrary figure of $3 billion which the government had decided was acceptable to public opinion, the operation was hardly a success.

The government had an indirect warning of the stance the unions would take in July, when the teachers' union federation (the CEQ) elected as their president Yvon Charbonneau, who had been jailed by Bourassa for defying an injunction ten years earlier. It was clear that bargaining would be tough.

However, in November, as the negotiations bogged down, the union leaders began to realize that (except in the CEQ) the members were not behind them. The Fédération des Affaires Sociales, which represented the hospital workers, went for a strike mandate, without letting anyone know that they did not have strong support. But that threat of a strike helped the government decide on stronger action.

On Thursday, November 18, Lévesque made it clear that he had lost patience with his own legislation. He told the Assembly that the urgency of the situation demanded that the government speed up the very process that it had extended three months. His reasoning was intriguing: it was necessary in order to protect the lowest-paid employees. However, the catastrophe he was moving to protect them from was the government's own law. If there was no settlement within three weeks, he said, the government would legislate. And if there was an illegal strike the government would legislate.

The result was Bill 105, which put an end to the negotiations and imposed 109 collective agreements on three hundred thousand public-sector employees. People could only guess how many pages were in the decrees, and some guesses were as high as eighty thousand pages: no legislator could read and absorb them in two days. Lise Bissonnette called it "the most enormous and most odious special law that the National Assembly has ever adopted".

The law was passed on December 11, and the ministers saw the bill not as a betrayal of union sympathies, but as proof that they had the courage to take hard decisions. "I feel," one minister told Bissonnette, "the serenity of the beaver who gnaws off his paw to free himself from a trap." Gérald Godin, the minister of immigration and cultural communities, felt no qualms. "The last time [in 1979], we were getting all kinds of pressure from union members. This time, all the pressure we are getting in our ridings is from people looking for work." But more than simply pressure, Godin had felt growing anger over the last few years at what he called "syndical-démocratie". By that he meant a stagnant self-protective complacency, an obsession with security, a business-union mentality. To the surprise of those who remembered an earlier Godin, a poet and left-wing journalist, he felt no need to apologize for the law.

About ten days earlier, when the final legislated result of the failed negotiations seemed inevitable, in one way or another, Robert Dean, a PQ MNA, talked about his frustration with the deadlock. He had been the Quebec director of the United Auto Workers, a vice-president of the FTQ, and a major organizer of the United Aircraft strike in 1975, but it was only since entering politics in 1981 that he had become very aware of how great the difference was between union contracts in the private and the public sector. When he looked at them, he was astounded. How many private-sector employees get four weeks' holiday after a year? he wondered. Or job security? "It may have been naive of me, but after the economic summit last spring, I had hoped that the union leadership in the private sector would speak to their colleagues in the Common Front," he said.

The debate on Bill 105 was long and intense. For the Liberals, the legislation was proof of the government's mismanagement for six years. For the government, whose control of the Assembly was never in question, it was a response to hard times. But, along with Guy Bisaillon, there were two important dissenters.

Louise Harel, who had abstained on Bill 70 the previous June, voted against Bill 105 on first and second reading. While stressing that she had no intention of leaving the caucus or the party, she was effective in her criticism, saying that no negotiations had ever taken place, since the government had a predetermined salary settlement. "What I refuse to countenance," she said, "is the idea that only brutal methods can make the employees and their unions listen to reason."

But the most effective and moving voice of dissent was that of Pierre de Bellefeuille. De Bellefeuille was a man of Lévesque's generation, not Harel's or Bisaillon's. He would be sixty the following spring. He had spent a decade as a National Film Board executive, was the first editor of *Le Maclean*, and a top official at Expo 67. He could not bring himself to vote against the government, so he made a point of being absent — but not before giving a moving cri de coeur. He had voted for Bill 70 in June and recognized that in all logic he could not break ranks in December. But he saw the bill as a betrayal of the members who had been told that there would be real negotiations, and a violation of the spirit of the Parti Québécois.

And yet the unions had been equally incapable of breaking the pattern of full-scale mobilization of the members, unlimited demands (the gap between the government offer and the union proposal was $8 billion), inflexible positions, and hardline tactics.

But worse was yet to come. The unions voted for a series of escalating strikes to begin on January 26. Bargaining continued, with energy focused on groups like the nurses, who could be split off from the Common Front. But the strikes began on schedule, beginning with the CEGEP teachers on Wednesday, followed by the elementary- and secondary-school teachers and then the hospital workers.

On Saturday, January 29, between twenty-five and thirty thousand public-sector employees marched in what the newspapers called the biggest demonstration ever held in Quebec City. It was a peaceful crowd, but for the first time popular rage was being directed, not at Trudeau, or "les bosses", or even, as in 1979 and during previous demonstrations in the fall, at Parizeau and Bérubé — but at Lévesque himself. There were taped chants and songs, with an accusing voice booming out over the loudspeaker saying "Enfin René, on voit ton vrai visage"; there was an effigy of Lévesque on a toilet bowl, of Lévesque's head on a stick with red streamers hanging down, and marchers struck at the effigies with sticks. Shown on the television news, the images had a brutal, shocking quality.

Things got worse.

Over that weekend, the government did strike a deal with the nurses, and, in the days ahead, the Fédération des Affaires Sociales, representing the hospital workers, agreed to call off their strike before the chronic-care hospitals were to go out. The teachers were left on their own in a strike that dragged on for three weeks.

At that point, the teachers were doubly betrayed: by their leaders, who were convinced that the government would not dare touch the question of teacher workload, and by a party they had overwhelmingly supported.

On February 9, Lévesque made a final offer to the teachers: less money than had been offered on January 21, but a slower introduction of the increased workload. The offer was accompanied by a threat. If it was not accepted by Sunday, February 13, the teachers would be legislated back to work. It was rejected by an 87.4 per cent vote. On Monday, February 14, Lévesque announced that the National Assembly would be recalled to approve what he called "extremely rigorous" back-to-work legislation. Asked why the teachers would obey, since their strike was already illegal, he said, "It will include prescriptions that will force people to think."

It certainly did. The legislation, Bill 111, called for firings without recourse or appeal, salary loss, seniority loss, and, in clause 28, suspension of the Quebec Charter of Rights and Freedoms and the federal Charter of Rights. On Tuesday morning, February 15, the PQ caucus met at 10.30 and Lévesque gave an outline of the legislation, but did not mention clause 28.

At two o'clock, the Assembly met to debate first the urgency of the legislation, and then the bill itself. The PQ backbenchers only became aware of clause 28 and its suspension of rights when Gérard-D. Lévesque began attacking the bill.

Suddenly, the moral advantage had shifted. From a position of apparent selfishness, the teachers were now fighting for human rights and freedoms. The provisions of the back-to-work law angered and appalled them, and stiffened their resolve.

The debate continued through the night. Louise Harel told

the party whip, Jacques Brassard, of her intention to vote against the law, but about 2 a.m. decided that if she did, it meant sitting as an independent. About 3.45, Lévesque called her into the office behind the speaker's chair and told her that he had canvassed her colleagues and they did not want her to remain in caucus if she voted against the bill. She told him that she had already decided to abstain. At 4.15, she spoke and said so.

That morning, Gérald Godin bumped into an acquaintance who told him that he thought the law was appalling. "Sure, it's tough," Godin replied calmly. "But you know the old English proverb. If you've swallowed an ox, you don't choke on the tail."

At four o'clock in the afternoon, Lévesque made an offer to the National Assembly to hold a parliamentary hearing on teacher workload and job security. Yvon Charbonneau, armed with a sixty-four per cent vote to defy the law, telephoned Lévesque at eleven o'clock that night to suggest naming a mediator. Lévesque was in no mood for mediation. "La médiation, c'est *out*! C'est de la marde!"

Lévesque then spoke to the National Assembly before the final vote and said that, on reflection, the government was prepared to go to the people for a judgement. In a final desperate attempt to stop the law from getting royal assent, Charbonneau and Claude Ryan (now opposition education critic) tried to get through to Lieutenant-Governor Jean-Pierre Côté to persuade him not to sign the bill into law. But it had already been slipped in through a side door and signed.

The next day, Thursday, as speculation increased that Lévesque might call a snap election against the unions, he backed away from his remark of the night before, saying that everything was returning to normal. But it took almost another week before the schools opened. The government had succeeded in making those teachers who had refused to go out on the illegal strike feel ashamed of themselves. On Friday, Robert Bisaillon of the CEQ told a press conference that "when Dr. Laurin, in his sinister way, lists off all the effects of the law, it makes our members realize they are dealing with a gang of chainsaw maniacs."

For the teachers had seen the ugliest side of the government. Incapable of negotiating, it either folded and gave in or imposed its will. The teachers learned how far it was prepared to go. However, on Saturday, March 5, they threw away the moral advantage they had gained. Several hundred demonstrators gathered outside the Concorde Hotel, where the PQ National Council was meeting. A limousine window was smashed, Camille Laurin was punched in the face and kicked in the legs, other cabinet ministers were roughed up, delegates were pushed around.

The National Council responded by criticizing the executive, which had dissociated itself from Bill 111. The meeting showed something of the direction the party had taken. Ernest Boudreau, a teacher in Terrebonne, resigned from the regional executive; Michel Bourdon had already torn up his card. At the press conference after the meeting, René Lévesque revealed something of his feelings when he said that while it was true that people had left the party because of the conflict, there were other people who had joined it because of the way the government had dealt with the situation. What kind of people? he was asked. "Normal people!" he replied.

The rest was anticlimax. A conciliator was appointed, a parliamentary committee heard presentations, an agreement was struck which reduced the number of teaching jobs to be eliminated from 5,000 to 3,800, and the CEQ signed a three-year contract on April 18.

But the illusions of thousands of Quebecers that the Parti Québécois government represented a different kind of labour-management relationship and a rooted respect for civil liberties was destroyed. In L. Ian MacDonald's memorable phrase, Bill 111 was "nothing less than the moral equivalent of the War Measures Act".

What conclusions can be drawn from the distressing conflict of 1982-3? According to Gérard Bergeron, it was "perhaps without precedent in any Western political system". Certainly, the confrontation confirmed how rigid and inflexible both sides had become.

On the union side, the strike was the climax of almost twenty years of unbending intensity of "mobilization". Before the negotiations began, Marcel Gilbert had tried to break this cycle, saying that it led to "a sort of microclimate capable, if not of repressing all independent reflection, at least of preventing it by making it 'politically' very costly".

Moreover, he pointed out, this climate of repression was counterproductive. It could dominate the organization, but not the membership — it simply separated the leadership from the members.

Gilbert suggested that the union's conception of mobilization had left an organization whose primary job, after all, was negotiating vulnerable to the leftist slogans "To negotiate is to be screwed" (Négocier c'est se faire fourrer) and "Talking to the bosses means betrayal" (Parler aux boss, c'est trahir).

The price for taking a moderate position became very high; Jean-François Munn pointed out that the executive of the junior-college teachers' union was nearly defeated for supporting the CSN counter-offer of April 1982, which would have kept them the status quo; nine months later, they were on strike to try to save this status quo and would lose. "We were prisoners of our rhetoric and of our method," he observed sadly. Both rhetoric and method were classic, but not only did they fail to work, they backfired.

Both Gilbert and Munn left the CSN; both ended up working for the government. It remains to be seen if their lessons can contribute to breaking the impasse.

But though the unions were losers, the government cannot be called a winner. It revealed a fundamental misunderstanding of the negotiating process, since it began by writing the salary settlement into its budget before talks began, and an equally profound misreading of the determination of the union movement to resist. What it could not obtain by persuasion in what Gérard Bergeron called "this bizarre upside-down negotiation", it obtained by threats and coercion.

As a result, the government isolated itself from its most idealistic, progressive, and active roots in the party. It degraded the law into a tactical instrument; it showed contempt for fundamental rights; it shook its own credibility as a responsible government. As Bergeron put it, "it will be impossible to do worse next time."

Yet, as Lévesque showed in his impatient remark about "normal people", he was not unhappy that the party had detached itself from people whom he had always considered irresponsible radicals. As he indicated in an interview with Peter Desbarats in 1969, he assumed that after independence the Parti Québécois would split into two separate parties, one on the left and the other on the right. In the 1960s, he had felt comfortable with dissidence and dissent; twenty years later, he increasingly found it abnormal and selfish.

The conflict virtually ended the party's hunger to identify
with the labour movement; simultaneously, it accelerated its
tendency to think in almost corporatist terms of "concertation": groups representing business and labour being brought
together and co-ordinated by government to plan economic
policy. Ideologically, the events helped force the party to
redefine itself in the directive centre.

WHEN THE NATIONAL ASSEMBLY BEGAN A NEW SESSION ON MARCH
23, 1983, Lévesque and his staff felt that the government was
at a critical point. It had reached a historic low in popularity;
the PQ poll in January showed that virtually every member
would have lost his seat had Lévesque called an election, and
in February PQ support had dropped below twenty per cent.
"We've got six months," one senior Lévesque aide said. "Either
we get a new start — or else phhhtt."

But things started badly. On March 17, *La Presse* accused
Lévesque of misleading the National Assembly on February
20, 1979, when he said that a $300,000 out-of-court settlement
of a $32-million lawsuit by the James Bay Energy Corporation
against a number of unions for sabotage had not been negotiated in his office.

When the Assembly gathered, the Liberals threatened to
block the election of a new speaker, Richard Guay, if Lévesque
did not agree to an inquiry. Immediately, angrily, he did so.

The new start quickly bogged down. The government also
had to deal with accusations that Rodrigue Biron, the minister
of industry and commerce, had engaged in patronage in over-
ruling the Société de Développement Industriel to approve a
$500,000 grant to a company in his riding, and nepotism in
approving loans to companies his brother represented as a
consultant. Even more embarrassing, Gilles Grégoire, the man
who had coined the name "Parti Québécois", was arrested on
charges of contributing to the delinquency of minors. He was
subsequently convicted of having had sex with seven girls
between twelve and seventeen.

The government was unprepared for the ordeal of the National Assembly committee hearings on the James Bay affair,
which were televised on cable. For nine weeks, the committee
grilled over twenty witnesses, including Lévesque, Jean-Roch
Boivin and another senior aide, every member of the board of

directors of the James Bay Energy Corporation, and the lawyers involved in the lawsuit.

For the Liberals on the committee, it was exhilarating. Every night and every morning they prepared questions and reviewed the evidence that had been produced; Liberal strategists studied and criticized the television tapes; every day, they worked on the strategy. The television exposure made them well-known figures inside the party. When John Ciaccia spoke at a fund-raising meeting in Baie Comeau, he had only to put on the half-glasses that he wore at the committee, and the hall burst into applause. Pierre Paradis, the shrewd young country lawyer from Brome-Missisquoi, had his dream of a leadership campaign become credible at the hearings.

After all the testimony, Lévesque's position remained the same. He insisted he had not lied — "on the essentials". He conceded that he had "completely hidden" the January 3, 1979, meeting in which Jean-Roch Boivin told the president of the JBEC, Claude Laliberté, that the premier wanted an out-of-court settlement.

But the Liberals became convinced that Lévesque had intentionally misled the Assembly on the basis of what they learned at the committee. Although inconclusive and sometimes circumstantial, all the evidence suggested that he had desperately wanted an out-of-court settlement, that he had used every tactic possible to get one, and that he had tried to give quite a different impression to the Assembly.

The tension grew: the Liberals on the committee were getting ready to "stake their seats" by formally accusing the premier of lying. By tradition, this would involve an examination of the evidence by the Assembly, and the expulsion of either the premier or his accusers. But the affair ended when Speaker Richard Guay astonished the Assembly by finding that there was no breach of privilege. The spectacle ended, and Lévesque sued *La Presse* for defamation. But the new start he had wanted was ruined.

JACQUES PARIZEAU SURVEYED THE POLITICAL SITUATION IN THE SPRING of 1983 with a rueful sense of political realities. The economic crisis had done terrible damage in Quebec, and the conflicts between governments had not helped. The federal government had tried to reduce the power of the Caisse de Dépôt by introducing legislation aimed at stopping it from acquiring more than ten per cent of Canadian Pacific. Parizeau had succeeded in forcing the federal government to back off, but for a long time he felt that he was the only person in cabinet who believed that they had lost the referendum.

"We lost, we were defeated," he told his cabinet colleagues. "As a result, we are weak. We haven't got the strength to fight Ottawa. We have got to retreat, until their engine runs out of gas."

Reminding them of the Russian general Kutuzov who kept retreating, drawing Napoleon's army deeper and deeper into Russia until the time came to turn, he would say with a chuckle, "It is not difficult to know to retreat — the difficult thing is to know when to turn."

The budget was certainly a kind of retreat. It was squarely and clearly pro-business: government encouragement for small businesses to go public, $26 million in tax breaks for research and development, and a promise to examine the tax levels for high-income earners in a White Paper. "The recovery must begin with business," he told reporters.

It was quite a contrast to his tone three years earlier, when he had been so scathing about the criticisms of the high taxes he had imposed in 1978 on those earning more than $30,000. In 1983 the entrepreneur was elevated to the pedestal previously reserved for poets and chansonniers. "In the longer run, it is investment in the manufacturing sector which reveals the imagination of a society and its ability to progress by surpassing competition," Parizeau said.

It was not a measure of the collective imagination that anyone would have used during the first term of the Parti Québécois in power.

WHEN JOE CLARK RESIGNED AS LEADER OF THE PROGRESSIVE CONservative Party on January 31, 1983, after a 66.9 per cent vote in a leadership review in Winnipeg, and became a candidate to get his job back, Parti Québécois hopes for an English-speaking prime minister were rekindled. For years they had felt that it was an unfair twist of fate that Quebec should be supplying the political leadership for two societies. "Give me a WASP!" said one cabinet minister privately. Asked his preference, he said simply "the one who speaks the least French". (Lévesque's personal preference was Clark, whom he called "the most open-minded English-Canadian politician that I've seen in Quebec".) The worst-case scenario was a victory of another bilingual Quebecer committed to a strong central government, Brian Mulroney.

But it soon became clear that the ability to speak French had become a basic prerequisite for national leadership, even in the Conservative Party. John Crosbie, a talented and witty man, discovered this to his embarrassment. As he passed through Quebec in late May, he became testier and testier as the questions kept coming. He is a proud man, and a shy man; he was clearly embarrassed to be plagued with questions, forced to turn to interpreters, and filmed groping to translate a headline in French.

Then, in Longueuil, Crosbie's judgement, if not his composure, snapped as he said that the bilingual of Canada should not think of themselves as an aristocracy, and compared the ability to speak French to Quebecers to speaking Chinese to the Chinese or German to the Germans. It was a gaffe of major proportions: Crosbie was the real PQ dream candidate.

Mulroney, on the other hand, was another Quebecer. Like Trudeau, he had a visceral commitment to bilingualism; like Trudeau, he knew the Parti Québécois leadership intimately, from his days at Laval law school in the early 1960s, his law practice in Montreal, and his work on the Cliche commission in the mid-seventies. He had run for the Tory leadership in 1976, and it was clear he would run again.

By dint of enormous personal effort and perseverance, Joe Clark had succeeded in changing the rules of Canadian politics. No longer would it be possible for someone to be elected leader without being able to speak French. His own French was not graceful or easy, but it was serviceable and broadcastable; it was now the minimum. But this was not enough; he never managed to shake his image as a bumbler, or to soothe the bitterness of Conservatives who never forgave him for losing power in 1980. Brian Mulroney managed to put together a coalition of resentment. When the fourth ballot was counted on June 11, he got 1,534 votes to Joe Clark's 1,325, and the convention exploded in the excitement of victory: for the first time in their history, the Conservatives had chosen a Quebecer. More than that, they had chosen an old-fashioned politician and a skilful conciliator. But, most important for the future shape of Canadian politics, they had chosen the first English-speaking Quebec politician acknowledged as a Quebecer by

French-speaking Quebecers. Overnight, the traditional equations in Quebec politics and the assumptions shared by the Liberals and the Parti Québécois seemed in danger.

With Mulroney's victory, a number of people in the PQ began to reconsider their feeling about a federal role for the party. Suddenly, the spectre of another prime minister with Trudeau's constitutional vision appeared. However, Lévesque remained reluctant, and the compromise that was hammered out over the summer was the creation, not of a federal wing of the Parti Québécois, but of a separate party with organic links to the Parti Québécois.

This compromise was announced at the annual three-day caucus retreat, held in Gatineau at the end of August. The new party, headed by Marcel Léger as interim leader, would be called the Parti Nationaliste. However, the organizers soon learned that their assumptions of support were flawed. The people polled had been asked if they would support the Parti Québécois if it ran candidates in a federal election, and some responses ran as high as thirty per cent. When the hypothetical federal wing of the PQ became a real Parti Nationaliste, the support for the idea in the polls plummeted to four per cent. Whether by accident or by design, all Lévesque's gloomiest predictions about a federal party seemed to be being borne out. Marcel Léger finally acknowledged this, and resigned as leader in May 1984.

ON OCTOBER 15, 1983, THE QUEBEC LIBERAL PARTY ELECTED ROBERT Bourassa as its leader. The result was a foregone conclusion; the only surprise was that Pierre Paradis, the right-wing rural populist, came second while Daniel Johnson came third.

How was it possible? How did Bourassa do it after being so hated seven years earlier?

He had matured, of course. He had become tougher and surer of himself, and had got rid of his Uriah Heep manner towards reporters, the sheepish grin at embarrassing questions. He had learned the hard way that reporters could lose respect for leaders they called "tu".

He was no less conscious of image and polls, but he had become sophisticated enough to know that he emerged with a better image if he let the wind blow his hair than if he hired a hairdresser as a bodyguard. But he remains more interested in politics than in policies. He resembles Brian Mulroney in many ways; like him, he smooths over differences, remembers friends, is fascinated by the techniques of politics. However, there is a difference. Bourassa no longer calls himself a social democrat, or a socialist — as he did in an interview as late as 1977 — but he is not a man of the right. Bourassa is one of the people who built the state in Quebec. It was his government that introduced Medicare, the system of social-service centres, and the first language legislation. He will modify the functioning of the state if he becomes premier again, but he will not dismantle it. In his second leadership campaign, he was the most left-leaning and the most nationalist of the candidates; Daniel Johnson, a former vice-president of Power Corporation, was the candidate of the rising francophone business élite, and Pierre Paradis was the candidate of the dissident farmers and agrobusiness interests attacking the farmers' union, the Union des Producteurs Agricoles.

On the personal level, Bourassa managed to win back the Liberal leadership because he wanted it more than anyone else — and he out-worked, out-hustled, out-campaigned, and out-toughed anyone who might have taken it from him.

But the subject that continues to shape and define the political mood in Quebec is the language debate, the political formulation of the relationship between the French-speaking majority and the minorities. The fall of 1983 saw the latest version of this debate when Gérald Godin held public hearings on the language law, Bill 101, as part of the process of reviewing and amending it. It was the clearest indication of how the political climate had changed in six years of PQ government.

Godin had promised a reassessment of Bill 101 as soon as he was given responsibility for it in September 1982; it was not until October 19, 1983, that an Assembly committee began hearing briefs. It seemed that all the old wounds of the language debate would be reopened.

On the one hand, nationalist groups were still smarting from the referendum defeat and the constitutional setback, and saw the language law as a sacred text to be defended. On the other hand, the minorities were becoming more organized and more vocal in opposition to the law. Some had seen the referendum as the end of language irritation: in the fall of 1980, one Montreal francophone was told by the woman at her neighbourhood bakery, "It's all over now. You will have to speak English again." For such people, the re-election of the

PQ had come as a traumatic shock; what they had thought was temporary now seemed permanent. In addition, a series of incidents aggravated the impression that the Office de la Langue Française and the Commission de Surveillance had created of petty, unreasonable, almost Kafkaesque bureaucracy. A nurse, Joanne Curran, failed a written French test three times and, despite Camille Laurin's promise that no-one would lose his or her job because of Bill 101, she was forced to resign. Since she was fluent enough in French to be able to be interviewed on French radio, she attracted wide attention and sympathy. And in 1982, the Commission investigated a complaint that Marie Marthe Larose had been unable to "die in French" at St. Mary's Hospital. This confirmed the worst fears of bureaucratic zeal, and implied that every employee of every English-speaking institution had to speak French.

The last weekend in May in 1982, Alliance Quebec was founded. It was a coalition led by a group of impressive young professionals who were temperamentally moderate — and it was a sign of how the mood had shifted that they no longer sounded moderate. Eric Maldoff, the president, insisted on the right to put up bilingual signs ("We have the right to be visible!") and demanded an end to the mandatory testing of professionals educated in Quebec.

At first apparently welcoming new spokesmen from the English-speaking community, the government stiffened its attitude; Lévesque bluntly denied their requests for changes in language policy, and Godin's tone began to change. In January 1983 he called Alliance Quebec "Keystone Cops" and "firemen without a fire". In April, under questioning in the National Assembly, he snapped, "Those who can't stand our smell should leave." Some people began to wonder how seriously they could take this man. For Godin was both a visceral nationalist and an intuitive cosmopolitan, and the two sides of his nature sometimes lived uneasily with each other. When Lévesque appointed him to the job, he eyed him sardonically and said, "I am looking forward to seeing how a guy caught between a rock and a hard place will get out of the jam."

Godin soon found the dimensions of the rock and the hard place. "I was caught between people in the nationalist movement, who said 'Any change to Bill 101 is unacceptable,' on the one hand, and on the other hand, people who said 'Godin is a new Goebbels.' " He was wrestling with a dilemma: his struggle between his pride and his fears, his commitment to diversity and his fear of cultural domination, his contradictory visions of the English presence in Quebec as a minority and a threat, an asset and a danger.

In his opening statement to the committee hearing, it became clear that he saw a solution. For he began by making a very important distinction between the English-speaking minority and the North American cultural presence of English. He pointed to the threat to French from the technological revolution. "When we need English, even in Quebec, to start the car, to turn on a television set, a computer, a video-cassette player, a camera, a photocopy machine and so on, isn't it inevitable that the Quebec francophone doubts the capacity of his own language to deal with the reality of the twentieth century and, very soon, the twenty-first?" he asked.

This was not an original point: French is under assault as a language of science and technology, as are German and Spanish. But Godin added another point rarely made in Quebec. "Let us be clear," he said. "Anglo-Quebecers have very little to do with this assimilation, and it is not they that we should consider responsible, or their institutions."

It was the crucial first step to cutting the Gordian knot of the language debate. After sixty-eight hours of hearings and sixty presentations, it was clear that there was a new consensus. On the one hand, there was still a strong nationalist desire to keep the face of Quebec French: signs, names, titles. There was a determination to maintain the rights of francophones to use French at work, and be served in French. But there was no longer a fear of an influx of English-speaking children from other provinces, and there was a new appreciation of the problems of English institutions.

After three amendments to his legislation in committee, and continuous private lobbying by Alliance Quebec, Godin finally succeeded in delivering what he had promised: institutional bilingualism for English-language schools, hospitals, and social service agencies. These institutions would guarantee to provide service in French, but not every employee would be required to speak French.

In addition, he broke the deadlock caused by the refusal of other provinces to negotiate reciprocal agreements with Quebec: Quebec would give access to English-language schools to people coming from provinces where services in French were available. This was granted to New Brunswick immediately. At the same time, Godin reinforced the francization process, making the committees in the workplace more effective.

It was not the end of the language debate, which will continue as long as francophones feel that their language is fragile in North America. But the changes did indicate a new maturity, and a new tolerance in Quebec.

ON NOVEMBER 24, 1983, PIERRE MAROIS RESIGNED FROM THE CABINET. He had been ill for several months in the winter of 1981-2, and had aged visibly, never really recovering either his strength or his intimate relationship with Lévesque. The welfare-reform program, which had been announced as part of the latest economic recovery package ten days earlier, was not his suggestion but had been imposed on him at a special cabinet meeting. Lévesque was increasingly annoyed with his lack of attendance at Question Period, and had lost his temper at him shortly before, accusing him of being unable to manage his ministry, of being worn out and useless. The latest embarrassment occurred after Marois had made his decision: that very afternoon, Lévesque had had to answer questions in the Assembly on the fact that Marois's ministry had given a $28,000 job-creation grant to a sex bar in Sept-Îles.

Marois's departure was another indication of the decline of the PQ as a progressive force, and the burn-out of the ministers who had personified the excitement and energy of the new government in 1976. Robert Burns, Louis O'Neill, Jacques Couture, Lise Payette, Guy Joron, Claude Charron, and now Pierre Marois—along with more conservative but still impressive figures like Claude Morin and Lucien Lessard. They were all gone, replaced by ministers every bit as flexible, colourless, and forgettable as the back row of the Trudeau cabinet, or the Davis cabinet in Ontario.

Before Lévesque completed his cabinet shuffle, another veteran resigned. When Lévesque told Jacques-Yvan Morin that he was dividing up Intergovernmental Affairs, giving the international responsibilities to External Trade Minister Bernard Landry and the federal-provincial responsibilities to Pierre Marc Johnson, Morin resigned on the spot, refusing offers of four other portfolios.

It was an honourable gesture, typical of the man. Sometimes naive, almost innocent, Morin was a man of taste and integrity who, like Marois but in a very different way, had come to be out of place in the PQ cabinet.

The March 5, 1984, cabinet shuffle was an extension of the September 1982 shuffle: an end to irritations. Camille Laurin's radical plan to make the school, not the school board, the focal point for decision-making had been under fire for months; Laurin became minister of social affairs, and Yves Bérubé became minister of education. On May 4, Bérubé announced that the school-board reform would be postponed indefinitely; one of the few radical measures of the second term was shelved.

Alain Marcoux's legislation to make waiters and waitresses pay taxes on their tips had stirred up anger and controversy; Robert Dean became minister of revenue, and Marcoux replaced Jacques Léonard, whose legislation penalizing municipalities for accepting direct federal grants was unpopular, as minister of municipal affairs.

Anyone involved in any controversy or unpopular legislation was moved. The result was enormously frustrating for the Liberals; as one opposition member complained privately, "We can't criticize Bérubé for not doing what Laurin wanted to do, or Dean for not doing what Marcoux wanted to do, or Marcoux for not doing what Léonard wanted to do."

The shuffle reaffirmed the conservatism of the government, and succeeded in putting the three likeliest candidates for succession to Lévesque on a balanced and equal footing: Jacques Parizeau in Finance, Pierre Marc Johnson in Justice and Interprovincial Affairs, and Bernard Landry, the first person to admit openly that he would seek the leadership when Lévesque retired, in International Relations and Commercial Trade.

As he had every time since the first cabinet in 1976, Lévesque tried to persuade Parizeau to move from Finance; this time to the new portfolio of International Relations and Commercial Trade. Parizeau agreed at first, but changed his mind: he wanted to finish the White Paper on Taxation he was working on. Had he not changed his mind, Landry was slated to become minister of finance, and Johnson was to become president of the Treasury Board.

For the first time in months, there was a renewed enthusiasm in the party, drawn, in part, from the polls, In the last three days of January and the first three days of February, the party asked francophones to rank sovereignty-association, renewed federalism, independence, and the status quo. Sovereignty-association was listed first by fifty-three per cent of those polled (which party strategists calculate would work out to forty-three or forty-four per cent in an election), renewed federalism came second, independence third, and the status quo fourth.

But more exciting to party activists than the polls was the growing confidence that René Lévesque would hold the next election on independence. It would be a whole new ballgame. For on February 29, 1984, only two days after the Progressive Conservative opposition in Manitoba had succeeded in forcing Premier Howard Pawley to withdraw his legislation recognizing certain French rights, Pierre Trudeau decided to resign. Suddenly a new horizon opened up, which Lévesque had been waiting for for years. With Trudeau gone, the debate on Quebec's future could resume in a very different fashion. The years of transition and humiliation since the patriation of the constitution seemed to be nearing a conclusion. A new era seemed to begin; but many of the old questions remained unanswered.

Epilogue

Our revels now are ended.
William Shakespeare

On Saturday morning, June 9, 1984, delegates gathered for the workshops at the Montreal Palais des Congrés. It was the ninth convention since the creation of the Parti Québécois, and once again delegates from across the province were working through resolutions to amend the party program. But this time the mood was different. That morning, *Le Soleil* published the results of a public-opinion poll that showed the PQ with 23 per cent and the Liberals with 68 per cent support of those polled.

At the opening on Friday night, René Lévesque had quoted Harry Truman's line, "If you can't stand the heat, get out of the kitchen" — and added "I accept to stay at the stove." Then he qualified this with the ambiguous phrase "jusqu'à nouvel ordre" — which might mean "until conditions change" or "until further notice". To muddy the waters further, he said, "I accept, in any case, until the inevitable day when a new kitchen requires a new chef." He was applauded, but without the fervour of previous years. For the first time, people who had always been loyal to Lévesque began to wonder out loud if the time had not come for the party's founder to step down.

The debate over the party program was almost devoid of controversy. The divisions of 1981-2 seemed forgotten; the party seemed to have embraced the new rhetoric of "la concertation", a jargon of social consensus which enabled the party to distance itself from the unions without embracing private enterprise, all in the name of co-operation, consultation, planning, and co-ordination. It was a kind of idealism that reminded Jean Francoeur, an editorial writer at *Le Devoir*, of Marshal Pétain's corporatism in Vichy France.

The only controversy was, in fact, spontaneously provoked by Lévesque himself, and to his annoyance it dominated the convention.

The executive had presented a motion in which the sentence "A vote for a Parti Québécois candidate will mean a vote for Quebec sovereignty" followed the statement that the next election would be held "principally" on the issue of sovereignty. Lévesque had been present at the executive meeting where this was discussed, and Gilbert Paquette, the sponsor, specifically asked him if he objected to it. Lévesque said that he didn't. "It's putting on a belt and suspenders," he said, using a phrase which describes Quebec habitant prudence, making doubly sure of something.

But at the workshop discussing the resolutions on sovereignty, Jacques-Yvan Morin argued vigorously against the motion. He pointed out that many PQ voters did not support Quebec independence. "I know that I was elected by a lot of people who are moving toward sovereignty," he said. "We are saying to the undecided, 'Believe or die.' We are saying to those who support our social program but do not support sovereignty, 'You have no choice, eh? If you don't support sovereignty, vote for our opponents.' "

This certainly struck a chord with Lévesque; he nodded vigorously, and said that he agreed with Morin's position. Paquette, on the other hand, said he wanted to be a candidate for a party clearly endorsing sovereignty.

When the motion was passed, Lévesque winced and grimaced, and left without speaking to reporters. Then, he asked his staff if they thought that the motion could be turned around in the plenary session. He was bluntly told that it was out of the question in four hours; this was a convention, not a National Council meeting, and it had been hard enough for Michel Carpentier to turn the National Council against an executive recommendation for Lévesque in four days.

The debate took place on Saturday night, and the motion was endorsed overwhelmingly. But the cat was among the pigeons. Several ministers were appalled at the party's tying its prospects so firmly to the sovereignty issue; Clément Richard told reporters that he would not be a candidate under those conditions. Michel Clair said he had "never seen turkeys so eager for Christmas". Pierre Marc Johnson, always prudent, said simply that he did not think that a party convention could redefine the meaning of an election.

But it was clear that the state of the opinion polls had given the party activists a sense of almost martyr-like conviction.

They had adopted the language of religious believers, and looked at the upcoming election with the serenity of lay missionaries, or Jehovah's Witnesses setting out to propagate the faith. "We must, at last, have the language of believers," André Auclair, a delegate, had told the workshop on sovereignty, and it seemed that many agreed with him.

Since Lévesque had not hidden his annoyance at the outcome of the debate, many had feared another scolding as he closed the convention. There was even a rumour on Sunday afternoon that he would not address the convention. Instead, he rallied to the motion he had originally endorsed at the executive. In fact, for the first time, he concluded a convention by attacking the Liberals instead of scolding his own party delegates. There was an almost pathetic feeling of relief in the hall.

But Lévesque could no longer afford the luxury of attacking his own party. Too many people who were too close to him had begun to mutter that he should resign. The Liberal leadership campaign had revived the Liberals in the polls, and more than one senior PQ member looked on enviously at this revival.

At the press conference, Lévesque was disconcerted at how direct the questioning was. "If the polls show you still low in the fall, will you quit political life?"

"I don't have to reply to a question like that," he said, clearly taken aback. Recovering, he made a facetious reference to Pierre Trudeau's walk in the snow on February 29. "If ever the chance is offered, I will go for a walk on a day of beautiful sunshine and make a decision," he said.

When the laughter had died down, another reporter said, "The whole convention is talking about it."

"Ah, the whole convention is talking about it," Lévesque said, his voice frosting with sarcasm. "Well then, do your assessment for me, as usual, with care and in detail, and I will draw the conclusion that seems to me to be appropriate."

His annoyance was understandable. The party had had its most serene convention ever, and the media's attention was centred on two things: an issue that he had accepted at the executive but had allowed to develop into a controversy, and his own future.

Certainly, the possible candidates for the succession were in evidence: Jacques Parizeau chatted with a group of young people who had been lobbying the delegates, Pierre Marc Johnson was omnipresent, chatting with delegates and reporters. Bernard Landry had toured the province twice as chairman of the financing campaign, and Gilbert Paquette had led the argument to make a vote for the PQ a vote for sovereignty. But these four had such different visions of the party and of the future that Lévesque and his advisers felt that a leadership campaign before the election might split the party.

In addition, the delegates were suffering from trauma: the party members from the polls, and the MNAs from a more profound shock.

ON MAY 8, ABOUT 9:30 IN THE MORNING, A MAN IN BATTLE FATIGUES drove up to radio station CJRP, the outlet for one of Quebec City's most popular and abrasive broadcasters, André Arthur. Arthur, who had performed the extraordinary feat of changing radio stations and bringing most of his listeners with him, was a constant critic of the government, abusing cabinet ministers and calling them vulgar names.

The man delivered a cassette tape to one of Arthur's researchers, Maritchu d'Abbadie d'Arrast, telling her that they were not to listen to the tape until 10 a.m. He would not give his name, saying only "For you, I am Mr. D." Later, someone would speculate that he was modelling himself on Mr. T. of the American television program "The A Team" — a story of a group of rebels in the army who, usually in very violent fashion, take the law into their own hands. Disregarding his instructions, the staff at the station played the cassette — and heard a rambling attack on the Quebec government, René Lévesque, and the Parti Québécois.

"What I am doing is not for me, but for future generations who speak French," he said. "It was being a French person who travels in Canada that I realized that people who speak other languages thought we were stupid.

". . . I respect my language. Fine, I speak English to get along. But I certainly do not renounce my language."

On he rambled: politicians were clowns, who argued all the time, and did so on our tax money; Quebec was beautiful, but people had never left the province and couldn't even say yes or no in English; the Parti Québécois only wanted one language, and they were destroying Quebec; he was going to fix things before Lévesque achieved independence.

When they heard that he was threatening to destroy the

Parti Québécois, the researchers phoned the police, but it was too late.

After he left the station, he drove to the Citadel, and fired off his machine gun. Then he drove up to the side door of the National Assembly, and went in shooting. The hostess at the door, Jacynthe Richard, fell in a hail of bullets, seriously injured. One bullet went through the door jamb of a room off the corridor, where a messenger, Camille Lepage, was filling an ice bucket at the ice machine. The bullet went through his skull; he was killed instantly.

The gunman headed up the corridor, around the corner at the front of the building, and reached the main hall. Firing off his machine gun, he went up the stairs as people fled in front of him in confusion. He turned and went up to the National Assembly's Salon Bleu. Assuming the Assembly would be in session, he went in firing. But it was Tuesday, and the Assembly would not sit until two. Roger Lefrançois, a member of the chief returning officer's staff who was preparing for a committee hearing on the estimates of the office, and Georges Boyer, a page, died, and thirteen people were injured.

The gunman was sitting in the speaker's chair, shooting off bursts of machine-gun fire, when the sergeant-at-arms, René Jalbert, came up on the elevator from his basement office to investigate. Jalbert called out to the man to stop shooting because he wanted to talk to him.

Coming around the corner, Jalbert saw a young man in fatigues; he was very pale, perspiring, and obviously very tense, waving his machine gun from side to side.

"I see you are a military man," said Jalbert, a retired major who had spent twenty-seven years in the army. "I am a military man too."

He produced his certificate of release from the army, and asked the gunman to show him his identification card.

Jalbert then learned he was dealing with a corporal named Denis Lortie. He persuaded him to release the terrified pages who were hiding behind the seats, offered him a cup of coffee, and led him down to his office. For the next three hours, he gradually succeeded in building a relationship with him.

It was a masterly job. Sometimes Jalbert called the soldier by his first name, and used the familiar form "tu"; sometimes he called him "vous"; sometimes he told him how wrong he had been; sometimes he spoke to him in the kindly avuncular tones of an older man trying to help a younger one, telling him he should let himself weep when he started to cry. Twice, Jalbert put him on the telephone to senior army officers. It was all a careful exercise to bring the corporal back in touch with military reality.

Finally, Jalbert felt that this had been done. "Look, you are a military man and I am a military man," he said. "You are a corporal and I am a major. From now on, you are going to talk to me and you will only address me as 'Major'; I will address you as 'Corporal'."

It was a crucial turning point. At 2:15 in the afternoon, the gunman surrendered.

The status of the sergeant-at-arms had lately been reduced by the speaker, Richard Guay; his office had been moved to the basement, the security force at the National Assembly had been taken out of his control and transferred to the Ministry of Justice, a new job of director of protocol had been created, and Jalbert had been left with little more than administration of the pages and the ceremonial duty of carrying in the mace at the opening of each sitting. Suddenly, he was a hero; at the funeral for the three victims, people came forward from the crowd outside the church to touch him.

The tragedy showed something more than the aberration of a deranged soldier and the courage of a former army officer charged with the protection of the Assembly. It revealed the depth of disillusionment with the political process in Quebec.

The first hint of this came the next day, when the Montreal radio station CFCF asked listeners if they agreed with those who had expressed sympathy with the gunman's motives. To the surprise of those who asked the question, seventy-six per cent of the 1,268 callers indicated that they did.

This reaction was not restricted to English-language radio listeners. Quebec politicians were shocked and hurt at the number of people who said, "What a shame he was early," or "What a shame innocent people died instead of politicians." This was a kind of hostility that no poll on voting intention would reveal, and many politicians, PQ members in particular, were stunned. Low popularity in the polls was one thing; public sympathy for a man who had tried to exterminate them was something else. The shock may have contributed to the fact that in the month that followed, eight MNAs went to the hospital with stress-related ailments.

It was a kind of grotesque symbol of the inadequacies of the PQ's achievements as compared to what it had promised. It had promised a dream, and it could not deliver. It had promised to be a new kind of government; it had become like other governments. A young man who enlisted in the Canadian army found that he was mocked and handicapped because of his poor English, and his rage turned, not against Ottawa, the federal government, and the dream of bilingualism, but against Quebec, the PQ, and the dream of an independent Quebec.

Despite the referendum, many members of the PQ thought that they had succeeded in transforming French Canadians — members of a defensive minority in Canada — into Québécois — a confident majority in Quebec. The public reaction to the May 8 killings made some reflect that they had been wrong.

IN MAY 1976, PIERRE TRUDEAU HAD ANNOUNCED THAT SEPARATISM was over. In April 1984, Marc Lalonde said more or less the same thing: "It has become literature. . . . It will continue to be there, it will still be talked about in the next election, but as a political force that carries away the new generations, in my opinion, it is dead."

The years in between those two remarks have been part of a major struggle between two traditions that have fought for dominance in Quebec for over a hundred and fifty years; during those eight years, each side won two major victories. The Parti Québécois won two elections; their federalist opponents won a referendum and a constitutional battle.

The achievements of the PQ in power were considerable. The face of Montreal and Quebec was transformed and rendered French, letting thousands of chips of resentment slide off thousands of shoulders; the volunteer ethic of the early years of Parti Québécois fund-raising was made the law. Long-neglected matters like libraries and sewage-treatment plants, women and minorities in the civil service became, however partially and belatedly, part of the public agenda.

At the same time, for better or for worse, the role of the state in the economy expanded as the crown corporations played an ever more important role as investors and partners; the English-speaking community wrestled, sometimes awkwardly, with the pain and difficulty of coming to terms with a shrinking minority status. The economic decline of Montreal, a phenomenon that had started years before, accelerated during these years as head offices withdrew to leave regional offices to function in French.

Throughout this period, English Canadians have been largely spectators — sometimes envious of Quebecers for their indisputable identity and the vigour of their debate over how best to define and protect it, sometimes fearful of the effects of the nationalist victories.

The nationalism of the Parti Québécois that came to power in 1976 was complex, varied, and often contradictory: by turns, it touched emotions that were idealistic, narrow, generous, defensive, open, manipulative, ennobling, and vengeful. The emotions it provoked oscillated between courage and fear, pride and humiliation.

The nationalist intellectual tradition in Quebec has dwelt on the threats and dangers facing the future of the French language in North America: assimilation, loss of language, economic subordination, social domination, personal humiliation. The White Paper on the French language in 1977 was a classic example of this, using out-of-date statistics and distorting some of them to make the case for the fragility of French. The advances of the French language have often been overlooked in the desire to justify more stringent regulations to protect against new threats.

On the other hand, the anti-nationalists have tended to see only the narrowness and none of the depth in Quebec nationalism, to see the manipulation but miss the openness, to attack the defensiveness but ignore the very real sense of personal humiliation, insecurity, and pain that many Quebecers have felt, and to exaggerate the progress that has been made in the rest of Canada in coming to terms with the French fact. At the same time, they have ignored the genuine, if sometimes clumsy, attempts by the PQ and by French-speaking Quebec as a whole to welcome minorities, and to make them a part of the party and the society.

The debate over Quebec's future has shifted: with the return of Robert Bourassa and the PQ's move to the right, both parties are trying to rationalize the role of the state and encourage the growth of the private sector. Lines that seemed so sharp in 1976 have been blurred.

The patriation of the constitution ended a twenty-year debate on whether Quebec would be able to get more powers inside Confederation; the National Assembly did not gain, but lost power. The great fear in Quebec after the double defeat of the referendum and the patriation of the constitution was that Quebec would no longer count in Canada.

However, the ensuing transition of leadership in the federal parties, with the election of Brian Mulroney as Progressive Conservative leader in June 1983 and of John Turner as Liberal leader in June 1984, made one thing clear. Canadians now use Quebec as a test of leadership. It is now a criterion for leadership in Canada that a person should not only be able to speak French, but be comfortable in Quebec. John Turner was able to win a majority of delegates from the province partly because he represented a promise of continued alternation and a hope of winning seats in the West — but also partly because he had spent a decade practising law in Montreal, and it showed.

His so-called campaign gaffes on the language question were, in fact, echoes of the Pepin-Robarts language recommendations: recommendations which had been shelved by Pierre Trudeau, and which called for provincial responsibility for language and greater economic centralization.

The Manitoba language debate of 1983-4 made it clear that the debate over minority-language rights in Canada is far from over. The challenge that René Lévesque presented to Canada in 1967 when he left the Quebec Liberal Party and formed the Mouvement Souveraineté-Association remains intact. But it remains to be seen how it will be tackled during the last fifteen years of the century.

On June 18, two days after Turner's election as Liberal leader, the Parti Québécois lost three more by-elections: Marguerite-Bourgeois, Sauvé, and Marie-Victorin. Marie-Victorin, Pierre Marois's old riding, was the most telling: it bordered on Lévesque's own constituency, and the PQ candidate got only thirty-eight per cent of the vote. The results — the PQ's nineteenth, twentieth, and twenty-first consecutive by-election defeats since 1976 — renewed speculation that Lévesque might be forced to step down.

At his end-of-session press conference, on June 21, Lévesque made it clear that he did not intend to quit. It was not the time to leave the ship, he said.

What he did not say was that the PQ had done polling on the Monday, Tuesday, and Wednesday of that week, to see if the defeat of Jean Chrétien had affected Liberal popularity in Quebec. It hadn't.

For three months, the PQ polls had found the federal Liberals had over fifty per cent in Quebec, rising to fifty-five when those polled had been asked to consider the Parti Nationaliste. Right after the Liberal convention, the party's lead over the Conservatives was at least twenty per cent. At those percentages, Lévesque's advisers figured, the Liberals would keep their seventy-four seats in Quebec, threaten the only Tory seat, and stay in power.

So Lévesque saw two glimmers of hope: the traditional Quebec reluctance to vote "rouge à Québec, rouge à Ottawa", and what he saw as Robert Bourassa's vulnerability. They were slim chances, he knew, and he would not dodge from the suggestion that in an immediate election the PQ would be defeated.

But he didn't want to quit, and he didn't plan to quit — at least not yet. He was still more popular than the party, a leadership campaign might prove more destructive than unifying, and anything might happen. He had proved that in 1981. Experience had shown the value of patience. As long as the party's popularity did not drop below twenty per cent in the polls in the fall of 1984, he could stay on, and fight the election on his own ground, at his own choosing. The old fox had not given up hope.

As Quebec and Canada began the post-Trudeau era, there was a general assumption that Lévesque and the Parti Québécois were facing automatic defeat. The "national question" seemed less and less relevant in Quebec, and economic priorities seemed more important. Personally, Lévesque seemed to be losing his sureness of touch. He had become even less direct with his cabinet ministers; he had never told Camille Laurin that he simply didn't like his proposals to restructure the school-board system, and had failed to make a decisive enough cabinet shuffle in September 1982. He had misjudged the effect of supporting Jacques-Yvan Morin in the workshop on sovereignty at the convention. He had allowed his anger at André Arthur to develop into such a vigorous controversy that he gave a local broadcaster a national reputation. He could be childishly rude to people he thought of as adversaries.

There were ways in which eight years in power had embittered Lévesque. At times, his resentment against the media would flash out; similarly, he sometimes felt betrayed by the lack of political commitment of the younger generation, whose intensity he had always counted on.

Lévesque was also bitter at his failure to overcome the bureaucracy. He had spent an enormous amount of time and energy in the first year or so on the question of decentralization. He had even ordered that the offices dealing with fisheries be transferred from Quebec to Gaspé—and the civil servants had dug in their heels and refused. A quieter attempt to establish the automobile-insurance headquarters in Trois-Rivières had similarly failed. In the weeks following his threat to resign in December 1981, those two failures seemed to nag at him most.

But René Lévesque remains potent, unpredictable, and a man, like Pierre Trudeau, of extraordinary resourcefulness and recuperative power. Those who dismiss him as a spent force do so at their peril.

In the spring and summer of 1984, the prospect of Quebec independence seemed more distant than it had for twenty years, But as the next election draws nearer, the debate on Quebec independence will intensify again. Whether the PQ wins or loses, the challenge that a French-speaking society represents to Canada and to North America will remain, and the dream of an independent nation will stay as an ideal for thousands of Quebecers.

The Parti Québécois may be defeated — yet, despite its fatigue and its dismal showing in the polls, the 1981 election proved how quickly its fortunes could revive—and the nationalism that it articulates may subside. But Quebec's collective emotions remain too strong for its nationalist idealism to vanish.

GRAHAM FRASER
Quebec, June 24, 1984

Acknowledgements

In the summer of 1976, John Macfarlane remembered my interest in Quebec and recommended me to Peter C. Newman as Montreal bureau chief for *Maclean's*. Newman not only agreed, he suggested to me that I write a book. I owe them both thanks.

This book was researched in three different ways. The major part was done in the course of doing my job: first at *Maclean's*, then at the Montreal *Gazette*, which granted me two leaves of absence, and, in the final weeks of completing the manuscript, at the Toronto *Globe and Mail*. Where possible, I kept tapes of my interviews and found, as the years passed, that they often yielded more than I had grasped or understood in my first rush to deadline. In addition, I worked to fill in the gaps with a systematic reading of the written material available. Finally, I conducted a series of interviews specifically for this book. Many of these were given on the understanding that the source of the information would not be identified. Where I have obtained the information from published sources or interviews on the record, I have tried to identify them. I apologize to some who took great pains to explain issues to me which, for one reason or another, are not dealt with in the final version of the book.

Since this work was done through some of the most difficult tensions felt in Quebec in this century, it is worth stressing that I was received with openness and co-operation by politicians and party officials both in the Parti Québécois and in the Quebec Liberal Party, by political aides and civil servants in Quebec and in Ottawa, and by party volunteers.

When I moved to Montreal, and later to Quebec City, I was welcomed and encouraged by a large number of people. Over the years that this project took, I was helped enormously by my colleagues: Robert Lewis, Ian Urquhart, and David Thomas at *Maclean's*; Joel Ruimy, Lewis Harris, Anthony Wilson-Smith,

Jonathan Mann, and, through it all, Marie-Louise Perron at the *Gazette*; Margot Gibb-Clark and Louise Gagnon at the *Globe and Mail*. I owe particular thanks to the staff of *L'Actualité* who made me welcome: Jean Paré, Yves Taschereau, and Yolande Rondeau. At the *Gazette*, a number of people were particularly supportive and understanding of my obsessive tendencies, and were the best of editors: in particular Mark Harrison and Joan Fraser.

Benoît Aubin and Michel C. Auger were a constant help throughout the project—reading, sharing, sparking, and reinforcing my enthusiasms with their own.

My colleagues in the National Assembly press gallery were all encouraging and helpful in passing on details, recollections, and suggestions to pursue. Particularly generous in their quite different insights were Normand Girard and Gilles Lesage. Like virtually every other journalist who has attempted to write about Quebec politics, I owe a particular debt to Bob McKenzie, whose generosity is unlimited. Mel Racine and his gallery staff were unfailingly helpful.

Friends provided emotional support and a place to stay, particularly Henry Aubin, Stephen Bornstein, Bob Rae, Jennifer Rae, Don Winkler, and Bruce Yaccato.

Jean Paré, Ramsay Cook, and Robert Fulford, in addition to their various forms of help and advice over the years, kindly agreed to recommend me for a Canada Council "Explorations" grant which helped cover my expenses during three leaves of absence to work on the book.

A variety of other people read parts of the manuscript at various stages of its evolution and made valuable, often crucial suggestions: Jeffrey Simpson, I. M. B. Dobell, Sheila Moore, Bernard Descôteaux, Sheila Fischman, Paige Woodward, Jennifer Robinson, Judy Steed, and Margot Gibb-Clark.

Doug Gibson, at Macmillan, nurtured this idea from its conception in August 1977 as a vague list of good intentions through all the various stages of rough drafts; his infectious enthusiasm never flagged. Anne Holloway remained both cheerful and realistic under the most trying circumstances. I owe a special debt to Ivon Owen. His knowledge, his rigour, and his professionalism as a translator and as an editor were invaluable.

Two final notes.

My father, Blair Fraser, gave me a love of the land and an affection for Quebec. He also gave me a sense of journalistic standards and personal integrity that I have tried to live up to. He died before he could write the book he wanted about Quebec; this represents a small tribute to his memory.

Barbara Uteck, my wife, kept an unwavering faith in this project, and hardly ever complained about the chaos of notes, clippings, and piles of seven-year-old newspapers I insisted was essential for its completion. Malcolm and Nicholas, our sons, were unfailingly supportive, if somewhat incredulous about this project, which has lasted most of their lives. I am grateful.

Graham Fraser
QUEBEC CITY

Chronology

1936
June 11: Liberal Premier Louis Alexandre Taschereau resigns, and is succeeded by Adélard Godbout.
August 17: Quebec election. The Union Nationale, led by Maurice Duplessis, is elected with 76 seats and 57.5 per cent of the popular vote. The Liberals win 14 seats and 41.8 per cent.

1939
October 23: Quebec election. The Liberals, led by Adélard Godbout, are elected with 70 seats and 54.2 per cent of the popular vote. The Union Nationale wins 14 seats and 39.2 per cent. Camillien Houde and René Chaloult are elected as independents.

1944
August 8: Quebec election. The Union Nationale, led by Duplessis, returns to power with 48 seats and 36 per cent of the popular vote. The Liberals win 37 seats and 37 per cent. The Bloc Populaire, led by André Laurendeau, wins 4 seats and 15 per cent. René Chaloult is elected as a Créditiste, and a CCF candidate wins Rouyn-Noranda.

1948
July 28: Quebec election. The Union Nationale wins 84 seats and 53 per cent of the popular vote; the Liberals win 6 seats and 36 per cent. René Chaloult and Frank Hanley are elected as independents.

1952
July 16: Quebec election. The Union Nationale wins 68 seats and 50.5 per cent of the popular vote; the Liberals win 23 seats and 46 per cent. Frank Hanley is re-elected as an independent.

1956
June 20: Quebec election. The Union Nationale wins 72 seats and 52 per cent of the popular vote. The Liberals, led by Georges-Émile Lapalme, win 20 seats and 44.5 per cent. Frank Hanley is re-elected as an independent.

1957
June 10: A federal election, in which the Progressive Conservatives led by John Diefenbaker win 112 seats, the Liberals 105, the CCF 25, Social Credit 19, and others 4. In Quebec, Conservatives win 9 seats and 31.1 per cent of the vote; Liberals win 62 seats and 57.6 per cent.

1958
March 31: Federal election. The Progressive Conservatives win a majority with 208 seats; the Liberals win 49 and the CCF 8. The Conservatives win 50 seats in Quebec and 45.7 per cent of the vote; the Liberals win 25 seats and 49.6 per cent.
May 31: Jean Lesage is elected leader of the Quebec Liberal Party, defeating René Hamel and Paul Gérin-Lajoie.
December 29: The producers' strike at Radio-Canada begins.

1959
March 7: The producers' strike ends; on the same day, Lévesque's angry statement on the strike is published in the *Montreal Star.*
September 7: Premier Maurice Duplessis dies of a stroke, and is succeeded by Paul Sauvé.

1960
January 2: Paul Sauvé dies of a heart attack, and is succeeded by Antonio Barrette.
June 22: Quebec election. The Liberals, led by Jean Lesage, win 50 seats and 51 per cent of the popular vote; the Union Nationale wins 44 seats and 47 per cent. Frank Hanley is re-elected as an independent.
July 25-7: Federal-provincial conference in Ottawa. Lesage proposes that the conference resume discussions of patriation and an amending formula for the British North America Act. This leads to what becomes known as the Fulton-Favreau formula.
September 10: The Rassemblement pour l'Indépendance Nationale is formed at a hotel in Morin Heights.

1961
April 4: The RIN has its first major public success, attracting six hundred people to a rally in Montreal the night of a hockey play-off final.
September 18: Marcel Chaput publishes *Pourquoi je suis séparatiste;* it sells 35,000 copies.
September 23: Daniel Johnson is elected leader of the Union Nationale.
October 4: Jean Lesage visits Paris, and is greeted like a head of state.
December 14: Pierre Laporte and Claire Kirkland-Casgrain are elected to the legislature as Liberals in two by-elections.

1962

June 18: Federal election. The Diefenbaker government loses its majority, winning 116 seats. The Liberals, led by L. B. Pearson, win 100 seats, Social Credit 30, the NDP 19. In Quebec, the Liberals win 35 seats and 39.2 per cent of the popular vote, the Conservatives 14 seats and 29.6 per cent, and Social Credit 26 seats and 26 per cent.

September 4: Quebec cabinet retreat at Lac-à-l'Épaule. Lévesque urges the acquisition of seven electricity companies, which produce 68 per cent of Quebec's power.

September 19: Lesage calls an election on the issue of taking over the electricity companies.

November 11: Televised debate between Jean Lesage and Daniel Johnson.

November 14: Quebec election. The Liberals win 63 seats, and 56.5 per cent of the popular vote. The Union Nationale wins 31 seats and 43 per cent. One independent, Frank Hanley, is re-elected.

1963

April 8: Federal election. The Liberals win 129 seats, enough to form a minority government. The Conservatives win 95 seats, Social Credit 24, the NDP 17. In Quebec, the Liberals win 47 seats and 45.6 per cent of the popular vote, the PCs 8 seats and 19.5 per cent, the Ralliement des Créditistes 9 seats and 27.3 per cent.

May 1: Quebec takes over the private hydro-electric companies.

July 22: Lester Pearson names André Laurendeau and Davidson Dunton as co-chairmen of the Royal Commission on Bilingualism and Biculturalism.

September 25: Eric Kierans is elected to the legislature as a Liberal.

December 11: Université de Montréal students, led by Bernard Landry and Pierre Marois, demonstrate against Donald Gordon, president of the Canadian National Railways, because of his defence, under questioning in parliamentary committee by Créditiste MP Gilles Grégoire, of the lack of French Canadians in senior management positions.

1964

February 5: Legislative Assembly approves Bill 60, setting up Ministry of Education.

March 31-April 2: Federal-provincial conference in Quebec. Lesage presents plans to withdraw from most joint federal-provincial programs and unveils pension plan.

April 20: Pension agreement between Ottawa and Quebec, which makes the creation of the Caisse de Dépôt possible, is announced.

May 9: Speaking at Collège Sainte-Marie, Lévesque endorses the idea of associate statehood for Quebec.

May 13: Paul Gérin-Lajoie becomes minister of education.

October 10: "Samedi de la matraque" — police attack separatist demonstrators protesting the Queen's visit to Quebec.

1965

March 18: Lévesque and Laporte debate Jacques-Yvan Morin on the Fulton-Favreau formula at the Université de Montréal.

September 10: Jean Marchand. Gérard Pelletier, and Pierre Trudeau announce that they will be Liberal candidates in the federal election.

November 8: Federal election. Liberals remain a minority government, with 131 seats, while the PCs win 97, the NDP 21, Social Credit 14, others 2. In Quebec, the Liberals win 56 seats and 45.6 per cent, the PCs 8 seats and 21.3 per cent, the Ralliement des Créditistes 9 seats and 17.5 per cent.

December 18: Jean Marchand enters federal cabinet as minister of citizenship and immigration, and John Turner as minister without portfolio.

1966

June 5: Quebec election. The Union Nationale, led by Daniel Johnson, win with 56 seats and 40.9 per cent of the popular vote The Liberals, led by Jean Lesage, win 50 seats and 47.2 per cent. The RIN, led by Pierre Bourgault, wins 5.6 per cent, and the Ralliement National, led by Gilles Grégoire, wins 3.2 per cent. Two independents are elected: Frank Hanley and Arthur-E. Séguin.

October 6: Daniel Johnson announces that an agreement has been reached between Hydro-Québec and the British Newfoundland Corporation (BRINCO) to undertake the hydro-electric project at Churchill Falls.

1967

April 4: Pierre Elliott Trudeau becomes minister of justice, Jean Chrétien minister without portfolio.

April 27: Expo 67 opens.

July 24: Charles de Gaulle ends his speech on the balcony of Montreal City Hall with the words "Vive le Québec libre!"

July 29: François Aquin leaves the Liberal Party, in protest against the party's critical reaction to the de Gaulle speech, and sits as the first indépendantiste member of the Assembly.

September 18: Lévesque presents his constitutional position to the Laurier riding association: the first statement of sovereignty-association.

October 14: Lévesque leaves the Liberal Party.

November 18-19: Four hundred people meet at the St. Albert-le-Grand monastery on Côte Sainte-Catherine Road, and found the Mouvement Souveraineté-Association. The provisional executive is

René Lévesque, Rosaire Beaulé, Gérard Bélanger, Marc Brière, and Reynald Brisson.

November 21-6: The Estates-General of French Canada meet at the Place des Arts; 2,500 delegates call for Quebec to have all the powers of a sovereign state.

December 7: The first volume of the Royal Commission on Bilingualism and Biculturalism is published.

1968

January 6: Lévesque's book *Option Québec* is published; it sells 50,000 copies.

February 7: Federal-provincial conference. Daniel Johnson calls for a new constitution; Pierre Trudeau debates with Johnson, getting national attention.

February 19: Canada breaks off diplomatic relations with Gabon after Quebec is invited to an international conference on education without Ottawa's being consulted.

February 22: Johnson announces the creation of Radio-Québec.

April 6: Pierre Elliott Trudeau is elected leader of the Liberal Party of Canada.

April 19-21: MSA policy conference, and a vigorous debate on language. An executive committee is formed of René Lévesque, François Aquin, Gérard Bélanger, Jean-Roch Boivin, Marc Brière, Doris Lussier, and Guy Pelletier.

April 20: Trudeau is sworn in as prime minister. Gérard Pelletier becomes minister without portfolio.

June 24: St. Jean Baptiste Parade riot.

June 25: Federal election. Liberals win a majority with 155 seats; the Progressive Conservatives win 72 seats, the NDP 22, the Ralliement des Créditistes 14; one independent is elected. In Quebec, the Liberals win 56 seats and 53.6 per cent of the popular vote, the Conservatives 4 and 21.3 per cent, the Ralliement des Créditistes 14 and 16.4 per cent.

July 5: John Turner is named minister of justice, Gérard Pelletier secretary of state, and Jean Chrétien minister of Indian affairs and northern development.

September 26: Daniel Johnson dies after the inauguration of the Manic V hydro-electric project.

October 12-14: Founding convention of the Parti Québécois, formally a fusion of the MSA and the Ralliement National. René Lévesque is elected president, Gilles Grégoire vice-president, and Fernand Paré treasurer; Marc-André Bédard, Gérard Bélanger, Jean-Roch Boivin, André Larocque, Marc Lavallée, and Camille Laurin are also elected to the executive.

October 26: A special convention of the RIN votes to dissolve the party, and the members join the PQ.

1969

March 28: "McGill français" demonstration in Montreal.

August 28: Jean Lesage resigns as Liberal leader.

September 19: Jacques Parizeau announces that he is joining the Parti Québécois.

October 7: Police strike in Montreal.

October 17-19: Parti Québécois convention. The executive elected is René Lévesque, president; Gilles Grégoire, vice-president; Fernand Paré, treasurer; André Larocque, program counsellor; Pierre Renaud, services counsellor; at large: Marc-André Bédard, Claude Charron, Camille Laurin (chairman of the executive), and Jacques Parizeau.

October 23: Bill 63, the Union Nationale legislation allowing parents to choose the language of education for their children, is tabled in the National Assembly.

October 31: Massive demonstration at the National Assembly against Bill 63.

November 11: Jérôme Proulx resigns from the Union Nationale and joins the Parti Québécois.

1970

January 17: Robert Bourassa is elected leader of the Quebec Liberal Party, defeating Claude Wagner and Pierre Laporte.

April 29: Quebec election. The Liberals, led by Robert Bourassa, win 72 seats and 44.4 per cent of the vote. The Union Nationale wins 17 seats and 19.7 per cent, the Ralliement des Créditistes 12 seats and 11.2 per cent, the Parti Québécois 7 seats and 23.1 per cent. The PQ members elected are Camille Laurin, Robert Burns, Charles Tremblay, Marcel Léger, Guy Joron, and Lucien Lessard.

October 5: James Cross, British trade commissioner in Montreal, is kidnapped by the Front de Libération du Québec.

October 10: The FLQ kidnaps Pierre Laporte.

October 16: The federal government invokes the War Measures Act.

October 17: The body of Pierre Laporte is found.

October 25: Jean Drapeau's Civic Party wins every seat in the Montreal civic elections.

December 3: Cross is freed, and his kidnappers obtain passage to Cuba.

December 28: Paul Rose, Jacques Rose, and Francis Simard are arrested and charged in connection with Laporte's murder.

1971

February 8: By-election in Chambly to fill Laporte's seat. Jean Cournoyer, the former Union Nationale labour minister who was defeated by Claude Charron in 1970, is elected as a Liberal. But the PQ candidate, Pierre Marois, receives 32.7 per cent of the vote – 0.8 per cent more than in 1970.

February 26-8: Third Parti Québécois convention. René Lévesque is challenged for the presidency by André Larocque, but wins easily. The rest of the executive is Camille Laurin, vice-president; Pierre Renaud, treasurer; Jacques Genest, program counsellor; members at large: Marc-André Bédard, Pierre Bourgault, Guy Joron, Pierre Marois, Jacques Parizeau, Charles Tremblay, and Maurice Tremblay.

April 29: On the first anniversary of the election, Robert Bourassa announces the "project of the century": the James Bay hydro-electric project, estimated to cost $6 billion.

June 14-16: Federal-provincial conference on the constitution in Victoria. The meeting ends with a tentative agreement on the "Victoria Charter", setting out terms for amending and patriating the constitution.

June 19: Gabriel Loubier is elected leader of the Union Nationale, defeating Marcel Massé.

June 23: After a strong public campaign against the Victoria Charter, including editorial attacks on it by Claude Ryan, Robert Bourassa announces he is rejecting the Charter.

October 29: Union march on *La Presse*. Eight policemen are injured, seven demonstrators go to hospital, thirty are arrested. One woman dies.

December 13: Pierre Vallières breaks with the FLQ and renounces violence, urging support for the PQ.

1972

April 5: Negotiations break off between the Common Front of public-sector unions and the Bourassa government.

April 11: An unlimited general strike in the public sector begins.

April 21: The 210,000 strikers are legislated back to work.

May 8: Union leaders Marcel Pépin of the Confederation of National Trade Unions, Louis Laberge of the Quebec Federation of Labour, and Yvon Charbonneau of the Centrale de l'Enseignement du Quebec, the teachers' federation, are sentenced to a year in prison for having encouraged workers to disobey court injunctions.

May 21: Claude Morin, former deputy minister of intergovernmental affairs, announces that he is joining the Parti Québécois.

October 30: Federal election. The Liberals, led by Pierre Trudeau, win 109 seats, and form a minority government. The Progressive Conservatives, led by Robert Stanfield, win 107, the New Democrats, led by David Lewis, win 30, and Social Credit, led by Réal Caouette, win 15. In Quebec, the Liberals win 56 seats with 49.1 per cent, Social Credit 15 seats with 24.4 per cent, and the Conservatives 2 seats with 17.4 per cent.

1973

February 2: Marcel Pépin, Louis Laberge, and Yvon Charbonneau enter Orsainville prison, where they remain until May 16.

February 23-5: Fourth Parti Québécois convention.

October 29: Quebec election. The Liberals, led by Robert Bourassa, win 102 out of 110 seats with 54.7 per cent of the vote; the Parti Québécois wins 6 seats with 30.2 per cent; the Créditistes win 2 seats with 9.9 per cent. The Union Nationale is wiped out, obtaining only 4.9 per cent of the vote. The PQ members elected are Jacques-Yvan Morin, Robert Burns, Marcel Léger, Lucien Lessard, Claude Charron, and Marc-André Bédard.

1974

February 28: *Le Jour* begins publication as a daily newspaper.

March 21: Violence and sabotage explode at the James Bay LG2 site.

July 8: Federal election. The Liberals, led by Pierre Trudeau, win a majority with 141 seats. The Progressive Conservatives, led by Robert Stanfield, win 95 seats; the NDP, led by David Lewis, wins 16 seats; Social Credit, led by Réal Caouette, wins 12; and there is one independent. In Quebec, the Liberals win 60 seats with 53.9 per cent of the vote, Social Credit wins 11 seats with 17.2 per cent, the Conservatives 3 seats with 21.1 per cent.

July 30: Bill 22, the Liberal government's language legislation, is adopted by the National Assembly.

August 28: Quebec by-election in Johnson, caused by the resignation of the Liberal Jean-Claude Boutin after accusations of conflict of interest in the Assembly by Robert Burns. Maurice Bellemare of the Union Nationale is elected.

November 10: Jean Drapeau is re-elected mayor of Montreal. However, the Montreal Citizens' Movement elects 18 councillors.

November 15-17: Parti Québécois convention. The convention adopts the idea of a referendum – but only if negotiations for independence break down, in order to ratify a constitution.

1975

September 26: Jérôme Choquette resigns as minister of education, and leaves the Liberal Party to found the Parti National Populaire.

October: A poll by CROP for *Le Dimanche* shows the PQ leading for the first time with 29 per cent, the Liberals with 24 per cent, and 33 per cent undecided. Two out of three polled say they are dissatisfied with the Bourassa government.

1976

January 12: Robert Bourassa says there will be no election in 1976.

March 2: James Livingston, president of the Canadian Air Traffic

Control Association (CATCA) warns that there will be a strike if the government continues with its plan to introduce bilingual air-traffic control.

March 8: Pierre Trudeau visits Quebec. He jokes with reporters after lunch with Robert Bourassa about the premier's taste for hot-dogs and, that night, attacks Bill 22 in a speech.

May 10: Pierre Trudeau says that separatism is dead.

May 24: Rodrigue Biron is elected leader of the Union Nationale.

June 20: Despite an injunction, air-traffic controllers walk off the job, closing down eight major airports.

June 21: With the threat of prosecution, the controllers return, but the pilots in the Canadian Airline Pilots Association (CALPA) refuse to fly.

June 23: The federal government names Mr. Justice W.R. Sinclair of the Court of Appeal in Edmonton and Mr. Justice Julien Chouinard of the Court of Appeal in Quebec City to study the safety aspects of bilingual air-traffic control in Quebec. Prime Minister Trudeau addresses the nation on the subject.

June 28: Federal Transport Minister Otto Lang signs an agreement of understanding with CATCA and CALPA, adding a third member to the Commission, and requiring that the commissioners not say that safety had been demonstrated "unless they can justify beyond a reasonable doubt why any contrary view by CATCA or CALPA should not prevail".

June 29: René Lévesque accuses the federal government of "backtracking in front of a group of anglophone racists".

June 30: Jean Marchand, minister of the environment, resigns from the federal cabinet. The National Assembly unanimously endorses the position of the Gens de l'Air and calls for bilingual air-traffic control.

July 7: The Olympics open in Montreal.

August 25: *Le Jour* suspends publication.

October 18: Robert Bourassa calls an election for November 15. By mid-November, the PQ has over 130,000 members.

November 15: The Parti Québécois, led by René Lévesque, wins 71 seats with 41.7 per cent of the popular vote; the Liberals win 26 seats with 33.7 per cent; the Union Nationale 11 seats with 18.2 per cent; the Ralliement des Créditistes 1 seat with 4.1 per cent; the Parti National Populaire wins 1 seat.

November 19: Robert Bourassa resigns as Liberal leader.

November 25: René Lévesque is sworn in as premier.

November 26: The Parti Québécois cabinet is sworn in.

December 6: Federal-provincial finance ministers' conference on the fiscal accords in Ottawa.

December 13: First ministers' conference in Ottawa; Lévesque and Trudeau meet for the first time since the election.

December 14-21: Mini-session of the National Assembly to pass necessary financial legislation.

1977

January 25: Lévesque addresses the Economic Club of New York.
February 6: Driving home from a party, Lévesque hits and kills Edgar Trottier, a derelict lying in the road.
February 22: Pierre Trudeau speaks to the American Congress, and says that separation would be "a crime against humanity".
March 4: Pierre Trudeau asks the CRTC to conduct an inquiry into the CBC to see if it is fulfilling its mandate.
March 8: The National Assembly session opens.
March 23: Robert Burns tables Bill 2, the election-financing legislation.
April 1: Camille Laurin tables the White Paper on language policy.
April 12: Jacques Parizeau presents his first budget, which is quickly dubbed "the banker's budget".
April 15: Lise Payette tables her proposal for automobile insurance.
April 27: Laurin tables Bill 1.
May 24-5: Economic summit at La Malbaie.
May 26-8: Parti Québécois convention. The PQ has 188,885 members.
July 6: Pierre Marc Johnson becomes minister of labour.
July 12: Laurin introduces Bill 101.
July 29: Johnson tables anti-scab legislation.
August 18-19: Premiers' conference at St. Andrews. Lévesque presents reciprocity offer on minority language.
August 26: Bill 101 is passed.
October 21: Lévesque announces plans to acquire Asbestos Corporation.
November 2-4: Lévesque visits Paris, and addresses the National Assembly.

1978

January 6: Sun Life announces it is leaving Montreal and moving its head office to Toronto.
January 10: Claude Ryan announces his candidacy for the leadership of the Quebec Liberal Party.
February 15: Federal-provincial conference on the economy. Lévesque walks out shortly after a shouting match with Urban Affairs Minister André Ouellet. Jean Garon surprises Trudeau in a debate over turkey farmers.
February 20: Signing of the so-called Cullen-Couture agreement, giving Quebec some responsibility in selecting immigrants.
February 21: Second Inaugural Address.
April 10: Jean Chrétien presents his first budget as federal finance

minister, laying out federal-provincial agreement on sales-tax cuts, gambling that Quebec will agree.

April 13: Parizeau announces the abolition of the sales tax for clothing, textiles, shoes, furniture, and hotel rooms.

April 15: Claude Ryan becomes Liberal leader, defeating Raymond Garneau.

May 15: Chrétien introduces legislation to send an income-tax rebate to Quebec taxpayers.

May 16: The Quebec National Assembly passes a unanimous resolution urging federal MPs to reject the Chrétien approach.

May 19: PQ House Leader Robert Burns suffers heart attack.

October 3: Television begins transmitting debates in the National Assembly, live on cable and in replay on Radio-Québec.

October 10: Lévesque makes statement in Assembly on sovereignty-association, establishing the hyphen between the two.

October 16: Federal Liberals lose 13 of 15 by-elections.

November 9: Garon tables agricultural-zoning legislation.

December 13: Claude Ryan announces he will be a candidate in Argenteuil.

December 15: Yves Bérubé tables legislation to expropriate Asbestos Corporation.

December 20: Raymond Garneau announces he is leaving politics.

1979

January 25: Jean-Luc Pepin and John Robarts submit their Task Force Report on Canadian Unity to Pierre Trudeau, arguing that language policy should be left to the provinces, but economic powers should be centralized. Trudeau disagrees.

February 5-6: First ministers' conference on the constitution. Trudeau offers more than ever before or since; the premiers refuse.

February 12-15: French Prime Minister Raymond Barre visits Quebec.

February 19: Justice Minister Marc Lalonde says that four-fifths of the PQ program is realizable inside Confederation, and the other fifth is negotiable.

February 22: The Pro-Canada committee folds, with president Michel Robert accusing Ryan of sabotaging it.

February 23: The Parti Québécois publishes a manifesto on sovereignty-association, *D'Égal à Égal* (Between Equals).

March 30: Fabien Roy resigns from the National Assembly to lead Social Credit in the federal election.

April 30: Claude Ryan is elected in Argenteuil, and Jean-Claude Rivest in Jean-Talon, Raymond Garneau's old seat.

May 17: The story breaks that Burns intends to quit.

May 22: Federal election. The Progressive Conservatives, led by Joe Clark, win 136 seats, with 35.9 per cent of the vote. The Liberals win

114 seats with 40.1 per cent, the NDP wins 26 seats with 17.9 per cent, and Social Credit 6, with 4.6 per cent. In Quebec, the Liberals win 67 seats, with 61.7 per cent of the vote, the PCs 2 with 13.5 per cent, Social Credit 6 with 16.0 per cent.

June 1-3: Seventh Parti Québécois convention. The delegates endorse Lévesque's "hyphen" policy for sovereignty-association. Louise Harel is elected vice-president of the party. The PQ has over 200,000 members.

June 21: Lévesque tells the National Assembly that the referendum will be held in the spring of 1980, and that the question will be known before Christmas.

September 21: Cabinet shuffle. Rodrigue Tremblay and Louis O'Neill are dropped from the cabinet.

November 1: The government tables the White Paper on sovereignty-association, *Quebec-Canada: A New Deal.*

November 14: The Quebec Liberals sweep three by-elections in Beauce-Sud, Prévost, and Maisonneuve. Prévost and Maisonneuve were PQ seats.

November 21: Pierre Trudeau announces he is resigning as federal Liberal leader.

December 11: Federal finance minister John Crosbie brings down his budget, with an 18-cent-per-gallon excise tax.

December 13: The Clark government falls in a vote of non-confidence on the budget.

December 14: Clark calls an election for February 18.

December 17: Trudeau announces he will lead the Liberals into the election.

December 20: Lévesque announces the wording of the referendum question to the National Assembly.

1980

January 10: The Quebec Liberal Party publishes its constitutional policy, quickly dubbed the Beige Paper.

February 18: Federal election. The Liberals, led by Pierre Trudeau, win 146 seats and 48.9 per cent of the vote. The Progressive Conservatives, led by Joe Clark, win 103 seats and 28.8 per cent of the vote. The NDP, led by Ed Broadbent, wins 32 seats with 18.6 per cent. In Quebec, the Liberals win 74 out of 75 seats, with 68.2 per cent of the vote, and the PCs win one seat with 12.6 per cent.

March 3: Rodrigue Biron resigns as Union Nationale leader, announcing he will support the Yes campaign in the referendum.

March 4: The debate on the referendum question begins in the National Assembly, and continues until March 20.

March 5: The new Trudeau cabinet is sworn in, and Jean Chrétien becomes minister of justice and minister responsible for federal-provincial relations.

March 7: A Radio-Canada poll shows a 52 per cent No vote and a 41 per cent Yes vote – but more francophones voting Yes than No (48 per cent to 46 per cent).

March 9: Lise Payette says in a speech that Claude Ryan married an Yvette – referring to a stereotyped passive figure in a school textbook. This provokes an editorial by Lise Bissonnette, and massive reaction.

March 25: Parizeau brings down his fourth budget.

April: At the end of the annual financing campaign, the PQ has 238,220 members.

April 7: Fifteen thousand "Yvettes" fill the Montreal Forum in support of the No campaign.

April 15: Pierre Trudeau makes the first of his four speeches in the referendum campaign, in the House of Commons.

May 5: Eric Kierans resigns from the board of the Caisse de Dépôt.

May 14: Trudeau promises Liberals will "put their heads on the block" to get constitutional change, in a speech at Paul Sauvé Arena.

May 20: The referendum. The No vote wins 59.6 per cent; the Yes vote 40.4 per cent.

June 9: Pierre Trudeau summons the ten premiers to 24 Sussex Drive to discuss the constitution. This begins a summer of discussions of ministers and officials across Canada.

September 3: Jacques Couture and Guy Joron resign from the cabinet.

September 12-16: A first ministers' conference in Ottawa on the constitution ends in failure. The conference sees the leak of the so-called "Kirby Memo", which lays out the tough federal strategy.

October 2: In an address to the country, Trudeau announces that he is going to proceed with unilateral patriation, and ask the British Parliament to amend the BNA Act by approving a Charter of Rights.

October 3: Rodrigue Biron joins the PQ.

October 3-5: At a National Council meeting Lévesque attacks the Trudeau plan as a betrayal of the referendum promise. The National Council agrees to an election commitment not to hold a referendum on sovereignty-association in the next mandate.

October 10: A public-opinion poll shows the PQ almost neck and neck with the Liberals, 41 per cent to 42 per cent – but pulling dramatically ahead by 44 to 35 per cent if they renounce their option for four years.

October 14: Lévesque meets with dissident premiers in Ottawa, and the first steps towards resisting unilateral patriation are taken.

October 16: Lévesque announces that there will be no fall election, but a massive campaign against the federal proposals.

November 6: Cabinet shuffle. Gérald Godin is named minister of immigration, and Clément Richard minister of cultural affairs – the only additions.

November 12: Lévesque presents a motion opposing unilateral patriation to the National Assembly.

November 17: Quebec Liberals win four by-elections: Outremont, Johnson, Mégantic-Compton, and Brome-Missisquoi.

November 19: Lévesque makes a last attempt to win Ryan's support for the motion in the Assembly. He fails.

December 7: A rally opposing unilateral patriation at the Montreal Forum draws 15,000 people.

1981

January 9: Roch LaSalle becomes the new leader of the Union Nationale.

January 21: The British Foreign Affairs Committee, chaired by Sir Anthony Kershaw, completes its report, urging that the British Parliament not grant Trudeau's request. A week later, the report is published.

February 5: Lise Payette announces she won't seek re-election.

March 10: Parizeau presents his fifth budget.

March 12: Lévesque calls the election for April 13. The Parti Québécois has 292,600 members.

March 28: Two polls are published showing the PQ with a substantial lead over the Liberals.

April 13: Quebec election. The PQ wins 80 seats with 49 per cent of the vote; the Liberals win 42 seats with 46 per cent.

April 16: Lévesque meets with dissident premiers, and signs accord, setting out conditions for patriation of the constitution.

September 28: Supreme Court decision on the provincial challenges of the federal plan for unilateral patriation. They rule it is legal, but say the "process itself offends the federal principle," and that "the passing of this Resolution would be unconstitutional in the conventional sense."

September 29: Lévesque calls the Assembly to debate a resolution calling on the federal government to renounce unilateralism.

October 2: Ryan leads the Liberals to vote with the government, but nine Liberal MNAs break ranks and vote against.

November 2-5: First ministers' conference on the Constitution in Ottawa. After an all-night private session, from which Quebec is excluded, an agreement is reached between the federal government and nine premiers. Quebec refuses to sign.

December 4-6: PQ convention. The delegates vote down all references to association. In his closing remarks to the convention, Lévesque threatens to resign.

December 13: The PQ executive announces an internal party referendum.

1982

January 30: Claude Charron steals a sports jacket from Eaton's.

February 2: Ted Tilden addresses the Chambre de Commerce de Montréal, and calls Bill 101 "garbage".

February 9: The PQ "renérendum" results are announced. The party members endorse Lévesque's position with a 95 per cent vote. Lévesque does not quit.

February 13-14: The second part of the December convention is held, to deal with the unfinished business. At the conclusion of the financing campaign, the PQ has 211,632 members.

April 5-7: Economic summit in Quebec. Lévesque says there is a $700 million gap in government finances, and hints at some form of salary freeze. Louis Laberge suggests a crash housing program.

May 25: In the budget, Parizeau announces the government will honour its contract, but roll the increases back in 1983.

May 26: Yves Bérubé tables Bill 70, which does this.

May 29-30: Alliance Quebec is founded.

June 8: Corvée-Habitation, a tripartite housing program, is announced.

June 12-13: National council in Hull decides the PQ should participate in the next federal election.

June 21: Guy Bisaillon quits PQ caucus.

June 22: Parizeau announces that banks who do not participate in Corvée-Habitation will be penalized by a special tax.

August 10: Claude Ryan resigns as Quebec Liberal leader.

September 2: Lucien Lessard resigns from the cabinet.

September 9: Cabinet shuffle. Marcel Léger is dropped, the ministries of state are abolished, Bernard Landry becomes minister of external trade.

September 29: Claude Charron announces he is resigning from the National Assembly after being charged with impaired driving.

October 30: The PQ National Council defers question of federal participation after Lévesque changes his mind.

December 11: Bill 105 is passed, ending negotiations in the public sector and imposing 109 collective agreements.

1983

January 26: Illegal strikes in the public sector begin.

January 29: Public-sector employees demonstrate in Quebec.

January 31: Joe Clark resigns as leader of the Progressive Conservative Party, and announces he will be a candidate.

February 15: National Assembly is called to pass Bill 111, which Lévesque calls "extremely rigorous" back-to-work legislation.

March 5: Teachers rough up cabinet ministers at a National Council meeting.

March 11-13: Cabinet meeting at Mont-Sainte-Anne begins planning for economic recovery, with an attempt to mobilize municipal investment, Hydro-Québec investment, and investment in public transit.

March 23: National Assembly resumes, and Lévesque's inaugural address calls for a new start. Liberals demand hearings on James Bay out-of-court settlement.

March 25: Gilles Grégoire is arrested for sexual offences with teen-age girls.

April 18: After parliamentary committee hearings and a concilia-tion report, the teachers sign a three-year contract.

May 28: Claude Charron talks publicly about being a homosexual.

June 11: Brian Mulroney is elected leader of the Progressive Con-servative Party, defeating Joe Clark on the fourth ballot.

June 18: Gilles Grégoire is found guilty.

June 20: Liberals win by-elections in Charlesbourg, Saguenay, and Saint-Jacques. PQ vote collapses from 19,878 to 3,273 in Charlesbourg, from 17,069 to 6,130 in Saguenay, and from 15,727 to 6,436 in Saint-Jacques. In contrast, the Liberal vote only increases from 13,982 to 17,586, and from 8,139 to 9,375 in Charlesbourg and Saguenay, and actually drops from 8,142 to 6,911 in Saint-Jacques.

July 16: Grégoire is sentenced to two years less a day.

August 31-September 1: PQ caucus meeting announces support for new federal party, the Parti Nationaliste.

October 15: Robert Bourassa is elected leader of the Quebec Liberal Party on the first ballot, defeating Pierre Paradis and Daniel Johnson.

October 19: Hearings begin on revisions to Bill 101.

November 13: Lévesque announces economic recovery program.

November 24: Pierre Marois resigns.

November 29: Pauline Marois replaces Pierre Marois as minister of manpower and revenue security; Denise Leblanc-Bantey replaces Pauline Marois as minister responsible for the status of women.

December 5: The Liberals win by-elections in Mégantic-Compton and Jonquière.

1984

February 29: Pierre Trudeau announces he is retiring as prime minister.

March 4: Jacques-Yvan Morin resigns from the cabinet and the Na-tional Assembly.

March 5: Cabinet shuffle. Camille Laurin becomes minister of social affairs, Yves Bérubé minister of education, Pierre Marc Johnson minister of justice.

March 28: Gilles Grégoire is released from prison.

March 29: Lévesque's chief of staff, Jean-Roch Boivin, announces he is resigning at the end of June. He is succeeded by Martine Tremblay.

May 8: Shooting at the National Assembly. Three are killed, thirteen injured.

May 22: Parizeau brings down budget, accusing the federal government of trying to destabilize Quebec's finances through equalization formula.

June 5: Gilles Grégoire tables document in National Assembly, arguing he was unjustly treated when he was convicted of contributing to the delinquency of seven girls, and jailed.

June 8-10: PQ convention. Before the fund-raising drive, there are 150,319 members: the lowest number since the spring of 1976.

June 16: John Turner elected federal Liberal leader on the second ballot, defeating Jean Chrétien and Don Johnston.

June 18: Liberals win by-elections in Marguerite-Bourgeoys, Sauvé, and Marie-Victorin.

Appendix
Members of the Lévesque Cabinets 1976-84

November 26, 1976

René Lévesque, premier.[1]

Jacques-Yvan Morin, minister of education.

Claude Morin, minister of intergovernmental affairs.

Jacques Parizeau, minister of finance and minister of revenue.

Marc-André Bédard, minister of justice.

Robert Burns, minister of state for parliamentary reform.[2]

Camille Laurin, minister of state for cultural development.[2]

Pierre Marois, minister of state for social development.[2]

Jacques Léonard, minister of state for land-use planning.[2]

Bernard Landry, minister of state for economic development.[2]

Lucien Lessard, minister of transport and minister of public works and supplies.

Lise Payette, minister of consumers, co-operatives, and financial institutions.

Jean Garon, minister of agriculture.

Denis Lazure, minister of social affairs.

Guy Tardif, minister of municipal affairs.

Jacques Couture, minister of labour and manpower and minister of immigration.

Louis O'Neill, minister of cultural affairs and minister of communications.

Yves Bérubé, minister of natural resources and minister of lands and forests.

Rodrigue Tremblay, minister of industry and commerce.

Yves Duhaime, minister of tourism, fish, and game.

Denis de Belleval, minister of the public service.

Marcel Léger, minister responsible for the environment.[2]

Guy Joron, minister responsible for energy.[2]

Claude Charron, minister responsible for the high commission for youth, leisure, and sports.[3]

July 6, 1977

Jocelyne Ouellette, minister of public works and supplies.

Pierre Marc Johnson, minister of labour and manpower.

February 28, 1978

Denis Vaugeois, minister of cultural affairs.

1. Sworn in on November 25, 1976.
2. Sworn in on February 2, 1977, after the enabling legislation creating the new positions was passed.
3. Sworn in on February 17, 1977, after the enabling legislation creating the new position was passed.

September 21, 1979

Lise Payette, minister of state for the status of women.
Marc-André Bédard, minister of state for parliamentary reform.
Claude Charron, minister responsible for parliamentary affairs.
Denis Vaugeois, minister of communications.
François Gendron, minister of the public service.
Yves Duhaime, minister of industry, commerce, and tourism.
Lucien Lessard, minister of leisure, fish, and game.
Michel Clair, minister of revenue.
Denis de Belleval, minister of transport.
Guy Joron, minister of consumers, co-operatives, and financial institutions.

November 29, 1979

Marcel Léger, minister of the environment.

November 6, 1980

Jacques-Yvan Morin, minister of state for cultural and scientific development.
Lise Payette, minister of state for social development.
Guy Tardif, minister of state for land-use planning, and minister responsible for housing.
Jacques Léonard, minister of municipal affairs.
Pierre Marc Johnson, minister of consumers, co-operatives, and financial institutions.
Clément Richard, minister of communications.
Camille Laurin, minister of education.
Gérald Godin, minister of immigration.
Pierre Marois, minister of labour and manpower.

April 30, 1981

René Lévesque, premier.
Jacques-Yvan Morin, minister of state for cultural and scientific development.
Camille Laurin, minister of education.
Claude Morin, minister of intergovernmental affairs.
Jacques Parizeau, minister of finance and minister of financial institutions and co-operatives.
Yves Bérubé, minister responsible for administration.
Claude Charron, minister responsible for parliamentary affairs.
Marc-André Bédard, minister of justice and minister of state for electoral reform.
Bernard Landry, minister of state for economic development.
Denis Lazure, minister of state for social development.
François Gendron, minister of state for land-use planning.
Pauline Marois, minister of state for the status of women.

Pierre Marois, minister of labour, manpower, and revenue security.
Michel Clair, minister of transport.
Clément Richard, minister of cultural affairs.
Jacques Léonard, minister of municipal affairs.
Jean Garon, minister of agriculture, fisheries, and food.
Marcel Léger, minister of the environment.
Lucien Lessard, minister of leisure, fish, and game.
Yves Duhaime, minister of energy and resources.
Guy Tardif, minister of housing and consumer protection.[1]
Pierre Marc Johnson, minister of social affairs.
Denise Leblanc-Bantey, minister of the public service.
Jean-François Bertrand, minister of communications.
Alain Marcoux, minister of public works and supplies.
Rodrigue Biron, minister of industry, commerce, and tourism.
Raynald Fréchette, minister of revenue.
Gérald Godin, minister of cultural communities and immigration.[2]

February 17, 1982
Jacques-Yvan Morin, minister of intergovernmental affairs.

September 9, 1982
Bernard Landry, minister responsible for external trade. (Ministry formally established on January 12, 1983.)
François Gendron, minister responsible for land-use planning and regional development.
Denis Lazure, minister responsible for citizen relations.
Alain Marcoux, minister of revenue.
Raynald Fréchette, minister responsible for labour. (Ministry changed formally on December 17.)
Guy Chevrette, minister of leisure, fish, and game.
Adrien Ouellette, minister of the environment.
Gilbert Paquette, minister responsible for science and technology. (Ministry created on August 18, 1983.)

September 15, 1982
Pauline Marois, minister responsible for the status of women.

November 29, 1983
Pauline Marois, minister of manpower and revenue security.
Denise Leblanc-Bantey, minister responsible for the status of women.

---

1. Originally sworn in as "minister responsible" on April 30, until the enabling legislation for the new ministry was passed, and he was sworn in again on June 18.
2. Sworn in on May 13, 1981.

March 5, 1984

Camille Laurin, minister of social affairs.
Marc-André Bédard, minister responsible for electoral reform.
Yves Bérubé, minister of education.
Michel Clair, minister responsible for administration.
Bernard Landry, minister of international relations.
Pierre Marc Johnson, minister of justice and minister responsible
   for Canadian intergovernmental affairs.
Jacques Léonard, minister of transport.
Alain Marcoux, minister of municipal affairs.
Robert Dean, minister of revenue.

Notes

Many of the events described in this book I witnessed and wrote about as a reporter. Many of the interviews were for feature articles or columns, and I have respected the confidences that I undertook at that time. In addition, I did separate interviews for this book: some for the record, and others for background, or not for attribution. In these notes, I cite the published or broadcast sources for quotations where possible, and, at the beginning of a chapter, describe the background journalistic research that went into the preparation of the chapter. Fuller references can be found in the bibliography. Unattributed quotations were given on a confidential basis. However, all remarks that suggest that someone thought or talked in a particular way have been confirmed, either directly or indirectly.

Page   Line

Preface

x   19   *Maclean's* article: "René Lévesque: The Anglais cheer as he calls for Canada's break-up", *Maclean's*, May 1969, republished in *Canada From the Newsstands*, edited by Val Clery.

Prologue: November 15, 1976

This prologue was based on observation, a reviewing of Radio-Canada's election night broadcast, the film *Le Quinze novembre*, and a series of interviews.

Chapter One: The Greenhouse Years

3   20   "The rebellion . . . came as a climax to the economic crisis of the 1830s": See Fernand Ouellet, *Economic and Social History of Quebec, 1760-1850*, chapter 14.

3   22   ". . . the defeat of the Patriotes 'hastened the process of inferiorization in French-Canadian society' . . .": Monière, *Ideologies in Quebec*, translated by Richard Howard, p. 118.

3   27   ". . . the dominant ideology in Quebec would reflect the clergy's world view . . .": Monière, p. 120.

3   31   Durham: "I expected to find a contest between a government and a people: I found two nations warring in the bosom of a single state": *Lord Durham's Report*, pp. 22-3.

3   41   "… the Ministry of Public Instruction … was abolished …": See Linteau, Durocher, and Robert, *L'Histoire du Québec contemporain*, p. 242.

4   7   "agriculturalism, anti-statism, and messianism": Brunet, *La Présence anglaise et les Canadiens.*

4   10   Tardivel: "Tardivel can be considered the father of separatist feeling in Quebec. In fact, Jules-Paul Tardivel was the first French Canadian to develop the idea of separatism and argue the ideal of a distinct nation, separate from English Canada." Girard, "La Pensée politique de Jules-Paul Tardivel". *Revue de l'histoire de l'Amérique française*, décembre 1967. See also Monière, p. 167, and A. I. Silver's introduction to Tardivel, *For My Country*, translated by Sheila Fischman.

4   20   "Mercier 'gave official status and impetus to the idea . . .'": Monière, p. 171.

4   26   Henri Bourassa: Quoted by Cook, *Canada and the French-Canadian Question*, p. 117.

5   9   ". . . sang the songs of outrage penned in Quebec to the tune of 'La Marseillaise'. . .": George F. G. Stanley, in LaPierre, *Four O'Clock Lectures*, p. 107.

5   18   ". . . anti-Semitism . . .": See "Letter to M. Lamoureux", quoted in Gaboury, *Le Nationalisme de Lionel Groulx*, p. 34, "It is obvious that Christian charity forbids us any form of anti-semitism. On the other hand, does this mean that we have to be easy-going and imprudent with the Jew? History and daily observation have only too often shown his revolutionary tendency. Rootless wherever he is, refusing any assimilation, he is indifferent to the political and social order around him. . . ." ". . . cannot be called a fascist": However, there was considerable pro-fascist feeling in Quebec in the 1930s and 1940s. Mayor Camillien Houde of Montreal told a group of representatives of the Youth Conference against War and Fascism in 1934, "But you forget that I am for fascism!" *Le Canada*, July 26, 1934, quoted by Olssen in "The Canadian Left in Quebec during the Great Depression", p. 184. For pro-Vichy feeling, see Paul M. Couture, "The Vichy–Free French Quebec Propaganda War, 1940-1942", *Historical Papers*, Canadian Historical Society, London, Ont., 1978.

5   30   "a sort of spiritual hyphen . . .": Ryan on Groulx in *Le Devoir*, le 24 mai 1967. However, Groulx didn't like Ryan, and wrote bitterly in 1961, "I have always held this poor Ryan to be one of those men who will have contributed, with his moralizing Catholic Action, to the disabling of a whole generation of French Canadians (those between 40 and 50 today) who believed themselves to be without job or future in a Quebec they had begun to detest." Quoted by Benoît Aubin in *L'Actualité*, février 1978.

5   33   ". . . practical and enlightened patriotism . . .": René Lévesque in Filion, ed., *Hommage à Lionel Groulx*, p. 143.

5   38   ". . . political implications . . .": Historians have debated vigorously whether or not he was a separatist. For Denis Monière,

"in spite of a brief fling in the 1920s with the notion of La Laurentie, an independent francophone state, Groulx kept the faith with the old nationalist dogma of Quebec within Confederation." *Ideology*, p. 196. But according to Ramsay Cook, "Abbé Groulx's nationalist doctrine was strongly separatist in its implications." *Canada and the French-Canadian Question*, p. 108. Linteau, Durocher, and Robert (p. 612) describe "a brief indépendantiste phase" of the group around Groulx and describe it as "whims about independence". In his thesis on the early indépendantistes (p. 88), Robert Comeau quotes Groulx as continuing to believe in "the juridical equality of the two nationalities before the federated constitution" in 1935, and concludes, "Lionel Groulx never believed that complete political independence was absolutely necessary to assure a sufficient mastery of the economic and cultural life of a minority people." Susan Mann Trofimenkoff points out that Groulx "tended to deny separatism as fast as he proclaimed it" and would then wonder why no-one understood what he meant. "No-one could understand because Groulx never elaborated. He obviously feared the revolutionary import of the very term separatism, yet he relished its revolutionary fervour." (*Introduction to Abbé Groulx*, p. 9.) And in *The Dream of Nation* (pp. 231-2), she observes that after he and his followers "toyed with the idea of a separate state" in 1922, they "rarely mentioned it again and Groulx spent the rest of his life denying he was a separatist." However, Gaboury points out (p. 156) that Groulx "gave his tacit support to all his disciples" and writes, "it flows clearly from the global thinking of the nationalist master that his 'French state' is more than eventually [but] necessarily an independent state. Thus, his reputation as a separatist is deserved." Gaboury acknowledges that Groulx never explicitly endorsed this position. Mason Wade wrote pointedly in *The French Canadians, 1760-1967* (p. 908) that "if Groulx was not a separatist at heart — and the whole tendency of his work indicates that he was — many of his followers undoubtedly were."

5   41   "Les Jeune-Canada": On April 20, 1933, the leaders of Jeune-Canada gave speeches at the Salle du Gésu, published as *Politiciens et Juifs*, Les Cahiers des Jeune-Canada. Laurendeau made an eloquent apology and renunciation of the anti-Semitism that "had polluted the atmosphere", saying, "our speeches were dreadful." "Pourquoi nous rappeler à chaque instant qu'il est juif?" *Le Magazine Maclean*, janvier 1963, published in *Ces choses qui nous arrivent*, and, in English, in *André Laurendeau: Witness for Quebec*. Monière describes and analyses the incident in *André Laurendeau et le destin d'un peuple*, pp. 58-61.

6   10   ". . . liberalism . . . 'an essentially Anglo-Saxon institution'": O'Leary, p. 177; "leads to communism and anarchy", p. 173; "The corporate state must be . . . authoritarian", p. 182. Andrée

Lévesque Olssen points out in her thesis (pp. 174-5) that "corporatism enjoyed a much greater vogue than fascism itself", appealing to a much wider range of intellectual opinion, from the Jesuits to the Action Libérale Nationale, who saw it as an acceptable form of non-Marxist economic planning.

6   24   On the formation and the policies of the Action Libérale Nationale, see Conrad Black, *Duplessis*, pp. 72-6, and Jean-Louis Roy, "Réflexions sur deux départs: Québec 1935 et 1960", in *Essays on the Left*, ed. Laurier LaPierre et al.

6   34   Groulx: "To have used three men . . ." Letter to René Chaloult, Sept. 1, 1936. Quoted in Chaloult, *Mémoires politiques*, p. 92, and by Black, p. 143.

6   40   On Bouchard, see Robert Comeau's thesis and Howard L. Singer, interview with Raymond Barbeau in *Contemporary French Civilization*, spring 1979.

7   4   Padlock Law: Black, p. 162. A journalist, Louis Francoeur, urged Duplessis to test the law by stopping André Malraux from speaking in Montreal. *La Patrie*, April 15, 1937. Olssen thesis, p. 194.

7   19   Marchand: "favouritism a political doctrine", quoted by Gérard Pelletier, *Les Années d'impatience*, p. 80. Pelletier gives a superb portrait of Duplessis, and the opposition to him during this period.

7   22   "the bishops eat out of my hand": Laporte, *The True Face of Duplessis*, p. 139.

7   23   "There is no great difficulty . . .": Black, p. 549.

7   35   "I don't sell you our natural resources . . .": Pelletier, p. 84.

8   8   On the ideology of the Bloc Populaire, see Comeau, *Le Bloc populaire*, chapter 3. Denis Monière called the Bloc "a mixture of traditional concerns and plans for modernization" in *Ideologies in Quebec*, p. 225, and Pierre Trudeau called it "a curious mixture of conservative money and progressive hopes, all under the banner of nationalism. Paul Gouin, René Chaloult, Philippe Hamel and Jean Martineau advocated the nationalization of public utility companies and other radical measures, while the national leader, Maxime Raymond, and the eventual party organizer, Édouard Lacroix, both adopted a position of extreme right-wing conservatism." "Quebec at the Time of the Strike", in *The Asbestos Strike*, p. 51.

8   14   On Drapeau and Trudeau, see *Drapeau* by Brian McKenna and Susan Purcell, chapter 11.

8   16   On André Laurendeau, see Denis Monière, *André Laurendeau et le destin d'un peuple*; "Portrait d'un nationaliste", *Le Magazine Maclean*, janvier 1968; and Ramsay Cook, "In the Bourassa Tradition", in *Canada and the French-Canadian Question*.

8   32   On Father Lévesque, see *Georges-Henri Lévesque: père de la renaissance québécoise*, by Robert Parisé; "The Fight over Father Lévesque", by Blair Fraser, *Maclean's*, July 1, 1950; and, for a good account of this era, chapters 2 and 3 of *Mandate '68* by Martin Sullivan.

9   1   "Quebecers under Duplessis . . .": Jean-Louis Roy, *La Marche des Québécois*, p. 11.

9   10   *Cité libre*: The best account of its birth is by Gérard Pelletier in *Les Années d'impatience*.

9   13   ". . . a crucial catalyst . . .": Marchand first became a special organizer for the CCCL in Thetford Mines in 1944.

9   18   "At a meeting on February 13 . . .": See "History of the Strike at Asbestos", by Gilles Beausoleil, in Trudeau, ed., *The Asbestos Strike*, p. 145. Also, "Priests, Pickets and Politics", by Blair Fraser, *Maclean's*, July 1, 1949.

9   25   Strike settlement: The union had asked for a fifteen-cent increase to $1.00 an hour.

9   28   ". . . not primarily for money . . .": Although he wrote that "the key issue was recognition for the union," Martin Sullivan suggested that "conditions were appalling; pay was poor," *Mandate '68*, p. 29. But Blair Fraser (*Maclean's*, July 1, 1949) talked to one striker who said it was the best mine he had ever worked in — but that they were fighting for the union. "If we lose this strike the union is smashed and then we'll have no protection." "links between the governments . . . and the asbestos industry . . .": Fernand Dumont points out that part of the disenchantment with the arbitration process came from the fact that the chairman of the arbitration board in 1948 had stayed in the hotel suite reserved for the president of the Johns-Manville Company. "Furthermore: for many years the union members had, in their disputes with the employers and their agents, found themselves caught up in a strange network of influence woven by the goings and comings of politicians and managers. The workers were aware of this network both before and during the strike. At the Asbestos Corporation, the legal firm of Duquette and Ralston was empowered to represent the company; Mr. Ralston had been, as we know, the Minister of National Defence. At Johns-Manville, the legal counsel of the Company was Yvan Sabourin, president of the Quebec wing of the Conservative party. . . . As for Hugh O'Donnell, whose actions on behalf of the company at East Broughton have been described, he was the son-in-law of Mr. St. Laurent, who was at that time Minister of Justice in the federal government." "History of the Trade Union Movement in the Asbestos Industry", in Trudeau, ed., *The Asbestos Strike*, pp. 138-9.

More immediately, as Gérard Pelletier pointed out, "all the professionals of Asbestos — doctors, lawyers, notaries, dentists — instinctively lined up on the side of the employers and the régime, from the first days of the conflict." *Les Années*, p. 117.

10   13   "Rioux was disqualified because he declared himself to be an atheist": *Marcel Rioux*, by Jules Duchastel, pp. 86-7.

10   21   ". . . his own bitterest memory . . .": Jean Marchand, interview, November 2, 1976.

10 39 Pierre Dansereau's memories of the telephone and the condescension: Interview, January 19, 1982.

11 11 Rioux and Trudeau call francophones Greeks: Duchastel, *Marcel Rioux*, p. 33.

Chapter Two: René Lévesque: Prelude to Politics

12 15 "Quebec's first lay teacher": Jacques Godbout, "Faut-il tuer le mythe René Lévesque?" *Le Magazine Maclean*, novembre 1964, and in *Le Réformiste*, p. 71.

13 8 "an original mixture of joual . . .": Gérard Bergeron, quoted in "Le Style de René Lévesque" by Robert Barberis, *Le Devoir*, le 15 janvier 1971.

14 7 "Ever since I began working with him . . .": *Témoignage de Camille Laurin: pourquoi je suis souverainiste*, quoted by Jean Provencher, *René Lévesque, Portrait of a Quebecer*, translated by David Ellis, pp. 263-4.

14 30 ". . . wear and tear of politics . . .": Interview with Lévesque, July 2, 1982.

15 31 "She must have been about seventy . . .": Quoted in William Stockton, "René Lévesque and the divided house of Canada", *New York Times Magazine*, May 20, 1979.

16 15 "atrocious . . .": Quoted by Provencher, p. 100.

16 21 "first expression of Quebec nationalism . . .": Interview, July 2, 1982.

16 39 "I won't kill another one": Interview, July 2, 1982.

17 35 "co-conspirators in practically everything": Interview, July 2, 1982.

18 12 "the radio discovery of the year . . .": Gérard Pelletier, *Le Devoir*, le 6 octobre 1961; Provencher, p. 77; Pelletier, *Les Années de l'impatience*, p. 44.

19 1 ". . . the golden age of television . . .": Godbout, *Le Réformiste*.

19 23 ". . . René didn't get involved . . .": Marchand interview, *Gazette*, March 7, 1979.

19 37 "You talk very well . . .": Pelletier recounts the meeting in *The Champions*, and in *Les Années de l'impatience*, pp. 48-50.

20 10 The producers' strike: For more details, see Jean-Louis Roux's essay in Lefebvre et al., *En grève*. Other factual details are from Bernard Trotter's essay, "The Montreal Producers' Strike — 1959". In addition to doing an undergraduate essay on it, I interviewed some of the key actors for a story on the twentieth anniversary of the strike, published in the *Gazette*, March 7, 1979.

22 4 *Montreal Star*: Pelletier translates the passage in *Les Années*, p. 304. Jean-Louis Roux quotes the text in English in Lefebvre et al., *En grève*.

22 26 Duceppe interview, *Gazette*, March 7, 1979.

22 37 "It is almost always this way . . .": Laurendeau, quoted by Michel Roy, "La grève des réalisateurs de Radio Canada", *Relations industrielles*, 14, 1959, p. 276.

23   24   "Lesage finally got in touch . . ." and "In the end . . .": Provencher, pp. 132-3.

24   19   ". . . the vote was extremely close": Richard Daignault in *Lesage* points this out, pp. 103-4. In "La Révolution en plan et le paradigme en cause", *Canadian Journal of Political Science*, XVI:4, December 1983, pp. 694-5, François-Pierre Gingras and Neil Nevitte point out the Union Nationale received only two per cent less of the popular vote in 1960 than in 1956—and a net increase of 21,000 votes. As a result, some of the sweeping interpretations of rapid change in 1960 have to be taken with a grain of salt.

24   29   "The people deserved this victory": *La Presse*, le 23 juin 1960.

Chapter Three: Whirlwind on the Margin

26   1   ". . . Lévesque . . . got a call . . .": Lévesque told this story at the University of Saskatchewan, February 11, 1969.

27   8   ". . . he telephoned Father Lévesque . . .": Father Lévesque told me this story, in an interview on January 18, 1980. On hiring experts, see Provencher, pp. 161-2.

27   28   ". . . Godbout . . . called the directors . . . bandits"; ". . . Shawinigan contributes . . .": Jean-V. Dufresne, "La Bataille de l'électricité", *Le Magazine Maclean*, novembre 1962.

28   10   "We'll show you, you bastard": Quoted in William Stockton, "René Lévesque and the divided house of Canada", *New York Times Magazine*, May 20, 1979.

28   18   "at any price": Dufresne, "La Bataille de l'électricité", *Le Magazine Maclean*, novembre 1962.

28   30   "Maîtres Chez Nous": According to Peter Desbarats the slogan was coined at the Reform Club when a drunken contractor threw his arm around Lesage's shoulder and uttered the phrase. See *René*, p. 34. However, its antecedents go further back. Maurice Duplessis used the phrase in a speech to a Union Nationale gathering on February 16, 1943, quoted by Conrad Black in *Duplessis*, p. 265. Laurendeau used the phrase "maître chez lui" as part of his definition of provincial autonomy in *Le Devoir*, le 24 janvier 1944; quoted by Monière in *André Laurendeau*, p. 158. Jean Provencher attributes the phrase to the Quebec economist Errol Bouchette (1863-1912) and quotes Lévesque as having used it in a speech on December 2, 1961, *René Lévesque*, p. 173.

28   37   ". . . regular sessions at Pelletier's Westmount house . . .": Desbarats, *René*, Chapter 1.

29   4   ". . . Johnson . . . promised to nationalize . . .": Pierre Godin, *Daniel Johnson*, vol. 1, p. 319. Later, Johnson commented privately that nationalization had, in fact, been a good thing. "Politics is the art of the possible," he said. "The electricity companies financed our campaign. If I said yes to nationalization, the companies threatened to finance the Créditistes." (Godin, *loc. cit.*)

29 10 "'Ten days after the election . . .'": For Douglas Fullerton's account of the nationalization, see his *The Dangerous Delusion*. For details of Quebec government recruitment, see *Financial Post*, September 23, 1961.

29 42 "When the RIN bogged down . . .": For an account of the birth of the first wave of RIN bombings, see Gabriel Hudon, *Ce n'était qu'un début*. See also Marc Laurendeau, *Les Québécois violents*, and Louis Fournier, *F.L.Q.: histoire d'un mouvement clandestin*.

30 9 "Less violent but almost as surprising . . .": See Michael B. Stein, *The Dynamics of Right-Wing Protest*, and Gilles Grégoire, *Aventure à Ottawa*.

30 26 "Lévesque continued to meet . . .": See Desbarats's *René* and Gérard Pelletier's *Les Années de l'impatience* for vivid descriptions.

30 35 ". . . Laval medical-faculty banquet . . .": Peter C. Newman, "The French Revolution, Quebec, 1961", *Maclean's*, April 22, 1961. ". . . keep this non-controversial": *Montreal Star*, January 14, 1964.

31 1 "Lâchez pas": Provencher, p. 209. Lesage was furious at this, and nearly fired Lévesque from the cabinet.

31 10 "The big problem . . .": Ken Johnstone, "The Man in the Middle of Quebec's New Deal", *Maclean's*, November 18, 1961.

31 21 "The ideology . . .": Peter C. Newman, *Maclean's*, April 22, 1961.

31 36 Léger interview, *Le Devoir*, le 5 juillet 1963. Text included in translation in *Quebec States Her Case*, ed. Frank Scott and Michael Oliver.

31 42 "wouldn't cry for long": *La Presse*, le 31 mai 1963.

32 2 "the time will soon come . . .": *Gazette*, January 1, 1964.

32 7 "associate state": *Le Devoir*, le 11 mai 1964.

32 11 ". . . vigorous criticism . . .": A *Montreal Star* editorial, June 1, 1964, accused Lévesque of complicity with terrorism, provoking an angry response from Gérard Pelletier, then editor-in-chief of *La Presse*, in an editorial headed "Quand le *Star* se déshonore", le 2 juin 1964.

32 11 ". . . Lévesque felt obliged . . .": See *Le Devoir*, le 1 juin 1964: "René Lévesque dénonce vigoureusement le terrorisme et se déclare solidaire du cabinet Lesage."

32 25 Laurendeau diary: Quoted by Monière, *André Laurendeau*, pp. 304-5.

32 37 The story of the fight over pensions is told in chapter 22 of Peter C. Newman's *Distemper of Our Times* and analysed in Richard Simeon's *Federal-Provincial Diplomacy*. It is also well summarized in Godin's *Daniel Johnson*, vol. 2, chap. 1, and dealt with in Claude Morin's *Le Pouvoir québécois . . . en négotiation*, in Judy LaMarsh's *Memoirs of a Bird in a Gilded Cage*, and in Peter Desbarats's *The State of Quebec*.

33 23 ". . . a small sensation": Simeon, *Federal-Provincial Diplomacy*, p. 55.

33   32   "With his long face . . .": Quoted in *Blair Fraser Reports . . .* , p. 121.

33   36   "I think we suddenly realized . . .": Simeon, *Federal-Provincial Diplomacy*, p. 171.

34   9   "For the past month I have lived . . .": Newman, *Distemper*, p. 315.

34   23   Lévesque comment on Caisse de Dépôt: Quoted by Pierre Fournier, *The Quebec Establishment*, p. 184.

34   31   On the birth of the RIN, see Pierre Bourgault, *Écrits polémiques, 1960-1981*, Marcel Chaput, *J'ai choisi de me battre*, André d'Allemagne, *Le RIN et les débuts du mouvement indépendantiste québécois*, and Howard L. Singer's thesis, "Institutionalization of Protest: the Quebec Separatist Movement".

35   22   For details of the Fulton-Favreau formula, see Jean-Louis Roy, *Le Choix d'un pays*, pp. 42-4.

35   40   Johnson accuses Lesage of betrayal: Roy, *Le Choix*, p. 48; Ryan, *Le Devoir*, le 4 mars 1965.

36   13   "I am neither a lawyer . . .": *Le Magazine Maclean*, juin 1962.

36   16   "We must be careful to avoid . . .": Provencher, p. 214, and Roy, *Le Choix*, p. 51.

37   15   On Lévesque's and Kierans's plans for social policy, see Peter C. Newman, *Distemper*, p. 319, and Louis Martin, "Tout sur la sécurité sociale", *Le Magazine Maclean*, février 1966.

37   32   ". . . Union Nationale . . . the only party capable of achieving independence in an orderly fashion": Johnson, *Égalité ou indépendance*, pp. 109-10.

37   36   Johnson's ambiguity: See Godin, *Daniel Johnson*, vol. 2, p. 39.

38   10   "If you take away the English-speaking vote . . .": Godin, *Daniel Johnson*, vol. 2, p. 118.

38   21   On Johnson's deal with Bourgault, see Godin, *Daniel Johnson*, vol. 2, pp. 91-3.

38   29   On the Ralliement National, see Michael Stein, *The Dynamics of Right-Wing Protest*, pp. 99-103. Among those who worked with the Ralliement National were three future Quebec cabinet ministers: Marc-André Bédard, Lucien Lessard (a candidate in Saguenay), and Jean Garon.

Chapter Four: Leader

39   14   "idealistic illusions" and "perfectionism": *Toronto Star*, November 21, 1966.

40   10   ". . . did not have the power . . .": See Dominique Clift, *Toronto Star*, November 21, 1966.

40   26   "Trudeau . . . advising . . . Sharp . . .": See *Globe and Mail*, October 31, 1966.

41   11   "Where does that lead us?": *Dimanche Matin*, le 2 juillet 1967.

41   29   "the essential components of independence . . .": *Le Devoir*, le 19 septembre 1967. Lévesque's statement was published in *Le Devoir* on September 19, 20, and 21. It was also the basis for his *Option Québec*. See p. 27.

41   39   "René, I can't join you": Jean Pelletier, "The Resurrection

of Robert Bourassa", *Saturday Night*, February 1984. For Lévesque's account of this meeting, see Provencher, *René Lévesque*, pp. 233-4. See also Desbarats's *René*, p. 129.

43   4   "Either we have to modify . . .": I am grateful to Bob McKenzie of the *Toronto Star* for playing me his tape of the speech, from which this passage was translated. A sparser version can be found in Michel Roy's report in *Le Devoir* and in Lévesque's *Option Québec*, p. 29, phrased slightly differently.

43   23   "I'm nervous . . .": Letter from Jean-Roch Boivin, January 9, 1984.

43   27   "Bourassa came up to him . . .": Desbarats, *René*, p. 137.

43   37   "like an American student burning his draft card": Blair Fraser, "René Lévesque and the Separatists", *Maclean's*, July 1968.

43   40   "That's enough . . .": Charron told me this story, December 13, 1979.

44   3   "I don't know . . .": Boivin letter.

44   9   "I'm going to make you all sign . . .": Boivin letter.

44   21   "if you *do* have to make me any kind of leader . . .": Letter to the author from René Lévesque, March 6, 1969.

45   11   ". . . no fixed address . . .": The phrase was used by Claude Ryan about René Lévesque and quoted by Benoît Aubin in *L'Actualité*, but it was literally true of Bourgault during part of this period.

45   11   ". . . a homosexual . . .": Bourgault discussed this part of his life in Andrée LeBel's *Pierre Bourgault: le plaisir de la liberté*, and in Benoît Aubin's "Le Mouton noir aux cheveux blancs", *L'Actualité*, juillet 1983.

45   31   ". . . careerist reasons": See Provencher, p. 233. According to Don and Vera Murray, Bourassa said privately that he had told Lévesque that "there is a damn good chance that I could replace Lesage as leader. I can't allow myself to waste that opportunity." *De Bourassa à Lévesque*, p. 41.

45   36   "The party will no longer be insured against . . . bourgeois complacency": Provencher, p. 243.

46   33   Debate at the MSA convention: This is all reconstructed from notes taken by Blair Fraser and Dominique Clift at the convention.

48   19   "Then, on June 24 . . .": The best description of the St. Jean Baptiste parade riot is in chapter 1 of Martin Sullivan's *Mandate '68*.

48   29   "They were right . . .": Howard L. Singer, "The Quebec Separatist Movement: From Educational Movement to Political Party", *Annales du Centre de recherche sur l'Amérique francophone*, Bordeaux, 1978.

50   27   ". . . by 1972 it was estimated . . .": Réjean Pelletier, *Les Militants du R.I.N.*, p. 50.

51   34   ". . . Desrochers . . . commissioned . . . Social Research Inc. . . .": Murray, *De Bourassa à Lévesque*, pp. 63-5.

52   17   "The rational functionalism . . .": *Le Devoir*, le 14 janvier 1970. Murray, *De Bourassa à Lévesque*, p. 102.

Chapter Five: Three Elections

53   1   For UN troubles, see Herbert F. Quinn, *The Union Nationale*, second edition, pp. 249-57, and Louis La Rochelle, *En flagrant délit du pouvoir*, pp. 132-7.

53   7   Beaulieu budget: Beaulieu gave reporters copies of what he said he would have presented to the National Assembly: a document that claimed a surplus of $16 million. This was not believed, was greeted with general derision, and further reduced the government's credibility. See La Rochelle, p. 136. Polls: on April 18, *La Presse* published a poll by the Centre de Recherche sur l'Opinion showing the Liberals with 25.6 per cent, the PQ with 24.9 per cent, the Union Nationale with 13.4 per cent, the Créditistes with 11.7 per cent, others 2.1 per cent, and undecided 22.2 per cent. On April 25, the CROP poll showed the Liberals with 24 per cent, the PQ with 19 per cent, the UN 10 per cent, the Créditistes 10 per cent, others 2 per cent, and undecided 35 per cent.

53   14   For Bertrand attack, see *Le Devoir*, *La Presse*, the *Globe and Mail*, and the *Toronto Star*, April 27, 1970.

53   27   "That's the result . . .": *Montreal Star*, April 27, 1970.

54   4   ". . . a hundred thousand jobs . . .": See *Le Devoir*, le 23 avril 1970: "Robert Bourassa s'engage: 100,000 emplois ou je quitte la vie politique."

54   6   Lévesque speech: Taped at Paul Sauvé Arena, April 27, 1970, for a radio documentary broadcast on CBC, April 30, 1970.

54   12   *Montreal Star* editorial: Quoted by Desbarats in *René*, p. 180. Lévesque speech: Quoted by Desbarats in *René*, pp. 190-1.

54   42   For PQ resentment, see Robert McKenzie, "So few seats for such a big vote angers separatists", *Toronto Star*, May 2, 1970, in which he describes a PQ supporter refusing to shake hands with him on being introduced as a correspondent for a Toronto newspaper the day after the election.

55   31   "provisional government": For the fullest account of this episode, see *Grits* by Christina McCall-Newman, pp. 281-6. For what is still the best account of the October Crisis, see *Rumours of War* by Ron Haggart and Aubrey Golden.

56   10   On the Bourassa years, see Don and Vera Murray, *De Bourassa à Lévesque*, and Jean Paré, *Le Temps des hôtages*.

57   9   On tensions in the PQ, see Vera Murray, *Le Parti québécois*.

57   37   ". . . with his face in his hands": Don and Vera Murray, p. 147.

57   38   "Ho Chi Minh . . .": Translated from a transcription of the Radio-Canada cassette of the sound track of the TV special on the PQ convention, February 29, 1971.

58   17   ". . . a neo-Marxist ideology and a sweeping critique": In October 1971 the CSN published "Ne comptons sur nos propres moyens" (It's Up to Us); in December the FTQ published "L'État, rouage de notre exploitation" (The State Is Our Exploiter); and in June 1972 the CEQ published "L'École, au service de la classe dominante" (The School, Serving the Dominant Class). The first two, along with a different CEQ manifesto, were translated and published in English as *Quebec — Only the Beginning: The*

Manifestos of the Common Front, ed. Daniel Drache. For an analysis of this radicalization, see Drache's introduction, pp. xxii-xxiii, in which he describes the publication of the manifestos as "a milestone in the development of indigenous Marxist thinking in Quebec"; and Jean Marc Piotte, "Le Syndicalisme au Québec depuis 1960", in *Le Syndicalisme de combat.* On the debate over the *La Presse* march, see Singer, "Internal conflicts within the Parti Québécois", *Dalhousie Review*, 1977. The lengthy statement is published in *Le Devoir*, le 29 novembre 1971, and quoted in McRoberts and Posgate, *Quebec: Social Change and Political Crisis*, revised edition, p. 193.

60   23   For a summary of the "scandals" of the Bourassa years, see Murray, *De Bourassa à Lévesque*, chapter 7.

60   33   ". . . building the Olympic Stadium": The Malouf Inquiry, set up by the Lévesque government to investigate cost overruns at the Montreal Olympics, completely exonerated the Bourassa administration and blamed Mayor Jean Drapeau — but this was not apparent in 1976.

60   40   "both creeps": Quoted in *Maclean's*, November 29, 1976.

61   26   "He only eats hot dogs . . .": Quoted by Pierre Dupont in *How Lévesque Won*, p. 16.

62   17   "We can't force Quebecers to learn English": *Globe and Mail*, June 26, 1976.

62   27   ". . . he could not stay . . .": *Maclean's*, July 12, 1976.

62   31   ". . . never been such unanimity . . .": John T. Saywell, *Canadian Annual Review of Politics and Public Affairs*, 1976, p. 74. Saywell gives a good summary of the fight. For a complete study of the issue, see Sandford Borins, *Language of the Skies.*

63   12   ". . . would end up being manipulated . . .": Lévesque later changed his mind on this, and the PQ used the Gens de l'Air issue in some of its advertising during the election campaign.

63   38   Bourassa's election plans: See Saint-Pierre, *Les Années Bourassa*, p. 202.

67   3   "Don't vote with your heads . . .": Bronfman's speech is quoted by Erna Paris in *Jews*, p. 107, and by Peter C. Newman in *The Bronfman Dynasty*, p. 275.

67   37   ". . . refusing to believe Michel Lepage and Pierre Drouilly . . .": In the first week of the campaign, Lepage had told the campaign committee that the PQ would win 70 seats. Abruptly, he was told that there was something wrong with his data, and that they could not be accurate. A week later, Lepage returned to the committee with a fulsome apology; there *had* been an error. The correct figure was 71 seats — and he read the list. The suggestion that the PQ might win Kamouraska-Témiscouata was the last straw for Michel Carpentier; as politely as possible, the committee told Lepage that they really wouldn't be needing his polling data any more during the campaign. Lepage spent the rest of the campaign doing riding-by-riding studies, picking the margins of victory — in some cases within a few hundred votes. On election night, he won the office pools

in Taillon, L'Assomption (Jacques Parizeau's riding), and the
National Office. His final tally, at the end of the second week,
had only two errors. He thought the PQ would lose in Hull
(it won by two votes on a recount) and would win in Saint-
Hyacinthe (the UN won by 58 votes).

Chapter Six: Forming a Government

72   12   "... old friends": Lévesque had known Giroux when he was a
Liberal minister and Giroux the head of the brokerage firm
Lévesque Beaubien. Moreover, Lévesque had borrowed $6,500
from Giroux in 1965 as a registered second mortgage on his
house at 5562 Woodbury Avenue in Outremont. Reported by
"As It Is", CFCF-TV, March 27, 1983.

72   20   "The stock market reflected this ...": The Toronto Stock
Exchange lost 4.29 points on Wednesday, the Montreal Stock
Exchange dropped 4.22 points, and the index of 149 key
industrial stocks dipped 4.29 points. For Quebec-based
stocks, the loss was more dramatic: Bell Canada dropped $1.75,
Noranda Mines $2.25, Asbestos Corporation $2.25, Alcan
Aluminum $1.87, and Consolidated Bathurst $1.25.

72   22   "At his press conference ...": The conference was taped and
broadcast on the Radio-Canada program "Aux 20 heures" that
night.

74   23   "... one of the few in the PQ not to shrink from calling themselves separatists ...": The word "separatist" has usually been
avoided or resented by those advocating independence for
Quebec, or sovereignty-association. When Marcel Chaput wrote
his book, he didn't want to call it *Pourquoi je suis séparatiste*
because of the pejorative connotation of the word, but his publisher, Jacques Hébert, insisted. More recently, when Robert
Guy Scully translated Peter Desbarats's book, he assumed
that this was only the case in French, and wrote in an accompanying note: "The English words *separatist* and *separatism*
have been translated here by *indépendantiste* and *indépendantisme*, which are closer to the neutral meaning intended
by the English words; over the last few years, *séparatiste* and
séparatisme have acquired in Quebec French a clearly pejorative meaning that English doesn't give them: an example of
living language!" However, in his introduction to *Must Canada Fail?*, Richard Simeon claims (p. 6) that the words do have a
pejorative sense in English as well as in French: "In this book
the terms 'separatist', 'separation', and 'separatism' have been
used sparingly. The PQ has seldom used these terms and they
represent not so much an accurate reflection of PQ goals as a
pejorative epithet imposed by their critics. 'Separation' implies
a total break, a fundamental fracturing, a cutting of all ties.
The PQ has always talked in terms of 'independence', 'association', and 'sovereignty'. All such abstract words are inevitably subject to many meanings, to different interpretations,
and to emotional loading. Our use of the words 'independence'

and 'independentist' may be criticized as hiding the reality of the PQ drive and blurring its danger. It may also be true that independence for Quebec would involve the cutting of all links, although that would be a decision not of the PQ alone but also of the remainder of Canada. 'Independence' is, here, the better and more accurate word."

74   30 "... only cabinet minister to call Lévesque 'tu' ": Claude Morin later observed that while he called Trudeau "tu", he called Lévesque "vous". When Margot Gibb-Clark of the *Globe and Mail* asked Lévesque about this, he said, "Hmm, that's true. French has an extraordinary advantage. It gives a chance not so much to keep distances, but to respect others, to bring in an element of non-intimacy." *Globe and Mail*, March 21, 1984.

74   32 "... one of the few to define himself clearly as a socialist": On November 6, 1974, Burns said in a speech to the Fleur de Lys club: "My political commitment rests above all else on my faith in democracy. My democratic commitment rests on my determination to contribute to an authentically Québécois socialism. Socialism here will come from the recovery of public power by people here — which is to say sovereignty. Without this fundamental framework, I don't see what I am doing in the Parti Québécois. Without this fundamental framework, I don't see what the Parti Québécois is doing in Quebec."

75   38 "... an enormous shock ...": See "Qui est Louis Bernard?" by Robert McKenzie, *Point de Mire*, August 10, 1970. He quotes a colleague of Bernard's describing the reaction: "He summoned us one Tuesday morning and he seemed a little strange. When he began by saying 'Messieurs, I must tell you that I have resigned ...' I said to myself, 'He's going to Ottawa.' Then, when I heard the words '... to become chief of staff for Dr. ...' I had the time to think that it must be Dr. Cloutier (the new Liberal minister of cultural affairs). When we heard 'Dr. Laurin', there was a silence of 25 or 30 seconds. Everybody was stunned. I think it was one of the most moving moments of my life. We are all pretty nationalist in the Ministry and if some kept a certain hope for federalism, it was perhaps in large part because of the admiration we had for Louis Bernard's competence.

"He is a rather shy, closed man, you know, but we all went to shake his hand and say a few words. I don't think anyone was able to stay and work in the office that day. You understand, we said to ourselves, 'This is the man who knows the files best from the federal-provincial point of view. So if he has taken that decision ...' "

Bernard himself made a similar analysis of the demoralizing effect on the civil service of the resignation of Claude Morin, a year later. See "Le Départ de Claude Morin, ou l'échec de la 3e voie", *Le Devoir*, le 10 septembre 1971.

The biographical information on Louis Bernard, and several other anecdotes in this chapter, were collected in preparing a series on the third anniversary of the election, published in the *Gazette*, November 11-15, 1979.

76   18   "the civil servant is to the politician . . .": Bernard, "La Fonction publique du Québec dans les années '80", conférence devant les membres de la section régionale du Québec de l'Institut d'administration publique du Canada, le 23 janvier 1979.

78   7   "Yes, but, Mr. Lévesque . . .": Pierre Godin, "Je sais que je suis capable d'atteindre la première place: Bernard Landry", *La Presse*, le 17 mars 1984.

79   23   Trudeau's feelings about Quebec nationalism: Trudeau deeply believed that nationalism of any kind was inevitably re-actionary, because it was based on the interests of a single ethnic ᵧroup. "That is why a nationalistic government is by nature intolerant, discriminatory, and when all is said and done, totalitarian," he wrote in 1962, in "La Nouvelle Trahison des clercs", published in *Cité libre*'s special issue on sepa-ratism, April 1962, and translated by Patricia Claxton as "New Treason of the Intellectuals" in *Federalism and the French Canadians*, pp. 168-9.

84   8   ". . . charges against . . . Morgentaler were dropped": *Le Devoir*, le 11 décembre 1976.

84   10   "a new social contract": *Le Devoir*, le 11 décembre 1976.

84   14   ". . . Quebecers would become their own environmental inspectors": *Le Devoir*, le 16 décembre 1976.

84   16   ". . . culture would be 'democratized'. . .": *Le Devoir*, le 6 décembre 1976.

84   19   ". . . compulsory two-year service in remote areas . . .": *Le Devoir*, le 11 décembre 1976.

85   2   "fiscal arrangements": The controversy revolved around the desire of the federal government to put an end to the set of guarantees introduced in 1972 which assured the provincial governments that they would have no loss in revenue from the tax reforms of the finance minister, Edgar Benson. Since all provinces but Quebec receive their income-tax revenue as a percentage of the federal revenue, the changes would other-wise have caused a drop in provincial revenues. *Maclean's*, December 27, 1976.

86   18   "There are Common Fronts of the provinces . . .": Interview with the author, December 9, 1976.

Chapter Seven: Camille Laurin and the Politics of Language

Much of the research for this chapter was done in preparing a profile for *Maclean's* and another for *L'Actualité*. This resulted in two lengthy interviews with Dr. Laurin. In addition, back-ground interviews were done for this book.

91   10   "in actual fact . . .": Interview, December 9, 1976.
92   36   "another career . . .": Interview, June 8, 1978.
93   1   "Sometimes, coming into the newsroom . . .": *Le Quartier Latin*, 1947.

93	8	"It's a question . . .": Special issue on Confederation, *Le Quartier Latin*, 1947.
93	36	". . . a commission of inquiry": Commission d'Enquête sur l'Administration de l'Institut Albert Prévost, quant à son personnel médical et hospitalier: André Regnier, Aristide Cousineau, Roland Parenteau, commissaires enquêteurs; Me Émile Colas, conseiller juridique. The report concluded that "the whole conflict . . . has its origins in a conflict of personalities between Dr. C. Laurin, full of initiative and audacity, and Nurse C. Tasse, a dignified but elderly woman, jealous of her authority, worried about the influence that Dr. Camille Laurin had over the medical staff and the power that he held over the granting of generously distributed grants, even to the fund over which he controlled the purse strings." (p. 73.)
94	8	". . . friendship with strong federalists . . .": When Laurin was editor of *Le Quartier Latin*, Maurice Sauvé was president of the Association Générale des Étudiants de l'Université de Montréal; when he went to Geneva, he succeeded Gérard Pelletier; when the doctors named a representative on the board of directors of the Institut Albert Prévost, the person they chose was Pierre Juneau.
95	10	"the creation of an independent French-speaking Quebec . . .": Guy Rocher, "Le Multiculturalisme au Canada", presented to the annual meeting of the Canadian Association of Sociology and Anthropology, May 30, 1972, reprinted in his *Le Québec en mutation*, p. 126.
95	19	". . . a widely eclectic thinker": Dumont classified his academic writing in the following categories: "Epistemology and sociology of culture", "sociology and economics", "religious anthropology", and "sociology in French Canada". Curriculum vitae, Cabinet du premier ministre, service de presse, le 7 décembre 1979.
96	14	"a collective inheritance . . .": *Témoignage de Camille Laurin: pourquoi je suis souverainiste*, p. 32.
96	25	"an envied and dreaded paternal substitute": Laurin, *Ma traversée du Québec*, p. 73.
96	35	"to its real proportions": *Le Jour*, le 6 mai 1977.
97	4	"The sociologists who have been shaped . . .": Interview, March 24, 1982.
97	13	"All developed language has a private core . . .": Steiner, *After Babel*, pp. 231-2.
97	18	". . . contrary to . . . Sapir and . . . Chomsky . . .": Laurin's Whorfian assumptions were directly confronted as such only once, by the McGill anthropologist John MacNamara, who used Chomsky's arguments in a lengthy piece published in *Le Devoir*, le 5 mai 1977. "If language . . . has an important role in the formation of the mind, what does one say about the bilingual? Does a French-English bilingual person always think with the mind that has been imposed on him by his mother tongue, English or French? If the mental differences constitute barri-

ers to communication, it follows that a bilingual person is incapable of understanding or being understood in his second language. Or does it mean that bilingualism imposes a bastard mind on a bilingual person, neither English nor French but something between the two? Or would the bilingual person find himself in a schizoid situation, with two minds, understanding both English and French but incapable of making the link between the two minds that were formed in his head?" But no one responded to MacNamara's questions.

98	7	"... law à la française ...": Rocher, interview, March 24, 1982.
98	34	"... champion boxer ... a very gentle man": Laurin, interview, April 18, 1977.
99	12	"... under-representation increased at higher salary levels": *The Position of the French Language in Quebec*: Report of the Commission of Inquiry on the Position of the French Language and on Language Rights in Quebec; Commissioners: Jean-Denis Gendron, Madeleine Doyon-Ferland, Aimé Gagné, Nicolas Mateesco Matte, Edward McWhinney; secretary, Jean-Guy Lavigne, 1972 (the Gendron Report), vol. I, p. 119.
99	25	Tetley: In "Once again, define a Francophone: French-born, or French-speaking?" *Gazette*, February 15, 1977.
99	38	Henripin: *Le Devoir*, le 4 novembre 1969.
100	7	Bill 22: For a detailed comparison of Bill 22, Bill 1, and Bill 101, see William D. Coleman, "From Bill 22 to Bill 101: The Politics of Language under the Parti Québécois", *Canadian Journal of Political Science*, XIV:3, September 1981.
102	26	"the French, like their language ...": The Charter of the French Language, English translation, p. 8.
103	27	"The Quebec we wish to build ...": Charter, p. 52.
104	24	"The time has come ...": Charter, p. 109.
105	19	"frankly abusive ...": Ryan, *Le Devoir*, le 2 avril 1977.
105	31	"The style ... often honey-coated": Ryan, *Le Devoir*, le 4 avril 1977.
106	1	Gérard-D. Lévesque's reaction: *Le Devoir*, le 4 avril 1977.
106	6	"narrow and retrograde": *Le Devoir*, le 6 avril 1977.
109	41	"For the love of God ...": *Le Devoir*, la 19 août 1977.
110	33	"the greatest moment ...": "La Montée vers un Québec maître de sa destinée", *L'Action nationale* 68, 1978, p. 28; quoted by Coleman.

Chapter Eight: Flying High

Much of the research in this chapter was initially done for an assessment of the government's first year, a profile of Pierre Marc Johnson, and a story on asbestos, all published in *Maclean's*.

114	35	"a year, let us say, of a lot of words": *Le Devoir*, le 24 septembre 1977.
115	42	"... no recommendation ...": *Le Devoir*, le 15 juin 1977.
116	12	"Do we permit ...": Press conference, December 9, 1976.
116	24	Tremblay's report: Claude Ryan saw the report as, in fact,

puncturing Quebec's arguments. "But how, faced with such figures, can serious public figures still try to make the population believe that a growing share of public revenues raised in Quebec is drained away by the federal government?": *Le Devoir*, le 29 mars 1977. In the *Globe and Mail*, William Johnson saw the coverage as an example of not only government manipulation, but journalistic willingness to be manipulated. *Globe and Mail*, March 28, 1977.

117   14   "When you don't have money . . .": *Le Devoir*, le 13 avril 1977.
117   16   Wall Street reaction: *Gazette*, April 14. AA rating kept: *Financial Times*, September 12, 1977.
117   40   "professional Cassandras . . .": *Le Devoir*, le 27 mai 1977.
121   29   Lise Payette's account of the cabinet meeting at Sainte-Marguerite is in her book *Le Pouvoir? Connais pas!*, p. 50.
122   31   ". . . a very good law for the victims of child abuse": *Maclean's*, June 8, 1981. The most complete appraisal of the strengths and weaknesses in the law was done by Anthony Wilson-Smith in the *Gazette*, May 30, 1981.
124   14   "The holes left in the ground . . .": Speech to the convention of the Prospectors and Developers Association, March 6, 1978.
125   25   "I was a nationalist . . .": Interview.
126   36   "to rid itself of colonization": *Le Devoir*, le 3 novembre 1977.
126   40   "Salut, espèce de chialeux": *Toronto Star*, November 3, 1977.
128   29   *Maclean's* note: Personal letter, October 31, 1977.
132   1   "we are fighting to preserve a great and precious country": *House of Commons Debates*, July 5, 1977, vol. 120, no. 157, p. 7316.
132   40   "much closer to sovereignty-association than to the status quo"; *Montréal Matin*, le 21 septembre 1977.
133   15   "We do not believe the separation of Quebec from Canada is likely": *Montreal Star*, January 7, 1978.
133   36   "'cowardice' . . . 'a political gesture'": *Le Devoir*, le 13 janvier 1978.
134   4   Bonin: *Maclean's*, January 23, 1978.
134   16   "We must emphasize . . ."; *Financial Post*, January 14, 1978.
134   42   ". . . Holden was jeered": *Gazette*, *New York Times*, April 26, 1978.

Chapter Nine: Mr. Ryan Goes to Gilford Street

The account of Ryan's decision-making on the leadership was originally researched for *Maclean's*, "Here Comes Mr. Ryan", January 23, 1978. In addition to covering the leadership campaign and the convention, I had a lengthy interview with Ryan, portions of which were published in *Maclean's* on July 12, 1978, and another in December 1979 for a profile published in the *Gazette* on January 5, 1980. Additional interviews were done for this chapter.

143   5   "If you think I'm going to win that for you . . .": Aurélien Leclerc, *Claude Ryan*, p. 24.
143   10   "I was too hard-headed and stiff-necked . . .": Benoît Aubin, "Le Père Ryan", *L'Actualité*, February 1978.

143   24   Theological influences on Ryan: See his text presented to the Journées Universitaires de la Pensée Chrétienne, Université de Montréal, quoted in *Cahier de Recherche Éthique* #6, Fides, 1978, p. 123.

143   41   "You're in Rome.": "Tu es à Rome.": Interview, January 10, 1978.

144   26   ". . . his insistence on hard work and intellectual rigour": Ryan wrote that "Action . . . is always a struggle, a combat, where there is an enemy, a real obstacle to fight and conquer." See *Un Type nouveau de laïc*, p. 66, and "Le Laïc d'Action Catholique dans l'église d'aujourd'hui", *Laïcat et mission*, no. 3, April 1959, pp. 134-5, quoted in André-J. Bélanger, *Ruptures et constantes*, p. 42.

144   37   "The real activist . . .": *Esprits durs*, p. 68.

145   22   "I was thirty-three, I was still a bachelor . . .": Aubin, "Le Père Ryan". Ryan later regretted his frankness with Aubin, and, despite the fact that Aubin had shown him the manuscript before publication and argued him out of his objections, accused Aubin of "making history with an off-the-record joke".

146   1   Filion's doubts: Jean Marchand also had reservations about Ryan for the job, saying "It will be the death of *Le Devoir*." See Denis Monière, *André Laurendeau*, p. 306. Lionel Groulx was also bitterly critical of Ryan. See Aubin, "Le Père Ryan". Nevertheless, despite their differences, Ryan wrote a stirring eulogy of Groulx after his death, calling him "the spiritual father of modern Quebec". *Le Devoir*, le 24 mai 1967.

146   22   "the thesis of two cultures": See *Le Devoir*, le 16 juin 1964.

146   31   "The Pierre Trudeau of the 1950s . . .": *Le Devoir*, le 8 septembre 1967.

147   5   "October Crisis of 1970": The best published account of the crisis remains *Rumours of War* by Ron Haggart and Aubrey Golden.

147   18   "Ryan . . . retorted in print that Trudeau was lying": See Ryan's introduction to *Le Devoir et la crise d'octobre*.

147   21   "provisional government plot": The fullest account of the story is in McCall-Newman, *Grits*. Peter Newman later apologized to Ryan.

149   29   "a psychological war": *Gazette*, March 6, 1978.

149   35   ". . . perfect salesman's kit . . .": See *Le Devoir*, le 25 mars 1978.

151   2   Léonce Mercier's "We'll get about eight hundred" and comments by Garneau are from Richard Cleroux's account in the *Globe and Mail*, April 17, 1978.

Chapter Ten: Jacques Parizeau and the Sales-Tax War

Some of the research for this chapter was initially done for a portrait of Jacques Parizeau, which I did with Michel C. Auger for *L'Actualité*, published November 1979. Unidentified biographical remarks by Parizeau are from the interview we did for that profile. Rodrigue Tremblay tells his version of the sales-tax decision in his memoir *Le Québec en crise*.

152	17	"I was simply tired of wasting my time": *Le Devoir*, le 16 février 1978.
152	22	For cabinet speculation, see *Le Devoir*, le 24 septembre 1977, le 7 janvier, le 13 février 1978.
153	6	Map incident: *Dimanche Matin*, le 5 février 1978.
153	12	The "dossier noir" is discussed at length in my article in *City Magazine*, July 1978.
153	14	Jean-Claude Picard: *Le Devoir*, le 18 mars 1978.
153	23	"Quebec: a grand design for a New Order": *Maclean's*, March 6, 1978. See also David Thomas's thesis, "Le Chapitre noir du livre blanc".
153	37	*Ici Québec*, février-mars 1978.
157	37	"the only professional Finance Minister in Canada": David Thomas, "The Right Hand Man," *Maclean's*, August 7, 1978.
157	42	"I am centre-left": Interview, December 10, 1976.
158	6	"... Lise Payette ... put down two dollars on the cabinet table": *Le Pouvoir? Connais pas!*, pp. 129-30.
160	5	"I went there mainly because my father ...": Ian Rodger, *Globe and Mail*, November 12, 1979.
161	26	"... part of the key group that provided the ideas to the Quiet Revolution": See Pierre Godin, *Daniel Johnson*, Jean Provencher, *René Lévesque*, Douglas Fullerton, *The Dangerous Delusion*, and Blair Fraser, "Quebec's New Power Elite," *Maclean's*, August 21, 1965.
162	10	Parizeau's speech at Charlottetown and the responses by Lalonde and Gordon are published in P.-A. Crépeau and C. B. Macpherson, eds., *The Future of Canadian Federalism/L'Avenir du fédéralisme canadien*.
163	24	"... given the job ... of rationalizing government salaries": Parizeau recounted this story in a speech to the CEQ in 1970.
164	15	"an extravagant pre-referendum Common Front settlement": See François Demers, *Chroniques impertinentes*.
164	33	"The only alternative ... independence": In *The Dangerous Delusion* (p. 105), Douglas Fullerton argues that Parizeau's decision was "in part a product of rebuffs from Ottawa" because he failed to get jobs that he deserved. However, Parizeau vigorously denied this, *Globe and Mail*, November 12, 1979.
164	39	"... a candidate in Crémazie ...": For a sardonic and sometimes cruel account of this campaign, see Carole de Vault's *The Informer*.
165	12	"For pretty long periods of time ..." David Thomas, *Maclean's*, August 7, 1978.
167	23	"the revolt of the rich": 1979-80 budget speech, p. 30.
167	33	"the most regressive tax structure ...": 1979-80 budget speech, p. 29.
167	37	"We will recall ... ": 1980-81 budget speech, p. 31.

Chapter Eleven: The Hesitation Waltz

169	2	"one step forward, one step back": "les valses, les hésitations, 'j'avance' et 'je recule' ". Press conference, April 27, 1978. I am grateful to René Lévesque for pointing out the phrase to me.

169   3   ". . . Pierre Trudeau hesitated . . . ": For details on the delay, see Christina McCall-Newman, *Grits*, p. 318, and Richard Gwyn, *The Northern Magus*, pp. 323-9.

169   9   "There could be nothing more confusing . . .": *La Presse*, le 28 août 1978.

171   15   "We have no intention . . .": Translation from Lévesque, *My Quebec*, p. x.

171   20   "Sovereignty-association is a single word": *La Presse*, le 14 octobre 1978.

171   38   ". . . Lévesque didn't bring . . . Kool-Aid": *La Presse*, le 4 décembre 1978.

173   23   "Ottawa was prepared to restrict . . . ": Louis Falardeau wrote a good summary of the initial positions in *La Presse*, le 3 février 1979; Lise Bissonnette pieced together the final impasse point by point in *Le Devoir*, le 12 février 1979.

174   2   "Pepin-Robarts had little impact": See Richard Simeon, *Montreal Star*, February 13, 1979.

174   33   Raymond Barre: For stories on the visit, see *Journal de Québec*, le 13 février 1979, *Globe and Mail*, February 15, 1979, *Le Nouvel Observateur*, le 19 février 1979. For a discussion of the contrast in the coverage of the Barre visit in English and French media, see David Waters, "The English Media and the New Quebec", in *The English of Quebec*.

176   2   "On March 26, 1979 . . .": The 1979 election has been remarkably well chronicled and analysed. See Jeffrey Simpson, *The Discipline of Power*, Richard Gwyn, *The Northern Magus*, Dalton Camp, *Points of Departure*, and, for the decisions leading up to the election call, Christina McCall-Newman, *Grits*.

187   4   "We had hoped to make labour our partner": *Toronto Star*, November 18, 1979.

Chapter 12: The Question

Much of the biographical information in this chapter was drawn from an interview with Claude Morin on April 8, 1980.

194   15   "unemployment insurance": quoted by Blair Fraser in "Quebec's New Power Elite", *Maclean's*, August 21, 1965.

195   7   "The achievement of independence . . ." and "You don't make a flower grow faster . . .": From paper quoted at length in Saywell, *The Rise of the Parti Québécois*.

195   23   ". . . no question . . . if the people don't want it": *Le Devoir*, le 23 septembre 1975.

195   26   "to dissociate taking power . . .": Quoted by Saywell, p. 120. The four agencies of sovereignty-association are described in: *Quebec-Canada: A New Deal*, pp. 61-2; reference to the Commonwealth, p. 57.

198   4   "Many English-Canadian personalities . . .": *Quebec-Canada*, pp. 70-1.

198   31   Poll: *Gazette*, September 28, 1979.

199   26   Vincent Lemieux, *Le Devoir*, le 2 octobre 1979.

200   30   William Davis, *Gazette*, November 12, 1979.

201   34   On CROP poll for *Reader's Digest*, see *La Presse*, le 27 septembre 1977.

203   25   ". . . he was furious . . .": *Gazette*, December 14, 1979.

205   27   "I don't believe my eyes or ears": Payette, *Le Pouvoir? Connais pas!* p. 77.

205   40   ". . . Bédard knew it by heart": This was no easy task. As a test, a Laval linguist, Conrad Bureau, gave the question to groups of students to memorize; none were able to do it. In a study of the question, he concluded that, although clear, it was more complex in one of its parts than Proust and almost twice as complex as Gide in its syntactical structure. See "Le référendum de mai 1980 au Québec: une analyse linguistique de 'la question'". *Langues et Linguistique*, No. 10, 1984.

Chapter 13: The Divided Elite

209   10   "Pierre Dansereau suggests that the optimists were sovereignists . . .": Interview, January 19, 1982; ". . . Guy Rocher thinks the reverse": Interview, March 24, 1982.

210   17   "On the contrary, I am happy": Interview with Georges-Henri Lévesque, January 18, 1980. For a study on the ideological differences between Yes voters and No voters, see Michael D. Ornstein, H. Michael Stevenson, "Élite and Public Opinion Before the Quebec Referendum: A Commentary on the State in Canada", *Canadian Journal of Political Science*, XIV: 4, December 1981.

210   24   "They massively entered . . .": Grand'maison, *La Nouvelle Classe*, p. 21.

210   40   For discussion of the state-in-waiting, or, as he called it, "a would-be state", see Alain Touraine, interview, *Le Temps fou*, février 1983.

211   4   *L'État du Québec en devenir*: See Bergeron et Pelletier in Bibliography.

211   13   Pinard-Hamilton poll, see *Policy Options*, vol. 2 No. 4, Sept.-Oct. 1981.

212   8   ". . . HEC had to turn away 1,150 applicants": *Le Devoir*, le 4 juillet 1978.

213   14   ". . . taught him everything he knew about administration": *L'Actualité*, juin 1980.

213   21   Blair Fraser on Bélanger: *Maclean's*, August 21, 1965.

214   9   Interview with Bélanger, February 6, 1981.

Chapter 14: The Campaign

216   13   "Today, I haven't changed . . .": Interview with Claude Ryan, December 28, 1979.

217   36   ". . . like punching a pillow": See *Le Devoir*, le 22 janvier 1980, on comment by Jacques-Yvan Morin.

222   6   "Guy is active in sports": quoted by Lise Payette in *Le Pouvoir? Connais pas!* p. 79.

222   18   "blunder of blunders": Payette, p. 80.

224   21   Quotations from Trudeau's speeches from transcripts produced
                  by the Prime Minister's Office.

224   38   "... a majestic performance ...": Sheppard and Valpy, *The National Deal*, p. 31.

229   18   "I'm not giving you the price in Italy ...": From the film *Le Confort et l'indifférence*, by Denys Arcand, National Film Board of Canada, 1982.

229   27   Lalonde, energy deficit: *Le Devoir*, le 17 avril; Bégin, welfare payments, *Le Devoir*, le 18 avril; Ouellet, social services, *Le Devoir*, le 23 avril 1980.

229   40   "not a war of slogans": Speech in Beaconsfield, April 29, 1980.

230   19   On the Caisse de Dépôt, see *Gazette*, May 10, 1980; *Les Affaires*, mai 1982, and "Caisse unpopulaire" by David Olive, *Canadian Business*, May 1982.

238   37   "... referendum ... a massive defeat for the 'national culture'": Michel Morin, *Gazette*, May 31, 1980.

239   7   "One can be disappointed...": *Le Soleil*, le 4 septembre 1982. François-Albert Angers on referendum, *Le Devoir*, le 17, 18, 19 septembre 1980.

Chapter 15: A Provincial Premier

An earlier version of this chapter appeared in the *Gazette* as "A Day in the Life of René Lévesque", November 15, 1980.

Chapter 16: Slump and Recovery

257   18   "... the chemistry wasn't there ...": In the closing summations, Brian Peckford said that he had heard both Trudeau's version of federalism and Lévesque's and he preferred Lévesque's. A federal official who had worked on the negotiations all summer concluded that they had made a mistake: that the potential for an agreement wasn't there.

258   11   "The Quebec National Assembly categorically opposes...": *Journal des débats*, sixth session, 31st legislature, November 12, 1980, p. 76.

259   32   "Lévesque goes on his knees ...": *Journal de Québec*, le 20 novembre 1980.

260   27   "a day of mourning": *Le Devoir*, le 25 novembre 1980.

261   34   "... Parizeau conceded ...": *Débats*, Commission permanente des finances, Questions avec débat, November 28, 1980. See especially p. B-12.

263   16   "... the British House of Commons ...": Quoted in "First Report from the Foreign Affairs Committee, Session 1980-81: British North America Acts: The Role of Parliament", Sir Anthony Kershaw, chairman, vol. 1, p. viii.

264   13   "the established constitutional position...": Kershaw, p. xlix.

265   39   "A good part of this deficit ...": 1981-2 budget speech, p. 12.

266   7   "In short ...": Budget speech, p. 13.

270 12 "...that the editors... had publicly called for...": See editorial, "Un Choix difficile", *Le Jour*, le 22 juillet 1977.

273 15 "He likes to think he's a superman": Benoît Aubin, "Le Triomphe et l'humiliation: Ryan", *L'Actualité*, juin 1981.

274 26 "Personally, I have given some pieces of advice...": *La Presse*, le 6 avril 1981.

275 40 "Provided we don't end up with eighty members...": Daniel Pérusse, "Le Triomphe et l'humiliation: Lévesque", *L'Actualité*, juin 1981.

276 11 "In the eighteen east-end ridings...": Benoît Aubin, *L'Actualité*, juin 1981.

278 23 "Contrary to other elections...": André Bernard and Bernard Descôteaux, *Quebec: elections 1981*, p. 195.

Chapter 17: The Constitution

I covered most of this process as a reporter, and filled in some of the gaps with interviews for this book. For a fuller description of the process of the amendment and patriation of the British North America Act, see Robert Sheppard and Michael Valpy's vivid account in *The National Deal*, David Milne's *The New Canadian Constitution*, and, for a wide range of academic opinions, *And No One Cheered*, edited by Keith Banting and Richard Simeon.

281 11 "If we threw that...": Interview, July 2, 1982.

282 37 "I've signed your damn ad": Sheppard and Valpy, p. 176.

283 3 Lévesque statement, *Globe and Mail*, April 18, 1981.

283 33 "The alliance...": *Le Devoir*, le 21 janvier 1982.

286 41 "It should be borne in mind...": *Constitutional Decisions*, September 28, 1981, Supreme Court of Canada, p. 20.

287 5 "Furthermore..." and "We have reached the conclusion...": *Constitutional Decisions*, p. 109.

287 19 "We won": Sheppard and Valpy, p. 251.

287 22 "On the political level...": *Gazette*, September 29, 1981.

287 37 "When you respect...": *Globe and Mail*, September 29, 1981.

289 21 "Metternich-like to the end": Sheppard and Valpy, p. 262.

300 39 "So it was with growing unease...": For the text of all but the last paragraph, see *Le Devoir*, le 17 novembre 1981.

Chapter 18: Morbid Symptoms

I covered the Parti Québécois convention for the *Gazette*, and watched the proceedings I describe here.

302 4 "a stab in the back... a night of long knives": Question Period, National Assembly, November 10; "a shameful betrayal": Inaugural Address, November 9, p. 4; "treachery", "contemptible", "banditry": *Debates*, November 19, 1981.

302 8 "'screwed left and right'... 'political sluts'": *Le Devoir*, le 16 novembre. More of Lévesque's bitterness can be found in his replies to questions in the National Assembly on Novem-

		ber 10, 11, 17, the inaugural address on November 9, his speech to the PQ National Council on November 14, and his speech in the National Assembly on November 19, 1981.
302	21	"Wolfe": *Debates*, November 12, 1981, p. 138.
303	9	"A general election . . .": *Le Soleil*, le 7 août 1981.
304	14	On the hyphen, see *Le Soleil* and *Le Devoir*, le 16 novembre 1981, and William Johnson's article "Sovereignty and the Elusive Hyphen", *Globe and Mail*, November 18, 1981.
308	38	"If you don't intervene . . .": Boudreau, *Le Rêve inachevé*, pp. 77-8.
310	6	"a rare humiliation": *Toronto Star*, December 9, 1981.
312	28	"After surrendering . . .": *Toronto Star*, December 20, 1981.
313	16	". . . 95 per cent voted Yes": *Gazette*, February 10, 1982.
315	1	". . . a good example . . .": *Gazette*, February 13, 1982.
315	25	"I frankly think . . .": "A Surviving Anglophone's Views on Montreal ", February 2, 1982, text, pp. 8-9.
315	42	"At least he could have had the competence . . .": *La Presse*, February 3, 1982.
316	8	"will have to have bloody good reasons": *Le Soleil*, le 6 février 1982.
316	9	". . . almost $800,000": Tilden received $507,936 in government business in 1980-1, and $264,000 for the first ten months of 1982, for a total of $771,936. *La Presse*, le 5 février 1982.
316	12	"the spontaneous reactions of citizens . . .": *Le Devoir*, le 6 février 1982.
316	17	"Tilden business . . . dropped fifty per cent . . .": *La Presse*, le 10 février 1982.
316	21	". . . speaking as a private individual . . .": *Gazette*, February 10, 1982.
316	23	A good summary of the reaction is in Nick Auf der Maur's column in the *Gazette*, Tuesday, March 8, 1982.
316	27	"On January 30 . . .": the events of the theft are summarized in *La Presse*, le 24 février 1982. Charron also describes what happened in his book, *Désobéir*.
317	20	"France had its Dreyfus . . .": *La Presse*, le 26 février 1982.
318	21	". . . a police investigation showed . . .": *Gazette*, December 11, 1981.
318	40	"During the summer of 1982 . . .": Charron, *Désobéir*, pp. 230-1.
319	17	". . . a strange, anonymous whispering campaign": As Quebec bureau chief for the *Gazette*, I had to check out these rumours several times in 1981-2. Finally, in the fall of 1982, I asked Corinne Côté-Lévesque if she would agree to be interviewed about the rumours. She agreed, and the article was published on November 20, 1982.

Chapter 19: Crisis Politics

		Parts of this chapter appeared, in slightly different form, as a series of letters from Quebec to *This Magazine*.
322	1	"I think it's rather funny": *Gazette*, December 21, 1981.
322	13	". . . the crown corporations . . .": By 1981, Hydro-Québec was

headed by Guy Coulombe, SOQUIP by Pierre Martin, the Société Générale de Financement by Jean-Claude Lebel, and the Caisse de Dépôt by Jean Campeau. All four were former senior civil servants, and three of the four were at the meeting with Louis Bernard on November 19, 1976, to discuss the new cabinet structure.

322   29   "the gross national product was dropping . . .": *Gazette*, March 4, 1982.

322   33   "Quebec's loss of 219,000 jobs . . .": Statistics Canada, 71-0001, quoted in "Un Aperçu de la situation économique courante", a paper for the Quebec Liberal caucus by Ghislain Fortin, quoted in the *Gazette*, October 1, 1982.

323   15   ". . . Claude Forget . . . told reporters . . .": Press conference transcript, November 16, 1981. Another economist who warned of the danger was Pierre Fortin. See "Un Coup de barre radical s'impose", *Le Devoir*, le 14 janvier; "Pierre Fortin: pour une stratégie anti-crise", *L'Actualité*, avril 1982. For a union response, see "L'Apocalypse selon Pierre Fortin", Pierre Beaulnes et al., *Le Devoir*, le 6 mars 1982.

323   22   Marcel Gilbert's analysis is included in "Bilan: Négociations du secteur public 1982-83, ou La Ronde des occasions man-quées", by Jean-François Munn, typescript, Montreal 1983. I am also grateful to Jennifer Robinson of the *Gazette* for her help in explaining the Common Front.

324   1   "At an economic summit . . .": The government's arguments at the summit are summarized in James Pottier, "L'Impasse, le gel et le naufrage", *Conjoncture et prévision*, juin 1982.

324   5   ". . . the way the government presented its case made it clear . . .": See *Le Devoir*, le 8 avril 1982.

325   1   "Ryan . . . support was deteriorating . . .": This can be traced easily in newspaper reports and features during the seven-teen months that he was leader after the election. The head-lines tell the story. See Lewis Harris, "For Ryan, the end of the beginning", *Gazette*, April 18, 1981; my *Gazette* pieces "Ryan prescribes a bitter pill for Quebec Liberals", September 22, 1981, "They won't get rid of me easily: Ryan", October 31, 1981, and "It may be too late now for Ryan to save himself", June 8, 1982; Claude Arpin, "Liberals sharpen tongues and knives for Ryan", *Gazette*, December 19, 1981; " 'Dump Ryan' Liberals pine for Garneau return", *Gazette*, January 30, 1982; Pierre O'Neill, "Ryan fera face au débat sur son leadership", *Le Devoir*, le 30 janvier 1982; Richard Daignault, "Ryan perçu comme le Lapalme des années 80", *Le Soleil*, le 30 janvier 1982; L. Ian MacDonald, "Ryan is Liberal issue that matters now," *Gazette*, May 5, 1982; Robert McKenzie, "I, Claude: Decline and fall of the Ryan empire", *Toronto Star*, June 12, 1982; Lewis Harris, "Ryan's last stand: He must convince Liberals that they still need him", *Gazette*, June 12, 1982.

325   20   ". . . on August 4 . . .": For a fuller description of Ryan's final deliberations, see L. Ian MacDonald's superb piece "Claude Ryan: the final days", *Gazette*, August 14, 1982. See his forth-

coming book on the Quebec Liberal Party, *De Bourassa à Bourassa.*

327   14   De Belleval paper: "Concertation, plein-emploi et fonds de solidarité", le 20 septembre 1982, typescript.

328   37   The best single published summary of the 1981-2 Common Front conflict is in Gérard Bergeron's *Pratique de l'État au Québec.*

334   19   "The rest was anticlimax": Raymond Désilets, director-general for labour relations in the Ministry of Labour, Louis-Marie Savard, former treasurer of the CEQ, and Jean-Claude Lebel, former secretary of Treasury Board, were named to a conciliation team. The Désilets Report was first rejected but finally accepted by the CEQ. The ensuing morale problems in the schools were such that Yves Bérubé tried without success to reach a new agreement on workload in May 1984.

334   31   "perhaps without precedent . . .": Bergeron, *Pratique de l'État*, p. 150.

334   38   "a sort of microclimate . . .": Annexe 8, in Jean-François Munn's "Bilan".

335   14   ". . . prisoners of our rhetoric . . .": Munn, "Bilan", pp. 30-1.

335   26   "this bizarre upside-down negotiation": Bergeron, *Pratique de l'État*, p. 169.

335   32   ". . . impossible to do worse . . .": Bergeron, *Pratique de l'État*, p. 171.

335   39   ". . . the Parti Québécois would split . . .": Desbarats, *René*, p. 222.

336   36   The committee hearings on the allegations that Lévesque misled the National Assembly were exhaustively documented, with enormous amounts of the documentation tabled and detailed daily coverage. The most scrupulously detailed coverage was, naturally, in *La Presse*, which started the story. The documents would provide a fascinating case study for students of the relationship between a government and a crown corporation.

338   24   "In the longer run . . .": 1983-4 Budget, May 10, 1983, p. 12.

338   41   "the most open-minded English-Canadian politician . . .": *Toronto Star*, May 1, 1983.

339   3   Brian Mulroney: See Martin, Gregg, and Perlin, *Contenders*; Murphy, Chodos, and Auf der Maur, *Brian Mulroney*; Gilles Lesage, "Le Rêve de Brian Mulroney", *L'Actualité*, juin 1983; the profile by Robert McKenzie in the *Toronto Star*, June 12, 1983.

339   22   ". . . his days at Laval law school . . .": Other students from that period at Laval include Liberal cabinet ministers Pierre de Bané and André Ouellet, Tory organizers and Mulroney loyalists Michel Cogger, Michael Meighen, Gary Ouellet, and Peter White, and labour lawyer Lucien Bouchard.

341   3   ". . . no longer calls himself a socialist . . .": See Saint-Pierre, *Les Années Bourassa*, p. 282: "Pourquoi vous disiez-vous socialiste?" "Parce que je le suis."

341   21   The two most useful summaries of the language issue from the vantage point of the English community are Mark Harrison's account in *Language and Society*, No. 10, Summer 1983, and the Alliance Quebec document, "The evolution of the language issue in Quebec, 1977-1983", produced for the National Assembly committee hearings in October 1983.

                      Laurin's promise: "I tell you vigorously and solemnly no one will be fired because he speaks only English. If it becomes necessary to put this into writing, somehow we will do it." *Gazette*, April 18, 1977.

342   26   ". . . bluntly denied . . .": See *Le Devoir*, le 6 novembre 1982.

342   28   "Keystone Cops", "firemen without a fire": *Gazette*, January 21, 1983.

342   30   ". . . can't stand our smell": *Le Devoir*, le 21 avril 1983.

Epilogue

                      I covered the events described here for the *Globe and Mail*.

347   28   ". . . reminded Jean Francoeur . . .": See *Le Devoir*, le 9 juin 1984.

353   17   "It has become literature . . .": Interview with *Le Devoir*, le 19 avril 1984.

356   5   ". . . Lévesque's advisers figured . . .": Lévesque was not so sure. In early July, he said privately that he expected to see a minority Progressive Conservative government. And, on returning from holidays in August, he told reporters that he liked Brian Mulroney's statement on federal-provincial relations, and hoped that "Liberal hegemony" would end in Quebec.

356   8   ". . . Lévesque saw two glimmers of hope": As the likelihood of a Liberal victory seemed to fade over the summer, he began to reflect on the possible advantages of a more "flexible" Conservative government.

Bibliography

André d'Allemagne. *Le RIN et les débuts du mouvement indépend-antiste québécois*. Préface de Marcel Rioux. Montréal: L'Étincelle, 1974.

Sheila Arnopoulos and Dominique Clift. *The English Fact in Quebec*. Montréal: McGill-Queen's University Press, 1980.

Keith Banting and Richard Simeon, eds. *And No One Cheered: Federalism, Democracy, and the Constitution Act*. Toronto: Methuen, 1983.

Robert Barberis et Pierre Drouilly. *Les Illusions du pouvoir: les erreurs stratégiques du gouvernement Lévesque*. Montréal: Sélect, 1980.

André J. Bélanger. *Ruptures et constantes: quatre idéologies du Québec en éclatement — la relève, la JEC, Cité libre, Parti pris*. Montréal: Hurtubise HMH, 1977.

Gérard Bergeron. *Du Duplessisme à Trudeau et Bourassa, 1956-1971*. Montréal: Parti-Pris, 1971.

———. *L'Indépendance: oui, mais . . .* Montréal: Quinze, 1977.

———. *Ce jour-là . . . le référendum*. Montréal: Quinze, 1978.

———. *Pratique de l'état au Québec*. Montréal: Québec-Amérique, 1984.

——— et Réjean Pelletier, sous la direction de. *L'État du Québec en devenir*. Montréal: Boréal Express, 1980.

André Bernard. *Québec: élections 1976*. Montréal: Hurtubise HMH, 1976.

——— et Bernard Descôteaux. *Québec: élections 1981*. Préface de Rodolphe Morrissette. Montréal: Hurtubise HMH, 1981.

Conrad Black. *Duplessis*. Toronto: McClelland and Stewart, 1976.

Sandford F. Borins. *Language of the Skies: The Bilingual Air Traffic Control Conflict in Canada*. Kingston: McGill-Queen's University Press, 1983.

Ernest Boudreau. *Le Rêve inachevé: le PQ, l'indépendance et la crise*. Préface de Pierre de Bellefeuille. Montréal: Nouvelle Optique, 1983.

Pierre Bourgault. *Écrits polémiques, 1960-1981: 1. La Politique*. Montréal: VLB, 1982.

Michel Brunet. *La Présence anglaise et les Canadiens*. Montréal: Beauchemin, 1964.

Dalton Camp. *Points of Departure*. Toronto: Deneau and Greenberg, 1979.

René Chaloult. *Mémoires politiques*. Montréal: Éditions du Jour, 1961.

Marcel Chaput. *Pourquoi je suis séparatiste*. Montréal: Editions du Jour, 1961.
—— . *J'ai choisi de me battre*. Montréal: Club du Livre du Québec, 1965.
Claude Charron. *Désobéir*. Montréal: VLB, 1983.
Val Clery, ed. *Canada from the Newsstands: A Selection from the Best Canadian Journalism of the Past Thirty Years*. Toronto: Macmillan, 1978.
Paul-André Comeau. *Le Bloc populaire*. Montréal: Québec-Amérique, 1982.
Robert Comeau. "Les Indépendantistes québécois, 1936-38". Thèse de maîtrise, l'Université de Montréal, 1971.
Ramsay Cook. *Canada and the French-Canadian Question*. Toronto: Macmillan, 1966.
Richard Daignault. *Lesage*. Montréal: Libre Expression, 1981.
Pierre Dansereau et al. *Politiciens et Juifs*. Discours prononcés le 20 avril 1933 à la Salle de Gésu, Montréal. Les Cahiers des Jeune-Canada, I, 1933.
François Demers. *Chroniques impertinentes du 3ième Front commun syndical, 1979-1980*. Montréal: Nouvelle Optique, 1982.
Peter Desbarats. *The State of Quebec*. Toronto: McClelland and Stewart, 1965.
—— . *René: A Canadian in Search of a Country*. Toronto: McClelland and Stewart, 1976.
Daniel Drache, ed. *Quebec — Only the Beginning: The Manifestoes of the Common Front*. Toronto: New Press.
Jules Duchastel. *Marcel Rioux: entre l'utopie et la raison*. Montréal: Nouvelle Optique, 1981.
Pierre Dupont. *How Lévesque Won: The Story of the PQ's Stunning Election Victory*. Translated by Sheila Fischman. Toronto: Lorimer, 1977.
The Earl of Durham. *Lord Durham's Report: An Abridgement of Report on the Affairs of British North America by Lord Durham*. Edited by Gerald M. Craig. Carleton Library. Toronto: McClelland and Stewart, 1963.
Maurice Filion, ed. *Hommage à Lionel Groulx*. Montréal: Leméac, 1978.
Louis Fournier. *F.L.Q.: histoire d'un mouvement clandestin*. Montréal: Québec-Amérique, 1982.
Pierre Fournier. *The Quebec Establishment: The Ruling Class and the State*. Montreal: Black Rose, 1976.
Blair Fraser. *The Search for Identity: Canada 1945-1967*. Toronto: Doubleday, 1967.
—— . "Notes on the MSA Convention". 1968.
—— . *Blair Fraser Reports. . . .* Edited by John and Graham Fraser. Toronto: Macmillan, 1969.

Douglas H. Fullerton. *The Dangerous Delusion*. Toronto: McClelland and Stewart, 1978.

Jean-Pierre Gaboury. *Le Nationalisme de Lionel Groulx: aspects idéologiques*. Ottawa: Éditions de l'Université d'Ottawa, 1970.

Jacques Godbout. *Le Réformiste: textes tranquilles*. Montréal: Quinze et Stanké, 1975.

Pierre Godin. *Daniel Johnson*. Montréal: Éditions de l'Homme, 1980.

Jacques Grand'maison. *La Nouvelle Classe et l'avenir du Québec*. Montréal: Stanké, 1979.

Gilles Grégoire. *Aventure à Ottawa*. Ottawa, 1969.

Richard Gwyn. *The Northern Magus: Pierre Trudeau and Canadians*. Edited by Sandra Gwyn. Toronto: McClelland and Stewart, 1980.

Ron Haggart and Aubrey E. Golden. *Rumours of War*. Toronto: New Press, 1971.

Gabriel Hudon. *Ce n'était qu'un début ou la petite histoire des premiers pas du FLQ*. Montréal: Parti-Pris, 1977.

Daniel Johnson. *Égalité ou indépendance*. Montréal: Éditions de l'Homme, 1965.

Judy LaMarsh. *Memoirs of a Bird in a Gilded Cage*. Toronto: McClelland and Stewart, 1969.

Laurier LaPierre, ed. *The Four O'Clock Lectures: French-Canadian Thinkers of the Nineteenth and Twentieth Centuries*. Montreal: McGill University Press, 1966.

—— et al, eds. *Essays on the Left: Essays in Honour of T. C. Douglas*. Toronto: McClelland and Stewart, 1971.

Pierre Laporte. *The True Face of Duplessis*. Montreal: Harvest House, 1960.

Louis La Rochelle. *En flagrant délit de pouvoir: chronique des évènements politiques de Maurice Duplessis à René Lévesque*. Montréal: Boréal Express, 1982.

André Laurendeau. *Ces choses qui nous arrivent: chronique des années 1961-1966*. Préface de Fernand Dumont. Montréal: Hurtubise HMH, 1970.

—— . *André Laurendeau: Witness for Quebec*. Essays selected and translated by Philip Stratford. Introduction by Claude Ryan. Toronto: Macmillan, 1973.

Marc Laurendeau. *Les Québécois violents*. Montréal: Boréal Express, 1974.

Camille Laurin. *Ma traversée du Québec*. Préface de René Lévesque. Montréal: Éditions du Jour, 1970.

—— . *Témoignage de Camille Laurin: pourquoi je suis souverainiste*. Montréal: Parti Québécois, n.d.

Andrée Lebel. *Pierre Bourgault: le plaisir de la liberté*. Montréal: Nouvelle Optique, 1983.

Aurélien Leclerc. *Claude Ryan: A Biography*. Translated by Colleen Kurtz. Preface by Jean Chrétien. Toronto: NC Press, 1980.

Jean-Paul Lefebvre et al. *En Grève! l'histoire de la C.S.N. et des luttes menées par ses militants de 1937 à 1963.* Préface de Jean Marchand. Montréal: Éditions du Jour, 1963.

René Lévesque. *An Option for Quebec.* Toronto: McClelland and Stewart, 1968.

————. *My Quebec.* Translated by Gaynor Fitzpatrick. Toronto: Methuen, 1979.

————. *Oui.* Montréal: Éditions de l'Homme, 1980.

Paul-André Linteau, René Durocher, et Jean-Claude Robert. *Histoire du Québec contemporain: de la Confédération à la crise (1867-1929).* Montréal: Boréal Express, 1979.

Christina McCall-Newman. *Grits: An Intimate Portrait of the Liberal Party.* Toronto: Macmillan, 1982.

Brian McKenna and Susan Purcell. *Drapeau.* Toronto: Clarke Irwin, 1980.

Kenneth McRoberts and Dale Posgate. *Quebec: Social Change and Political Crisis.* 2d ed., rev. Toronto: McClelland and Stewart, 1980.

Patrick Martin, Allan Gregg, and George Perlin. *Contenders: The Tory Quest for Power.* Toronto: Prentice-Hall, 1983.

David Milne. *The New Canadian Constitution.* Toronto: Lorimer, 1982.

Denis Monière. *Ideologies in Quebec: The Historical Development.* Translated by Richard Howard. Toronto: University of Toronto Press, 1981.

————. *André Laurendeau et le destin d'un peuple.* Montréal: Québec-Amérique, 1983.

Claude Morin. *Le Pouvoir québécois . . . en négociation.* Montréal: Boréal Express, 1972.

Jean-François Munn. "Bilan: négociations du secteur public 1982-83, ou la ronde des occasions manquées". Unpublished typescript, 1983.

Rae Murphy, Robert Chodos, and Nick Auf der Maur. *Brian Mulroney: The Boy from Baie Comeau.* Toronto: Lorimer, 1984.

Don et Vera Murray. *De Bourassa à Lévesque.* Montréal: Quinze, 1978.

Vera Murray. *Le Parti québécois: de la fondation à la prise du pouvoir.* Montréal: Hurtubise HMH, 1976.

Peter C. Newman. *The Distemper of Our Times.* Toronto: McClelland and Stewart, 1968.

————. *The Bronfman Dynasty: The Rothschilds of the New World.* Toronto: McClelland and Stewart, 1978.

Dostaler O'Leary. *Le Séparatisme: doctrine constructive.* Montréal: Éditions des Jeunesses Patriotes, 1937.

Andrée Lévesque Olssen. "The Canadian Left in Quebec during the Great Depression: the Communist Party of Canada and the CCF in Quebec, 1929-1939". Doctoral dissertation, Duke University, 1972.

Fernand Ouellet. *Economic and Social History of Quebec, 1760-1850:*

Structures and Conjunctures. Translated under the auspices of the Institute of Canadian Studies. Toronto: Carleton Library, 1980.

Michel Paradis, ed. *Aspects of Bilingualism.* Columbia, S.C.: Hornbeam Press, 1978.

Erna Paris. *Jews: An Account of Their Experiences in Canada.* Toronto: Macmillan, 1980.

Robert Parisé. *Georges-Henri Lévesque: père de la renaissance québécoise.* Montréal: Stanké, 1976.

Lise Payette. *Le Pouvoir? Connais pas!* Montréal: Québec-Amérique, 1982.

Gérard Pelletier. *Les Années de l'impatience: 1950-1960.* Montréal: Stanké, 1983.

Réjean Pelletier. *Les Militants du R.I.N.* Ottawa: Éditions de l'Université d'Ottawa, 1974.

Jean Provencher. *René Lévesque: Portrait of a Quebecer.* Translated by David Ellis. Toronto: Gage, 1975.

Herbert F. Quinn. *The Union Nationale: A Study in Quebec Nationalism.* 2d ed. Toronto: University of Toronto Press, 1979.

Guy Rocher. *Le Québec en mutation.* Montréal: Hurtubise HMH, 1973.

Jean-Louis Roy. *La Marche des québécois: le temps des ruptures (1945-1960).* Montréal: Leméac, 1976.

—— . *Le Choix d'un pays: le débat constitutionnel Québec-Canada 1960-1976.* Montréal: Leméac, 1978.

Claude Ryan. *Le Contact dans l'Apostolat.* Montréal: L'Action Catholique Canadienne, 1959.

—— . *Esprits durs, coeurs doux: la vie intellectuelle des militants chrétiens.* Montréal: L'Action Catholique Canadienne, 1959.

—— . *Un Type nouveau de laïc: problèmes et perspectives.* 2ième éd. Montréal: L'Action Catholique Canadienne, 1966.

—— , dir. Le Devoir *et la Crise d'Octobre.* Montréal: HMH, 1971.

—— . *A Stable Society: Quebec after the PQ.* Edited and translated by Robert Guy Scully with Marc Plourde. Montreal: Heritage, 1977.

John T. Saywell. *The Rise of the Parti Québécois, 1967-1976.* Toronto: University of Toronto Press, 1977.

F. R. Scott and Michael Oliver, eds. *Quebec States Her Case: Speeches and Articles from Quebec in the Years of Unrest.* Toronto: Macmillan, 1964.

Robert Sheppard and Michael Valpy. *The National Deal: The Fight for a Canadian Constitution.* Toronto: Fleet, 1982.

Richard Simeon. *Federal-Provincial Diplomacy: The Making of Recent Policy in Canada.* Toronto: University of Toronto Press, 1972.

—— , ed. *Must Canada Fail?* Montreal: McGill-Queen's University Press, 1977.

Jeffrey Simpson. *Discipline of Power: The Conservative Interlude and the Liberal Restoration.* Toronto: Personal Library, 1980.

Howard L. Singer. "Institutionalization of Protest: The Quebec Separatist Movement". Doctoral dissertation, New York University, October, 1976.

Michael B. Stein. *The Dynamics of Right-Wing Protest: A Political Analysis of Social Credit in Quebec*. Toronto: University of Toronto Press, 1973.

George Steiner. *After Babel*. London: Oxford University Press, 1975.

Martin Sullivan. *Mandate '68*. Toronto: Doubleday, 1968.

Jules-Paul Tardivel. *For My Country*. Translated by Sheila Fischman. Introduction by A. I. Silver. Toronto: University of Toronto Press, 1975.

David Thomas. "Le Chapitre noir du Livre blanc". Carleton University School of Journalism, 1979.

Rodrigue Tremblay. *Le Québec en crise*. Montréal: Sélect, 1981.

Susan Mann Trofimenkoff. *Introduction to Abbé Groulx: Variations on a Nationalist Theme*. Toronto: Copp Clark, 1974.

———. *The Dream of Nation: A Social and Intellectual History of Quebec*. Toronto: Macmillan, 1982.

Bernard Trotter. "The Montreal Producers' Strike — 1959". Prepared for John Meisel's seminar on French Canada, Queen's University, 1965.

Pierre Elliott Trudeau. *Federalism and the French Canadians*. Toronto: Macmillan, 1968.

———, ed. *The Asbestos Strike*. Translated by James Boake. Toronto: James, Lewis and Samuel, 1974.

Carole de Vault with William Johnson. *The Informer: Confessions of an Ex-Terrorist*. Toronto: Fleet, 1982.

Mason Wade. *The French Canadians, 1760-1967*. 2d ed., rev., 2 vols. Toronto: Macmillan, 1968.

Index